FURIOUS
Love

FURIOUS
Love

Elizabeth Taylor ★ Richard Burton
The Marriage of the Century

Sam Kashner & Nancy Schoenberger

JR
BOOKS

First published in Great Britain in 2010 by
JR Books, 10 Greenland Street, London NW1 0ND
www.jrbooks.com

First published in paperback, 2011

A catalogue record for this book is available from the British Library.

ISBN 978-1-907532-40-5

1 3 5 7 9 10 8 6 4 2

Printed by CPI Bookmarque, Croydon

CONTENTS

CONTENTS

PREFACE

"I am forever punished by the gods for being given
the fire and trying to put it out. The fire, of course, is you."
—RICHARD BURTON

"Since I was a little girl, I believed I was a child of destiny,
and if that is true, Richard Burton was surely my fate."
—ELIZABETH TAYLOR

When asked by *Time* magazine a few years ago to name the five great love affairs of all time, the Texas-born gossip columnist Liz Smith didn't even have to think about who would occupy first place. The Burtons, of course. Richard Burton and Elizabeth Taylor "were the most vivid example of a public love affair that I can think of. The Burtons and the Lindbergh baby being kidnapped and Kennedy's assassination—these are the biggest stories of our time. Whenever somebody says, 'So and so is a big star,' I say, 'Have they been condemned by the Vatican?'"

Their thirteen-year saga was the most notorious, publicized, celebrated, and vilified love affair of its day. Indeed, their ten-year marriage, followed by a divorce, remarriage, and a final divorce, was often called "the marriage of the century" in the press. Just thirty years earlier, the Duke of Windsor had embarked upon his own famous marriage, to Wallis Simpson, giving up the throne of England to marry the American divorcée from Baltimore. A nation wept, but the Duke and Duchess of Windsor went on to rule a shadow empire of jet-setters, aristocrats, gigolos, international bon vivants, in a floating world of yachts, dance floors, casinos, and the homes and hotels of the very rich. So famous were the Burtons in the 1960s and 1970s that the duke and the duchess were their only peers, the only other couple who knew what it was like to be pariahs for a time, to pay a high price for their choices, and to live the rest of their lives in isolated luxury. But the notorious Burtons managed to win their way back into the hearts of the American public through sheer talent, hard work, chutzpah, and glamour. "On the face of it," said columnist Smith, "Elizabeth Taylor was just totally arrogant. She'd walk out in capri pants and her Cleopatra makeup and her kerchief and go off to whatever local restaurant and drink up a storm with Burton. That's part of what excited the public: her vulgarity and her arrogance and the money. Oh God, their love story had everything."

It also brought us the modern accoutrements of celebrity: the relentless paparazzi, the continuous press exposure, the public airing of private grief. In short, it brought us "Liz and Dick," a tabloid shorthand that they hated but that stood for everything extravagant and over-the-top about their all-too-public lives.

In fact, you might say there were two marriages: the ballyhooed union of Liz and Dick and the private marriage of Richard and Elizabeth. More often than not, Liz and Dick overwhelmed the private marriage, holding it hostage and ultimately helping to destroy it. The yachts, the glamorous ports of call (Monte Carlo, Portofino), the grand hotels of the world, the fabled jewels, the homes in London, Gstaad, Céligny, and Puerto Vallarta, the hobnobbing with the Rothschilds, Ari Onassis, General Tito of Yugoslavia, and, of course, the Windsors. They were indeed Hollywood royalty. But like any other married couple, they had to deal with children coming of age during the cultural upheavals of the 1960s—communes, family squabbles, balancing two careers (even if their careers meant making some of the most remarkable films of the 1960s)—in short, the real marriage of two people trying to live their lives together.

If Burton had entered into the pact with impure motives, he quickly found himself utterly bewitched. He discovered in Elizabeth the embodiment of all the women in Wales he had loved or lusted after: from his sainted sister who had raised him to the dark-haired Welsh "tarts" he knew as a randy youth in the towns of Pontrhydyfen and Port Talbot. "My blind eyes are desperately waiting for the sight of you," he would write to her well into their marriage. "You don't realize of course, E. B., how fantastically beautiful you have always been, and how strangely you have acquired an added and special and dangerous loveliness. Your breasts jutting out from that half-asleep languid lingering body, the remote eyes, the parted lips."

For Elizabeth, this was the one true marriage. When she agreed to share with us letters that Richard Burton had written to her in the last few years of their life together, she wanted us to know the place he held, and continues to hold, in her heart. She wrote to us,

> Richard was magnificent in every sense of the word . . . and in everything he ever did. He was magnificent on the stage, he was magnificent in film, he was magnificent at making love . . . at least to me. He was the kindest, funniest, and most gentle father. All my kids worshipped him. Attentive, loving—that was Richard. The bond with all of us continued until he drew his last breath. We knew he was absolutely there for us no matter what. In my heart, I will always believe we would have been married a third and final time . . . from those first moments in Rome we were always madly and powerfully in love. We had more time but not enough.

Of the nearly forty letters Richard wrote to Elizabeth, perhaps the most important was written shortly before his untimely death on August 5, 1984, at the age of fifty-eight. He was in the attic study of his beloved house in Céligny, Switzerland, a home he shared with his fourth wife, Sally Hay Burton, when he wrote what would turn out to be his final letter to Elizabeth. He had recently completed work in Michael Radford's adaptation of George Orwell's *1984*, ironically the year of Burton's death, in what would be a brief but powerful performance. His costar, the English actor John Hurt, was staying with Richard and Sally for a few days, but Richard managed to slip away and sequester himself in the study. Surrounded by his treasured thousand volumes of The Everyman Library—a gift from Elizabeth—he wrote to her at her home in Bel Air in Los Angeles.

But by the time Elizabeth received the letter, Richard Burton was dead. He had gone to bed with a terrible headache, and sometime during the night he suffered a cerebral hemorrhage. Elizabeth was barred by Richard's widow from attending his funeral in Céligny, for fear of the disrupting crowds and paparazzi that still followed Elizabeth wherever she went. That letter would be her most cherished remembrance of the thirteen years, all told, they spent together in the whirlwind of their grand affair.

But what was in that letter?

FURIOUS LOVE

1

LE SCANDALE

"I did not want to be another notch on his belt."
—ELIZABETH TAYLOR

"How did I know the woman was so fucking famous?"
—RICHARD BURTON

The first time Richard Burton laid eyes on Elizabeth Taylor, he nearly laughed out loud.

It was 1953, and Burton had been plucked from the London stage where he was being hailed as the great successor to Sir John Gielgud and Sir Laurence Olivier, to make three dramas for 20th Century-Fox—*My Cousin Rachel*, *The Robe*, and *The Desert Rats*. He had swooped into Hollywood with his Welsh wife, Sybil, and had cut a swath through willing Hollywood wives, earning a reputation as an irresistible lover, a great raconteur, a rough and randy Welshman, a powerful drinker. At a party at Stewart Granger and Jean Simmons's house in Bel Air, the twenty-eight-year-old actor outdid himself in drinking and storytelling. It was the Welsh actor's first time in California, and his first visit to "a swank house," where he was agog at the suntanned beauties lounging around the largest swimming pool he had ever seen. The hot desert air was cooled by the sound of ice clinking in glasses, and Bloody Marys, boilermakers, and ice-cold beer kept the party well lubricated. "It had been a hell of a year," Burton would later write in his frank and colorful notebooks, his diary entries recorded for a possible autobiography. "Three big movies; drinking with Bogie; flirting with Garbo . . ." He recalled,

> I was enjoying this small social triumph, but then a girl sitting on the other side of the pool lowered her book, took off her sunglasses and looked at me. She was so extraordinarily beautiful that I nearly laughed out loud . . . she was unquestioningly gorgeous . . . She was lavish. She was a dark unyielding largess. She was, in short, too bloody much, and not only that, she was totally ignoring me.

Well, not "totally." That cool look took in a man she considered, at the time, swaggering and vulgar. She would have none of it. Besides, she was a year into her second marriage, to English actor Michael Wilding, a close friend of the Grangers. (Elizabeth, for her part, would recall that first meeting as having taken place at her and Michael's home in the Hollywood Hills; in her memory, she was nineteen at the time.) But Burton was already, let's say, intrigued. Reliving that first glimpse of twenty-one-year-old Elizabeth Taylor, he later described her as "the most astonishingly self-contained, pulchritudinous, remote, removed, inaccessible woman I had ever seen. . . . Was she merely sullen? I thought not. There was no trace of sulkiness in that divine face." And later still: "Her breasts were apocalyptic, they would topple empires . . ." They would also topple Burton.

He would not meet her again for another nine years.

By the time they met in 1962 on the set of *Cleopatra*—after the production's lengthy, expensive delays, a costly move from London's Pinewood Studios to Rome's Cinecittà, and a shuffling of studio heads, producers, directors, writers, and actors—Elizabeth Taylor and Richard Burton had already lived several lives. Elizabeth had survived child stardom, with all its demands and excesses. Having been wrenched from a bucolic childhood in Hampstead, England (complete with a pony), resettled in Los Angeles by her doting parents to escape the gathering storm of World War II, and thrust into filmdom by her ambitious mother, the former stage actress Sara Sothern Taylor, Elizabeth found herself famous at the tender age of ten, the diminutive costar of Metro-Goldwyn-Mayer's *Lassie Come Home,* and *National Velvet* the following year. (She would always have a fondness for animals, especially horses; since the age of three, she could jump without a saddle.) She learned early the value of her preternaturally beautiful, eerily adult face, though she treated her beauty cavalierly and had almost no personal vanity. She learned how the business worked: the fussing over by wardrobe and makeup and hair stylists and studio publicity agents, the constant fawning, the power struggles, the peaks and valleys of popularity. She became used to, and came to require, an entourage of helpers that would sink most ships. (Her even more beautiful brother, Howard, had wanted no part of it, so at fifteen he shaved his head the day before being hauled into Universal Studios to be tested for a boy-with-horse Western, thus assuring his escape into normalcy.) Elizabeth's rewards—fame, money, attention, studio animals to play with—balanced out her punishment: putting up with relentless control by her mother and her directors and tyrannical studio chief Louis B. Mayer, and a complete lack of privacy and independence. "I was so totally chaperoned," she recalled, "that I couldn't go to the bathroom alone." She was taught how to look and to speak and to walk and to stand and to breathe. But through it all, she learned about power: who had it, how to get it, how to keep it. When Louis B. Mayer once swore at Elizabeth's mother in a fit of rage, eleven-year-old Elizabeth shouted back, "You and your studio can go to hell!" She refused to apologize, and—amazingly—Mayer didn't fire her on the spot. Truly, at that moment, a diva was born.

At her second meeting with Burton, Elizabeth was at the height of her raven beauty but seemed older than her twenty-nine years. She had been married thrice and widowed once. Her first, brief marriage at age eighteen to the compulsive gambler, hotel heir Conrad Nicholson "Nicky" Hilton Jr., was a studio-arranged disaster from the start. When he wasn't jilting her for the gaming tables, he beat her; Elizabeth later claimed that he even kicked her in the stomach when she was a few months into a pregnancy, inducing a miscarriage. The studio had convinced her to marry the attractive but louche playboy as a publicity tie-in to *Father of the Bride*, MGM's 1950 film with Elizabeth as the young bride and Spencer Tracy as her put-upon father. Sara Taylor went along with MGM's plans; she knew it would help her daughter on her way to becoming a star, and, anyway, she'd wanted Elizabeth to marry wealth.

"When I met Nicky Hilton," Elizabeth later admitted, "I was ripe to get married. Dazzled by his charm and apparent sophistication, driven by feelings that could not be indulged outside of marriage, desperate to live a life independent of my parents and the studio, I closed my eyes to any problem and walked radiantly down the aisle." The ballyhooed wedding, designed and flogged by MGM and witnessed by a crush of fans, did what it was meant to do: *Father of the Bride* was a huge success for the studio. The marriage lasted six months.

The brief marriage was ended on February 1, 1952, on the grounds of mental cruelty. Nicky blamed his bad behavior on the goldfish life he had suddenly found himself plunged into. When a legion of reporters and photographers invaded their hotel suite—a frequent occurrence—one of the photographers aimed his camera at Elizabeth and barked at the bridegroom, "Hey, Mac, get out of the way, I want to snap a picture." It was too much for the immature, headstrong playboy to bear. His father, Conrad Hilton, agreed: "They never had a chance . . . Elizabeth is a princess who isn't allowed to lead a normal life, and those near her are affected, too. . . . [I]f she had been a counter girl at Macy's instead of a movie star . . ."

By the time Elizabeth took up the Queen of the Nile's headdress in 1962, she was already the mother of three. Her two sons, Michael and Christopher, were born during her second marriage, to Michael Wilding, the genteel English actor who was closer to Elizabeth's father's age than her own. It had been another marriage encouraged by MGM, to wipe out the bad publicity of her short-lived stint with Nicky, but Elizabeth had been attracted to Wilding, who seemed to offer stability and protection.

Mike Todd, Elizabeth's third husband, was the epitome of a self-made man: born into a poor rabbi's family, lacking in formal education, he made money as a peddler and in the construction business before becoming an independent film producer. He turned his considerable publicity skills toward producing one endlessly flogged hit, *Around the World in 80 Days*. He was part showman, part hustler, part genius, and was touted in the movie magazines as "the love of Elizabeth's life"; she had reveled in the manic showman's macho bluster and outsized personality. He was the complete opposite of her husband Michael Wilding, and thus the complete opposite of her mild-mannered father, art-and-antiques dealer Francis Taylor.

The writer and satirist S. J. Perelman, who wrote the screenplay for Todd's big movie, ended up with a less than sanguine impression of the diminutive mogul, pre-Elizabeth: "Todd's living up to his legend," he wrote in a 1955 letter to his wife, Laura, "standing off from himself and admiring this Napoleonic figure he's created who's . . . producing *War and Peace* and *The Life of Toscanini* at the same time he's releasing *Oklahoma!* and preparing *Around the World in 80 Days* and sleeping with sixteen dames alternately and flying back from Las Vegas and leaving for Paris tomorrow and returning from London yesterday." But his ultra-masculinity and total devotion were just what Elizabeth wanted. Having found her life controlled by others—her mother and MGM—she felt protected by his swagger and strength. And, as an independent producer, he could help her win her freedom from MGM. With Todd at her side, she could tell them all to go to hell.

Todd lived on chutzpah and hype and bought Elizabeth magnificent gifts, including a blinding, 27-carat diamond. He dazzled her with attention. He also knocked her around a few times. Her experience with Nicky Hilton notwithstanding, Elizabeth admitted that she relished the caveman attention—had even goaded him into it—because, in the old morality, it meant he was passionate about her. She needed someone who was tougher, more macho, and more in control than she was. She had tried goading Wilding into bossing her around, but he just wasn't up to it.

One morning, in the third year of her marriage to Wilding, Elizabeth had snatched the crossword puzzle from his hands and challenged him, "Go on, hit me! Why don't you!" But he demurred, too much of a gentleman. Or too passive. A big part of the problem in that marriage had been not only the age difference but the fact that Wilding's once-lively career in England as a light romantic lead had dried up in Hollywood, and Elizabeth was virtually supporting the family. But Elizabeth was an old-fashioned girl. She wanted to be the 1950s-era ideal of femininity that her lush beauty promised but her circumstances and commanding personality left no room for. She was born to rule, but she wanted a man's man, and in Mike Todd, she finally got one.

Tragically, her joy was snatched from her all too soon, on March 22, 1958, after thirteen months of marriage and eight months after the birth of her third child, Elizabeth Frances Todd, known as Liza. Todd had left for the East Coast on a publicity jaunt in the *Liz*, an eleven-seater, Lockheed Lodestar. Elizabeth planned to accompany her husband, but a 102-degree fever kept her at home. The *Liz* encountered a storm over the Nevada desert, ice formed on the wings, the engine failed, and the plane went down in a fiery explosion. Todd, the pilot, the copilot, and Art Cohn, who was writing Todd's biography, all died in the crash. When the news was brought to Elizabeth, she was inconsolable. She became ill with grief, refusing to eat, and MGM was worried that she would be unable to complete filming her role as Maggie the Cat in *Cat on a Hot Tin Roof*, the Tennessee Williams drama costarring Paul Newman and Burl Ives. But she did return to work, and Richard Brooks, her director, coaxed her back to health. The camaraderie of the film set and the demands of finishing the shoot probably saved her sanity and her life.

Soon after Todd's death, Elizabeth turned for comfort to Todd's closest friend and protégé: the crooner Eddie Fisher, who was, inconveniently, Debbie Reynolds's husband at the time. The Fishers were considered America's Sweethearts, and the bust-up of their marriage scandalized the country. Reynolds, whose kewpie-doll cuteness belied her tough-as-nails personality ("She's as wistful as an iron foundry," Oscar Levant once quipped), was now the poster girl for Jilted Wife, victim of the Other Woman, a role Taylor fit all too well, to the horror of her handlers. After a tremendous hue and cry from the press, Elizabeth and Eddie Fisher hastily married, on May 12, 1959, fourteen months after Todd's death.

Why such haste? It could have been that Elizabeth—who had been surrounded since childhood by a studio full of fawners—simply didn't know how to be alone. And, as the biographer Richard Meryman, who collaborated with Taylor on her 1964 memoir, *Elizabeth Taylor*, once observed, marrying Fisher was her way of holding on to Mike Todd. As Todd's best friend (he had named his son Todd, after his hero), Fisher was a bantam-weight substitute, but a substitute nonetheless, except in the bedroom. By several accounts (including Fisher's own), he was a lusty and enthusiastic lover, often making love to his gorgeous bride three and four times a day. Unlike other movie stars, such as Greta Garbo and Marlene Dietrich, Elizabeth really *was* a sex goddess—she adored sex, she loved inspiring lust and satisfying it, she loved the attention, she loved the excitement and the danger. (She had always been attracted to danger, ever since she'd learned to ride and to jump at the age of five.) As Fisher later wrote about their relationship, "She was a woman who loved men as much as they loved her, and she wasn't shy about it."

Elizabeth was vilified for breaking up the Fisher-Reynolds marriage, even though it was clear to all three involved that the connubial fires had completely gone out (if indeed they ever existed). Fisher would later admit that his marriage to the effervescent blond actress, whose girl-next-door image clashed with her real-life toughness, was mostly studio-arranged and had never been a love match. She had been Elizabeth's maid of honor at Elizabeth and Mike Todd's wedding, and she had affectionately washed the bride's hair the day before the nuptials. Now Reynolds, not surprisingly, went along with the studio publicity in portraying Elizabeth as a home-wrecker. She even appeared for newspaper reporters wearing diaper pins attached to her sweater, at the studio publicity department's insistence ("What's a diaper pin?" she'd allegedly asked). America definitely sided with the jilted blonde, not knowing, of course, that her marriage to Eddie Fisher had been stage-managed by Hollywood, just as Elizabeth's marriage to Nicky Hilton—and possibly Michael Wilding—had been. At the height of the scandal, Eddie Fisher received seven thousand hate letters a week. Elizabeth was vilified as a harlot, a viper, a Jezebel. One headline announced "Blood Thirsty Widow Liz Vampires Eddie," and she was denounced from pulpits across the country. When the moralizing gossip maven Hedda Hopper got into the act, Elizabeth fought back with the immortal words "Mike is dead and I'm alive!" (echoing the *cri de coeur* of her character, Maggie the Cat, in *Cat on a Hot Tin Roof*). Hopper, in fact, led the charge against what she perceived as Elizabeth's immoral behavior—an irony considering that the columnist had been crucial in touting Elizabeth as a child star.

The scandal of the Fisher marriage would have a long shelf life, invoked in 1965 when Jacqueline Kennedy was fighting her own public relations war over the publication of William Manchester's *The Death of a President*, commissioned by the Kennedys after the assassination but which Jacqueline, in the end, found too personally revealing. In a publicity battle against the writer and his publisher, Mrs. Kennedy appeared on the cover of *Esquire* with the pull quote:

"Anyone who is against me will look like a rat—unless I run off with Eddie Fisher . . ."

It didn't matter that Fisher's marriage to Debbie Reynolds had never been an affair of the heart. His marriage to Elizabeth brought the actress her first bad publicity. Some even speculated that it had cost her the Academy Award for her work in *Cat on a Hot Tin Roof*, a performance she had painfully—and affectingly—delivered from the depths of her grief.

Fisher had begun his career as a popular singer at Grossinger's, a resort in the Catskills, and had an early *Billboard* hit with "Oh My Pa-Pa." A popular recording star, he reached the pinnacle of his success with a weekly NBC variety show, *Coke Time* (named after its sponsor). Besides the bad publicity of his ruined marriage, the era of crooners was giving way to rock-and-roll stars like Elvis Presley and Buddy Holly. His career never recovered, but it didn't seem to matter—he was wildly, madly, dangerously in love with the grieving beauty. It was thrilling for him to try to follow in Todd's footsteps, as Todd was everything Fisher longed to be—authoritative, expansive, macho. A waiter at Chasen's in Beverly Hills recalled that when the Todds and the Fishers would dine together, Eddie always ordered exactly what Mike Todd ordered. "If Todd said steak medium rare, Eddie wanted steak medium rare. If Todd ordered sole slightly underdone, Eddie wanted the same thing . . . Fisher even ate the same way Todd did—fast." Alas, though Todd and Fisher shared similar backgrounds (both came from urban Jewish working-class families) and ambitions (Fisher hoped to be a producer, like his hero), Fisher would prove to be no Mike Todd. But then nobody could fill those shoes—the short, bulldoggish impresario was louder, more lavish, more passionate, more of a con man, more challenging than anyone Elizabeth had ever known.

By the time Elizabeth was ensconced in a fourteen-room villa on the Appian Way in Rome with an entourage of three children, a huge staff, and several pets, preparing for a role she had demanded and for which she had been paid a record $1 million (plus substantial overages and a percentage of profits), it was probably apparent to her that Eddie was not the kind of husband she needed. Having already stared down Louis B. Mayer and having learned how to handle alpha males like Todd, the last thing she wanted was someone she could boss around. His career as a pop singer in trouble, Fisher was kept on salary by 20th Century-Fox as a producer, really just another factotum hired to make sure Elizabeth showed up on time. His own plans to produce films starring his wife were not catching fire. So he hung on, picking up after Elizabeth's several dogs and sliding into the role of "Mr. Elizabeth Taylor."

Having learned always to get her way and to indulge her enormous appetite for life, in all its forms—food, love, sex, jewels, booze, attention, drama, joy—what Elizabeth needed was someone who could say no to her. Or at least stand up to her. Or at least knock her down a peg or two. Or match her in her Rabelaisian joie de vivre. Fisher just couldn't do it.

But, she would soon discover, Richard Burton could.

The dapper, newly appointed 20th Century-Fox producer Walter Wanger was chosen to produce *Cleopatra* by then-studio boss Spyros Skouras, who believed that a remake of the successful 1917 silent film starring Theda Bara would bring in much needed income to the studio, which had fallen on hard times. Wanger was a successful producer of over sixty pictures, most notably *Joan of Arc* in 1948 and Susan Hayward's tearjerker *I Want to Live!* in 1958. Though his private life had been a tad shaky (he had served time for shooting talent agent Jennings Lang in the groin when he'd discovered that the agent was having an affair with his wife, Joan Bennett), Wanger was up to the task. How hard could it be to add some dialogue to the silent-movie script, hire some attention-getting names, and bring the movie in for $2 million?

Their dream of a modestly budgeted movie was dashed when their top choice to play Cleopatra—Elizabeth—asked for $1 million, a fee she came up with because she really didn't want to make the picture. Her typical salary at the time was $125,000 (close to $900,000 today, adjusted for inflation). Skouras was outraged and told Wanger to jettison Elizabeth for Susan Hayward. But by then, Elizabeth had warmed to the idea, and when Wanger called to tell her the studio wouldn't pay her asking price, Elizabeth went into negotiation mode. First she cried. Then she got tough. She ended up with an even better deal—the $1 million originally offered, a $3,000 a week living allowance, $50,000 for every week over the production schedule, and 10 percent of the movie's gross profits. In addition, she insisted the movie be shot in Todd-AO, a cinemascopic process invented by Mike Todd, which would further enrich her, because, as Todd's widow, she had inherited the rights to the process. She had learned a lot from her third husband—how to ask for the moon and how to get it. The studio agreed. She also demanded director approval. Again, the studio agreed. Peter Finch was cast as Caesar; he had costarred with her in *Elephant Walk*, a jungle drama in which Elizabeth had replaced an ailing Vivien Leigh as the female lead. Stephen Boyd, fresh from his success in *Ben-Hur*, would, for the time being, be her Marc Antony. Wanger then made the odd choice of Rouben Mamoulian to direct the epic—odd, because, though he'd had many successes and was known as "a woman's director"—he had never brought in an epic before. And epic this was going to be.

Elizabeth then insisted on shooting the film overseas, for tax purposes. The studio had hoped to film in Rome, but the 1960 Summer Olympics were to be held in the Eternal City when production was slated to begin, so there would be no hotel rooms available for cast and crew. (It was the 1960 Olympic Games, incidentally, that bestowed the gold medal in light-heavyweight boxing to a young American boxer with a Roman-sounding name: Cassius Marcellus Clay. He would change his name a few years later to Muhammad Ali.) Skouras, however, discovered that he could film in Pinewood Studios outside of London—not only did they have excellent soundstages, they contributed funding to the production in exchange for employing British extras, costumers, hairdressers, and crew and construction workers. So entire sets depicting Rome and Alexandria were built on the Pinewood Studios lot, in a doomed attempt to transform England into Rome.

Massive set construction began, extravagant costumes and props were created, and an enormous cast of extras was assembled. Skouras, Wanger, and Mamoulian, however, didn't anticipate two things: the lousy English weather and Elizabeth Taylor's persistent health problems. The nearly constant rain, wind, and gloom delayed shooting and eroded the sets, which had to be constantly repainted. Living in London's luxurious Dorchester Hotel with Eddie Fisher, Elizabeth contracted bronchitis and missed weeks of shooting, virtually grinding the production to a halt, while extras, actors, and crew all had to be paid. While Wanger was still trying to turn a cold and rainy landscape into sun-baked Rome, Elizabeth's bronchitis turned into pneumonia, which was so intractable that the actress fell into a coma and had to be rushed to the London Clinic, where she famously underwent a tracheotomy to save her life. It left her with a scar visible in close-ups as Queen of the Nile, but it was the luckiest scar imaginable: she credited it with winning her the sympathy vote for Best Actress for her 1961 portrayal of good-time girl Gloria Wandrous in BUtterfield 8, a picture she'd completed the year before and had loathed. ("I lost to a tracheotomy," her rival for the award, Shirley MacLaine, bemoaned.) The world waited anxiously as she recovered from her near-fatal illness—one wire service even reported that she had died—and the international headlines finally turned around the bad publicity that had dogged her after her breakup of the Fishers' marriage. Elizabeth learned early how to make the most of her frequently dramatic illnesses and accidents. Sometimes it was the only way she could find respite from MGM's relentless demands on her; other times it was a surefire way to win sympathy in the face of criticism.

By the time she recovered, the entire set for *Cleopatra* had been disassembled and moved to Rome, where it should have been all along. At last, Rome would stand in for Rome, and the warm sun would hasten Elizabeth's return to health.

But problems persisted. Peter Finch and Elizabeth disliked the script, which had been rewritten by Sidney Buchman, Ben Hecht, and Ranald MacDougall. Mamoulian agreed, and he demanded a new script or else he'd walk off the picture. But the production was already behind schedule and horribly over budget. Elizabeth's pneumonia and tracheotomy had brought the production to a halt, costing the studio $100,000 a day. A year of production had produced only ten minutes of film and had increased the budget to $35 million. To Mamoulian's surprise, Wanger and Skouras accepted his resignation. Elizabeth— exercising her director-approval clause—asked that either George Stevens, who had directed her so magnificently in *A Place in the Sun* (and had driven her to tears in *Giant*) or Joseph L. Mankiewicz, who had directed her in *Suddenly, Last Summer* two years earlier, be hired to replace Mamoulian. Elizabeth knew how important the right director was, how good she had been in the hands of Stevens and Mankiewicz. Stevens wasn't available, so Mankiewicz got the call while he was vacationing on the island retreat owned by his friend, actor Hume Cronyn. Like Mamoulian, Mankiewicz was an esteemed director, but, also like Mamoulian, he had never before brought in an epic.

Cronyn's advice to his friend? "Don't do it."

A brilliant writer-director, Mankiewicz had won four Academy Awards, back to back, for writing and directing *A Letter to Three Wives* and *All About Eve*; like Mamoulian, he had a reputation as a "woman's director," so the studio thought he would help keep Elizabeth in line. Besides being prone to sickness and accidents, she contractually demanded time off from filming during her menstrual periods. She was chronically, famously late, and she suffered flus, infections, bronchitis, and injuries the way other people caught colds. She once stepped on a wire while dancing at a wrap party, injuring

herself and starting a fire. Mankiewicz had already wrestled into sub-
mission divas such as Bette Davis in *All About Eve* and Katharine
Hepburn in *Suddenly, Last Summer.* He was fascinated by "actresses,"
whom he regarded (perhaps a tad jealously) as neurotic, fabulous creatures, and he was writing a never-finished tome on the subject. The
studio tempted him with a $3 million payout (over $21 million in
today's dollars) for his services and an offer to buy him out of existing
commitments—more money than he had ever received in his long,
distinguished career—so he agreed to shoulder the burden, casting
his friend Hume Cronyn as Cleopatra's tutor, Sosigenes.

Mankiewicz would prove to have a strong influence on Elizabeth,
who would one day describe him as her favorite director. His own
view of women reiterated Elizabeth's feeling that a certain femininity
was lacking in her life. Mankiewicz, a stocky, pipe-smoking intellectual, was proud of his understanding of the human psyche and was
known to have his screenplays psychoanalyzed before shooting. The
lines he wrote for Bette Davis in *All About Eve* would later be appro-
priated by Elizabeth: "I can be an actress or a woman, but I can't be
both." Happy, fulfilled women served their men (and were supported
by them). With almost every new marriage, Elizabeth publicly announced that her main role in life was to be "Mrs. Michael Wilding"
or "Mrs. Mike Todd" or "Mrs. Eddie Fisher." It was good press in the
Eisenhower era, but it was also her genuine longing for a "normal" life.
On one rare occasion, she railed against her own movie-star status:
"Why couldn't they let me grow up like Suzy Smith with a house in
the suburbs, a husband who takes the 8:10, and three fat, saucy kids?"
Of course, she would have hated that. Too safe.

In some ways, their fates were intertwined. Mankiewicz had been
scheduled to accompany Mike Todd on his last, fatal flight on the
Liz, but his sister-in-law, Sarah Mankiewicz, had had a premonition
and warned him not to go. He took a different flight, but he had the
frisson of seeing his own death notice when he was mistakenly re-

ported as having been aboard the doomed plane. Mankiewicz lived, he accepted the offer of directing *Cleopatra*, and his choice to replace Stephen Boyd as Marc Antony would change the course of Elizabeth's life. The movie would also change the course of his own: his brilliant career lost all momentum and limped to its conclusion five years later; in the last twenty years of his long life Joe Mankiewicz never directed another film. He would blame Elizabeth and Richard for that.

Mankiewicz replaced Peter Finch (now committed to another film) with Rex Harrison, whom he'd loved directing in *The Ghost and Mrs. Muir*. To replace Stephen Boyd, the studio had to buy Richard Burton out of his successful Broadway run as King Arthur in *Camelot*, paying Alan Jay Lerner and Frederick Loewe a lump sum of $50,000. In addition to that payment, Burton was offered a contract guaranteeing him $250,000 ($1.7 million today), plus overages, plus extras, such as transportation for himself and his family, and $1,000 a week for what 20th Century-Fox's ledgers referred to as "small expenses." He and Sybil and their two girls were also given the use of a villa and household staff, which they shared with Roddy McDowall, Burton's *Camelot* costar and Elizabeth's childhood friend from their *Lassie* days. All of these perks, of course, further bloated the production budget.

Burton, his eye always on the prize and feeling he had botched his earlier attempt at conquering Hollywood (though he had acquitted himself rather well in *The Robe* and *My Cousin Rachel*, two prior Hollywood films), leaped at the chance. He was becoming bored after playing King Arthur, night after night, for nearly a year in *Camelot*'s long run, even though he reveled in the part and had kept libations flowing in his dressing room, which he'd dubbed "Burton's Bar." His final night in the role was September 16, 1961, and by then everyone knew the reason for his leaving the play. His last performance was triumphant, rewarded with a standing ovation. Julie Andrews (who played Queen Guinevere) left Burton alone onstage so he could bask in the waves of adulation that poured forth from the audience. There was the unspoken recognition that this boy from an unpronounceable Welsh mining town had made good, and the audience cherished their last night in his company, relishing each kingly gesture. This would be hard for Burton to give up: the seduction and acclaim of a live audience, fought for and won night after night.

When the houselights came on and the last theatergoer had left the Majestic Theater, Burton found himself in the midst of a farewell party. Among the celebrants was the playwright Moss Hart, who had directed the play, and who had suffered a heart attack ten days after opening. That last night, Hart, given to Polonius-like pronouncements, took Burton aside and cautioned him, "I beg you not to waste your wonderful gifts. You must know you have it in you to be one of the greatest stage actors of this century." But for now, the movies once again beckoned. For Burton, that's where real fame—and fortune—were to be made.

Burton generally disliked "tits and sand" epics, like *The Robe* and now *Cleopatra*, that required him to wear togas and tunics. He found prancing around barelegged or in tights decidedly unmanly, which is one reason his Broadway *Hamlet* two years later would be performed in street clothes. But in *Cleopatra*, Mankiewicz costumed Burton in the shortest soldier's tunic of all—a pleated skirt that showcases his muscular thighs and barely covers his manhood. Mankiewicz was impressed with Burton, whose intelligence, wit, and soulful masculinity attracted men and women alike. Like Burton, the twice-married Mankiewicz was given to having affairs with the actresses he directed (and some that he didn't, like a young Judy Garland), but he was dazzled by Burton, joking to the press later on that it was he, not Elizabeth, who was having the affair with him.

Burton exuded virility, but there was something in his past he was ashamed of. He had, reportedly, succumbed to advances by Sir John Gielgud and Sir Laurence Olivier as he made his stellar way through the hierarchical world of the English theater. He would later tell interview hosts like Dick Cavett and the BBC's Michael Parkinson that he had "tried homosexuality" and "it didn't take." It came down to this: men from mining towns don't have sex with other men. In the rugged world of coal miners, rugby players, and world-class drinkers, masculinity was something you earned, and you earned it in the eyes of other men. So the encounters of his youth troubled him; they may have fueled his relentless womanizing.

If Skouras and Wanger thought that Mankiewicz would stem the financial bleeding and put the production on an even keel, they were wrong. In Mankiewicz's hands, the production continued to spiral out of control. First, he agreed with Elizabeth that the script needed a major rewrite, and he felt that he was the only one up to the task. So he set about directing by day and writing all night. In order to both direct and rewrite the script, he began relying on twice-daily injections of amphetamines to keep going, administered by the notorious Max Jacobson, aka "Dr. Feelgood." His ambition was noble: to equal Shaw and Shakespeare in his sprawling, hybrid screenplay. Indeed, in the beauty of his language he sometimes comes close, but the thing was so gargantuan—a whopping 327 pages—and so impossible to wrestle into shape while simultaneously overseeing a vast cast and crew, that it seriously undermined his health. His eldest son, Chris Mankiewicz, who was hired to work on the production, feared his father might suffer a heart attack. The agitated state it left him in not only brought on a skin disorder that caused his fingertips to bleed, necessitating the wearing of white cotton film-cutter's gloves, it also brought about a common result of amphetamine abuse: grandiosity.

Everything about the production—the sets, the dressing rooms, the props, the number of extras, the script itself—took on gargantuan proportions. The entire production suffered from gigantism. The film would eventually take three years to complete, at a staggering cost of $44 million, close to $300 million in today's dollars; it's considered the third most expensive movie ever made. And because Mankiewicz was literally writing the screenplay as they were shooting, he was virtually directing his first draft—there was no time for streamlining and honing, and no shooting script was prepared, so they were forced to shoot everything in sequence, a costly process that kept all the actors on salary all the time. Just about everything that could go wrong went wrong. Reflecting back on the Herculean effort to get this story on film, Elizabeth described it in her 1964 memoir as "a nightmare." But what redeemed the experience, at least for her, was falling in love with Richard Burton.

When Elizabeth had first encountered Burton at Stewart Granger's Hollywood party in 1953, she'd disliked him—he talked too much, he was "rather full of himself," and she gave him "the cold fish eye." So she was prepared to treat him coolly on the set of *Cleopatra*, vowing that she would not be another notch on his gun belt.

So they met, for the second time, on the set on January 22, 1962, costumed and in full makeup. Elizabeth was already on her guard, even before meeting the notorious Welshman. She was well aware of his theatrical reputation for having all his lines and even his costars' lines memorized on the first day. She thought of him as not just "a movie star but a genuine actor." Taylor was well aware of her own technical limitations; the one thing MGM had failed to do was to provide her with acting lessons. She was what is known as "a natural," and her greatest talent was that unknown quality that leaps through the camera and goes directly into the audience's heart.

Elizabeth also knew of Burton's legendary conquests—he had bedded many of his leading ladies, including dark-haired beauties like Claire Bloom, and Susan Strasberg (a mere seventeen at the time), all the while married to his plucky and stalwart Welsh wife, Sybil Burton, whom he claimed he would never abandon. Legendary, too, was the Welshman's golden-throated voice, his bonhomie, his love of poetry and language and Shakespeare and liquor. His vibrant sexuality could heat up a room. His face was pockmarked from the testosterone-fueled boils that had plagued him during his hardscrabble youth in the Welsh coal town of Pontrhydyfen, but he had, nonetheless, a soulful and haunted beauty. Earth and air were mingled in him; he looked like "a boxing poet," according to his countryman Emlyn Williams, the playwright and actor whose early interest in Burton had helped launch his theatrical career in *The Druid's Rest* and his film career as the young swain in *The Last Days of Dolwyn*.

So when they first clapped eyes on each other on the oversized set of *Cleopatra*, Richard in his too-short tunic and Elizabeth in her dark Egyptian eye makeup and stunning Irene Sharaff gown, "there was a lot of hemming and hawing." Burton, the great seducer, tried to ignore her at first, then he edged over to Elizabeth and said fatuously, "Has anybody ever told you that you're a very pretty girl?" As recounted in her autobiography, Elizabeth couldn't believe the lameness of that gambit. She "couldn't wait to go back to the dressing room where all the girls were and tell them, *'Oy gevalt'*" (delighted to use the Yiddishisms she'd learned from Todd and Fisher), "here's the great lover, the great wit, the great intellectual of Wales, and he comes out with a line like that." It was actually a brilliant gambit—in a world in which everyone catered to Elizabeth Taylor, Richard Burton showed he was willing to make fun of her.

In another account, Burton also took one look at her overripe beauty and let slip the words "You're too fat." In actuality, he was so shaken by the sight of her looking "so bloody marvelous" that he'd wanted to knock her down a peg. Besides her overwhelming physical presence, Burton was impressed by the fact that she was earning four times his own considerable salary, and that she already possessed the thing that had so far eluded him—movie star status. He was also contemptuous of the hovering presence of Eddie Fisher on the set. A friend had joked with Burton that Fisher only came in third in Elizabeth's entourage, after her hairdresser, Alexandre de Paris, and her agent, Kurt Frings. Burton had taken in the absurdity of this overpaid, ripe beauty and her doting husband, and had meant to show that he was unfazed.

But fazed he was. And at their next meeting, everything changed.

Their first day of working together, Burton had showed up completely hungover from a night of carousing. "He was kind of quivering from head to foot and there were grog blossoms—you know, from booze—all over his face," Elizabeth remembered. "He ordered a cup of coffee to sort of still his trembling fists and I had to help it to his mouth, and that just endeared him to me. I thought, 'Well, he really is human. . . . so vulnerable and sweet and shaky and terribly giggly that with my heart I *'cwtched'* him—that's Welsh for 'hug.' " He then further disarmed Elizabeth when he blew a line. "If it had been a planned strategic campaign, Caesar couldn't have planned it better," she recalled.

But their early on-camera scenes together, in Eddie Fisher's understandably jaundiced view, were underwhelming. Fisher showed up on the set for Elizabeth's nude bathing scene. (Only a generous glimpse of thigh is actually visible onscreen. Elizabeth was too Old Hollywood to show more.) Elizabeth showed up three hours late, trailing a phalanx of makeup specialists and hairdressers. Fisher took a sip of the bottle of Coke Elizabeth was nursing, only to discover that it was brandy. He sat down next to Mankiewicz.

"Joe," he said, "what's going on here?"

"Eddie, she hasn't the faintest idea what she's doing."

After watching the early rushes, Fisher was struck by the difference between Burton's and Elizabeth's acting styles; he felt that, "with his big, sonorous voice and her little, squeaky one, their scenes together were ludicrous."

Burton himself was at first perplexed by Elizabeth's apparent lack of technique. "She's just not *doing* anything," he complained to Mankiewicz, until the pipe-smoking director took him aside and showed him Taylor's impact onscreen. It took his breath away. Burton—trained to move, to speak, to *act*—was struck by Elizabeth's absolute *stillness*, and he would later say that he learned an important film technique from Elizabeth: how to tone down his theatrical performances for the camera's cool eye. From that moment, Burton learned how the visual/spectacle element of film could trump the written/spoken element of theater. Under the influence of Elizabeth, Burton made the transition from stage acting to screen acting on the soundstage of *Cleopatra.* Later, when their relationship began to stagger under the weight of their fame and their excesses, Elizabeth would remind him of that fact.

If it was Burton's vulnerability that first attracted Elizabeth, there was a deeper siren call as well. Truth was, Elizabeth was having her own romance with alcohol, though not quite on Burton's level. At their sumptuous Villa Pappa on the Appian Way, Fisher watched as she took her first drink in the morning, followed by several glasses of wine at lunch, and "who knows how much for the remainder of the day? And as I discovered, she wasn't just drinking at home." She loved Bloody Marys and was in the habit of taking with her to the studio a case of vodka, tonic water, and tomato juice. Their liquor bill could reach as much as $700 a week (roughly $4,900 today). Fisher had been a heavy drinker once, but he wasn't drinking in those days, and he tried to curtail Elizabeth's alcohol intake, watering down her drinks as he anxiously watched over her. He had nursed her through her near-fatal pneumonia at the Dorchester Hotel, and her recovery from a tracheotomy, never leaving her bedside. Now he tried to monitor her alcohol intake. But that's not what Elizabeth had signed up for.

"At some point after working with Burton," Fisher later recalled, "I think she began to see me as a jailer. I was spoiling her fun. She didn't need me to monitor her medication and drinks and put her to bed at night." And now, suddenly, Elizabeth would be playing love scenes with this devastating Welshman, made vulnerable by drink, a god brought down to earth, whose need for alcohol translated into a ravishing thirst for life. In this, and in other areas, Burton left Elizabeth's anxious care-taker—whom he would later dismiss as "the busboy"—in the dust.

As for Burton, he reportedly set his cap for Taylor as just one of his usual conquests. He expected to bed all of his leading ladies (with the apparent exception of Julie Andrews, Guinevere to his Arthur in *Camelot*, who remained beyond his reach). At least that's what Jack Brodsky and Nathan Weiss, 20th Century-Fox publicity agents attached to the first incarnation of *Cleopatra*, wrote in their chronicle of the production, *The Cleopatra Papers*. They suggest that her star power was what impressed him most—her million-dollar salary, her fourteen-room villa, the shipments of her favorite food, Chasen's chili, flown in from Los Angeles. He thought an affair might elevate his own status in the industry—and he was nothing if not ambitious—but Burton had no intention of falling in love. "I must don my armor once more," Brodsky and Weiss report him as saying, "to play against Miss Tits." That bit of bravado suggests that Burton had no idea what was about to engulf him.

Protected by his marriage to Sybil, a sane, witty, and intelligent woman who kept him grounded in his Welsh life, Burton felt he could fall in and out of affairs with no possibility of becoming ensnared. His affair with Claire Bloom, begun while they were both still in their twenties and making their names as extraordinary Shakespearean actors at the Old Vic, had probably come closest to threatening his marriage. But Burton needed Sybil and the stability she provided. In his own way, he loved her, though Sybil's prematurely silver hair made her appear, at times, more like his mother than his wife. Burton adored their five-year-old daughter, Kate, and their toddler, Jessica, who seemed to need special care.

And there was this basic fact: Welsh men did not abandon their families.

But the heat and lightning of Burton's scenes with Elizabeth were beginning to be noticed. Burton would later claim that he was first smitten when he watched the scene of Elizabeth naked in her bath, lolling like a mermaid, tended by a bevy of handmaidens. In their first deep kiss, in Cleopatra's boudoir, just after confessing their mutual love, Burton found himself caught up, almost drugged, in her presence. They repeated the scene several times, their kiss lasting longer with each take. Finally, Mankiewicz shouted, "Print it"—but the scene continued. "Would you two mind if I say cut?" he asked again. And then, "Does it interest you that it is time for lunch?"

Burton didn't have a chance.

It was not just Elizabeth Taylor who was casting her spell over him, it was Cleopatra herself, who ruled by divine right, descended from the Egyptian goddess Isis. "I am Isis," she had revealed to Caesar in their first love scene. "I am the Nile. I am worshipped by millions who believe it." Taylor already identified with Cleopatra. She felt that "Mike Todd . . . had been to her what Julius Caesar had been to Cleopatra." Now Marc Antony—Burton—would take his place.

And there were those words of love Mankiewicz had written for Cleopatra and Antony to speak—Richard himself was especially vulnerable to the beauty of words: "From that first instant I saw you entering Rome on that fabulous beast, crowned in gold . . . I envied Caesar . . . I envied him *you*," Antony confesses. And, later, when the destruction of their empire looms, Cleopatra cries to Antony, "To have waited so long, to know so suddenly. Without you, this is not a world I want to live in." And Antony answers her: "Everything that I want to love or hold or have or be is here with me now."

When their first love scene finally ended, Burton reportedly called for a beer and Elizabeth nonchalantly handed off her wig and walked away. In his dressing room, where he had resumed "Burton's Bar" for cast and crew, Burton lunched with a bevy of actors, writers, and adoring females. Suddenly, he called out across the empty soundstage for Elizabeth to join them.

She turned and smiled. She walked into his crowded dressing room, where he promptly ignored her, except to bend down low and whisper an off-color story into her ear, one which made her blush and laugh in delight. Later, when they returned to the soundstage, he dragged her director's chair next to his, where it would remain throughout the rest of the shoot.

Still, Burton kept his guard up—at first by keeping on hand a girl-friend, Pat Tunder, a Copacabana dancer Burton had met during the run of *Camelot* whom he'd brought with him to Rome. But Taylor had already discovered that Eddie, for all his ministrations and devotion, could not take Mike Todd's place. She had tamed him, and therefore he was now unchallenging. He couldn't match her increasingly brilliant star status. It didn't help Fisher's case that Burton looked like a younger, taller, and handsomer version of Todd: the squarish face, the broad shoulders, the roughness of skin, the working-class background, the sheer virility.

"Elizabeth was not used to assertive men," observed Ron Berkeley, Elizabeth's makeup artist on many of her early films. "Oh, they might put on an act for a while, but they nearly all ended up showing love by deference, paying tribute to her beauty. Only one other man had taken her by sheer force of personality. When she encountered Richard Burton, it must have seemed to her that she had rediscovered Mike Todd." The moment Burton had shown up, hungover, on the soundstage of *Cleopatra*, Fisher was history. He just didn't know it yet.

Fisher should, perhaps, have been on his guard. "Even if he hadn't destroyed my marriage," he later wrote about Burton, "I would have disliked him." He claimed that he and Elizabeth had at first made fun of Burton behind his back, put off by his roughness and lack of grooming. "I thought he was an arrogant slob. Elizabeth and I . . . compared him to the great producer of MGM musicals, Arthur Freed, about whom it was said he could grow orchids under his fingernails."

Fisher must have been reassured by the fact that he and Elizabeth were in the process of adopting a nine-month-old German girl whose parents could not afford the series of operations needed to correct her crippling hip deformity. Elizabeth's heart had gone out to this needy infant, whom she and Fisher renamed Maria (after the actress Maria Schell, who had located the child for them). Unable or unwilling to bear more children after her cesarean delivery of Liza Todd, in which she had almost lost her baby, Elizabeth had longed for a child to consecrate her marriage to Fisher. But by the time the adoption papers were signed, Fisher's days were numbered.

On a few occasions, Sybil accompanied Burton to Villa Pappa, the expansive Italian villa on the Appian Way rented by Fox studio for Elizabeth and her entourage. The pink marble mansion came complete with swimming pool, acres of pine forests, two butlers, and three maids. The entourage included the couple's two secretaries and Elizabeth's three children, ten dogs, and four cats. Dick Hanley, a former secretary to Louis B. Mayer and now Elizabeth's majordomo, was set up in a nearby flat with his companion. In Rome, Taylor lived in Cleopatra-like luxury, insisting that all the beds be made daily with fresh linen. For each meal, full place settings were provided by the maids—complete with a glass for white wine, one for red, one for champagne, and one for water. When she wasn't dining luxuriously, she made sure Hanley had her favorite chili flown in from Chasen's. For dinner parties, the table settings were color-coordinated with Elizabeth's outfit (no doubt to bring out the violet hues in her changeable, blue-violet eyes). Fisher watched his wife's drinking, instructing their servants to stop serving her after five drinks. But the first time Burton dined with them at the villa, the actor surreptitiously refilled her glass. "I adore this man," Elizabeth thought at that moment; with or without Mankiewicz's dialogue, she knew she was falling for him.

At a New Year's Eve party at Villa Pappa to celebrate the impending adoption of Maria, Fisher was surprised to see Elizabeth sitting with Burton on a small couch, whispering and giggling. Feeling excluded, he sat down at the piano and started to sing, to attract her attention, but Elizabeth just glared at him and he left the room.

Elizabeth and Richard probably first made love in Burton's dressing room, and then found stolen afternoons in Dick Hanley's flat near Villa Pappa. What began as a thrilling conquest for Burton quickly deepened into infatuation, then an inexplicable thirst for her. He was a celebrated cocksman with a string of women in his past—and a wife very much in his present—yet in Elizabeth he found a woman who matched him in sexual fire. Later, Burton would pour out his emotions in love letters to Elizabeth, describing how "I lust after your smell and your paps and your divine little money-box and your round belly and the exquisite softness of the inside of your thighs and your baby-bottom and your giving lips & the half hostile look in your eyes when you're deep in rut with your little Welsh stallion . . ." Rumors of the affair began to swirl around the set, finally reaching Fisher, who confronted her. "Tell me the truth," he asked Elizabeth. "Is there something going on between you and Burton?"

"Yes."

Elizabeth simply couldn't lie—not to herself, not to Eddie. The truth just smacked her in the face—she was in love with Richard Burton. Elizabeth had always been a truth-teller.

Fisher, like Burton, couldn't escape what was happening to him. At one point, he left Rome to nurse his wounds at the chalet Elizabeth had purchased in Gstaad. When he returned to Rome, he was severely depressed, wandering around Villa Pappa all day in his pajamas, drinking vodka and wondering what had happened to his career. At one miserable dinner at the villa in March of 1962, Burton, deep in his cups, had brutally demanded that Elizabeth declare, in front of Eddie Fisher, to name the one she loved.

"Elizabeth," he'd growled in his best theatrical voice, "who do you love? *Whooo do you love?*"

She looked at both men and said to Burton, "You."

Burton then picked up a silver-framed photograph of Mike Todd, Elizabeth, and their daughter, Liza, and he turned to Fisher. "He didn't know how to use her!" Burton shouted, pointing to the picture of Mike Todd. "You don't know how to use her, either! And what's that fucking picture here for?" He continued to rage—all of this remembered and recorded by Eddie Fisher in both of his memoirs—

until Elizabeth ran out of the villa in tears. The two men were left alone in the empty room, where they continued to fume over snifters of brandy. "Burton did most of the talking," Fisher wrote, "flattering me, insulting me, laying little traps, charming and apologetic one moment, crude and abusive the next."

Unnerved by his encounter with Burton, Fisher sought out Sybil at their rented villa and told her about his suspicions. "Eddie broke the cardinal rule as the cuckold in any affair," Walter Wanger later confided in the producer and agent Edward Heyman. "He called the wife." Sybil admitted that she had known about the affair for weeks. Fisher asked her how she managed to cope with the situation, and she answered, "Ever since Richard and I have been married, he's had these affairs. But he always comes back to me. The thing with Elizabeth is over."

"It isn't over, Sybil. They're seeing each other constantly," Fisher informed her. Sybil, however, refused to believe it. Fisher left, admiring Sybil's powers of denial. But she wasn't as sanguine as she'd appeared. Shortly after her encounter with Fisher, she reportedly stormed onto the soundstage and created a scene, which shut down production for an entire day, costing the studio another $100,000.

Fisher tried to escape the madness by traveling to Florence, where he called Elizabeth at their villa. But it was Richard who answered the telephone.

"What are you doing there?" Eddie Fisher asked Richard Burton. "What are you doing in my house?"

"What do you think I'm doing?" Burton answered. "I'm fucking your wife."

Mankiewicz was also aware of what was happening and was leery of the new complication, confiding in Wanger, "Elizabeth and Burton are not just *playing* Antony and Cleopatra!" Studio publicists like Jack Brodsky tried to suppress rumors of the affair, but it was too late. Hordes of photographers camping out at Cinecittà got wind of it, adding to the general chaos of the production. They hounded the couple, snapping their photo outside Tre Scalini in Piazza Navona, even following them on a brief escape to Elizabeth's chalet in Gstaad. Whenever the lovers escaped to the fashionable Via Veneto, they were followed by wildly snapping photographers, eager to sell their photos to newspapers and magazines. Their constant buzz inspired Federico Fellini, who was filming *La Dolce Vita* on the streets of Rome at the time; he named his intrusive reporter "Paparazzo," which means "buzzing insect." The name stuck.

Wanger saw how "incredibly patient and well informed" the paparazzi were, these young Italian men on Vespas and in low-slung sports cars, their Rolleiflexes slung over their shoulders. They had found out even before the lease was signed just which magnificent villa would house the Taylor-Fisher household, and they climbed into the trees along one of Villa Pappa's two swimming pools. They seemed to be everywhere, one day disguising themselves as priests boldly knocking on the Burtons' door, sometimes dropping from the trees to grab a photograph of a startled Richard or Elizabeth or Eddie Fisher, their eyes blinded by the sudden white light of the flashcubes. "It seemed like everybody who worked for Richard or me in Rome made a fortune selling their stories to the press," Elizabeth believed. "A woman Richard hired for his children turned out to be a fake Italian countess, and she sold her story in America."

For a time, the two lovers did make an attempt to stay away from each other. Elizabeth couldn't bear the idea of going through another highly publicized divorce and world disapprobation, so there were occasions when they showed up on the set and barely spoke to each other. But not for long. Their happiest moments were when they managed to escape for a few days, hiding out in a pink stucco villa they had secretly rented at Porto Santo Stefano. She always relished those rare occasions when she could pretend to be an ordinary woman: "We'd spend weekends there. I'd barbecue. There was a crummy old shower, and the sheets were always damp. We loved it—absolutely adored it." On one occasion, their disappearance sent their beleaguered director into an amphetamine-fueled tizzy. He began searching the hospitals before Burton finally showed up, pretending ignorance. Then Elizabeth suddenly appeared, tapping Mankiewicz on the back. He was furious—but relieved—to welcome them back on the set.

By February, Brodsky and Mankiewicz took Burton aside and pleaded with him to come to his senses, but the real pressure was from Sybil, who was packing her bags for New York. Unable to face the loss of his family, Burton—wracked with guilt and terrified over the intensity of his feelings for Elizabeth—informed her that he would never leave Sybil (nor would he give up his girlfriend, Pat Tunder, for that matter). Elizabeth, not used to being denied anything, was devastated. On February 17, 1962, she took an overdose of sleeping pills and had to be rushed to Salvator Mundi International Hospital to be resuscitated.

Wanger and Mankiewicz had come for lunch to Villa Pappa and found Elizabeth being tended to by a physician, Dr. Coen. She seemed unusually pale, Wanger thought, and after lunch she confided how terrible she felt about hurting Sybil. "I feel dreadful," she'd said. "Sybil is such a wonderful woman." Wanger had tried to comfort her by talking about how difficult it was to swim against the tides of life. "How funny you should say that," Elizabeth said. "Richard calls me 'Ocean.'" She then retired to her bedroom and slipped into a pale gray Christian Dior nightgown, claiming exhaustion. A few minutes later, when he checked on her, he was told that she took some sleeping pills. That's when one of her entourage called an ambulance, and word got out to the press that Elizabeth had attempted suicide.

Wanger tried to make light of the event, asking Brodsky and Weiss to make up a story of food poisoning to avert the bad publicity already dogging the star-crossed production. Wanger had put the blame on "a tin of bully beef" they had shared for lunch at the villa, then on a handful of Seconals Elizabeth had taken to help her sleep. Their cover-up seemed to have worked, but it really didn't matter: a few days later, the Burton-Taylor affair resumed.

In April, Sybil flew back to Rome from New York, once again forcing the issue. When Richard received word of his wife's imminent arrival in the Eternal City, he and Elizabeth drove from Rome to their beach hideaway in a small, two-seater Fiat, leaving early in the morning to escape the paparazzi. It was the Easter weekend, and their beachside town was half-deserted. They enjoyed caffe lattes and cognac in a small bar-café, but their idyllic weekend quickly turned into a nightmare when they wandered into the small café, deserted except for a sleeping dog, a bored waiter, and a few idle customers. It seemed the perfect haven for a couple hounded by the world, but as it happened, one of the idle customers was, in fact, a local newspaper reporter, there to cover the arrival of a minor member of the Dutch royal family. He quickly recognized the two most famous people in the world. They finished their cognacs and drove to their isolated, half-finished villa with its glorious view of the Mediterranean. There they played in the surf, made love, clambered over the rocks as if they were any pair of lovers delighting in each other's company.

Suddenly, they looked around and discovered that the paparazzi had found them out and were hiding in the bushes and among the rocks. The newspaperman had notified the press of Richard and Elizabeth's whereabouts. They escaped back to their small villa, trapped in their guilty paradise, where there was nothing to do but drink, play gin rummy, and wait for the paparazzi to go away.

Burton later recalled that weekend in his notebooks:

> We drank to the point of stupefaction and idiocy. We couldn't go outside. We were not married. . . . We tried to read. We failed. We couldn't go out. We made a desperate kind of love. We played gin rummy. E. kept on winning and oddly enough out of this silly game came the crisis. For some reason—who knows or remembers the conversation that led up to it?—E. said that she was prepared to kill herself for me. Easy to say, I said, but no woman would kill herself for me, etc. with oodlings of self pity . . . out of it all came

E. standing over me with a bottle or box of sleeping pills in her hand, saying that she could do it. Go ahead, I said, or words along those lines, whereupon she took a handful and swallowed with gusto and no dramatics.

Burton at first didn't believe she had swallowed sleeping pills— he thought Elizabeth had probably just taken a handful of vitamin C. But when she went to sleep, Burton couldn't wake her. That's when he realized she had not been acting. He managed to drag her into the car and sped back to Rome, where, for a second time, she had her stomach pumped at Salvator Mundi. Burton then slunk back to his villa, ironically named "Beautiful Solitude," and then on to Paris, where he was shooting a scene for Darryl Zanuck's World War II epic, *The Longest Day.*

Still hoping to deflect rumors of the affair, Wanger warned Burton to stay away. "I think Burton had finally begun to understand the consequence of being with Elizabeth," Wanger later wrote about the incident. "He had complained when the reporters hounded him in Paris, 'It's like fucking Khrushchev. I've had affairs before—how did I know the woman was so fucking famous?' "

When Elizabeth was again released from the hospital, her face was bruised and she couldn't appear on camera for several days. Other accounts suggest that Elizabeth was hospitalized for a bloody nose, caused by being thrown forward in the Fiat when the car suddenly stopped short. Given that Wanger was putting out cover stories, Burton's diary entry is probably the most reliable account. Years later, Elizabeth would ruefully admit to the suicide attempt, saying that at the time, "I was a very sick girl," in agony over what to do, unwilling to relive the kind of public shaming she had received over her breakup of Eddie Fisher's marriage, and equally unwilling—and unable—to give up Richard. "Everyone's unhappiness," she later said, "had reached a point of no return."

* * *

Meanwhile, Fisher was deep in denial. It took a column by Louella Parsons, one of the two leading gossip columnists in Hollywood, and headlines such as the *Los Angeles Examiner*'s "Row Over Actor Ends Liz, Eddie Marriage," to force Fisher to finally act, though by now he must have known his marriage was over.

"I knew it before she did," he later confessed. "Elizabeth desperately needed excitement, and our relationship had settled into a marriage. Comfort wasn't enough for her. She was addicted to drama, to the fights and making up, to breaking down doors. There was no possible way she could have given up what she'd found in Burton."

Nonetheless, Fisher and Taylor continued to deny the rumors ("LIZ, EDDY DENY SPLIT"). He left for New York, heartbroken and humiliated, and landed in the arms of Dr. Jacobson, who kept him supplied with drugs. In one attempt to put the swirling rumors to rest, he agreed to appear as a mystery guest on the popular quiz show *What's My Line?*, ostensibly to publicize *Cleopatra*-inspired cosmetics that the studio was marketing. It didn't help. The gossip columnist Dorothy Kilgallen, a regular panel member on the show, had already written a damning story about the affair. To add to his humiliation, Fisher wound up predicting that "Elizabeth Taylor Fisher" would win an Academy Award for her role in *Cleopatra*. "I was lost," he later wrote, devastated by Elizabeth's betrayal. He wound up in a small private hospital in New York, having overdosed on vodka and amphetamines. The rumor mill went overboard, announcing that he was locked up in a psychiatric ward, so when he was released, he held a press conference to show that he wasn't confined to a padded cell.

Fortified with a shot of methamphetamine, he strolled into a feeding frenzy at the Sapphire Room of the Pierre Hotel on Fifth Avenue, where reporters were practically hanging from the rafters. The press conference was his last-ditch ploy to persuade the public that his marriage was still intact. He'd even asked Elizabeth to speak to the press by telephone from Rome, believing that she still wanted to deny the rumors of their breakup. But that was not to be.

Fisher was called into the hotel manager's office, where Elizabeth delivered the news—with reporters listening in on the call—that she would no longer participate in the fiction of their marriage. It was over. Instead of a reconciliation, he was treated to a headline: "Eddie Fisher Dumped."

Deep down, Fisher had known all along that Burton had what Elizabeth wanted: "[t]hat marvelous voice, his knowledge of acting, and his ability to teach her. I also believed she mistook his weaknesses, his alcoholism, his bitterness, and the anger that led to violence, for independence and self-confidence. She thought he was a hero." In his desperation, Fisher at one point bought a gun, ostensibly to protect the family because of a deluge of threatening letters they were receiving. Years later, Elizabeth would reveal things she had left out of her memoir because she felt they were too hurtful. One of them was that she had awoken in the villa one night to find Eddie watching over her, pointing the gun at her head. "Don't worry, Elizabeth," she heard him say. "I'm not going to kill you. You're too beautiful."

That's when she fled. She gathered up her children and took them to Dick Hanley's place and never went back.

Their divorce was handled by the influential lawyer Louis Nizer, but it would take years to untangle their financial dealings—the chalet in Gstaad, their expensive cars and Elizabeth's jewels, their business enterprises. Meanwhile, Fisher attempted to salvage his career by making a number of nightclub appearances, opening his new act with the song "Arrivederci, Roma." He later appeared in New York's Winter Garden Theater with the South African dancer Juliet Prowse, who slithered on-stage as Cleopatra, singing "I'm Cleo, the Nympho of the Nile." But his once-fabulous career, like his once-famous marriage, never recovered. The former singing sensation would be remembered by the public as Elizabeth Taylor's fourth husband, the one between Todd and Burton. And yet, for a brief time, they had been happy together.

In mid-June, 20th Century-Fox sent cast and crew to the south-ern Italian island of Ischia, in the Bay of Naples, to film the Battle of

Actium. Richard and Elizabeth arrived by helicopter, and once there, hired a yacht. They were, of course, surrounded by the paparazzi, who trained their telephoto lenses on the couple from a flotilla of small boats. A photographer, Pat Morin, shot a now-famous picture of the two kissing on the bow of their rented yacht, published in the Italian newspaper *Oggi*. It was the shot seen around the world: she's in a striped one-piece bathing suit, her dark hair tumbled over the dazzling white of the yacht; he's lying beside her, kissing her, their two packs of cigarettes (one of them Marlboro) resting near their naked feet. They are lost in each other, moored, hiding in plain sight.

The grainy, black-and-white photograph ushered in a brave new world of invasive publicity, the forerunner and prototype of photographs of Diana, Princess of Wales, and Dodi Fayed; Sarah Ferguson, the Duchess of York, having her toes sucked by a boyfriend.

"Le Scandale"—Burton's term—was born.

2
VERY IMPORTANT PEOPLE

"I was damned helpless . . ."
—RICHARD BURTON

"Gstaad is a lonely place out of season."
—ELIZABETH TAYLOR

Elizabeth and Richard's grand passion launched a new industry: celebrity culture on a scale never before seen. Suddenly, their images—usually costumed as Cleopatra and Marc Antony—appeared on the covers of countless newspapers and magazines. The Burton-Taylor affair was so famous that even Jacqueline Kennedy asked the publicist Warren Cowan, "Warren, do you think Elizabeth Taylor will marry Richard Burton?" One chronicler wrote, "They had moved off the show biz pages and into the hard news. They were up there with Kennedy and Khrushchev and the Cuban missiles." Louella Parsons wrote that the massive amount of publicity "ought to have killed them."

Quickly written paperback books were published, such as *Cleopatra in Mink* by entertainment writer Cy Rice and *Richard Burton, His Intimate Story* by Ruth Waterbury; even Walter Wanger got into the act by publishing his production diary, *My Life with Cleopatra* ("FOR THE FIRST TIME! The complete, true, behind-the-scenes story of the most talked-about movie of our time by the man who produced it!"). Wanger wrote in those pages: "Tried again to get Elizabeth to make some kind of statement to counteract the bad press she has been receiving. *Paris Match, Life, News of the World, France Soir,* and many other European papers are violently attacking her," and noted how the "paparazzi, that raffish group of photographers so well portrayed in Fellini's *La Dolce Vita,* have been the bane of our existence since we came to Rome."

Il Tempo, the *Los Angeles Times,* the *Herald Examiner, Hollywood Reporter,* and *Variety* all weighed in, as did the Vatican, which published a reader's letter in the Vatican weekly *Osservatore della Domenica,* denouncing Elizabeth Taylor's "erotic vagrancy" and calling into question Elizabeth and "her fourth ex-husband's" fitness to adopt Maria, the German infant. In America, a U.S. congresswoman from Georgia named Iris Faircloth Blitch called on Congress to make "Miss Taylor and Mr. Burton . . . ineligible for reentry into the United States on the grounds of undesirability." Congressmen in New York and North Carolina joined the fray, blaming the nation's "moral slide" on the Taylor-Burton affair.

Wanger was afraid that the bad publicity would destroy *Cleopatra,* causing audiences to boycott the picture. He sent in nine plain-clothed policemen to keep the paparazzi from sneaking onto the set. But "Liz and Dick" had had enough. They told their producer that they were "sick of being chased by the paparazzi" and they were going to turn the tables. So, one night, Burton and Taylor—who was chicly dressed in a leopard-skin coat and cloche hat—strolled hand-in-hand down Via Veneto, while the paparazzi went wild. They kissed publicly, flaunting their affair and letting the frenzy go on around them. They met their friend Mike Nichols, then known for his satiric comedy routines with Elaine May, at a Via Veneto nightclub.

An Evening with Mike Nichols and Elaine May had run on Broadway next to Burton's *Camelot,* and Nichols had befriended both Richard and Elizabeth. (Though he would appear with the model

Suzy Parker in a series of Richard Avedon's photographs spoofing Burton and Taylor's newfound notoriety, in fact, Nichols was at the beginning of a long and fulfilling friendship with Elizabeth that would change the direction of his career.)

Another close friend during the feeding frenzy was Roddy McDowall, who had had an important supporting role in *Cleopatra* as Octavian, the wily third member of the Roman triumvirate who outwits and ultimately defeats Antony. He had an important supporting role in Elizabeth's life as well—one of the gay actors, like Montgomery Clift and Rock Hudson, whom she would rely upon and count among her dearest friends. Elizabeth was well ahead of her time in her complete acceptance and love for her gay friends. When McDowall returned to New York at the end of that summer and regaled Monty Clift with stories of *Le Scandale*, Clift was amazed. "It's lunatic. Bessie Mae [his pet name for her] is now the most famous woman in the world!" He believed that Burton was the driving force behind the scandalous headlines: "Richard wants to be famous at any cost," he complained.

But it was Elizabeth, more than Richard, who could handle the press and the paparazzi—she was practically born to it, and she'd learned from Todd the importance of always being in the public's eye. It wasn't so for Burton, who still had a bookish sense of privacy, and though he had often basked in the adulation of theater audiences, he wasn't used to this kind of constant public attention. At first, it was intoxicating. "In a few weeks," Fisher noted, "Burton had been transformed from a well-respected British actor to a world-renowned celebrity—and he loved it. Suddenly he couldn't walk down the street without being recognized. . . . What he didn't yet understand," Fisher wrote years after the fact, "was that he couldn't turn off this fame when it was convenient to him."

After her marriages to the "sullen, resentful, and ultimately violent" Nicky Hilton, and to "sweet Michael Wilding, to whom I was more a sister than anything," and "to Mike [Todd] whom I adored but had only two marvelous years with," being with Burton was like a revelation to Taylor. "Richard and I had an incredible chemistry together," she later said. "We couldn't get enough of each other." She loved best of all when they would slip off to their hideaway outside of Rome. "Even with paparazzi hanging out of the trees and hearing them tramping over the rooftops above us, even with all that going on, we could make love, and play Scrabble, and spell out naughty words for each other, and the game would never be finished. When you get aroused playing Scrabble, that's love, baby."

Through it all, Elizabeth prevailed. It had been a gamble. Thirteen years earlier, Ingrid Bergman had derailed her career by leaving her husband, Peter Lindstrom, and running off with the Italian director Roberto Rossellini, with whom she had an illegitimate child. She was hounded by the Hollywood gossip mavens and denounced on the floor of the Senate. But Elizabeth had been through all this before, when the public had sided with Debbie Reynolds in the Fisher-Taylor-Reynolds scandal, a mere two years earlier. If anything, that notoriety had continued to fuel the unstoppable engine of Elizabeth's white-hot career. If the paparazzi were camping outside Villa Pappa and the Cinecittà studios, what did she care? She was already used to crowds—ten thousand fans had gawked at her at Mike Todd's funeral, where she'd collapsed, weeping on his grave.

Indeed, it was Mike Todd himself—the ultimate showman, who had taken Elizabeth along on an endless series of hyped premieres for *Around the World in 80 Days*—who had shown her the transformative power of publicity. She had learned from a master: there's no such thing as bad publicity. The world's disapproval was nothing more than its newest incarnation, and publicity she could handle. And if she had any doubt that the public would cease to love her, would turn away from her in moral outrage, she got her answer when shooting began on Cleopatra's grand entrance into Rome.

In the spectacular scene, Cleopatra enters the city in a $6,500 gown of pure gold, perched atop an enormous, golden sphinx pulled through the Roman gates by scores of Nubian slaves, preceded by a legion of writhing snake dancers, splendid archers, horses, elephants, and fire-eaters. Elizabeth later confessed that the scene terrified her. Given the frenzy of bad press over the affair, she confided in Mankiewicz, "Being pulled through that mob—alone up there—who knows? They'll jeer at me and they'll throw rocks at me." The director had received anonymous bomb threats and had taken them seriously enough to place toga-clad detectives among the extras on the set. It's a testament to Elizabeth's courage that she endured the scene.

And then something amazing happened. The crowd of six thousand extras—Romans playing Romans—were meant to yell in jubilation, "Cleopatra! Cleopatra!" as she entered Rome.

Instead, they yelled, "Leez, Leez! *Baci, baci!* [Kisses!]"

Tears sprang to her eyes. When the scene was completed, she thanked the crowd of extras—standing in for all of Rome—for their love and approval.

By the end of July 1962, the ten months of filming *Cleopatra* were over.

"After my last shot," Elizabeth recalled, "there was a curiously sad sort of aching, empty feeling—but such astronomical relief. It was finally over. It was like a disease, shooting that film—an illness one had a very difficult time recuperating from." The Roman sets were taken down at Cinecittà. In September, Elizabeth decamped to her Swiss villa with her four children, having installed her parents at a nearby hotel. Richard returned with his family to Le Pays de Galles, the villa he and Sybil had bought in Céligny, on the west side of Lake Geneva in Switzerland, to avoid Britain's high taxes.

Conveniently, perhaps, Elizabeth's Chalet Ariel in Gstaad was on the other side of the lake, an hour's drive away over hairpin turns. For four months, the lovers tried to let the fires that had burned so intensely in Rome die down. "We tried to stay away from each other," Elizabeth later explained. "We were too aware of the pain we were causing others to stay together. But it is a hard thing to do, to run away from your fate. When you are in love and lust like that, you just grab it with both hands and ride out the storm."

Unable to tell him in person, Elizabeth wrote an agonizing letter to Richard, admitting that their affair was causing too much suffering, "making too many people unhappy" and that they should separate. She also decided to start divorce proceedings to dissolve her marriage to Eddie Fisher.

On her thirtieth birthday, which Elizabeth remembered as "the most miserable day of my life," she had already known it was over when Eddie gave her a pair of yellow-diamond pendant earrings, a brooch, and a matching ring. "It came as a total surprise," she'd recalled, "but you know something? The whole time I was just looking for something from Richard. I felt miserable, I thanked Eddie, but all I wanted was some sign from Richard. There wasn't even a bouquet of flowers." Later, a few months after their separation, Fisher sent her a bill for the jewelry. "I probably paid it," Elizabeth remembered. Now she was trying to stay away from Richard.

Burton was just as unhappy. He missed Elizabeth and he, perhaps, equally missed the attention of the world. He finally broke their enforced silence and telephoned, admitting that he was concerned about her and arranging a meeting at the Château de Chillon, a twelfth-century castle on Lake Geneva. She agreed.

Even though she was with her children in Gstaad, her parents, Francis and Sara, staying in a nearby villa, Elizabeth had not lived without a man in her life since her first, ill-advised marriage to Nicky Hilton. She was lonely. She later wrote in her autobiography: "I was dying inside and trying to hide it from the children with all kinds of frenzied activity." Her children seemed to miss Burton almost as much as she did, whereas, Elizabeth later noted, "When Eddie left, the children didn't even ask where he'd gone." She credits her younger son, Christopher, with helping her make up her mind when he confided, "I prayed to God last night that you and Richard would be married."

So Burton drove eastward from his villa, alone, while Elizabeth was driven by her parents. It's surprising that Sara Taylor went along with this plan; as the prime mover of Elizabeth's rise at MGM, she had sanctioned her daughter's earlier marriages as good for her career. But the terrible publicity over *Le Scandale*, she feared, would ruin all those years of hard maneuvering. It shows that Elizabeth was standing up for her own desires, no matter the cost, and finally taking the reins of her career—and her life—away from her mother.

"Richard and I arrived at exactly the same moment," recalled Elizabeth. "The top of his car was down, he was terribly suntanned and his hair was cut very short. I hadn't seen him since *Cleopatra*. He looked nervous, not happy, but so marvelous." Suddenly shy, Elizabeth had a hard time getting out of the car. Sara leaned over and whispered to her, "Have a lovely day, baby," and her father, Francis, kissed her on the cheek.

"Oh, doesn't he look wonderful!" Elizabeth said. "I don't know what to do! I'm scared."

Richard ambled over to their car and sheepishly said hello. The Taylors practically pushed Elizabeth out of the car—as she remembers it—and she and Richard blurted out simultaneously, "You look marvelous!" Then a peck on the cheek, then a quiet lunch at a lakeside restaurant.

Sitting at an outdoor table without the attendant fussing of publicists and the blinding flashbulbs of the paparazzi, Elizabeth and Richard found themselves in an awkward silence. Suddenly alone, they discovered they didn't really know each other all that well—the mad attention had distracted them, perhaps, from true intimacy. Even the loquacious Burton, who could recite reams of verse at the drop of a hat, found himself surprisingly without words. But eventually, they began to find things to talk about—their children, the now-completed movie, the beauty of Lake Geneva. Her parents having by now departed, Burton drove Elizabeth home. They parted without a kiss, but agreed to see each other again. If Elizabeth had indeed intended to reconcile with Fisher—not likely—she changed her mind. She knew now that she still wanted Richard. The flame still burned, though Burton would continue to publicly say that he had no intention of leaving his wife.

And he had good reason to stay with Sybil. There were reports that she had tried to commit suicide while Burton was in Gstaad with Elizabeth—surprising for one as grounded and sane as Sybil. But her entire world had been shaken. Besides Burton's betrayal, their youngest daughter, Jessica, was alternately identified as "severely retarded" or possibly autistic and faced the possibility of lifelong institutionalization. It was too much to bear. Burton would learn of Jessica's condition later that summer, and it would add another layer of guilt to his already wounded psyche. He would stay in Céligny, with his family, though he still longed for Elizabeth.

They would continue to see each other for chaste lunches every few weeks. Elizabeth finally came to the conclusion that she would be with Burton any way he would have her—she wouldn't insist on marriage, she wouldn't insist that he leave Sybil. "I loved Richard so much that for the first time it was an unselfish love," she'd later write. "I didn't want to marry Richard because I didn't want him to be unhappy. I didn't want Sybil to be unhappy. I would have been perfectly content to just talk to him on the phone every once in a while."

They would, however, soon have their chance to be together again, in London, where they would resume their passionate affair while filming their second movie together, *The V.I.P.s.*

If Wanger, Skouras, and Zanuck had worried about the box office effects of *Le Scandale*, there was another producer who knew instantly that a new era had dawned since Ingrid Bergman was chased out of Hollywood, and he set out to capitalize on the biggest sex scandal of the day. Anatole "Tolly" de Grunwald, a Russian-born producer, had produced Emlyn Williams's *Last Days of Dolwyn* fourteen years earlier, which had showcased the youthful Richard

Burton. De Grunwald, like Williams before him, knew a good thing when he saw it.

Working with a screenplay by the eminent English playwright Terence Rattigan (*Separate Tables*, *The Winslow Boy*) about a number of VIPs stranded at Heathrow Airport during heavy fog, de Grunwald cast Burton and Taylor in the leading roles and began shooting even before *Cleopatra* was completed.

Richard, for one, was relieved. He, too, was worried that his affair with Elizabeth, arguably intended to elevate his stature in Hollywood, had instead made him unemployable—he had gone several months without a job offer. De Grunwald had originally wanted Sophia Loren to play opposite Burton, but Elizabeth would have none of it. Though they were still working out the ramifications of their living arrangements—Eddie Fisher was now permanently out of the picture, but Burton still clung to his marriage, and Sybil still seemed convinced that he would tire of Elizabeth and return to her—it dawned on Elizabeth that the two stars might create a new, powerful alliance in filmdom, along the lines of Mary Pickford–Douglas Fairbanks in silent films and the Barrymores and Lunts in the theater. "Let Sophia stay in Rome!" she magisterially proclaimed, so, despite the fact that she was now uninsurable due to her calamitous health (her tracheotomy was the coup de grâce), de Grunwald signed her. As the producer was making the movie for MGM, with the stroke of a pen, Taylor was returned to the studio that had virtually owned her for most of her film career. But that was about to change.

A canny businesswoman, who had learned early at the feet of masters—including Louis B. Mayer, Mike Todd, and her own mother—Taylor had formed her own company, Taylor Productions, Inc., which then lent Elizabeth's services to MGM for $500,000, with an additional $50,000 per week over the shooting schedule, plus per diem. Budgeted at $3.3 million, the production would end up paying Burton $500,000—which was $300,000 more than the combined salaries of all the other players. Burton—who had feared that *Le Scandale* had ruined his career—now saw his *Cleopatra* salary doubled (as Eddie Fisher had predicted). Elizabeth left her children in Switzerland, where they were in boarding schools, and joined Richard in London.

The couple would play Paul and Frances Andros, a powerful shipping magnate and his about-to-be-unfaithful trophy wife. During the twenty-four hours they are trapped at Heathrow, Elizabeth/Frances nearly runs off with her gigolo lover, played by Louis Jourdan. Once Burton and Taylor agreed to star in the film, Rattigan set about adapting his screenplay to take advantage of their notoriety. *The V.I.P.s* would be a disguised film version of their lives, this time with the emphasis on Elizabeth Taylor's penchant for eye-popping jewelry. In the film, we first see the couple descending from the heavens, like gods, in their private helicopter. On the way to the airport terminal in their Rolls-Royce, Richard/Paul gives Elizabeth/Frances an exquisite diamond bracelet. Already Burton was fulfilling one of Taylor's basic requirements in a lover: a willingness and the ability to drape her in stupendous jewelry. She had learned early how to extract gifts from her directors and producers, like tributes paid to royalty by their subjects. Queens are meant to accept tribute, and, having already become the first actress in history to be given a million-dollar-plus salary for her services, she was the closest thing America had to royalty. She had become accustomed to deference. Even her name befitted a queen. Her love of jewelry—diamonds especially—would be a leitmotif running throughout her life, apotheosized in the publication of *Elizabeth Taylor, My Love Affair with Jewelry*, a coffee-table book replete with vivid photographs of her most famous jewels and the circumstances surrounding them. One of Elizabeth's early chroniclers, the literary biographer Brenda Maddox, speculated that Elizabeth's attraction to diamonds was a kind of atavistic need to deflect the rapt gaze of her admirers. Her penchant for jewels was not lost on Andy Warhol, who believed that women live longer than men because they wear diamonds, which—because of the mystical powers of crystals—intensify and protect the life force. Perhaps he was on to something: Elizabeth has so far outlived four of her seven husbands, despite her often perilous health.

One of her few pleasures in Rome, besides falling in love with Richard on the set of *Cleopatra*, had been Elizabeth's discovery of the Italian jeweler Bulgari's "nice little shop" on Via Condotti. "I used to visit Gianni Bulgari in the afternoons," she later recalled, "and we'd sit in what he called the 'money room' and swap stories." One day, when they'd managed to evade the paparazzi, Richard told Elizabeth, "I feel like buying you a present!" Off they went to Bulgari's back room, where Richard announced his intention to buy a gift, but it had to be under $100,000. Gianni showed them a pair of lovely but rather small earrings. Richard and Elizabeth exchanged glances—by now he knew her tastes. "Try again," he told the jeweler.

By the end of the afternoon, they departed with a stunning, emerald-and-diamond necklace with a pendant that could be detached and worn as a brooch. The diamonds surrounding the pendant were 10 carats each, and the necklace cost well over $100,000, but Elizabeth pointed out to Richard that with the detachable pendant, "it's really like getting two pieces for the price of one." She would later complete the set (or, rather, Richard would) with a matching emerald-and-diamond ring, pendant earrings, and a beautiful bracelet—all part of what Bulgari described as "the Grand Duchess Vladimir Suite."

Elizabeth would later have a little fight with Anthony "Puffin" Asquith, the director of *The V.I.P.s*, over wearing the brooch as part of her Givenchy-designed costume. The producer, who had accepted the uninsurable Elizabeth Taylor, would now have to insure the fabulous jewel. However, the quick-thinking director persuaded her to allow a copy to be made for filming.

After Burton's and Taylor's work was done on *Cleopatra*, the real power struggle began. Horrified over the movie's tremendous cost, which had forced Skouras to sell off 260 acres of 20th Century-Fox's back lot to the real estate developer William Zeckendorf (turning the vast acreage into present-day Century City), the studio's founder, Darryl F. Zanuck, swooped in to save his company from destruction. In a stockholders' takeover, he forced out Skouras, reclaimed his former title as studio head, and fired *Cleopatra*'s producer, Walter Wanger. After being ignominiously fired, Wanger would never produce another film. Zanuck then turned his attention to Mankiewicz.

Burdened with twenty-six hours of film, the director had planned to bring out two parallel movies: *Caesar and Cleopatra* and *Antony and Cleopatra*, and he set about editing the two epics. Zanuck, however, hated the idea. First, it was not yet clear how the worldwide publicity surrounding Taylor's adulterous affair with Burton would play out at the box office. Hedging his predecessors' bets and trying to salvage what he could, Zanuck fired Mankiewicz and took over editing the film himself. While Mankiewicz had been wrestling with the myriad disasters of *Cleopatra*, Zanuck had smoothly overseen production of *The Longest Day*, flying in Richard Burton from Rome, with none of the Sturm und Drang. Zanuck took over the final edit and produced one four-hour epic, served up with an intermission. Its final price tag, including distribution costs: $62 million ($434 million today), the most ever spent on a Hollywood movie at that time. The final cut ran slightly over four hours, making it the longest film ever released. It was not just the longest, it was also the heaviest: each print of *Cleopatra* weighed six hundred pounds. Even the publicity kit weighed more than ten pounds. Finally, when all was said and done, Wanger sued 20th Century-Fox for breach of contract, and the studio sued their two stars for $50,000, claiming that the bad publicity of their "scandalous conduct" had harmed the value of the film. They countersued, and the lawsuit was eventually dropped.

Mankiewicz was heartbroken. With the film taken from his hands and drastically cut, he felt that some of his finest work was sacrificed, and that the final product—though it had its spectacular moments, such as Cleopatra's grand entrance into Rome—lacked cohesion. Elizabeth, too, felt that the truncated version did Richard a disservice, leaving some of his best scenes unseen. Instead of portraying a strong character who gradually gives in to his weaknesses, Elizabeth complained, "they cut the film so that all you see is him drunk and shouting all the time, and you never know what in his character led up to that. He just looks like a drunken sot."

It was a disappointment that would haunt Mankiewicz the rest of his life, eventually turning him into a rather bitter recluse, nursing his grudges in a baronial country house in Bedford, New York, being trotted out to various film festivals toward the end of his life to receive honors for movies he'd made decades earlier. Elizabeth, in later years, was very much aware that Mankiewicz blamed the demise of his career on her and Burton's "indulgences," though she would speak graciously about her former director whenever she had the opportunity.

Signed by de Grunwald and free of the onerous work of *Cleopatra*, Burton and Taylor arrived in London on a cold morning in December of 1962. The hoopla that had surrounded the couple in Rome continued, but now it was mostly excited fans hounding them. They were mobbed at Victoria Station and fled in separate cars (Elizabeth in a blue Jaguar and Richard in a blue station wagon). When they arrived at the Dorchester Hotel on Park Lane, where they had taken adjoining penthouse suites, the lobby was awash with journalists and photographers. (Elizabeth had always stayed at the luxurious Dorchester, beginning with her days as a child actress. It was home to her.) Other actors signed to the film, including Rod Taylor, Linda Christian, and even Orson Welles, checked into the hotel virtually ignored by the press, which continued to swarm around Burton and Taylor.

Burton was still married to Sybil and he agonized over his dilemma. There was no doubt that he was infatuated with Elizabeth. What had begun as a conquest quickly became an obsession—Elizabeth's body was a marvel to him, the eighth wonder of the world. He reveled in her voluptuousness. And Elizabeth was in thrall to him sexually as well—his rough skin, his intense, blue-green eyes, his voice, his smell, his "arrogant hair" all delighted her senses. "Imagine having Richard Burton's voice in your ear while you are making love," Elizabeth later recalled. "It drowned out the troubles, the sorrows, everything just melted away." She found Richard "an incredibly sexy man. I was the happy recipient of his reputation as a man who knew how to please a woman. Being unfaithful to Richard was as impossible as not being in love with him." In short, they made love everywhere they could—in boats, in dressing rooms, once in a catamaran, once in a photographer's studio. Burton was phenomenal in that way. Alcohol didn't seem to tamp his ardor or his gifts as a lover, at least in the beginning of their grand affair.

And she had already catapulted him into a higher sphere of fame, opportunity, and wealth. He was heady with the sheer dazzle of the life they had begun together, unreal as it seemed to one who might have otherwise entered the Welsh mines. Sir Laurence Olivier, whom Burton greatly admired, had earlier sent him a telegram, demanding, "Make up your mind—do you want to be a great actor or a household word?" To which Burton famously replied, "Both." Now, it seemed as if both fates were within his grasp. But could he sacrifice Sybil—and his two beloved young daughters, Kate and Jessica—on the altar of his ambition?

It turned out that he could, though, in the words of his friend, the actor Robert "Tim" Hardy, "it left him with an incurable wound."

Burton had met Sybil Williams in 1949 on the set of *The Last Days of Dolwyn*, Emlyn Williams's movie about Welsh villagers under threat of being bought out and relocated to England so their valley can be flooded to bring drinking water to London. Like the 1986 movie *Local Hero*, the film has a moral dilemma at its heart: should the Welsh villagers give up their valley, their way of life, their centuries-old homes, their birthright, in exchange for modern flats in a big city and a little pocket money? Burton plays an earnest young villager who's desperate to improve his English in order to impress the daughter of the English landowner. (Burton himself—when he was still known as Rich Jenkins—had fallen in love with the English tongue and the opportunities it offered a poor Welsh lad; he had practiced his diction as much as eight hours a day, reciting reams of poetry and speeches from Shakespeare's plays.) The villagers, led by Burton's adoptive mother in the film, played by Dame Edith Evans, resist the lure of easy money and cling to their beloved valley, until an accidental murder seals their fate. Burton is heartbreaking in the film—a poetic, virile youth full of hope and idealism, a country swain in love with a woman above his station, reciting his English verses to the wind, whose right action brings about a wrong result.

Sybil Williams had been hired as an extra to play one of the Welsh villager girls. Though not a beauty, she was lively and intelligent. Robert Hardy, who capped his distinguished stage and film career by playing the irascible Siegfried in the long-running BBC adaptation of *All Creatures Great and Small* and is known to a new generation of fans as Cornelius Fudge in the Harry Potter movies, knew and admired Sybil. "She came from the valleys, but her brother was quite a smart lawyer. As a family and financial stratum, they were above [the Jenkinses]." Her father had been an official at the mines where Burton's father, and all of his brothers, save one, had toiled. She was nineteen when she married the twenty-three-year-old Burton, and because she was Welsh, she kept Burton grounded in his Welsh life throughout his meteoric rise in the London theater and their more modestly successful jaunt in Hollywood. Burton's huge family loved her, especially Burton's idolized older brother, Ifor Jenkins. Indeed, everyone who knew her loved her, and despite Burton's dalliances (including an intense love affair begun with Claire Bloom), Burton and Sybil seemed devoted to each other. "It was admirable, that marriage," recalls Hardy, who used to visit the couple in their Hampstead home.

Sybil adored Burton, but she must have known about his constant philandering. She allowed him his flings with actresses high and low, as long as he returned to her in the end. It wasn't that she was masochistic, necessarily; she was realistic. His fame, attractions, and gifts were prodigious in an era when men drank and played hard and ruled the roost and got away with it all—at least for a time. A certain amount of tomfoolery was tolerated—even expected—as long as the paterfamilias supported his family and stayed devoted to his wife and children. That was the Welsh—and not only the Welsh—code of behavior. And, for a time, it worked.

Now Burton agonized over the decision staring him in the face. "One just hoped he would come back to Sybil," Hardy recalled. "Then it became bit by bit obvious that he wouldn't and that was just awful." Burton's prodigious capacity for drink seemed to double.

Two weeks after Burton's arrival in London, Sybil brought her two daughters to their cottage in Hampstead, inviting Burton's beloved older brother, Ifor, and his wife, Gwen, to stay with them. Sybil was sure her Lothario husband would tire of his new paramour, as he had of past lovers, and return once again to his family. So, for a time, Burton was trapped between two households: the adjoining penthouses he and Elizabeth shared in the Dorchester Hotel while making *The V.I.P.s*, and the Hampstead cottage to which he would slink when Elizabeth was occupied elsewhere. He usually spent days, when he wasn't needed on the set, in Hampstead, but his nights were spent with Elizabeth.

Occasionally, Sybil would show up on the set of *The V.I.P.s*, throwing everyone in a tizzy. Peter Medak, the Hungarian director of later acclaimed films *The Ruling Class*, *The Krays*, and *Romeo Is Bleeding*, was a twenty-five-year-old assistant director on *The V.I.P.s* at the time. He recalled that Burton would "show up for wardrobe fittings with Sybil, and the next day he'd suddenly show up with Elizabeth. I don't know how he did it. Sybil would say, 'No, you can't wear those trousers—it doesn't look right.' And Elizabeth would appear and she would countermand it." As comic as this might seem—the two women trying to dress their man according to their own tastes—it was devastating to all parties. Burton called it his period of "suspended animation," but it was more dramatic than that. Ifor—the man among men whose masculinity and good character Burton most admired— was furious with his brother for putting Sybil through the public horrors of his affair. Ifor spent time with Sybil at the Hampstead cottage, and at one point the two men found themselves in a shouting match, screaming through the mail slot of the cottage's white door.

Disheartened, Burton returned to London and promptly drank himself into a stupor. His old friend and fellow Welshman, the actor Stanley Baker, found him passed out and plied him with three pots of black coffee to bring him around. Graham Jenkins, Burton's youngest brother, who would often serve as his stand-in on movie sets, beginning with *The V.I.P.s*, worried that Burton was close to a complete breakdown, drinking suicidal amounts of alcohol.

Sybil, for her part, was not unmoved by her husband's suffering, and she accompanied Burton to an intimate dinner party given by Stanley Baker and his wife. During the course of the evening, Elizabeth pestered the Baker residence with constant phone calls, interrupting their dinner and reminding Burton of her own vulnerability. "He was one haunted boy-o," Baker said about his friend. Adding to his burdens was the disapproval of his entire Welsh family, who adored Sybil.

"The family wasn't happy about the affair," recalled Graham. "He was ordered to come down to Wales to face them. We were Welsh Baptists. Divorce was not in our vocabulary." But Burton refused, claiming that his shooting schedule on *The V.I.P.s* made a visit impossible. That's when Graham offered to stand in for him, launching his occasional work as Burton's stand-in: "We looked quite a bit alike, except he was five feet ten and a half inches and I was five feet eight and a half inches. I'm in several of the long shots, and not even my wife, Hilary, could tell us apart in the movie."

Ifor tried to persuade Burton that his obligation was to his family. Ifor was the closest Burton had to a father figure, replacing Dadi Ni, his feckless, whiskey-sodden father, but even he couldn't persuade

Burton once he'd resolved to divorce Sybil and marry Elizabeth. "If Ifor couldn't get him back," recalled Graham, "no one could. But I do think that if he could, he would have been married to both women." Needless to say, he couldn't.

So, Elizabeth sent Richard to Hampstead to ask Sybil for a divorce. When he arrived at Sybil's door, however, all his resolve melted. Sybil asked him if he planned to stay, and he answered, "Yes," and he probably meant it at the time. When he was with Sybil, he vowed to stay with Sybil. When he was with Elizabeth—well, she was an unstoppable force, a force of nature, a gale-force wind. Nothing, no one, could resist her once she'd made up her mind. Robert Hardy himself, though devoted to Sybil, felt Elizabeth's immense charm and power when Burton first introduced them. "At her best, she was immensely impressive," he recalled. "The color of her eyes was enough to turn a saint into a devil, and I wouldn't say that Richard was a saint."

By now, Burton was drinking more than ever—Bloody Marys before noon, straight vodka for lunch. As one of Burton's biographers observed, "the boozing was prodigious, but, for reasons which escaped the doctors who checked him out at the time, he seemed to be walking through the furnace of alcohol unscathed. The system took everything he threw at it." And he wasn't the only one. "The drink was the problem," Medak believed, "with both of them. I remember Elizabeth in the dressing room, sitting in a makeup chair, and she'd be drinking a glass of water. And she'd say, 'Can you fill this up?' And I'd put some water in it, and she'd say, 'No, I didn't mean water. I meant vodka.'"

But then, almost everyone on the set was drinking. After all, it was 1963, but in essence it was still the 1950s, in terms of the complete acceptance of alcohol and cigarettes as relatively benign, grown-up pleasures. In fact, it was a sign of character—certainly of masculinity—*to* drink. Teetotalers were looked upon with suspicion, as health food faddists, or moralists or namby-pambies or goody-goodies or, worse than all of that, as *bores*.

Elizabeth would accompany Richard on pub crawls through London, where he would introduce her to his old theater and rugby chums—those who were still talking to him, like his Oxford friends, which included Hardy and writers Terence Rattigan, Robert Bolt (who wrote *A Man for All Seasons*), and John Morgan, a journalist and intellectual. She kept Burton's "Welsh hours," devoting herself to Richard as Sybil had done before her, impressing him with how well she fit into his world. She could drink and swear and sing bawdy limericks with the best of them. That always won them over.

And she could also make fun of herself with Burton's crowd. At one point, she'd sat silent during a long discussion of the theater. Finally, in a melodramatic gesture, she threw her head back and declaimed, "I know nothing about the theater. But I don't need to. I'm a star!"

Rod Taylor, the strapping Australian actor best known for his roles in H. G. Wells's *The Time Machine* and Alfred Hitchcock's *The Birds*, was cast in *The V.I.P.s* to play an Aussie businessman, head of a tractor company who writes a bad check to save his company from a hostile takeover. He recalled, "Everybody was extremely thirsty on the set. It wasn't like going to Hollywood lunches and having iced tea. I mean, the bar inside the studio was constantly packed. You definitely did not get through lunch without a bottle of wine . . . And, of course, Dickie [Burton was called by a number of names by his friends and family: Dick, Dickie, Rich, and—by Elizabeth—the more dignified Richard] would say, 'Have a tot of brandy,' and this would be ten thirty in the morning. Which seemed perfectly normal to everybody." Medak remembered Burton coming back to the set after lunch completely drunk, and very much the worse for wear. He'd rip into Asquith, demanding, "What kind of fucking shot is this? This is ridiculous!" Asquith, a gentlemanly, upper-class fellow who hated confrontation, would visibly crumble. "Puffin was very slight," Medak recalled, "and when Burton was yelling at him, he would just cringe until he practically disappeared into himself. There was nothing he could do, because the guy was absolutely out-of-his-mind drunk. So Asquith decided to handle it by barely saying anything as long as he got [Burton and Taylor] in the frame and let them say their lines. Burton wasn't always like that, though—just when he was drunk. We all knew that after lunch—look out!"

It didn't help the equanimity of the set that Elizabeth enjoyed Richard's alcoholic outbursts and encouraged them whenever she could. She loved passion and drama; as one brought up on fawning compliments, she needed the bracing reality of a good fight. It made her feel alive. "Richard loses his temper with true enjoyment. It's beautiful to watch," she once said. "Our fights are delightful screaming matches, and Richard is rather like a small atom bomb going off." They fought explosively off set and on.

"I think the effect Burton had on her was beyond even that of Mike Todd," Eddie Fisher—now out of the picture—wrote in retrospect. "Her relationship with Mike had been animalistic—she had never met a man like him. It was a great love affair. Mike was very clever, very shrewd, and very strong and possessive. But Burton went far beyond that. Burton was crazy. She needed his approval as an actress and as a woman, and by withholding it, he made her need him desperately." Fisher was right about one thing. "Mike [Todd] was a bit of a madman," Elizabeth admitted, "and, in his way, so was Richard Burton. I truly believe I can be content only with a man who's a bit crazy."

Richard and Elizabeth seemed to particularly enjoy having an audience, and they enjoyed heaping insults upon each other. Burton was fond of calling Elizabeth "my little Jewish tart" (because she had converted to Judaism to marry Mike Todd); Elizabeth trumped that by ridiculing his pockmarked skin. "I think they had fights for the glory of making up," Rod Taylor believed. "It was foreplay to them." Their reconciliation would sometimes take the form of extravagant gifts, including a Van Gogh Elizabeth had bought at Sotheby's for $257,000 (a mere $1.8 million in today's dollars), which she lugged up the Dorchester elevator, kicked off her shoes, and hammering a nail into the wall, hung the painting over Burton's penthouse fireplace herself.

Elizabeth was proud of the fact that she could keep up with Richard—even drink him under the table. She was truly a man's woman, and she could drink, belch, and swear with the best of them. It was, for her, an important antidote to her staggering beauty and hothouse upbringing. It made her human. It kept her *real*.

Despite the amount of vodka she was consuming, and the fact that she loved food and would easily put on excess weight, she was still stunning on film. The camera, as they say, adored her. "You couldn't have been more beautiful or a bigger movie star than she was then," Medak believed. "When I saw her at six in the morning, when she used to come in for makeup, I often wondered, what was the point of making her up? She was breathtaking in some of those outfits, fantastic in that fur-lined coat and hat." Even so, Medak recalled, "everything had to be incredibly lit, which took forever. That's why we never did that many shots. We had a wonderful cameraman, Jack Hildyard, and the way he photographed her, he must have been in love with her. But I remember, even then, her weight went up and down. One week she was chubby, and the next week she was thin. You can almost see it in the film."

Finally, after five weeks of shooting at the Pinewood Studios, where a giant replica of Heathrow's new, modernist Terminal 5 had been constructed, complete with massive staircase and modern décor, Burton made up his mind. In January, he asked Sybil for a divorce, and she agreed.

He would throw his lot in with the gods of fame—or infamy. It did not seem to bring him peace of mind, however; throughout the film, torment is visibly stamped on his boxer-poet's face.

In later scenes, that baleful stare may have also been the result of a sound drubbing he received at the hands of some London hooligans. It was a Saturday. He had slipped into Cardiff to see a rugby match with Ifor Jenkins, his beloved older brother, and when he returned to London's Paddington Station, he was set upon by thugs. "I was caught off-balance and felt my feet giving way," he later wrote about the incident. "I was damned helpless . . . lying on the snow unable to move . . . They just kicked and kicked me." The street toughs nearly forced his eye from its socket, and injured Richard's neck and back. He was rescued by a taxi driver, but he refused to be taken to the hospital. The thugs who beat him probably didn't recognize the actor, but the taxi driver who drove him back to the Dorchester did, asking en route, "Are we in a film?" Once again, at that moment, life and artifice had become interchangeable.

Burton had to wear an eye patch for several days, and his neck injuries would plague him in later years. Of great interest to Medak, Burton contacted the notorious Kray brothers, brutal twin gangsters from East London, and asked them to hunt down his attackers. They lurked around the set for several days, keenly interested in the whole motion-picture business. Whether they succeeded in finding Burton's attackers is unknown, but Medak was impressed enough to make a celebrated film about the twins in 1990, *The Krays*.

In April of 1963, *Life* magazine put its imprimatur on the adulterous couple, in a stunning cover photograph of the two—Burton brooding into the camera, Taylor in dramatic profile against a black backdrop—to accompany the feature, "CLEOPATRA, Most Talked About Movie Ever Made." The apotheosis was complete. Elizabeth had won her dangerous game of courting the press and the paparazzi, of grabbing with both hands what she most desired. "Burton and Taylor in their public adultery," Burton's biographer Melvyn Bragg reflected, "seemed to be saying, 'We love each other, we know we are destroying marriages and disrupting families, but love is all you need and all that counts. And we are not going to hide it. Furthermore, folks, we don't give a damn.'"

When *Cleopatra* opened at last, on June 11, 1963, the trade press and the *New York Times* gave it mixed reviews, though Brendan Gill, writing in the *New Yorker*, loved the film's spectacle. His review is virtually an effusive love letter to Elizabeth Taylor, describing her as

> less an actress than a great natural wonder, like Niagara or the Alps, and it was right of the director to deal with her as the thing she has become—the most famous woman of her time, and probably of all time, who . . . is set pacing from bed to bath and from Caesar to Mark Antony not as the embodiment of a dead ancient queen but as, quite literally, a living doll, at once so sexy and so modest that her historical predecessor, seeing her, might easily have died not from the sting of an asp but from the sting of envy.

Several critics offered up howls of disdain. Judith Crist, in the *Herald Tribune*, jeered, "The mountain of notoriety has produced a mouse." *Time* magazine complained, "When [Elizabeth] plays Cleopatra as a political animal, she screeches like a ward heeler's wife at a block party." But the most damning verdict of all was delivered by Elizabeth Taylor herself after an advance screening in London. Upon viewing the film, Elizabeth rushed back to her penthouse suite at the Dorchester Hotel and promptly threw up.

But audiences loved it. They lined up around the block to see the picture, and, in fact, it made $15.7 million domestically—the top-grossing film of 1963, though not enough to earn a profit. That would take three more years, when, in 1966, Fox was paid $5 million [$35 million today] by ABC for two television-network showings. And in the forty-eight years since it was made, *Cleopatra* has grown in stature. In retrospect, there is much to admire in the movie's lush production values, its passionate performances, its rich language and ambitious storytelling. It's truly a feast for the senses, and the Burton-Taylor affair adds another layer of cultural history to the various interwoven versions of the story (Pliny's, Suetonius's, Shakespeare's, Shaw's, Mankiewicz's). And though Rex Harrison is a superbly poised and cunning Caesar, you can't take your eyes off Burton and Taylor. They smolder and ignite; their fatal beauty infuses their self-wrought tragedy. They are, truly, comets unleashed.

Some of Elizabeth's biographers have noted the almost eerie way in which her films often mirrored her private life as she was living it, often blurring the boundaries between what was real and what was imagined. It's true that she had learned from MGM how to choose scripts that reflected the life she was living, but she was also swept away by the intense make-believe of whatever role she found herself playing. It was a kind of reverse method acting, in which she drew on her theatrical roles to provide direction and add luster to her life. Mankiewicz saw it. He commented: "She was the reverse of most other stars . . . For her, living life was a kind of acting." Bragg observed that as Mankiewicz wrote the script by night while *Le Scandale* exploded all around him, he "wisely tried to ride it and was accused of putting in lines which were deliberately ambiguous." Elizabeth's anger when Cleopatra slashed Antony's clothes after hearing of his marriage to Octavian's sister is often cited as a moment when real life intersected the opulent fantasy of the movie: Elizabeth was heard to cry out "Sybil!" and she accidentally cut herself in her fury.

"These were larger-than-life humans," Mankiewicz said about his fated heroes, but he may just as well have been describing Burton and Taylor themselves. "They lived against larger-than-human backgrounds . . . I meant to focus interest upon the foreground, where those humans destroyed themselves in the end, or were destroyed, because it turned out that they were all-too-human after all."

But if Mankiewicz was, consciously or unconsciously, weaving the threads of their affair into his screenplay, he could not have known how closely *Cleopatra* would anticipate the arc of Elizabeth and Richard's thirteen-year love affair, begun on that Roman soundstage. It's all there, like a blueprint: their unstoppable lust, which deepens into love. Antony's jealous supplanting of Caesar, as he rips Caesar's necklace of gold coins from Cleopatra's throat, demanding, "Has it been his name you cry out in the dark?" (Richard resented the many framed photographs of Mike Todd in Elizabeth's villa, and saw the ghost of Todd—not Eddie Fisher—as his true rival. He noticed, too, that Elizabeth still wore Todd's wedding ring on her finger, a memento mori blackened and twisted from Todd's fatal air crash.) The opulence of Cleopatra's palace would pale next to the extravagance of Burton-Taylor's life together, with its yacht, its jewels, its furs, its entourages, its champagne and caviar, the five-star hotels, the Van Goghs and Matisses and Pissarros. And just as Antony and Cleopatra had plotted to rule together a third of the Roman empire, Burton and Taylor would form a company to produce movies that would capitalize on their notoriety, becoming—for a time—Hollywood's royalty. Antony is introduced in the film as a man redolent of wine; as his world collapses, he feeds his despair with more and more alcohol. Just so, Burton. When Cleopatra reproaches him and slaps his face, Antony knocks her to the ground. Elizabeth was already familiar with this apache dance.

Indeed, Mankiewicz created for Burton, in the role of Antony, the prototype for what would endure as the actor's greatest theatrical persona: his embodiment of self-pitying despair. The director saw Antony as essentially weak, a man "who stood always in Caesar's footsteps—right up to and into Cleopatra's bed." In an interview for *Life* magazine, Mankiewicz described Antony as "a masculine façade, constantly threatened by Caesar, the all-powerful father figure. His love for Cleopatra was, in the beginning, as guilt-ridden and frightening as that of a son in love with his father's mistress." Burton embraced that vision of Antony, explaining to the English drama critic Kenneth Tynan that the director/screenwriter had fashioned a man "who talks incessantly to excuse his own failure to become a great man. . . . The fury is there and the sense of failure is there, but sometimes all that comes out is a series of splendid words without any particular meaning."

After Antony abandons his soldiers to follow Cleopatra's departing barge at the disastrous Battle of Actium, all he has left is his shame. When his remnant of an army finally deserts him and he and Cleopatra are defeated by Octavian, Antony can find no one to dispatch him with an honorable death. He cries out, "The ultimate desertion? I from myself! Is that what I aimed for all my life? Will you finish me now?"

In art and in life, Burton would often feel he had made the ultimate desertion: "I from myself."

Perhaps Mankiewicz could sense the arc of their grand passion, and the current of injurious self-censure that lay within Burton. At one point, when Antony has foolishly dismissed his closest lieutenants before the Battle of Actium, Cleopatra realizes that something fateful has just occurred.

"Antony, what has happened?" she demands of him.

To which he replies, "To me? *You* have happened to me."

Once he made up his mind to be with Elizabeth, two years would pass before Richard would see his children, Kate and Jessica. And Sybil, whom he once cherished, would never speak to him again, not ever, not for the rest of his life.

3

A YEAR IN THE SUN

"My father would never say he drank a lot.
He'd say he was a man of vast drinking habits."
—RICHARD BURTON

"Ever since I'd been ten, I'd been a child star with no privacy."
—ELIZABETH TAYLOR

lizabeth Taylor was born to an upper-middle-class family with doting parents and an adored older brother, and was raised on an estate in Hampstead Heath, where she had her own pony and wanted for nothing. Originally from Arkansas City, Kansas, Francis Taylor—a shy but dapper man with a good eye for paintings—had moved to England to buy Old Masters for his wealthy uncle, an art dealer named Howard Young. It was Young who had launched Francis in the business, setting him up in one of his galleries in New York before sending him abroad. Francis Taylor opened his own gallery in London's Old Bond Street. Francis and Sara's two children, Howard and Elizabeth, were thus Americans born in England.

For a while, the Taylors lived well—some would say well beyond their means—partly on the generosity of others. Howard Young kept an eye out for his nephew (and his own vested interests), and Sara and Francis were invited to make use of a spacious, sixteenth-century cottage on an estate in Kent belonging to Victor Cazalet, a wealthy art collector and well-liked Conservative Member of Parliament, who had bought paintings from Francis Taylor. Cazalet and Sara were both keen believers in Christian Science.

Elizabeth lived a fairy-tale life, given her own horse at the age of five, sent to the same ballet school as Princess Elizabeth and her sister Princess Margaret. She was fussed over not only by her mother but by Cazalet himself. It was rumored that his generosity to the Taylors stemmed from an affair he was having with Sara, and it was also rumored that the bachelor MP was having an affair with Francis; either scenario would have added to the unreality of Elizabeth's storybook childhood.

Elizabeth later wrote about her early years, "The happiest days of my childhood were in England, because I rode—that's where I learned to ride bareback . . ." But once the family decamped to Los Angeles before the outbreak of World War II, leaving her beloved horse behind, the sweet unreality of her English life would take on another kind of unreality—one full of triumphs, but not so sweet. "I never cared whether or not I was an actress, especially when I was a very little girl," she recalled. "When I was first acting, I just liked playing with the dogs and the horses. Riding a horse gave me a sense of freedom and *abandon*, because I was so controlled by my parents and the studio when I was a child that when I was on a horse *we* could do whatever *we* wanted. Riding a horse was my way of getting away from people telling me what to do and when to do it and how to do it."

In a way, it was a horse that changed the direction of Elizabeth's extraordinary life. Sara Taylor knew that the role of Velvet Brown in MGM's *National Velvet* would be a star vehicle for her beautiful little eleven-year-old. She was born for the role of an English girl who loved horses and who trained her horse, "Pi," to win the Grand National Sweepstakes, while she rode him to victory disguised as a boy jockey. Abetted by her mother, Elizabeth came to feel that "National Velvet was really me," and she began decorating her bedroom with statues of horses and to dream of playing Velvet Brown. The only problem was that Elizabeth was too small for the role, looking more like a first-grader than an eleven-year-old. Elizabeth reportedly told the producer, Pandro S. Berman, "I will grow—I will grow in the part." Again, with her mother's encouragement and her intense belief in Christian Science, the two prayed together that Elizabeth would shoot up in time to be cast as Velvet. Sara also plied her with farmer's breakfasts—heapings of pancakes, fried eggs, bacon, all washed down with jugs of fresh milk—in an effort to add three inches to Elizabeth's height. Amazingly, it did the trick (without adding three inches to her waist), but it may also have unleashed a hedonistic love of food that would wreak havoc with Elizabeth's tiny frame in later years. Sara Taylor credited the re-markable growth spurt to two things—their prayers and Elizabeth's amazing willpower. They both believed that Elizabeth had actually *willed* herself to grow three inches. It was the beginning of Elizabeth's sense that she was ultimately in control of her fate, and if she wanted something badly enough, she would find a way to have it.

She also learned at an early age that movie-making was hard, backbreaking work. "I worked harder on that film than on any other movie in my life," she later said, spending hours riding a tempera-mental horse named King Charles, who would be Velvet's horse, Pi, in the movie. Through it all, Francis Taylor said little, though he did put his foot down after the studio pulled two of Elizabeth's baby teeth and replaced them with false stubs in order to put a set of braces in her mouth, which the role called for. *That* she endured, but Francis backed her up when she refused to have her long, lustrous hair cut for the role.

When *National Velvet* was released in 1943, it was a tremendous success, which made the now twelve-year-old a star. It also brought her an amazing salary for a child—negotiated by her mother—$30,000, plus a bonus of $15,000 (close to $450,000 in today's purchasing power). But, more important for Elizabeth, it brought her a horse. She asked Berman if she could have King Charles for her own, and the studio decided to make her the gift (provided she would lend the horse back to the studio whenever it was needed). From then on, Elizabeth would come to expect—and even demand—expensive, meaningful gifts from her producers and directors at the end of a shoot. And she usually got them.

But Elizabeth continued to chafe under Sara's watchful control. She adored her mother, and the two were very close, but she would eventually have to rebel against such closeness. Margaret Kelly, Elizabeth's body double in *National Velvet*, recalled cringing every time she heard Sara Taylor call out, "Oh, Elizabeth, darling. Come along," to which Elizabeth would meekly reply, "Coming, Mother dear."

The differences in Elizabeth's and Richard's upbringing brought about a curious paradox: Elizabeth, raised as an upper-class girl, would delight in acting the vulgarian, with a lusty joy in using four-letter words and winning belching contests, which she indulged in with her costar Rock Hudson on the set of *Giant*, thirteen years after making *National Velvet*. Yet Richard, son of an impoverished miner, saw himself as nobility. Of all the major Shakespearean roles he would play in his life—Prince Hal, Henry V, Othello, Iago, Hamlet, Petruchio—he most identified with the noble Roman warrior Coriolanus, who disdained the treacherous crowds of Rome. "I'm the son of a Welsh miner," he later told Kenneth Tynan, "and one would expect me to be at my happiest playing peasants, people of the earth, but in actual fact I am much happier playing princes and kings . . . I'm never really comfortable playing people from the working class."

Another contrast: Elizabeth would have her parents with her for a very long time (Sara Taylor, in fact, died in her nineties). Richard was virtually orphaned by his parents, raised by his sister, Cecilia "Cissy" James, and later taken under the wing of Philip Burton, a Welsh teacher and dramatist who gave Richard his name. When Richard Burton was informed in 1957 that his father had died, the first words out of his mouth were, "Which one?" Indeed, there were at least two fathers Burton could claim to have lost.

His first, of course, was the man who sired him, a hard-drinking coal miner named Richard Jenkins, known as Dic Jenkins and called "Dadi Ni" by his seven boys and four girls—Tom, Ifor, Cecilia, Will, David, Verdun (named after the great battle of World War I), Hilda, Katherine, Edith, Richard, and Graham. Burton was named Richard Walter Jenkins, after his father, and called "Rich" by his family. He was the twelfth of thirteen children (two daughters died in infancy), born on November 10, 1925 in the mining-and-smelting town of Pontrhydyfen in South Wales. His mother, Edith Thomas, had married Jenkins at sixteen and raised her large brood with resourcefulness and hard work, taking in washing, making and selling sweets and nonalcoholic beer, and making sure her children were well fed and attended church regularly. All but Graham, Richard's youngest brother, would toil long hours in the coal pits. As Hilda Jenkins Owens, one of Richard's sisters, recalled, "the seven boys born to Dic and Edith between 1901 and 1927 survived. They grew tall like their mother, rugged and strong like their father, and the first five went down to the mines like their ancestors before them."

Robert Hardy, who knew several of Burton's siblings, described the Jenkinses as "remarkable. Each and every one of them had an extraordinary ability about them, a sort of ancient dignity. That was wonderfully true of the eldest brother, Thomas, who had been a miner all his life. His face was pocked with all these little blue marks, and he was the gentlest and most dignified, charming, and easy man." Yet they were tough. "To have Dadi Ni's boys against you was something to shy away from," Hilda recalled. Richard himself had to earn his place among his six brothers. They would sometimes walk along the highest ledge of the bridge that gave Pontrhydyfen its name, a terrifying height. "I did it, even though I was frightened," Burton recalled. "After all, I had to prove I was a full-fledged member of the Jenkins family."

Dic Jenkins often worked from six thirty a.m. to seven thirty p.m. six days a week, which meant he saw daylight only on Sundays. Burton's brother Verdun lost half of his foot in a mining accident. Besides the long hours in the pits and the hard poverty of the 1920s and 1930s, there were also the twin perils of malnutrition and tuberculosis. Pontrhydyfen means "bridge over the ford across two rivers," but very few sons of the valley crossed those rivers into the greater world. (Of Burton's era and just after, the Welshmen who crossed over included the poet Dylan Thomas, the playwright Emlyn Williams, the pop singer Tom Jones, and the actors Stanley Baker, Thomas Owen Jones, and Anthony Hopkins.) This Welsh valley of roughly two thousand souls was sustained by three enterprises: the mines, the pubs, and the churches. The women of Pontrhydyfen would habitually climb to the top of the mines each payday, waiting for the men to surface so they could pluck the paychecks out of their hands before the local pubs took it all.

Nonetheless, Richard—and Hilda and Graham—looked back on their hardscrabble early years as happy ones. "It was our parents who had the hard time, not us," Graham Jenkins wrote in his memoir, *Richard Burton, My Brother.* "We ate plentifully and with great gusto. The main diet was fresh fish but there was a joint once a week and on Saturday we had cockles and lava bread—a huge treat." Burton, in fact, never developed a sophisticated palate and never lost his taste for lava bread, a Welsh dish consisting of the froth of boiled seaweed plunked down on the plate "like a cow pat," or for a dish called *siencyn,* a "delicious mush" made from pieces of fried bread, bacon, and cheese, with sugared tea poured over it. Graham may have put too cheerful a spin on his memories, as another chronicler reported that Edith Jenkins often fed her family "by dribbling [two] eggs over fourteen slices of bread, particularly when the bread had turned moldy," as it often did in the clammy Welsh air. All the family meals were washed down by gallons of hot, sweetened tea.

Graham remembers his father as a man who drank no more than other miners, and who was never cruel nor violent while drunk. Others recall a more prodigious appetite: "Dic was a real sweet man.

No harm in him at all, but a right terror for his booze. Only this size, tiny, couldn't be five-two out of his boots. But drink! Bloody hollow legs," recalled one of the miners who had grown up in Pontrhydyfen with the Jenkinses. The village was full of pubs, then, with names like Bird in Hand, Heart of Oak, Boar's Head, Miners Arms, British Lion, where "the drinking was tremendous and cheap . . . There were only two ways of life. You were either going to the chapel or to the pub, and most of the miners went to the pub, and the women understood, because miners' work is hell."

Barely five feet two inches tall, proud, hardworking, highly intelligent, full of stories and swagger, Jenkins bore his hard life stoically. Burned in a mine fire, he was treated at home by two of his daughters. Hilda remembers rubbing olive oil on his burned arms, which were then bandaged to his torso so he couldn't use them at all—which didn't keep him from showing up at the pub, where he'd have a pint of bitter poured directly into his mouth. On his way home from the pub one night, his ruined arms strapped to his side, he was horribly beaten by an old adversary; his teeth were knocked out and he was thrown over a wall where he wasn't found until the next morning. Still, he survived, hardened and darkened like a piece of coal, retelling the story with relish at the local pubs well into his eighties.

Jenkins, a masculine role model for Richard, wasn't pleased by Richard's choice of a profession. The fame and the money were to be admired, yes, but prancing around in costumes and wearing makeup and being bullied by women? Or perhaps Jenkins was resentful of his next-to-youngest son's extraordinary renown, seeing how he bore not his own name but the name of another.

Edith Jenkins died at the age of forty-four just after giving birth to Graham, her youngest. Richard was only two years old at the time, though he would claim that he had vivid memories of his mother. Jenkins farmed out the younger boys—Graham and Rich, an infant and a toddler—to their older, married siblings. Graham would be raised by Tom and his wife, Cassie, and Jenkins put Rich into the hands of his twenty-one-year-old sister Cecilia, who was married and living on her own in nearby Port Talbot. Richard thrived in her care.

Cecilia was a striking, green-eyed, dark-haired woman known in the family as "Cis." She would become, for Burton, the paragon of female perfection. In *A Christmas Story*, Burton's autobiographical short story, he described his sister as "no ordinary woman—no woman ever is, but to me, my sister less than any."

> When my mother had died, she, my sister, had become my mother . . . I was immensely proud of her. I shone in the reflection of her green-eyed, black-haired, gypsy beauty. She sang at her work in a voice so pure that the local men said she had a bell in every tooth, and was gifted by God. . . . She was naïve to the point of saintliness, and wept a lot at the misery of others. She felt all tragedies except her own. I had read of the Knights of Chivalry and I knew that I had a bounden duty to protect her above all other creatures. It wasn't until thirty years later, when I saw her in another woman that I realized I had been searching for her all my life.

First published in 1965, three years after the beginning of his affair with Elizabeth, the story makes it clear that the other woman in whom he sees the reflection of his adored sister is Elizabeth, another dark-haired, gypsy beauty. If Sybil had kept him moored to his Welsh life and family, Elizabeth supplanted her in representing a type of raven-haired, lavishly shaped woman that he associated with the comeliest women of his Welsh childhood.

Cis doted on her young brother, even after her own two daughters were born a few years later. Cis and her gruff husband, Elfred James, had only been married for four months when two-year-old Richard came to live with them. Elfred often resented the care and attention Cis lavished on Richard. "He was never smacked," Graham recalled, but he at times had to be shielded from Elfred's temper. "Nothing is good enough for that boy," Elfred often complained. Graham reports that his sister tried to be fair-handed, but "when it came to a choice between Elfred and Rich, as it often did, Elfred lost out."

Part of Cis's preference was due to her strong family loyalty, but it was also because Richard, as he would prove to be his entire life, was catnip to women. He was charming, he was playful, he was smart. He delighted not just Cis but his entire family—although apparently not Elfred—with his playacting. He loved to imitate the local preacher by giving mock sermons in the family parlor. He was, according to Graham, "quick to discover the power of language—the Welsh language, to be precise, since our patch of South Wales remained loyal to its mother tongue."

Richard didn't speak English until he was six, but he learned the beauty of language from attending chapel. Graham recalls, "The chapel was our other world. Within that simple building we let our emotions rip. We sang lustily, prayed fervently, and listened in awe to the thunderous declarations of moral judgment. A good preacher was a poet in action. He could spin words into a story of such power as to stop the mind." Men who would be actors found their niche in the church, where, as preachers, they could indulge all their penchants for drama, language, passion.

Hardy observed that Burton "spoke the most perfect Welsh, coming from that part of Wales where the most sonorous, the deepest kind of Welsh is spoken—pure, classical Welsh. He felt very attached to that." Burton would never lose his love of the language, which he described as "a wild, breathy, passionate, powerful tongue. I once heard Shakespeare's *Macbeth* recited in Welsh, and it shook me to the core."

It wasn't just the beauty of the Welsh tongue, it was the quality of the Welsh voice as well. The Welsh have had a long, passionate tradition of choral societies. Young men often resorted to fisticuffs to win singing contests. Byrn Davies, another Welsh miner, who used to drink with Burton's father, once observed, "The Welsh gift of language is a sad gift of God. He inclined us all towards poetry and then buried us in coal."

Graham thought his older brother might join the clergy. In his parlor-room sermons, Richard often played for laughs, exaggerating the fire-and-brimstone, but he and other boys of the village were also invited, from the age of seven, to read scripture at Sunday sermons. Rich easily memorized long passages from the Bible and recited them to the congregation, mesmerizing them with his voice. He was a born performer. But when Richard—still known as Rich Jenkins—came of age and had an opportunity to continue his secondary school studies in Port Talbot, Elfred put his foot down. They had already locked horns over various adolescent outbursts—Rich was smoking at eight, drinking at eleven, and at fifteen going with girls—now it was time for the boy to work and earn his keep, even though Cis was willing to pay the money to keep him in school. But he was set up as a clerk in a local haberdashery, where he was misplaced and miserable.

Meredith Jones, one of Burton's teachers and a brilliant, thundering Welshman who had escaped the mines as a "scholarship boy," came to Rich's rescue. He taught Rich at Dryffen Grammar School and recognized the boy's quickness and gifts, particularly in local theater. He encouraged and inspired Rich, and made it possible for him to leave the hated work as a haberdashery clerk at Mr. Maynard's Co-op. Rich, now a year or two older than all the other boys, returned to finish his education at Port Talbot Secondary School. That's where he met—or rather re-met—Philip Burton, whom Richard would consider his second father.

Philip Burton had taught the boy English his first year of grammar school, but had not been especially impressed, put off by Rich's atrocious accent and noticing that "the boy had spots." Rich suffered from cystic acne, which left scars on his cheeks and back, and an enduring sense of shame. A Welshman, Philip Burton had taught himself to speak perfect English. He was an officer in the Air Training Corps and a director and actor in local theater. Besides teaching English, he wrote and performed radio dramas for the BBC Welsh radio. He was plump, demanding, beautifully dressed, and highly cultured. He was also gay, though probably celibate—or mostly celibate, given the time and place. When he cast Rich in *Gallows Glorious*, one of Philip Burton's local productions, he first realized what he had on his hands. He offered Rich another role, in a radio drama he had written called *Youth at the Helm*, and the man and boy traveled to Cardiff to record the play. Graham remembered hearing his brother's performance, for the first time, over the radio: "Not having to act, physically, he concentrated on voice. And what a voice . . . I was bowled over by the melodious, seductive tones of the *Welsh* Welsh, deeper and stronger than anything you will hear in the north." Aware of his impact and no doubt blossoming under his mentor's approval, Rich knew then he wanted to be an actor.

Philip was pleased to have a new protégé. He had earlier on nurtured the career of another young Welsh actor, Thomas Owen Jones, who had won a scholarship to the prestigious Royal Academy of Dramatic Arts (RADA), but had become a fighter pilot in the Second World War and died in the Battle of Britain. In a sense, Rich Jenkins would replace the lost Thomas Owen Jones, and, if anything, young Jenkins, now fifteen, seemed even more gifted. As Graham noted, "he had the rough good looks of a warrior, a stubborn jaw and compelling blue eyes. He was strong and intelligent and he could act." (Richard's eyes would variously be described as blue or green.)

Philip wanted Rich to have extra tutoring, but Cis and Elfred couldn't afford it. There was no other way; Philip suggested that Rich move into his lodging house in Port Talbot, essentially sharing his rented rooms, while the older man continued to mentor him.

Cis had prayed for such an opportunity for her gifted brother— but there were unspoken concerns. It wasn't lost on the other Jenkins men that Philip was a fortyish bachelor, and they wondered what other interest he might have in the fifteen-year-old, but the fact that Burton's new lodgings in Connaught Street were part of a respectable household consisting of a widow and her two daughters put everyone's mind at ease. And so Rich moved in with Burton and the great project began, Philip drilling Rich on his English for hours a day, teaching him Shakespeare and elocution and theater. He smoothed Rich's rough manners and dressed him, at his own expense, better than he had ever dressed himself.

Rich knew this was a way to stay out of the mines forever, if he could only pass his exams and apply to RADA, as his predecessor had done. In later years, he would say that it was *he* who had adopted Philip Burton, and not the other way around, though Rich surely must have known that his benefactor was in love with him. It would remain, apparently, an unrequited love.

Philip made plans to adopt his protégé, but was technically too close to Rich in age to legally do so. But he could make the young man his ward, so Philip Burton approached the Jenkinses about becoming Rich's legal guardian, which, he explained, would smooth his way academically and professionally. He had already realized that he could put Rich up for a Royal Air Force (RAF) officer's training program, which would include a six-month stint at Exeter College, Oxford. Oxford! The son of a coal miner could only dream of such an opportunity, but the ward of a teacher, writer, and director just might pull it off. But permission was needed from Rich's true father, Dic Jenkins, for the legal guardianship to go forward.

Rich would have to repudiate his family name and take Philip Burton's name as his own.

But there was a problem. "However often the advantages of the Burton connection were explained to him," Graham recalled, Dadi Ni "could never quite reconcile himself to Rich assuming another name. To him, it was a renunciation of a birthright. And the Welsh miners of the old school were very strong on birthright." Indeed, in his whole life, his name was the only thing Jenkins had been able to give his seven sons. It was all he had.

So, when the time came to meet with Philip Burton at Hilda's cottage in Pontrhydyfen to finalize the arrangements, Dadi Ni just didn't show up. He'd stopped in at the Miners Arms and got drunk, his own, time-tested way of avoiding what must have seemed like a repudiation. So Richard Walter Jenkins became Richard Burton that December in 1943, and from then on would refer to Philip Burton as his father. Years later, in a documentary about Burton titled *In from the Cold*, directed by Tony Palmer, Joe Mankiewicz commented on Burton's abandonment of his father's name. "Burton's tragedy," he explained, "was that he couldn't go beyond Philip Burton to access his true ancestry." It would seem that the only thing he would inherit from his scrappy, original father was his alcoholism.

The devil's bargain paid off. In 1951, the influential London drama critic Ken Tynan wrote of Burton, ". . . a shrewd Welsh boy shines out with greatness" as Prince Hal in *Henry IV*, Part I.

"Before I met her," Burton confessed to Tynan in a *Playboy* interview, "I was making any kind of film in sight, just to get rich. Then Liz made me see what kind of rubbish I was doing. She made me do the film *Becket* when I didn't want to—and it was a turning point in my career. She also made me do *Hamlet*." It was to Elizabeth's credit that she wanted to see Richard in prestigious roles, not just Hollywood money-makers. Cast as Thomas Becket in Hal Wallis's screen version of Jean Anouilh's play, opposite his good friend Peter O'Toole as the swaggering young Henry II, Burton found himself not just in the company of esteemed theatrical talents—including Sir John Gielgud and Pamela Brown—but in the company of a fellow actor with a capacity for drink that matched his own. Though Burton refrained from imbibing on the set, he and O'Toole would usually knock off around noon and begin their consumption—wine and champagne at lunch, then, after work, they'd go pub-hopping where Burton switched to hard liquor with beer chasers.

Taylor joined them on these merry jaunts and made sure Burton returned home safely each night to the Oliver Messel Suite at the Dorchester, where they had taken up semipermanent residence after completing *The V.I.P.s*. The director, Peter Glenville, was mostly tolerant, in part because his lead actors' carousing was in keeping with the debauched bonhomie of the two characters depicted onscreen. Beyond that, *Becket* would admirably illustrate just what Richard had learned from Elizabeth about film acting. In contrast to the theatrical, scenery-chewing O'Toole, Burton radiates cool control onscreen. He had learned, from Elizabeth, how to underplay and how to be *still*, and indeed his performance is hard, brilliant, powerful. Where O'Toole is *acting*, Burton is *being*. The gemlike performance endures as one of Burton's best. It's all there—the voice, the control, the depth of feeling, the ease with which Anouilh's and screenwriter Edward Anhalt's rich dialogue falls from his tongue, his effortless, graceful masculinity. Richard was entering his great period of screen acting, beginning with *Cleopatra* and *Becket* and continuing through his next several films.

If Taylor influenced Burton's screen acting, she, too, was influenced by her now-famous paramour. Oddly enough, the rough-hewn son of a miner was having a civilizing influence on the coddled daughter of privilege. She began to adopt a British accent. Though she was born in England of American parents, her slight English accent had been something she could put on or take off, like a designer gown; under Burton's influence, her plummier tones returned. And, though Burton loved her earthiness, he was not overly fond of her sailor's vocabulary, and he wanted her to tone it down. That was harder to do: since early years, Elizabeth had felt liberated by uttering four-letter words—it was her spell-breaking rebellion against the imprisonment of praise. Her newly dusted-off English accent was on display in *Eliza-*

beth Taylor in London, a CBS special for which she served as tour guide while Burton was busy filming *Becket*. Another record broken: she had been paid $500,000 to do it. It had also strengthened her ties to the country of her birth. Burton would seek to strengthen his ties, but not to England. To Wales.

After filming was completed, Burton returned to Port Talbot and Pontrhydyfen, with Elizabeth by his side. It was an act of boldness: he knew that his entire family—including Philip Burton and Cis—had taken Sybil's side. Sybil was one of their own, and they loved her. But if they were baffled by Burton's taking up with this notorious Hollywood princess, this "third-rate chorus girl," in Emlyn Williams's words, they were too proud to show it. *Let her speak for herself* seemed to have been the prevailing attitude. The couple arrived in mid-June, driving from London in a Rolls-Royce, and headed straight for a large, two-story house Burton had bought for Cis and Elfred James in the town of Aberavon. Cis kept a bedroom on the main floor available for Burton's rare return visits to Wales.

For the grand couple's arrival, Cis had prepared Burton's favorite meal of scrambled eggs, hot tea, and lava bread. They ate enthusiastically, then Burton left the two women together while he met his old cronies at a local pub. The two women, surprisingly, bonded immediately. For all their differences in upbringing and circumstance, Elizabeth had genuine warmth, and when she wanted to please, she dazzled. She got Cis to regale her with stories about Burton's childhood, his boyhood triumphs on the rugby field, his scholastic successes. When Burton returned, he whisked Elizabeth off to the pub to meet his pals, where she was even more of a success. The hard-bitten miners sitting in those dark pubs knew royalty when they saw it, but didn't she drink with the rest of them, and laugh at their stories, and fit right in! Later, Burton bought Elizabeth supper (beef and kidney pie), and treated her to a sixpence ride on a carousel. She was in heaven. For a woman who had been raised on a country estate surrounded by art and antiques, and who, since the age of ten, had never experienced a normal life, this was the one thing her fame, her beauty, and her wealth could not provide. This was *real*.

Exhausted by *Cleopatra* and happy to stop working for a while to enjoy being with Burton, Taylor put her own career on hold for two years. She watched with immense pride as his film career began to soar. His next movie would provide him with another great role and another occasion for a powerful performance: Tennessee Williams's *The Night of the Iguana*, directed in Mexico by John Huston with a challenging cast that included a middle-aged and still beautiful Ava Gardner, the refined English actress Deborah Kerr, and a young Sue Lyon, following up her debut performance in Stanley Kubrick's *Lolita* the year before.

The movie business had noticeably changed in the five years since Elizabeth appeared as Maggie the Cat in Tennessee Williams's *Cat on a Hot Tin Roof*, when Production Code censors dogged the set. "It's hard to believe how strictly we were supervised in those days when it came to anything involving sex. It wasn't just homosexuality that was concealed; heterosexual behavior was subject to almost as many restrictions," Elizabeth recalled about the experience. One day when she was on camera for a wardrobe test, the "inspectors" showed up. "When a BI (that's a Bust Inspector, if you can believe it) appeared, he took one look at me and called for a stepladder. He climbed up, peered down, and announced that I needed a higher-cut dress, too much breast was exposed." The costume designer, Helen Rose, had to pin Elizabeth's bodice with a brooch, but as soon as the "BI" left, she pulled the pin off. She knew what looked good on camera—and off.

The Night of the Iguana would be more sexually explicit than *Cat on a Hot Tin Roof*, involving a man-hungry hotelier cavorting with her cabana boys and an alcoholic priest being tempted by a seductive teenager. Burton plays the desolate, defrocked priest who sinks deeper and deeper into alcoholic disgrace, till he's redeemed by the ministrations of two women: one spiritual (Deborah Kerr) and the other sensual (Ava Gardner). It's pure Tennessee Williams—intensely lyrical, sharply insightful, and full of bitch-wit, all brought to bloom under the Mexican sun and the canny direction of John Huston (who wickedly outfitted his volatile cast with gold-plated derringers and a handful of bullets that bore the name of each key member of the cast). Elizabeth had no role in the film, though she would have given Ava Gardner a good run for her money as the sex-starved, big-hearted earth goddess who runs the tourist hotel where most of the action unfolds. Nonetheless, she accompanied Burton to Puerto Vallarta, Mexico. Some speculated that it was to keep an eye on Burton, surrounded as he was by three kinds of female beauty: the nubile (Lyon), the refined (Kerr), and the lushly ripe (Gardner). Added to that was the sensuality of the place itself.

Huston's friend and assistant on the shoot, the actress Eloise Hardt, described it as being "like Never Never Land. Everyone was on edge from the heat and the sickness. Scorpions and iguanas hopping in your bed. You never knew if you were going to be bitten by something or stranded by a storm. There were all these emotions and egos . . . It got to be ridiculous. If you wanted to get in a sexy mood, just go to the Malecón and listen to the waves. Even if you didn't want it, your body felt it, the atmosphere was so primeval."

It was Ava Gardner, in fact, with her bold, sensuous beauty, her strong sexuality, and her ability to drink like a man, who posed the greatest threat to Elizabeth. They were uniquely alike, Ava and Elizabeth: both hothouse flowers raised by Hollywood studios, both known for their many marriages and love affairs, both "made equally unfit for normal life," as Gardner's latest biographer has noted, by their unreal upbringing. Indeed, the cast and crew noticed a certain mutual attraction between Richard and Ava, how Ava seemed to come alive in Richard's presence, how they seemed to exchange meaningful glances. The press were not just covering a congregation of some of the world's greatest talents and personalities in a remote Mexican village, they were waiting—hoping?—that Burton and Taylor's vaunted love affair might founder on Ava Gardner's dangerous shoulders. So Elizabeth was especially present on the set during Richard's steamy scenes with Ava, standing just out of the camera's range, dressed to kill in clingy blouses, tight slacks, and—of course—dazzling jewels.

But Richard's brother Graham felt that Elizabeth went to Mexico for other reasons.

"She wanted to be with Rich," Graham Jenkins recalled, "but also by showing that his career came first, she hoped to overcome his sense of inferiority. Elizabeth knew well enough how Rich smarted at the cheap jibes. In public he joked about his junior status in the partnership . . . but in private his anger at journalists who called him Mr. Cleopatra was terrible to behold." Sometimes he'd turn his fury against Elizabeth, making fun of her "MGM education" and challenging her to give him any line from Shakespeare, so that he could roll out the rest of the speech it came from. Of course, she couldn't, beyond "To be or not to be." Elizabeth usually enjoyed the spectacle of his rages, but not always. Jenkins describes one such scene that ended with Elizabeth getting up and leaving the room, pausing to warn Richard, "You should be more careful, love. One day you might harm more than yourself."

"When she left the room," Jenkins noticed, "Richard was close to tears."

Their Mexican hiatus, despite their loudly escalating spats, would prove to be a golden time for Richard and Elizabeth, one in which their volatile love affair deepened into something far richer. As Jenkins observed,

In Mexico . . . Richard discovered how much he really needed her . . . His surrender to Elizabeth was total. Once he came to terms with this, the sheer joy of knowing spilled over into every other part of his life. There were still rows, of course. With two such mercurial people, it could not have been otherwise. But taking a wider view, I could see that in his love for Elizabeth, Rich was at last beginning to understand his own character, which in turn gave him a sense of contentment he had never known before.

Contributing to this deepening of their bond was, no doubt, the enchantment of the place itself. At the time Puerto Vallarta was a sleepy fishing village on the Banderas Bay, surrounded by steep, green mountains and long, empty beaches. It has since become a thriving tourist town—in no small part due to Elizabeth and Richard's presence—but if they expected the remoteness of the area to make it a safe haven from paparazzi and prying eyes, they were disappointed. When they first flew into Mexico City on September 22, 1963, they were met by a swarming crowd.

Having placed Elizabeth's two sons in a boarding school in California, and leaving Maria temporarily in London to undergo further operations on her malformed hip, they arrived with seven-year-old Liza Todd amid the usual chaos that continued to surround them wherever they traveled. Elizabeth panicked when she saw the mob awaiting her, and when a man in a sombrero with pistols on his hip attempted to corral them through the crowd, they both panicked. "Get this maniac off the plane or I'll kill him," Richard reportedly yelled, before realizing the man, a volatile actor, filmmaker, and local character named Emilio "El Indio" Fernández, had been hired by John Huston to usher the famous couple to safety. In a Beatlemania-like frenzy, the crowd surged around them; they passed Liza over their heads to whisk her to safety. Elizabeth lost her shoes and her purse in the fracas before making it through the crowd. But the ordeal continued.

When they finally arrived in the overgrown jungle that would be the location for *The Night of the Iguana*, "there were more reporters on the site than iguanas," recalled John Huston in his 1980 memoir. They came from all over the world, hanging around the sleepy fishing village, just waiting for "the great day when the derringers were pulled out and the shooting started." Of course, they were really there for the continuing drama of Burton and Taylor's romance. After all, they were infamously cohabiting, still technically married to other people. In 1963, that was still a shocking state of affairs, but the public couldn't get enough of it.

Back in New York where Sybil had relocated, she at last gave up any hope of reconciliation when Richard declined to visit her and his two children before decamping to Mexico. He had already consulted Aaron Frosch, Elizabeth's attorney, about possible settlements, including $1 million to be deposited in Sybil's Swiss bank account, plus an annual $500,000 for ten years. Burton's divorce from Sybil was finally announced on December 5, 1963, on the grounds of "abandonment and cruel and inhumane treatment." Burton was at last free to marry Elizabeth, who considered his divorce from Sybil "the best Christmas present" she had ever received. But Elizabeth was still not free.

Eddie Fisher was dragging his feet over signing the final divorce papers, holding out for a better settlement. She wanted to keep the chalet in Gstaad, which Fisher had actually bought for her for $350,000, and she wanted to keep all the jewelry he had given her, as well as a dark green Rolls-Royce she had given him as a birthday present. To complicate their financial matters, Elizabeth and Fisher had formed a production company, MCL Films, for the purpose of freeing her from MGM servitude by lending her services to 20th Century-Fox for *Cleopatra*. She had insisted on keeping all the profits from MCL Films.

Elizabeth finally agreed to release some of the profits in exchange for an agreement with Fisher to refrain from "embarrassing her publicly" (she had been incensed by his "Cleo, the Nympho of the Nile" specialty number developed for his nightclub act). He agreed, and that was one reason he didn't publish his first memoir until 1981. There was also the issue of Fisher's name on Maria's adoption papers. Taylor hoped to replace his name with Burton's, and Fisher agreed only after insisting that he maintain legal ties to Liza Todd, as his only remaining connection to his lost friend and mentor, Mike Todd.

Elizabeth got her way: she managed to convince the German authorities that Eddie had never been Maria's adoptive father in the first place (though he had signed the adoption papers), and that she had always been the sole adoptive parent. But then, who could deny Elizabeth anything?

Michael Wilding, Taylor's second husband and father of her two sons, accompanied her to Puerto Vallarta as Richard's agent. It was perhaps a tribute to Wilding's geniality and their amicable divorce that he was able to work for his ex-wife's current paramour.

Delighted with the dazzling, white-hot sun and the turquoise-green of the sea, they first rented and then bought a four-story white stucco villa called Casa Kimberly, with access to ten acres of beach. "There is no more delectable place on the face of the earth, but don't come because you'll spoil it," is how Burton described their newly discovered paradise. For the first time, perhaps, since her early childhood in England, Elizabeth felt at home. She loved the heat, the verdant green of the jungle, the brightly colored macaws that flew across her balcony in the mornings. She bought a blue launch named *Taffy* to cross the Banderas Bay to the film set, precariously built on a perch overlooking the bay. She also flew in her secretary, her chauffeur, and her cook, and hired two maids from the village and a retired slot-machine repairman to serve as Burton's masseur. She was so happily ensconced in Puerto Vallarta, and so ubiquitous on the set, she was practically part of the crew. In order to keep for himself a shred of privacy so he could continue his habit of voracious reading, Burton bought a second villa and had a bridge built to connect them, modeled on the Venetian Bridge of Sighs.

In addition to Liza Todd, Maria soon joined the family in Puerto Vallarta. Liza—an extraordinarily beautiful child—had been virtually raised without formal education, and at seven was still unable to read. Elizabeth tried to teach her with the use of primers she had bought, but without much success, given her devotion to Richard and the amount of time she spent with him on the set and in various bars. So they hired a live-in tutor, a twenty-two-year-old named Paul Neshamkin. "I used to spend all day with the kids, and then I would spend the evening entertaining the Burtons . . . I drank with them every night, until about four in the morning," Neshamkin told Kitty Kelley for her 1981 biography *Elizabeth Taylor: The Last Star.* "We'd start drinking and talking and reciting poetry," he recalled, "and, of course, debating Jews versus Protestants." On school holidays, Michael and Christopher joined the family, and Richard and Elizabeth could be seen dining *en famille* in a village restaurant.

With or without Elizabeth's children in tow, Richard continued his dangerous dance with alcohol, drinking enough to cause even the hard-drinking John Huston to shake his head. Elizabeth continued to serve as his drinking companion. After one such five-hour bout of drinking, Elizabeth told a reporter, "Richard lives each of his roles. In this film, he's an alcoholic and an unshaven bum, so that explains his appearance and liquid intake."

Budd Schulberg, the author of the Hollywood novel *What Makes Sammy Run?* and the screenplays *On the Waterfront* and *The Harder They Fall,* was also on the set, spending time with his good friend Ava Gardner. A steady stream of friends, former and current lovers, and personalities flocked to Mismaloya, including Deborah Kerr's new husband, the screenwriter Peter Viertel, who had once been involved with Gardner during the making of *The Sun Also Rises* and was the author of *White Hunter Black Heart,* a thinly disguised, unflattering portrait of John Huston. (Viertel had also been married to Budd Schulberg's ex-wife.) Tennessee Williams arrived with his lover of the moment, soon joined by his longtime companion Frank Merlo (whom the playwright affectionately called "The Little Horse"), and his poodle, Gigi. The randy but genteel Southern playwright spent much of his time donning a bathing cap and swimming with Burton and Taylor, bobbing like a wet seal in a cove just below the set that had been hastily constructed on a bluff overlooking the bay. It was an extraordinary collection of actors, writers, filmmakers, hangers-on, and heavy drinkers.

"Everyone was drinking quite a bit," Schulberg recalled. "Richard hit it very hard and Huston always did. And Ava—yes, she was pretty good, too. I stayed out with Richard Burton several nights. It would be past three in the morning, and he would be in his cups and want to talk about Dylan Thomas or—he was a big fight fan. We'd be yakking about the fights. And Elizabeth would come storming out in her bathrobe looking for him, giving him hell—'What do you think you're doing, you've got to work in the morning!' They were all having a good time. It was a happy company. You couldn't believe they were making a movie."

The veteran Hollywood reporter James Bacon was among the many journalists covering the movie shoot. Free to roam the set, Bacon spent time with Richard and Elizabeth, often accompanying them on their long afternoons of drinking. "She can outdrink any man I've known, including Burton," Bacon reported about Elizabeth, with a certain respectful amazement. He recalled one night when, oddly, Burton remained sober until Taylor taunted him with, "Richard, take a drink. You are so goddamned dull when you're not drinking." She had apparently touched a nerve—Burton lived in fear of "boring the piss out of everyone. Without alcohol, when I'm stone-cold sober, I feel I belong in a university town somewhere teaching literature and drama to grubby little boys." Bacon remembered that that was the night he watched Burton down twenty-three straight shots of tequila, "with a few bottles of Carta Blanca beer as chasers."

If the American press were mostly fawning, interested in every bit of minutia about the famous couple, the Mexican press expressed outrage. In an editorial, the *Siempre* called for the ousting of the whole *Iguana* cast and crew, complaining about the "sex, drinks, drugs, vice, and carnal bestiality by the garbage of the United States." The local Catholic convent broke their vow of silence to protest Elizabeth Taylor's presence in Puerto Vallarta, as she was "living in sin" with Richard Burton.

But by now the couple was impervious to the pronouncements of the press. Elizabeth fussed over Richard on the set, combing and recombing his hair. (At one point, exasperated with her constant ministrations, Burton poured a pitcher of beer over his head.) When she wasn't on set or bar-hopping with Burton, Elizabeth lolled on the beach, clad in a bikini, a green-and-white Mexican shift, and gold-and-turquoise-beaded sandals. On another occasion, she showed up in a bikini bottom and sheer top, wearing a stunning pearl-and-ruby ring given to her, she said, by the king of Indonesia. Burton was thoroughly delighted, taking the occasion to mischievously describe her as looking like "a French tart." Her outrageous displays of bounty—gifts of nature and of men—only made her more desirable in his eyes, more extraordinary, more loved. No wonder he called her "Ocean," to describe her deep, overpowering presence.

In 1971, Burton recalled his Mexican hiatus in an article titled "Dauntless Travelers" for *Vogue* magazine, capturing the euphoria of that time. By then married to Elizabeth, he wrote in his typically lavish style,

> . . . the street we live on is a bewitchment invented by a genius with taste, endlessly fascinating, pastelled in blues and terra-cottas, blazing whites and duns, and there are laden burros and men from the hills going home asleep on walking horses and I could sit here forever as long as someone feeds me from time to time and plies me with drinks and if one's wife hangs around for another forty years or so and God knows none of us have long to live.

He describes a day on which a traveling circus trailed in over the "Bridge of a Hundred Days," led by a baby elephant. Burton first glimpsed it from Casa Kimberly's balcony, mistrusting his own eyes, till he heard "the thrilling still music blast[ing] out, and children [weeping] with delight." Though it was an unusually hot day even for Puerto Vallarta, Elizabeth wanted to go, and of course Burton couldn't deny her. Once they assembled in the dusty town square to watch the circus acts (all but the high-wire artist—Burton had a morbid dread of heights), the master of ceremonies noticed their presence among the villagers. He called out, *"Tenemous sta noche los muy famosas actors del mondo,"* Burton wrote in a kind of pidgin Spanish. "What can you do? My wife undulated exquisitely into the arena without any apparent qualm and addressed herself to the task of having scimitars thrown at her by a Mexican man she'd never met." The daggers were thrown within a hair's breadth of Elizabeth's famous face. Like a brave soul staring down a firing squad, she barely blinked. By now, she was used to the spectacle of having daggers thrown at her in public. When it was Burton's turn to be pinned to the board, they turned him sideways and stuck a balloon in his mouth and in each hand. The "dagger man," Alejandro Fuentes, successfully punctured the balloons, sparing Burton's profile, amid roars from the crowd. "I looked, in short, like an idiot," Burton wrote, "as the daggers went true to their targets—three for the balloons and one each side of my head . . ."

Later that evening, Richard and Elizabeth sat on their balcony with their neighbors, the American actor Phil Ober and his wife, Jane, looking over their humble, resplendent town. "We must have been out of our minds," Elizabeth said about the day's events, and, later, in bed before dousing the light, "Ah well, another day, another drama." It had been a curious metaphor for their circus life together: on display, cheered by crowds, while a professional knife-thrower hurled stilettos at them, missing them by inches.

The day before Richard Burton turned thirty-eight, he started celebrating early by drinking with Ava Gardner, who had presented him with a fifth of bourbon. It was nine thirty in the morning, and the heat in Mismaloya was already crushing. Burton held forth in his costar's dressing room, reciting poetry and then reminiscing about his father—his first father, the miner who sired him. Elizabeth had yet to arrive at the set.

"My father would never say he drank a lot," Burton told the sultry actress and Joseph Roddy, a visiting journalist who later described the occasion. "He'd say he was a man of vast drinking habits." He laughed. He described how his father would come up out of the coal mines on paydays—"days of decision," he called them—trying to decide if he should first head for the dog track or the tavern. He would reappear days later to apologize to his eleven surviving offspring, saying, in Burton's spirited telling, "I . . . am . . . pro-foundahleeee . . . sawree . . . For one torn second a week before Friday last, I nearly came home directly." Burton loved to tell that story, making a fine joke out of his father's fecklessness.

He then regaled his audience with another favorite tale about the night Dadi Ni, with dreams of making a killing on the dog races, came home leading an ancient, toothless, winded dog on the end of a leash. "Boys," he said, pointing to the panting wreck, "our troubles are over!" But what was curiously revealed during Burton's raucous birthday celebration was another side of Dic Jenkins, and a hint of the high regard Burton still carried for his broken father, who had nonetheless managed to make it to the age of eighty-one. He had often joked that his father rarely saw his films because "there were too many pubs between the house and the cinema." Yet he knew that his love of poetry—and of the English tongue itself—came to him through his father.

"My father could give bad verse a ring of great quality," he told Ava Gardner, then launched into several stanzas of verse to illustrate the point.

"So do you," she replied.

"Ah, love, but you should have heard my father do it."

"I'm sure that I just did."

For father and son, alcohol opened up the floodgates of poetry. Burton described how he would bring home books from school that his father would ravenously pore over, memorizing the English poetry he found there. "He was never the man to use a short word when there was a long one that would do," Burton recalled, explaining that the first time his father talked to him about the sun, it was to explain the "dichotomies between the Copernican and heliocentric cosmologies." He related a conversation he'd had with his father over who was the most courageous poet of World War I, "after he had worked out the answer at the pub. 'Not Alan Seeger. Not Rupert Brooke. Not Wilfred Owen. No, my boy, no one of them. The most courageous poet of that war was Mister Thomas Stearns Eliot in *The Love Song of J. Alfred Prufrock*. At the bloody height of the whole bloody battle, Mr. Eliot wrote that he had measured out his life in coffee spoons. Now that took what I call courage.' "

It had long been assumed that Richard's adoptive father, Philip Burton, had introduced Burton to poetry—English and Welsh—and had encouraged that talent. But it had been a paternal inheritance all along—poetry and storytelling and drinking, and as Burton grew older and his father's memory hardened into a series of tragicomic anecdotes, the residue of that original gift—or debt—survived.

Despite the torrid heat, the abundance of reporters and scorpions, the chiggers that left painful bites all over Elizabeth's feet because she went everywhere in her gold-strapped sandals, their time in Puerto Vallarta had been deeply happy. A pattern had emerged. Elizabeth would use her star power to help Richard achieve the world acclaim she knew he deserved. And she would be sure that he appeared only in the best vehicles: *Becket*, *The Night of the Iguana*—because it was by Tennessee Williams, America's greatest living playwright—and then a Broadway production of *Hamlet*. They would show the world that they were not tarnished celluloid adulterers, but artists of the highest order, and they belonged in a realm where ordinary codes of behavior no longer applied. They were beyond bourgeois morality now.

They would no longer let each other out of their sight, if they could help it. They'd both suffered too much to let their embattled love slip away, and their passion for each other showed no signs of abating. Elizabeth knew that Richard "loved my shape—my body appealed to him. He teased me, but I knew he loved my body. I loved being admired by Richard. It was the kind of admiration that mattered to me. I felt adored, worshipped."

And her power over Burton made him tremble. "Bewitched" is how he would describe it, "bewitched by her cunt and her cunning." He would be drunk when he said it, but as his closest friends knew, he only lied when he was sober. In letters home, Burton wrote to his brother Graham about his happiness and the close bond he felt with Elizabeth.

"Where I was wrong," Jenkins recalled in his memoir, "was in believing it would last."

4
NO MORE MARRIAGES

"You're the one they've come to see.
You're the Frank Sinatra of Shakespeare."
—TAYLOR TO BURTON

"I say we will have no more marriages."
—BURTON QUOTING SHAKESPEARE

Elizabeth was supremely happy to step back and let Richard take center stage. It wouldn't be the first time she'd announced her plans to be a wife first, an actress second. She'd resented being the principal breadwinner in her marriage to Michael Wilding. With Todd, she'd informed her public, "Mike and I hope to have many children. I think it's much more important for a woman to be a mother than an actress." She had wanted to consecrate her marriage to Eddie Fisher by adopting a child. Now, above all, she wanted to make Richard happy. She could see that he chafed at being occasionally referred to as "Mr. Taylor," or even worse, "Mr. Cleopatra." There were still critics who loudly lamented Burton's defection from legitimate theater, where Olivier and Gielgud's laurels waited to be permanently attached to Burton's brow, and she knew there were critics who blamed her. They had to be silenced.

Plans to produce a new *Hamlet* with Burton in the title role and

Gielgud directing had been discussed as early as 1963, when Burton had appeared with Sir John in *Becket*. Burton had played Hamlet before, in Edinburgh and at the Old Vic Company in 1953–1954, among some complaints that he had rushed his lines and thrown away the poetry of the Bard—surprising, for one as devoted to poetry as Burton. Gielgud's own Hamlet, performed in London's Old Vic, had been, in Burton's eyes, the greatest in his lifetime, and to be directed by Gielgud in the quintessential actor's role was truly a passing of the baton. After all, it was Gielgud who had helped launch Burton's stage career, casting and directing him in three plays by Christopher Fry— *The Lady's Not for Burning*, *The Boy with a Cart*, and *A Phoenix Too Frequent*—which garnered Burton early enthusiastic reviews. Gielgud himself said about Burton's performance in *The Boy with a Cart*, "He was simply splendid . . . It was a wonderful *succés d'estime*." In a 1967 interview with Kenneth Tynan, Burton remarked, "I can never repay him for the debt of casting me in *The Lady's Not for Burning* and *The Boy with a Cart*. He made me into what is casually known as a leading man."

The only problem was, Burton didn't particularly want to go back onstage. It helped that both he and Gielgud agreed that the play would be mounted with minimal sets and in modern dress, "so the beauty of the language and imagery may shine through unencumbered," as Gielgud explained in a program note. The idea was that the performance take the form of a last rehearsal, before the actors donned their costumes and sets were rolled into place. Burton would wear black trousers and a black sweater for the role. Nonetheless, he was reluctant. He was, in fact, terrified.

It had only been two years since he'd walked away from playing King Arthur to don Roman general Marc Antony's breastplate, but he feared the public would be waiting to judge him, eager to see him fail. Behind that was the sheer terror of live performance, which he had never completely overcome, made more intense, perhaps, by a dislike of being touched while performing onstage. When the London drama critic Tynan said that Burton seemed "isolated, apart, in a world of [his] own" onstage, Burton confided, "I do feel that on the stage it's quite literally every man for himself. I don't think anyone wants to help you particularly . . . you have to look after yourself. And I think that particular loneliness, solitude, that idea of carrying on in your own private room is not . . . unique to actors . . . I have it perhaps more than most. When I go out there, onstage, I'm battling the world—I have to beat the world. I have to be the best, as far as I can make it."

It was Elizabeth who urged him to face up to his fear of live performance. In this, and in other aspects of their life together, she was his courage-teacher. For example, she noticed that in interviews he tended to speak with his hand close to his mouth, to shield his pockmarked right cheek from the intrusive camera. She would have none of that. It was her philosophy to drag secrets and fears into the pitiless light, and she called him out on it, teasing him with seemingly cruel endearments like "my pockmarked Welshman."

Burton, in fact, like many stage actors, had a number of phobias and conditions he hid from the public. One was that acute fear of heights, which he only began to reveal under Elizabeth's influence. The other secret he'd nurtured was the fact that he was a hemophiliac, though to a mild degree, remarkable in one so athletic and so physically engaged with the world. In fact, his sword fights each night in *Hamlet* put him at risk, because he never held back. John Cullum, the actor who played Laertes, recalled that sometimes the fight was so intense that he would get quite banged up, eventually losing a thumbnail as a result. "I bleed more than Laertes," Burton said. "Of course, I'm a wilder duelist. But he stops bleeding within twenty-four hours. It takes me five days."

In spite of it, there wasn't a pub brawl he ducked from if it came his way; he'd had dreams of being a rugby player for Wales long before he'd hoped to become an actor. It was Elizabeth who urged him to stop hiding his hemophilia, which Richard felt was unmanly. She urged him to go public with the inherited condition, and later he would take it on as a cause, touting the benefits of vitamin K in treating the blood disorder. (Elizabeth would later say that taking up this cause with Richard was a precursor to her AIDS charitable work, long before the AIDS-related death of her friend and costar in *Giant*, Rock Hudson.) In a press release announcing the establishment of the Richard Burton Hemophilia Fund, Burton told the press, "I've been a bleeder all my life," though his own case was relatively slight. Two of his brothers, however, had the condition in a more severe form, and had almost died undergoing tonsillectomies in their youth.

Another condition that haunted Richard was epilepsy. He had suffered a mild seizure when he was a young actor in London and was reportedly set to rights by a couple of brandies. Since then, he feared its recurrence and felt that alcohol kept the seizures at bay—as if he needed another reason to drink. He would be free of attacks for some time, but they would recur toward the end of his career, during a period when he was not drinking, sending him twice to the hospital.

Elizabeth gave him the courage to face the abominable crowds that now pushed against them whenever they ventured out in public. Though he would later admit to liking the perks of fame—"the best seat at the restaurant, the best seat on the plane; you're treated like a kind of demigod"—Burton disliked the hurly-burly of fandom, with its prying journalists and relentless paparazzi. He would never quite learn how to manage the crush of fame, unlike Elizabeth, who, as he later marveled in a BBC interview, "had a kind of private veil she put on in public, where she didn't seem to notice photographers or journalists. She walked through them as if through a vacuum. [Her] public persona was aloof and enormously difficult to break." Elizabeth would have to teach Burton how to be private in public, now that she had brought him into her world.

Elizabeth would need her "private veil" when the couple flew to Toronto on January 28, 1964, to rehearse *Hamlet* at the O'Keefe Theater. When they checked into a five-room suite on the eighth floor of the King Edward–Sheraton Hotel, they were met by huge crowds, not all of them fans. One hostile picketer carried a sign that read, "Drink not the wine of adultery." Except for rehearsals at the O'Keefe, Taylor and Burton were virtual prisoners of the eighth floor, afraid to go out and be overwhelmed by adoring or hostile crowds. An armed guard was placed outside the door of their suite, for their own protection, and Elizabeth, who had arrived with two poodles, had to walk her dogs on the roof of the hotel.

John Gielgud was appalled at this American form of worship. He wrote in a letter to his partner, Paul Anstee, "Ghastly crowds of morons besiege the hotel where Burton and Taylor are staying—every drink and conversation they have is paragraphed and reported. It really must be hell for them, and now some Ohio congressman has demanded that his American visa be rescinded for moral turpitude . . . !"

Elizabeth came to only two of the Toronto rehearsals, recalls the actor Richard L. Sterne (who appeared as "A Gentleman" in *Hamlet*), during the entire three-city run of the production. "Mostly, she stayed in the hotel. It was dangerous for them to go out. I've never seen anything quite like that. I suppose some of the rock musicians get that treatment, but it's exceptional for theater people. There was always a crowd outside the theater trying to just see them, to get a glimpse of the two of them."

At the first company meeting in Toronto, Sterne recalled the cast sitting down at a large table to read through the script. Burton "read with such enormous energy. Usually, at first readings, you're just studying the words. Richard was giving an all-out, rip-roaring reading that amazed everybody."

The young actor was particularly taken with Burton's voice: "He had an amazing projection. The timbre of it was quite penetrating and carried all the way to the last row of the theater. We weren't microphoned then. One of the reviewers said he had a voice that could outshout Times Square traffic." Years later, when asked by British TV interviewer Michael Parkinson, "Is there such a thing as a 'Welsh voice'?" Burton had said, partly tongue-in-cheek, "It's the deep, dark answer from the valleys, to everybody." But he also said, "I can't help the voice. . . . It was given to me. I'm very lucky to possess it, I suppose. It's not a gift I would wish on anybody else."

Sterne remembered that Elizabeth "was very quiet during rehearsals." This was her first up-close exposure to classical theater, and she wanted to learn. "She steeped herself in the play and its various interpretations." Sterne was also struck by how "awesomely beautiful" she was. "I can still see her coming into the rehearsal hall for the first time. It was maybe a week or so after we'd started rehearsing; she was dressed in a purple pantsuit. You couldn't miss those violet-colored eyes. She sat very quietly; she barely moved, and she watched very attentively. Then we didn't see her again until we were in performance."

Gielgud was immensely pleased with the advanced booking for the play ("We shall be sold out for the entire engagement," he wrote to his friend), and equally pleased with his assembled cast: "Rehearsals have begun unbelievably well . . . Richard looks pretty gross and red, but he is so beguiling and gifted that one succumbs the moment he begins to act, and he is utterly amenable to every suggestion and extremely skilled in adapting any idea one gives him. I really think he will be wonderfully moving and affecting."

Sterne knew that "Richard adored Sir John and thought he was the greatest Shakespearean actor of all time, the best Hamlet he'd ever seen; he was in awe of him, as we all were in that cast." Nonetheless, Burton seemed to have mixed feelings about Gielgud's direction, explaining to Tynan that in theater, which is essentially a writer's medium, "directors are relatively unimportant. They're not much more than jumped-up stage managers [who] should show you the place on the stage where you will be best seen. Then, assuredly leave the rest up to you." Nonetheless, he praised Gielgud to Tynan as "the best director I've ever worked with on the stage . . . He was as dominating as a director could be, with somebody like myself" because he understood, Burton felt, that he needed to be left alone onstage. "I do think he thinks I'm an undisciplined actor. . . . I wouldn't want to be that kind of disciplined actor who goes onstage every night and gives the same cadence to every speech, every night for days and days and days on end. I would prefer to be free so that I'm invited to be bad some nights . . ."

However, Elizabeth noticed that Richard was not completely at ease with Gielgud's direction, nor with the physical and mental demands of the role. Perhaps he'd just been away too long, and though he'd played the part many times before, he couldn't find his footing. Just before the play was to open, Elizabeth took it upon herself to call Richard's "father"—his second father, the one who had plucked him from obscurity and set him on the path to fame—Philip Burton—to come to Richard's aid.

It was a bold thing to do. Philip was now living in New York City, where he had launched an acting school, the American Music and Dramatic Academy, and he had sided with Sybil over the scandalous affair and subsequent divorce. It had been two years since Philip, now fifty-nine, had even spoken to his protégé. Whether Sybil graciously encouraged him to fly to Toronto, or he just wanted another chance to instruct and influence his brilliant ward, Philip agreed to step in. According to Sterne, Philip took over from Gielgud, taking an active role in shaping Burton's performance. Gielgud was not happy about it, but, if nothing else, Philip's presence seemed to calm Burton and give him confidence, and he stayed on for a few days as an unofficial, and unpaid, adjunct to the production.

Philip Burton arrived a few days after the play opened on February 26, 1964, to mixed reviews, though Burton fared much better than the production itself. Though the *Toronto Daily Star* called the pre-Broadway opening "an unmitigated disaster," the *Toronto Telegram* lauded Burton as "magnificent" and described him as "the only thing of consequence" in Gielgud's production. "We've seen in Toronto only two other such brilliant displays. Sir Laurence Olivier's *Becket* in 1961 and Sir Alec Guinness's *Dylan* two months ago." The pared-down, minimalist approach came in for the biggest criticism—audiences apparently wanted the trappings of Denmark, not modern-day dress. Luckily, two days after opening in Toronto, Burton's *Becket* was released in New York, to strong reviews.

Despite the production's mixed reception and the nightly strain of performing onstage, Burton was gracious to the entire cast and crew. ("The crew adore him," Gielgud had observed.) Sterne, fresh from Philadelphia and embarking on his first major theatrical production, noted that Burton "treated everybody, from the producer down to the doorman, the same. We had this rather odd character named Peter Green, who was the stage doorman," Sterne recalled. "He was a very old man, and he had a wooden leg. . . . Richard's dressing room was one floor up, so every message that came to the stage door, Peter Green had to get up those stairs with his wooden leg and hand it to him. Richard adored him; he was very, very kind. His dressing-room door was almost always open. Anybody could go by and say hello."

As he had while appearing as King Arthur in *Camelot*, Burton held court in his dressing room, regaling cast and crew with his storehouse of anecdotes, jokes, and bawdy songs. Once the play opened and his dressing room was thronged with well-wishers, security guards, and Burton's growing entourage, Gielgud found it next to impossible to get in to see Burton to give him performance notes. He had to wait in line, like everybody else. "There was one performance in Boston where he couldn't even get backstage afterward," Sterne remembered. "The police were posted at the door, and he went up and said, 'I'm the director of this play!' and they told him to move along. So, Richard had to get the notes the next day before the matinee."

The sheer enormity of Burton's fame greatly outshone Gielgud's, and seeing Philip Burton swoop in to add grace notes to his own direction must have created a strain between the two men. Added to that, Burton, of course, was intent on putting his own stamp on the role. In commenting on the difference between his 1953 *Hamlet* performed at the Old Vic and his 1964 *Hamlet,* Burton told Tynan, "The first time I played it as if I'd like to be John Gielgud. The second time . . . I played it absolutely as myself."

Even so, Burton altered his performance vastly from show to show, Sterne recalled. "You never knew what he was going to do. He was always in character, and it was always fascinating and exciting to watch him. Maybe a few performances he was down and not completely into it, but for almost all of them, he was electrifying." One night he recited the "To be or not to be" soliloquy in German, to acknowledge some important German-speaking people in the audience—social workers who had come to New York to decide if Burton and Taylor were fit parents to adopt Maria, whose adoption was not yet finalized. (Burton had easily picked up a smattering of languages, German, French, and Spanish.) He was even capable of reciting "To be or not to be," backward. Despite the enormous amounts of alcohol Burton put away, his memory never seemed to fail him.

Offstage, Richard and Elizabeth "couldn't keep their hands off each other," recalled Robert Misil (who played Horatio in the production). "She was captivated by his poetic brilliance and he was—to the extreme—inordinately proud that he, Richard Burton, the twelfth of thirteen children born to a barmaid and a Welsh coal miner, had married the most beautiful and most famous woman in the world." John Cullum, the tall, rugged actor who played Laertes (and Sir Dinadan in *Camelot*) saw that "everybody wanted to be around them. They were so charismatic, so much in love, so generous to everyone in the production." Sterne thought so, too. "Physically, Burton was magnetic. He had an aura about him."

Sterne was also impressed by the enormous amounts of alcohol Burton was able to consume without affecting his performance. "Richard belonged to that school of British actors who were big drinkers. Richard and Peter O'Toole. I would say, just from my own observation, that he actually drank a fifth of scotch during the performance. It seemed to have no effect on him whatsoever." Gielgud wrote to

Burton's longtime friend and supporter, the playwright Emlyn Williams, "Richard is at his most agreeable—full of charm and quick to take criticism and advice—but he does put away the drink, and looks terribly coarse and heavy—gets muddled and fluffy and then loses all his nimbleness and attack."

It's mind-boggling that Burton was able to perform nightly while downing a fifth of scotch. Cullum, who was a drinking buddy of Burton's when they were in *Camelot*, couldn't keep up with him (Cullum no longer drinks). Though he did notice that while Burton's dresser, Bob Wilson, always had a full glass of scotch waiting for him just off-stage, he didn't think Burton always finished each drink. Throughout the run of the play, Burton only missed two performances, and that was because he was beginning to have severe bursitis in one shoulder. His performances were consistently brilliant and physically energetic. "Richard was so energetic in his fencing," Sterne recalled, "the foil broke three or four times during performances." (When the pianist Oscar Levant saw the New York production, he commented to his wife, June, that Burton's Hamlet was so energetic he actually felt sorry for Claudius.)

Sterne was one of the actors who carried Burton off at the end of the play after Hamlet is slain by Laertes. "There were six of us carrying him out in a sort of funeral procession," Sterne recalled. "Drums in the background. Hamlet gets a short break during the fourth act while Ophelia is doing the mad scene. Richard would go up and take a shower in his dressing room and put on a clean, fresh costume to do the last act. So, he always smelled very, very fresh, that he'd just come out of the shower. Maybe he sweated the alcohol out."

Sterne was well aware of Burton's need for physical space around him onstage: "He didn't like to be touched . . . he let us know that, and people were very respectful. There were a few times when we had to touch him, pulling him out of the grave. I think it broke his concentration. Some of the old-time actors were like that, too. They would stand in the center of the stage, in the limelight, and everybody else had to work from outside that circle. It could have been a fear too, because of the crowds who tried to grab at him."

Once the play opened, Sterne recalled, "Elizabeth was always there with him. Every night, never missed one. I think she only saw it once in the audience, after that she saw it from the wings or heard it over the monitor." That was because when she arrived on opening night, her very appearance caused such a ruckus it delayed the curtain by a half hour. Audience members actually climbed onto their seats to get a better look at her. Rather than upstage the actors, from that night on she either slipped in and sat at the rear or wings of the theater or watched the performance from backstage. But she was there every night.

Elizabeth celebrated her thirty-second birthday with the cast and crew of *Hamlet*. She showed up backstage, dressed in black, exactly like Richard, and everyone sang "Happy Birthday" and then broke into a chorus of "Danny Boy" for Burton. She then cut the birthday cake with a sword. It was one of the happiest moments of her life. "She couldn't have been lovelier," Sterne recalls. "She was kind of a prisoner of the whole crowd because she couldn't go out in public without being molested," but she was safe with Burton and the actors. And Burton gave her a stunning birthday present, an emerald-and-diamond necklace from Bulgari. It gave him, this miner's son, as much pleasure to buy her jewels as it pleased her to have them. He admired the way the jewels, brought up from the great mine of his fame and wealth, shone between her breasts. He felt as proud of bedecking Elizabeth in jewels as of anything else in his life.

On March 5, 1964, two years after falling in love with Richard, Elizabeth was finally granted her divorce from Eddie Fisher on the grounds of abandonment. Ten days later, Elizabeth and Richard chartered a Viscount turbo-prop airliner to Montreal, where they were met by three limousines. The couple and a few members of their entourage—including their publicist John Springer, their lawyer and tax specialist Aaron Frosch, and Burton's dresser Robert Wilson and his wife—were then whisked to Montreal's Ritz-Carlton Hotel, where Elizabeth and Richard registered under the name of "Smith." That Sunday afternoon, they were married in a private ceremony.

Though Elizabeth now considered herself Jewish, they were married by a Unitarian minister who agreed to take on the much-divorced couple. It was a hurried ceremony. The bride wore a yellow chiffon dress designed by Irene Sharaff, who had fashioned her stunning costumes for *Cleopatra*. She wore hyacinths and lily of the valley in her coiled hair, and the $150,000 emerald-and-diamond necklace Burton had given her, and matching earrings as his wedding gift. Newsmen were barred from the hotel; the only official statement given was Richard's: "Elizabeth Burton and I are very happy."

It was Richard's second marriage; it was Elizabeth's fifth.

They returned to Toronto the following day and Burton resumed his role as the Prince of Denmark. When the performance was over, after his curtain calls, Burton held his hand out as Elizabeth joined him onstage. In his thrilling Welsh voice, he reprised Hamlet's line to Ophelia: "I say, we will have no more marriages." The audience cheered.

Their triumph was complete.

On March 22, the production company flew to Boston for out-of-town tryouts at the Shubert Theater. "We thought there was going to be less commotion in Boston," Sterne recalled about their landing at Logan Airport. "There's a picture of Richard and Elizabeth getting off the plane. They were the first ones to come out; someone had presented them with flowers, and then this huge crowd of several thousand people broke through the Cyclone fences. They broke them down and ran out onto the airfield, so the Burtons had to get back on the plane." The plane had to be towed into a hangar, but the fans had overrun the police barriers and rushed the plane. Two limousines were quickly brought into the hangar to whisk the Burtons to their hotel (one was a decoy).

An even bigger mob of fans became unruly when Elizabeth and Richard checked into the Copley Plaza Hotel. If their adulterous affair had made the couple notorious, their marriage, announced in headlines around the world, had made them idols. A thousand "shouting, clawing admirers" poured into the hotel lobby. What had been mere hysteria was now frenzy, as fans grabbed at the couple's clothing and tore hair from Elizabeth's head. An eyewitness reported that Elizabeth "was being pulled in opposite directions at the same time. People were tugging at each arm and even crushed her face against the wall when she attempted to free herself." Burton had to fight his way through the crowd to rescue Taylor and safely usher her into the hotel elevator. Near collapse, Elizabeth broke down in sobs. A doctor was summoned. Elizabeth was treated for back and arm injuries and given a sedative before being put to bed in the first-class suite that had formerly been used by Presidents Kennedy and Eisenhower.

Burton was furious. "My wife was almost killed," he roared, and he threatened to lodge a complaint with the Boston police commissioner. "I've never seen anything like this before. It's outrageous. We had crowds like this in Toronto, but the police gave us adequate protection," he complained. Elizabeth, recovering from the crowd's attack, agreed that even she had "encountered mobs all over the world, but never anything to this extent."

Burton sufficiently recovered to give a brilliant performance at the Shubert two days later. The production was hailed by drama critic Elliot Norton as "a theatrical experience of much power and excitement, frequently tender, sometimes deeply moving, often wildly and honestly passionate." Norton wrote, "Richard Burton . . . has moments of greatness." Elinor Hughes of the *Boston Herald* noted that Burton had "poetry and passion in his bones, and in his voice . . . he gave us the music, the meaning, and the passion of this extraordinary role."

The Canadian-born character actor Hume Cronyn had been with Burton and Taylor in Rome, playing Cleopatra's tutor and prime minister, Sosigenes ("an Egyptian Polonius," in Mankiewicz's phrase).

Cronyn played Polonius in Gielgud's *Hamlet*, where he saw more of Elizabeth and Richard, close-up, than he had on the set of *Cleopatra*. He remained impressed—even awed—by Burton's gifts as an actor. Cronyn had seen all of the great Hamlets of the first half of the twentieth century—John Barrymore's, Maurice Evans's, John Gielgud's, Laurence Olivier's—so he was in a unique position to judge Burton's performance. He was "one of the very few actors I've known," Cronyn recalled later, "who was truly touched by the finger of God: his appearance, despite the pockmarked face; his quick intelligence, beautiful voice, and, above all, a Welsh lyricism of spirit that only money, notoriety, and an overweening ambition to be a film star could waste." But he knew that audiences were not lined up to see *Hamlet* just to see Burton; the entire production "was enveloped in the mystique of the Burton-Taylor romance." He had seen the hysteria play out two years earlier in Rome—the photographers hiding in the trees, the paparazzi on Vespas buzzing up and down Via Veneto. "Poor old Shakespeare didn't stand a chance" against the "Dickenliz" hoopla, a term first used by the Toronto newspapers when the production came to town.

On April 9, 1964, the play opened at the Lunt-Fontanne Theatre, where it would become the longest-running production of *Hamlet*—and the most profitable—ever staged in New York. Burton, who received six curtain calls on opening night, would perform the role 136 times. Taylor would attend 40 performances. The entire block surrounding the theater—46th Street from Eighth Avenue to Broadway—was thronged every night after the show with fans trying to get a glimpse of the famous couple. Barricades were set up, and policemen on horseback kept the crowds at bay. Sterne recalled having to wait until the Burtons left the theater before anyone else in the cast or crew could venture out.

Some weeks into the run, Hamlet invited Polonius to lunch. Cronyn and his wife, the acclaimed actress Jessica Tandy, joined the Burtons for a meal between the matinee and evening performances. Leaving the theater alley and turning onto West 45th, they had to run a gauntlet of over two thousand people waiting to see the Burtons. When they appeared, "a great roar" went up, as Cronyn recalled. Traffic came to a complete stop, and police on horseback had to open a passage for the two couples, just to cross the alley and enter a waiting limousine. Hands snatched at them, as people in the crowd cheered and waved autograph books in the air. Some even jeered. "Liz is a bad, bad girl!" someone called out. Cronyn felt that if they had stopped to sign one autograph, they would have been trampled to death by the crowd. It was as bad as anything the Beatles had to endure when they arrived in New York for the first time, to tape *The Ed Sullivan Show*. But it didn't end there. Once in the limousine, with Elizabeth and Richard tucked safely into the backseat, Cronyn saw that a couple of teenage fans had thrown themselves onto the roof of the car and were hanging upside down, peering into the limousine's windows. With fans hanging off the roof, the limousine pulled out into the street and slowly made its way through the mob. "It was the only time in my life," Cronyn recalled, "that I remember being frightened by a crowd." As the limousine picked up speed, Elizabeth sweetly smiled and waved to the crowd like royalty—all the while silently mouthing the words "Fuck you—and you—and you, dear!" She'd simply had it—it was worse than Rome—and her usual patience had been tried beyond bearing. "There came a point," Cronyn recalled, "when 'Dickenliz' would have sold their souls for a couple of days of peace, quiet, and solitude."

The production was widely praised by reviewers, though Walter Kerr groused in the *New York Herald Tribune*, "Mr. Burton is without feeling . . ." and *Time* magazine faulted Burton for being "more heroic than tragic." But elsewhere, Burton's energy, irony, and mastery of the stage were praised. "Burton . . . leaps to action with a tigerish snarl," wrote *Life* magazine's reviewer. "I do not recall a Hamlet of such tempestuous manliness . . . full of pride and wit and mettle," wrote Howard Taubman in the *New York Times*. And the *New York Post's* theater critic, Richard Watts, praised Burton as "a very fine Hamlet, indeed. His Prince of Denmark is forceful, direct, unpretentiously eloquent, more thoughtfully introspective than darkly melancholy, with the glint of ironic humor, and decidedly a man of action and feeling." All words, indeed, that could have been written about Burton himself, in the thirty-ninth year of his life, at the peak of his powers, the world spread out before him like a glittering jewel.

And yet—despite the recognition of Burton's superb performance, he did not get nominated for a Tony Award. Cronyn would win his first and only Tony for Polonius, but Richard was, apparently, still being punished—deserved prizes withheld—for daring to snatch fire from the gods.

During one matinee performance, something unsettling happened. Sterne remembered, "We could tell something was wrong because Burton wasn't really concentrating on the words. He got into the third scene, and he left the stage. The curtain came down, and [the producer] Alexander Cohen was there for that performance. He came out and made an announcement that Richard was indisposed and couldn't go on, and that they were sending on his understudy, Robert Burr. Anybody who wanted a refund, he would gladly give it to them." Burton would later blame it on arthritis, made worse by the attack he suffered at the hands of thugs in Paddington Station while filming *The V.I.P.s.*

In an interview the following year, Burton recalled, "I was tearing along, waving my arms and ripping out the lines when the arthritis struck me. I stopped absolutely rigid in mid-flight, one arm raised above my head. You can't imagine the pain . . . I shuffled off stage sideways like an old man." He also blamed "the weak Jenkins bones," but after being tended to by a doctor Elizabeth found for him, he forgot about the incident. He didn't know then that his affliction—little helped by his high intake of alcohol—would return to bedevil him.

And then, one night, during a performance, a man in the audience stood up and booed Richard Burton. He had never been booed before, and it shook him to the core. He reportedly stopped the play, stepped out of character, and announced to the audience, "We have been playing this production in public for over eighty performances. Some have liked it, some have not. But I can assure you, we have never before been booed!" After the performance ended and Richard returned to their suite in the Regency, he vented his anger on Elizabeth, who was coolly watching television. In his fury, Burton kicked in the television screen, slicing his toe to the bone. It set off an enormous row between the newly married couple—not the first, and decidedly not the last.

Sterne was present on one of those occasions, when he had dropped by their hotel to interview Burton for a book he was writing about the production. "I had been asking him to do it ever since the opening of the show. He always said yes. He promised he would do it, but he couldn't come up with a time. Finally, the last week, he told me to come up to the Regency Hotel where they were staying. I arrived there with my tape recorder. Richard and Elizabeth were having the most tremendous row you could imagine; they were yelling and screaming at each other. Their lawyer was there, Aaron Frosch and his secretary, and Bob Wilson. Finally, he said, 'Well, look, we're going to have to go off into another room here if we're going to do this interview.'"

When the interview was half-over, Bob Wilson stuck his head in the door and said, "Richard, we've got to leave; we've got to get to the theater. It's almost time to do the show." So they finished the interview in the back of a limousine on their way to the theater.

"As we were pulling around 46th Street," Sterne recalled, "these small street children—three or four little boys, rather ragamuffin and dirty—ran up to the car window. One of them held up a nickel and I said, 'Hey, Rich.'" Burton became morose and told the boy, "I don't have any money; I never carry any money." In that moment, Burton looked into the face of his past—the kind of boy he had once been, rough and dirty and scrambling for money. What had happened to that boy, Rich Jenkins, now that he had become Richard Burton, the most famous actor in the world?

By the end of his long run in *Hamlet*, Burton had apparently grown bored with the role. He'd try out different interpretations—not just reciting a speech in German but playing Hamlet as a homosexual one night, or substituting lines from Christopher Marlowe to entertain himself and to see if anyone noticed. As Melvyn Bragg observed, "It was always hard for him to sustain an interest once he had cracked a problem. He went out to conquer, did so, and was then often indifferent. Elizabeth and money and writing—they were the infinitely interesting matters." So when Philip Burton confessed that his American Music and Dramatic Academy was facing a financial setback, Burton agreed to give a special performance to raise money for the school. But not of *Hamlet*—this would be a poetry reading, and Elizabeth Taylor would join in, making her theatrical debut alongside him.

It was an extraordinary event, and the Lunt-Fontanne Theatre glittered with boldfaced names—Mayor Lindsay, Eunice Kennedy Shriver, Montgomery Clift, Carol Channing. Elizabeth had made an effort to bring Burton's Welsh friend and mentor Emlyn Williams back into the fold, and he, too, was there. Nervous about appearing live onstage, Elizabeth had asked Philip to coach her through a handful of canonical poems by Robert Frost and Elizabeth Barrett Browning, as well as her favorite poem, Thomas Hardy's "The Ruined Maid." Burton answered her with Andrew Marvell's "To His Coy Mistress" and D. H. Lawrence's "The Snake." They traded lines in English and Welsh. Elizabeth dazzled in a Grecian gown and diamonds, and her readings were convincing enough that one wag in the audience quipped, "If she doesn't get bad pretty soon, people are going to start leaving." In act two, appearing in another splendid gown, Elizabeth muffed the first line of the Twenty-third Psalm, then blurted out, "Sorry. Let me begin again. I sure screwed that one up." She knew they were gunning for her. But when the evening ended, the couple were rewarded with a standing ovation. She had done it. She had entered Burton's world and had held her own. They could be equals now. Within a week of the event, Richard and Elizabeth received more than half a millon dollars' worth of offers to give poetry readings. Poetry!

Afterward, Elizabeth and Richard got magnificently drunk and retired to their suite at the Regency, where they reverted to their favorite pastimes, fighting and having sex. Or having sex and fighting.

Soon after, in the middle of an argument, Eddie Fisher turned up. He later described, with some bitterness, what he saw there: "Her makeup smeared, her voice loud and shrill, Elizabeth was furious about something, and I thought, I was married to that woman, that wild thing. Burton was trying to soothe her and as I watched him walk around her suite, apologizing, straightening up, retrieving things she had dropped, I saw myself. . . . He was doing the same things I had done, the same things Mike [Todd] had done. The battle was over and they both got what they wanted. Burton was a superstar. And Elizabeth had someone else to pick up after her."

Two years later, when Sterne saw the Burtons in *Who's Afraid of Virginia Woolf?*, he "was reminded of that time up in the hotel room when they were having their row. It seemed like the film was a replay of what I had seen over in the hotel." And yet, Sterne believed, "I had this feeling that they really, deeply loved each other."

5

IN FROM THE COLD

"I love not being me, not being Elizabeth Taylor,
but being Richard Burton's wife."
—ELIZABETH TAYLOR

"How would you like to travel from Paris to Geneva with
two nannies, four children, five dogs, two secretaries, a
budgerigar, and a turtle . . . and a wildcat, and 140 bags . . . ?"
—RICHARD BURTON

If part of Richard's job description was to pick up after Elizabeth,
it was worth it, at least in the passionate weeks and months and
early years of their marriage. Their life together was shaping into
one lived in constant travel, the fate of "professional itinerants"—in
Burton's phrase—spent in five-star hotels, fawned over by their own
expanding entourage and by hoteliers, wine stewards, and porters.
For Elizabeth, it was only her due: a continuation of the life she had
lived since the age of ten, fussed over by MGM publicists, hairdressers, makeup people, and various handlers. She knew no other way to
be. Hotel security also afforded them a measure of protection from the
crowds of fans (and not all fans) that still dogged their every move.

In *Vogue* magazine, Burton recalled what it was like to travel with
Elizabeth ("Travelling with Elizabeth, by Her Husband Who Loves

Her in Spite of It"). He opens and closes his article with the mock *cri de coeur,* "Gawd 'elp me!"

> Travelling with Elizabeth is a kind of exquisite pain. Let me ex-
> plain why this is: I am ferociously overpunctual whereas Elizabeth
> is indolently the opposite. I love Elizabeth to the point of idolatry
> but—let's repeat that "but"—she will unquestionably be . . . late
> for the last bloody judgment. And, infuriatingly, she is always
> breathtakingly on time. She actually misses no train or plane or
> boat, but, of course, misses the fact that her husband has had
> several minor heart attacks waiting for her while he shifts a shiver-
> ing scotch from his trembling hand to his quivering mouth to his
> abandoned liver, waiting, waiting, waiting for her to come out of
> the lavatory. . . . there is my stupendously serene lady, firmly be-
> lieving that time waits for no man but will wait for her.

Burton goes on to describe how he was born to the class of those who "watched the train go by and lusted for London . . . I finally caught that train and never went back and never will." Had he remained that "original boy," he imagines that he'd be one of the baggage handlers that Elizabeth might have honored with a tip or a pat on the head. ("Let's face it," he writes. "She wouldn't have tipped me. She would have arranged for one of her minions to do so.") Instead, he has the privilege of sharing, with Elizabeth, the spoils of the world, even if it means being "doomed nomads," unable to stay in any one place for more than three months at a time, shuttling among New York, London, Paris, Rome, San Francisco, Puerto Vallarta, Gstaad, Ireland, and that "rough country of my heart, Wales . . ."

The advantages of constant travel? The service ("porters and stew-ards and even stewardesses reward her with enormous over-attention and therefore I get a little on the side"). And the food! "We separate countries into foods," Burton writes, in a comic discourse on how the national diet of various countries reflects the physiognomy of their citizens. At night, alone at last in their hotel bedroom—the Lancaster, the Dorchester, the Regency—they dream of the cuisines in countries left behind: hamburgers and egg-topped corned-beef hash from American delicatessens, dreamed of in Paris; or, in New York, memories of that Swiss bistro or Italian trattoria with "a turbulent red wine and salami and fava and a cheese that crumbles in the hand falling down its own face like a landslide." He writes,

> I will allow nobody but me to take Elizabeth, tardy as she is, to Evian or Austria or Aston Clinton or Tor Vaiannica or Le Coq Hardy or La Méditerranée or the Oak Room at the Plaza or the Top of the Mark or The Savoy Grill or the Terrace at the Dorchester or the Hotel de La Poste at Avallon or that delicatessen on Sixth Avenue where they serve beer in steins and where you can have split and grilled frankfurters with appalling French fries on the side, and Rumplemeyer's for breakfast with a daughter around; or how would you like to stop your Phantom Rolls outside a fish-and-chips shop in Flask Lane, Hampstead, and munch greasily and happily away in the back of the car, watching television while waiting for the traffic to ease with two enchanting daughters and an enchanting wife beside you . . . ?

The drawbacks? Besides waiting eternally for Elizabeth to show up at the last minute, they are, nearly three years past *Le Scandale*, still stalked by paparazzi and hordes of fans. Richard recalls when a shoe was stolen off of Elizabeth's foot at an airport (in Puerto Vallarta), and another time when a photographer punched Elizabeth in the stomach. "How would you like to pass your small daughter," he writes, "over the heads of the madding crowd to a friend, all of us shouting in a language we didn't know?"

By now, Elizabeth was essentially stateless, a citizen of the world, who lived almost entirely in hotels; she had even considered renouncing her American citizenship after her rough treatment following the scandal. She had left her childhood home at the age of nine, had lived in Los Angeles, virtually residing at MGM until her first marriage, but you can't put MGM on a passport. She owned a chalet in Gstaad and a villa in Puerto Vallarta, but while in the States or in England, she lived in hotels (mostly the Regency and the Dorchester). Not surprisingly, she was drawn to Burton's deep connection to Wales and to his large, sprawling family. For Burton, the life of the world traveler was thrilling, but also exhausting. He, too, would soon miss the sense of belonging to a place, a permanent home.

Another obstacle to their peace of mind was Burton's attention to their box-office rankings. Burton was well aware that Elizabeth still outdrew him and outearned him, and as any proud Welshman would, he dedicated himself to balancing the equation. It was beginning to happen. When the reviews came out for *The Night of the Iguana* in June of 1964, Burton's performance as the louche Reverend Shannon was generally lauded, making him "the new Mr. Box Office." Not surprisingly, perhaps, given the mixed reviews of *Cleopatra* and The *V.I.P.s*, and the two years she spent away from the camera, Elizabeth Taylor dropped from first place to seventh in box-office ratings. She didn't care much. She was tired of being a movie star and was increasingly interested in just being with Richard. Let her coast for a while—she'd earned it.

Elizabeth's surprisingly good performance reciting poetry onstage with Burton had been a glorious welcome home from the country she had come close to renouncing. As early as May of 1964, Burton was planning a stage production of Christopher Marlowe's *Doctor Faustus* in Oxford, with Elizabeth to make a brief appearance as Helen of Troy. But, finally, Elizabeth knew how fickle movie audiences could be: it was time to make another film, in America.

In 1964, her image was changing and hardening into a new incarnation: no longer the pampered ingénue or the world-conquering beauty, she was now the vixen, the vamp, the sexually dangerous woman of the world, the ultimate femme fatale. The role she'd hated, the good-time girl Gloria Wandrous in *BUtterfield 8,* had been a harbinger of things to come.

The Burtons plowed through legions of scripts and considered a number of projects: Elizabeth as Anne Boleyn and Richard as Henry VIII in Maxwell Anderson's *Anne of the Thousand Days* (not to be, for Elizabeth); a film adaptation of *This Property Is Condemned* by Elizabeth's favorite playwright, Tennessee Williams; and, among other possible productions, Carson McCullers's novella *Reflections in a Golden Eye*, which she planned to star in with her dear, damaged friend, Montgomery Clift. Elizabeth even contemplated a Broadway run with Clift in *The Owl and the Pussycat.* She would, of course, play the prostitute.

Instead, they settled on making a picture titled *The Flight of the Sandpiper* for MGM-Filmways Studio, based on a story by the highly successful producer Martin Ransohoff, with a screenplay by Michael Wilson and the formerly blacklisted writer Dalton Trumbo. (The film would be released as *The Sandpiper.*) Ransohoff had conceived of the story as a vehicle for Kim Novak, for whom he created the lead role of a free-spirited artist living in Big Sur. At the time, Novak was known in Hollywood for her bohemian ways and love of painting. She was also living in Big Sur, but when the relationship she'd had with Ransohoff soured, he offered the role to Elizabeth.

As usual, the Burtons made a shrewd bargain: Elizabeth received her $1 million salary, Richard was offered $500,000, and the couple's production company would earn 20 percent of the gross, which would net them additional millions of dollars. Burton hated the script but reportedly said, "For the money, we will dance."

Though *The V.I.P.s* had inspired a certain degree of critical scoffing, it had begun to enrich Burton at a level he had only dreamed of. With his wealth increasing exponentially, his brilliant reviews in New York for the most successful run of *Hamlet* in theater history—136 performances—Burton now set his cap for directing. He planned, among other films, to direct Elizabeth in a forthcoming production of *Macbeth*, and he'd hoped to make his directorial debut on *The Sand-piper*, but in the end—after turning down William Wyler—Elizabeth asked for and got Vincente Minnelli, who had directed her years ear-lier at MGM in *Father of the Bride* and *Father's Little Dividend*. Now she would be back at her former studio, but not as chattel, but as a free agent loaned to the studio by the Burtons' production company. Burton already planned to co-direct a stage production of *Doctor Faustus* as a kind of favor to his early Oxford mentor, Sir Nevill Cog-hill, who presided over the Oxford University Drama Society and who had given Burton his first Shakespearean role. (Coghill had deemed Burton one of only two "geniuses" he'd had the privilege to teach; the other was poet W. H. Auden.)

The Sandpiper was the perfect vehicle for the juggernaut that was now Burton-Taylor. One of the movie's tag lines was: "From the Begin-ning, They Knew It Was Wrong. Nothing Could Keep Them Apart." Whether it was pure exploitation of *Le Scandale* or Elizabeth's canny understanding of what the public wanted—or both—*The Sandpiper* capitalized on the now-married lovers' scandalous history, telling the tale of an adulterous headmaster (the Reverend Dr. Edward Hewitt, played by Burton), who falls madly in love with a beautiful bohemian artist named Laura Reynolds (Taylor). Her nine-year-old illegitimate son was played by Morgan Mason, the son of actor James Mason and his wife, Pamela. In a curious footnote, Sammy Davis Jr. was under consideration to appear as "Cos," a "beatnik artist" and former lover of Laura's. Deciding, no doubt, that a mixed-race love affair was too much even for Elizabeth Taylor in 1964, the part went to a sinewy, rough-hewn Charles Bronson. Eva Marie Saint is poignant (and soignée) as Claire, Hewitt's abandoned wife; in her respectable, blonde suitability, she might as well have been a stand-in for Sybil Burton. Burton played, yet again, a tortured man torn between duty and passion: his duty to his wife and children and to his calling as the headmster of an Episcopal school, and his passion for Laura/Elizabeth. It was the second, but not the last time, he would portray a defrocked man of the cloth.

Also featured prominently in the film is a nude sculpture of Elizabeth, carved out of a 2,200-pound redwood log by a sculptor named Edmund Kara. In the movie, it's the work of the bohemian sculptor played by Bronson, and it's the flashpoint for Dr. Hewitt's (Burton's) jealousy and passion. In real life, it was the closest the moviegoing public would ever get to seeing Elizabeth onscreen in glorious nudity, beyond the generous glimpses of thigh and cleavage in her bathing scene in *Cleopatra* and a nanosecond of Elizabeth's partial nudity as her character, Laura, poses for the sculpture in *The Sandpiper*. Though Elizabeth crashed through the puritanical strictures of her day, becoming a vanguard of the sexual revolution in spite of herself, she was still a product of MGM's morals code, at least onscreen. In 1965, other, younger actresses were beginning to bare their breasts on camera in mainstream films, but Edmund Kara's rather demure nude sculpture would have to do, mostly, for Elizabeth. The sculpture serves the additional purpose of being fondled, disrobed, manhandled, and gawked at by the various ex- and would-be lovers that enter her seaside abode.

Shot in the spectacularly beautiful Carmel Highlands near Big Sur, MGM spent $35,000 constructing Laura's glass-and-driftwood house overlooking the sea, a perfect setting to show off nature's—and Elizabeth's—spectacular scenery. (The entire production costs to MGM were reported at $5 million.) Mr. and Mrs. Burton (as she now preferred to be called) arrived in Carmel Heights with their usual large entourage—their four children (Michael, Christopher, Liza, and Maria), Burton's trusted dresser, Bob Wilson, and his wife, a cook, and a staff of lawyers and secretaries.

The film writer Peter Bart visited the location and noticed that, unlike the frenzy their appearances created in Puerto Vallarta, Toronto, New York, and Boston, their impact on Carmel and Big Sur was rather negligible. Perhaps it was because the Monterey Jazz Festival was in full swing at the time, absorbing the attentions of a decidedly more mellow citizenry. The Burtons rented "one of the biggest homes in the area," wrote Bart, and were able to visit the local shops, bars, and restaurants without incident.

On October 5, the *Hollywood Reporter* noted that MGM-Filmways prepared to leave for six weeks, to shoot the interiors for *The Sandpiper* in Paris. Two months later, they reported that the move overseas was made to protect Richard Burton's growing fortune, as he "would have ended with less money than he began with if all of the film were made in its natural locale." So the Burtons left on the *Queen Elizabeth* and checked into the Lancaster Hotel in Paris; they had by now truly become tax exiles, unable to stay in America or Britain for more than a few months at a time without becoming liable for whopping tax bills. Burton was taxed at the highest rate in Britain, but he could keep his British passport and considerably reduce his taxes as a "nonresident" if he didn't stay in Britain more than ninety days a year. Taylor, with dual citizenship in England and America, had similar tax advantages if she kept moving.

Kara's massive sculpture, incidentally, was shipped to Paris in a temperature-controlled stateroom on the *Queen Mary* and insured for $100,000 with Lloyds of London. It was treated like a religious icon, made the subject of a film short and "a special unveiling" for the Parisian press corps when it arrived safely in France.

When the film opened in July of 1965, it was not well received. The *New Yorker* called it "soggy, woolly, maundering, bumbling" and "a very silly movie"; *Life* magazine sneered—hooted—at the Burtons' second foray into showcasing their guilty passion onscreen. Some audiences reportedly laughed when Burton's tortured headmaster utters the words, "I've lost all my sense of sin." The *Saturday Review* derided "the mess of windy platitudes and stale stereotypes." Trumbo, years later, would complain that his "nice, taut little drama" was derailed by the opulence of the Burtons ("twenty-two smashing costume changes" for Elizabeth and "an $85,000 bungalow"). But the beautifully photographed, lushly produced film does have its guilty pleasures, not least of which are Richard's and Elizabeth's presence onscreen, made more exciting by the whiff of scandal that still clung to them.

The film's main problem, despite its gorgeous scenery, high production values, and good performances by the entire cast, is a certain lack of authenticity. There was already a small but burgeoning counterculture in Big Sur, and *The Sandpiper* tried to make use of the social phenomenon that was stirring in America—the subculture of beatniks, hippies, free-love advocates, jazz enthusiasts, pagans, naturalists, and all-around free-thinkers that would take center stage as the decade marched on. The problem with the movie, under Minnelli's too-tasteful direction, is that he doesn't quite get it right. On paper, the role of Laura Reynolds, an artist who defies social proprieties by refusing to marry her son's father and by having affairs as she pleases, should have suited Elizabeth perfectly. But she seems miscast as an iconoclastic, proto-feminist artist: she is both too glamorous, too diva-like, and too angry, and her artist's "shack" is far too *Architectural Digest* for a struggling painter (one that "any poor soul could probably buy for forty or fifty thousand dollars" in 1965 currency, as one reviewer wrote). By 1965, Elizabeth Taylor was just too famous to disappear into another character, and her lush, glossy beauty and increasingly voluptuous figure made her unsuited to play the newly emerging American woman who came into being in the "swinging 1960s"—sexually adventurous, guilt-free, sometimes androgynous, and full of a kind of joyful innocence—a spirit then embodied by younger actresses such as Julie Christie, Vanessa Redgrave, and Jane Fonda. Elizabeth may have helped usher in that seismic shift in the sexual landscape, but by the age of thirty-two, with five marriages, four children, thirty-one films, and world infamy behind her, she simply had too much history to play a "new woman." She was a queen, and there would be few queenly roles for women in the next three decades.

Burton fared much better. Unhappy with the screenplay, he tinkered with lines, but it's hard to know how much he contributed to the final script. However, when Dr. Hewitt confesses, "It was my betrayal of myself that began years ago," the line carries a remembrance of Marc Antony's "I from myself—the ultimate betrayal." What Richard, perhaps, had not counted on was the psychic toll of reliving, onscreen, his abandonment of Sybil. He was awash with guilt—for turning his back on Sybil and his two girls, especially Jessica, the one who most needed him, and before that, for turning his back on his true father, and therefore the core of his Welsh identity. By now he was sending thousands of pounds to his brothers and sisters in Port Talbot and Pontrhydyfen, supporting their families with annual checks and Christmas bounty, as a kind of devotion, or reparation. He was rescuing his brothers from a life in the mines, but he was also assuaging his conscience for having been the one who had escaped. He had given work to his brother Graham as his movie stand-in; he had hired his worshipped elder brother Ifor as a kind of caretaker of his home in Céligny, which he retained after his divorce from Sybil. He would even take Brook Williams, the son of his early mentor, Emlyn Williams, into his entourage, but it wasn't enough. And now to relive that guilt onscreen was a further torment, one that sex and money and fame and alcohol could assuage, up to a point.

As for Elizabeth's psychic burden, she does have one speech in *The Sandpiper* that is revelatory, and she delivers it from the heart. When she tries to explain to Hewitt the source of her distrust of men, she confesses, "men have been staring at me and rubbing up against me since I was twelve. . . . I have been *had* by men," she says, "but not loved." No wonder she clung to Burton, as she had to Mike Todd, believing that of all the men she had known, only these two loved her in the way she wanted to be loved.

Despite the dismissive reviews (and some sniping about Elizabeth's exposed cleavage and her weight, which fluctuated throughout the film), *The Sandpiper* was enormously profitable, earning $14 million and beating out MGM's blockbuster for the year, *The Unsinkable*

Molly Brown, starring Elizabeth's former "rival" Debbie Reynolds and proving that sex trumps effervescence, at least at the box office. The public couldn't stop reliving the drama of the couple's world-shaking adultery.

While in Paris, the Burtons occupied two floors at the Lancaster, making room for their gypsy children—the wild Wilding boys, Michael and Christopher; Liza Todd; and four-year-old Maria Burton, still enduring hip operations. The tutor who had accompanied them in Puerto Vallarta, Paul Neshamkin, was also in residence, and he expressed concern that the children were being overlooked by their parents, relegated to the care of "an elderly governess." When they did look in on the children, it was more like "a royal visit." Burton felt that the boys would be better off in a boarding school than traipsing around the globe with their itinerant parents, but Elizabeth wanted her family around her.

According to Gianni Bozzacchi, who would become the Burtons' friend and in-house photographer throughout the next decade, Elizabeth wanted Burton to bring Jessica into their household, where she could be looked after by a hired nurse. After all, they were already surrounded by an entourage that now included Dick Hanley and his companion, John Lee; Burton's dresser, Bob Wilson, and his wife; Elizabeth's makeup man, Ron Berkeley; a bodyguard and ex-boxer named Bobby LaSalle; Gaston, the French chauffeur; and, of course, the tutor, the governess, and a live-in nurse for Maria. The Burtons could afford it. They set up two companies, which brought in an estimated $50 million a year in royalties and salaries—equivalent to approximately $350 million in today's dollars.

But Burton refused to let Elizabeth bring Jessica out of the institution on Long Island, where she was being kept. For one thing, Sybil would not have allowed it. Jessica's existence remained, possibly, the one hold she still had on Richard, Bozzacchi thought, and that may have been a reason why Sybil would not give her up. It may have been that Jessica was unable to live outside of an institution, but Elizabeth, tough and shrewd as she was, always had a soft spot for wounded things. And she knew that Burton suffered over Jessica's fate and blamed himself for his inability to care for her, except financially.

So Burton acted, made money, brooded, drank, and suffered bouts of depression. "The Black Dog—that's very Welsh," said the English actor Michael York, who is half-Welsh himself, recalling Burton when he knew him in the mid-1960s. (They would meet on the set of Franco Zeffirelli's *The Taming of the Shrew* in February 1966.) "He was of a generation of actors, like Peter O'Toole, who were famous for self-destruction—it was part of their aura. They seemed to be hanging by a thread." Burton used the Welsh word *hiraeth*, which he translated as "a longing for unnamable things," to describe his black moods. Bragg described it as "a melancholy that was impenetrable . . . the Celtic gloom of many a grounded drunken poet," like Burton's hero, Dylan Thomas. Some of Burton's friends, Bragg suggests, suspected "a chemical imbalance," noting that Burton, besides hemophilia, also suffered from mild epilepsy. So the alcohol was, among other things, a form of self-medication that only deepened his depression.

Perhaps as an effort to cheer him up, Elizabeth bought Burton thirty-seven tailored suits in Paris. It gave her pleasure to bestow gifts upon him.

In January 1965, the couple moved back to London and took up residence at their favorite hotel, the Dorchester on Park Lane. They were greeted by Marjorie Lee, the hotel's concierge, who became indispensable to the Burtons. She made the trains run on time, so to speak, while they were in London, getting them reservations at restaurants, helping to bring relatives in from Wales, making sure they had everything they wanted in their suites. She also made sure there were rooms available to the Burtons whenever they needed them, even if it meant kicking out royalty to accommodate the famous couple.

Burton was to begin filming *The Spy Who Came in from the Cold* with his former costar and inamorata Claire Bloom, a situation Elizabeth was not at all happy about. She knew of their one-time affair; she must have known that he had been in love with the actress, and that this was the only relationship, pre-Elizabeth, that had threatened his marriage to Sybil.

Like Elizabeth, Claire Bloom is a dark-haired beauty and a fine actress, but unlike Elizabeth, she made her reputation on the London stage. She first met Burton in 1949 at the audition for *The Lady's Not for Burning*, which was conducted by John Gielgud on the stage of the Globe Theatre on Shaftesbury Avenue in the heart of London's West End. A young Burton auditioned with her, and he made a powerful impression just by sitting down. Bloom remembered her first sight of him forty-six years later, when she wrote her 1995 memoir, *Leaving a Doll's House*: " . . . even today I can remember the way he sat in his chair," she recalled, "his rather pockmarked skin, his green eyes. He was an extraordinarily beautiful man." And, at twenty-three, a soon-to-be-married one. The play went on an eleven-week tour, and the two actors knew they were smitten, even after Burton's brand-new marriage to Sybil, who occasionally showed up on the tour. "Long after the curtain had come down," Bloom wrote,

> Burton, who had an encyclopedic memory for poetry, would recite poems to me late in the night. He would be seated in my room, very properly on a chair pulled away from the bed, on which I silently lay, fervently listening to the sound of his beautiful voice. We never touched each other, never physically shared more than the rather chaste kiss that I looked forward to every night on the stage; and yet we had unquestionably fallen deeply in love.

Throughout the run of the play, they continued their chaste affair, and Burton stayed faithful to Sybil. A few years later, at the Old Vic on Waterloo Road, Bloom appeared in four Shakespearean productions with Burton, beginning with playing Ophelia to Burton's Hamlet (he also played Philip the Bastard, Sir Toby Belch, Henry IV, Caliban, Othello, and Iago in a series of roles that by the age of twenty-seven established him as the preeminent actor of his generation). This time, their old feelings overwhelmed them, and they began their affair.

By then, Richard had had his first stint in Hollywood and had returned with the reputation of a ladies' man. They would meet in her mother's home, with Burton sneaking in at night and leaving before dawn, or they would sometimes make love in their dressing rooms at the Old Vic between the matinee and evening performances. When Burton and Sybil left again for Hollywood, where Burton was to film *My Cousin Rachel* with Olivia de Havilland, they exchanged love letters, with Burton writing twice a day on some occasions. In one letter, he wrote, "I haven't looked at another woman. This has never happened to me before. You have changed me so radically. I have almost grown up." Bloom eventually burned most of his letters on the eve of her marriage to the actor Rod Steiger, another brilliant, rough-hewn actor given, like Burton, to bouts of depression.

As a lover, "Richard was tender and considerate," Bloom wrote, and their off-again, on-again romance lasted five years. Eventually, it was clear that Burton would never leave Sybil, and the necessary secrecy became too much for the young actress, still in her twenties, to bear. The affair ended, but Bloom later wrote that Burton was "the only man to whom I have fervently given all of myself. To feel so much pleasure from the body, mind, voice, mere presence of another is a gift I am profoundly grateful to have received."

However, her feelings would change when she and Burton were again cast opposite each other, this time in Tony Richardson's film adaptation of John Osborne's blistering, kitchen-sink drama *Look Back in Anger*, which ushered in a new kind of theater protesting the genteel drawing-room comedies and dramas that dominated the West End. Burton was cast as the quintessential "angry young man," Jimmy Porter, and Bloom as his lover Helena. She thought she would resume her affair with Burton, only to walk in on him in the arms of a young Susan Strasberg, with whom he had had a brief affair when they appeared together in *Time Remembered* in New York in 1957. That finally ended it, as Bloom wrote that she castigated herself for being drawn in again by the still-married, and still-womanizing, Burton. They parted rather bitterly. (In her own autobiography, titled *Time Remembered*, after the play that launched her stage career, Susan Strasberg remembered hiding in that dressing room bathroom and watching Bloom and Burton embracing, a scene that sent the nineteen-year-old actress back to her hotel, shattered and humiliated.)

Despite her disappointment, Bloom saw that Burton was brilliant in the role of Jimmy Porter—born to it, in fact.

As Jimmy, he was able to draw on his own sense of social injustice, to remember the Great Depression, the poverty of his family, the illnesses suffered by his brothers from the years spent underground in the Welsh coal mines. Richard was always extremely aware of his own good fortune in escaping from such physical labor; however, I always thought that he suffered from a feeling of inadequacy in the face of his family's stoic endurance; that he believed the life of an actor was "cushy," and that he had been emasculated by his profession.

Which may have been one reason for his incessant womanizing, until he met Elizabeth.

They met for the fourth time in January 1965 to appear together in the screen adaptation of John Le Carré's first best-selling novel, *The Spy Who Came in from the Cold*, directed by the once blacklisted Martin Ritt. Filmed at the Shepperton Studios in London and on location in Dublin, it wasn't a happy experience. In Bloom's view, Burton was again transformed. By 1965, he was world-famous, at the top of his game, the highest-paid actor in the profession, and very much married to "one of the most beautiful women in the world." But she felt that he had not fulfilled his earlier promise of greatness, and she told gossip columnist Sheilah Graham that Burton "hadn't changed at all, except physically. He was still drinking, still boasting, he was still late, still reciting the same poems and telling the same stories as when he was twenty-three . . . it was obvious that he was going to be a huge star, which is not the same as being a great actor. He has confused them." Her opinion, however, would change after seeing his performance as the raincoated, world-weary Alec Leamas in *The Spy Who Came in from the Cold*—one she would call "brilliant."

After a lunch with Martin Ritt and Claire Bloom in London, Burton confided in the leather-bound diary he had begun keeping that year that Claire was "nervous, but all right." The real problem would come not from Bloom but from Elizabeth Taylor's jealousy. "Burton was in the ring with both of them and it was raw-knuckled stuff," wrote Bragg. Bloom's character's name was even changed from "Liz" to "Nan" to avoid an unnecessary evocation of Burton's famous wife. Early on, when the idea of having Elizabeth play Claire's role came up, it was decided that she was just too grand a star to convincingly play a librarian—she would have thrown the whole production off-kilter.

"Taylor was extremely upset by my reappearance in Richard's life," Bloom observed. "Subsequently, she was always on hand during our scenes together. Her commanding if unmusical call for 'Richard!' sent him scurrying to her side." Elizabeth took to yelling Richard's name throughout the shoot, and Claire took some delight in imitating that call for attention. She was, Bloom thought, "extremely uncomfortable having me around." Elizabeth may have feared that the younger actress was still smitten with her one-time lover. Did she trust Burton?

Bloom also observed that Burton's drinking had begun to take its toll. "Like the spirit of the sturdy miner's son I had known and loved, the muscle tone had vanished." She noticed a tremor in his hand that was only cured by his midday drinks. She thought that his once-prodigious memory for poetry was not quite what it used to be, and he required cue cards to be placed strategically throughout the set.

This last observation, however, was disputed by Frank Delaney, a writer who spent time with the Burtons during the making of *Spy*. He was impressed by Burton's memory for great literature—"not just Shakespeare and the Welsh poets, you'd expect that, but 'Tintern Abbey,' I remember, reams of it, and Joyce, the opening of *Ulysses*, paragraph after paragraph, word-perfect."

Delaney also noticed that Burton in particular seemed oppressed by melancholy. Perhaps it was the role of Alec Leamas itself that infected Burton's mood. The character is a disillusioned and joyless pawn in a Machiavellian game of espionage, a character written in stark contrast to the unrealistic glamour of James Bond. Or perhaps the tensions between Claire Bloom and Elizabeth were taking their toll. And there was always the crush of crowds and Richard's realization that no matter how brilliant he was onscreen, Elizabeth was more famous than he. At a pub lunch with Le Carré (David Cornwall's nom de plume), Burton was in a particularly self-pitying mood. He groused to the novelist, "I can't go to a pub anymore. Elizabeth is more famous than the queen. I wish none of it had ever happened." Le Carré observed: "They were living out their marriage in public. There were shouting matches in restaurants."

During a break in filming, Burton whisked Taylor off to Wales to reconnect with his roots, which usually lifted his spirits. They checked into the Queens Hotel, and at Cardiff Arms Park, Elizabeth donned the traditional Welsh color by wearing a red bowler. They cheered as the Welsh rugby team trounced England, then joined in a rousing chorus of the Welsh anthem, *"Cwm Rhondda."* It was a glorious afternoon, until they returned to their hotel, where they were nearly trampled by an overly enthusiastic crowd of fans celebrating the Welsh victory. Graham Jenkins, who accompanied the couple, recalled, "It was without doubt one of the worst experiences of lack of crowd control that I have ever known. The crowd just wouldn't let us get out." The Burtons were used to mobs, but this was like a repeat of what had met them in Boston or outside the stage door during their

Hamlet year. They were saved by a legendary Welsh rugby star, the tackler Haydn Mainwaring, who barreled into the hotel kitchen and cleared a path for the Burtons.

In Port Talbot, Burton took special pride in showing off his voluptuous wife, parading her in front of the stalwart Welsh miners who thronged the pubs. One of them reached out and pinched Elizabeth's derrière; she turned around and thwacked him on the jaw, which completely delighted Burton. It was all in good fun. She loved the Welsh people and felt at home among them. For someone as stateless as Elizabeth, this, and being in Puerto Vallarta, was as close as she would come to feeling at home.

As usual, trips to Burton's sisters were accompanied by lavish gifts. Elizabeth had gotten into the habit of sending them armfuls of her cast-off clothes—silk and sequined movie star gowns with labels from shops on Rodeo Drive, which they would wear to the market in Pontrhydyfen and Port Talbot. Burton's sister Hilda Owens recalled, however, that it was often hard on them, and the village itself, when the Burtons came into town unannounced. "It was like a fair here" whenever the Burtons arrived in their Daimler. Aside from the press and the BBC, there were "busloads coming to see them," she recalled, and "they were so hospitable they would invite many of them in. Even the chauffeur. . . . Even the press came in. That's how we are in the village, we couldn't keep them out." Once at home, Burton relished playing hymns on the piano and speaking to his brothers and sisters only in Welsh. His sisters would make the traditional Welsh dishes that Burton so loved, lava bread and gooseberry tart.

The trip so lifted his spirits that Burton even considered resettling in Britain, even if it meant paying the dreaded British taxes. He'd had it with living out of suitcases, traipsing from one hotel to another. But instead, he and Elizabeth flew to Dublin and immediately checked into the penthouse suite of the Gresham Hotel, to resume location shooting for *The Spy Who Came in from the Cold*. Once again, they were thronged by crowds, stirred up in part by the fact that *Cleopatra* was being shown at a theater across the street from the Burtons' hotel (they could see the giant marquee through their window).

It was not a happy time for them. The weather was bleak, the theme and tone and look of the movie Burton was making was grim. Maria Burton came down with the measles. Bad things started to happen. Their faithful, stalwart chauffeur, Gaston Sanz, lost his sixteen-year-old son, killed in a shooting accident. Sanz, who had been with Elizabeth for twelve years, was a decorated war hero of the Free French Commandos, but it was Elizabeth who bolstered him, accompanying him to Paris for the inquest and funeral. ("I wouldn't be here now if it wasn't for her," he later admitted.) In Paris, $50,000 worth of Elizabeth's jewels were stolen from her hotel room. It got worse. Back in Dublin, Elizabeth was with Sanz when the chauffeur accidentally hit and killed a pedestrian. And then, on March 12, in Los Angeles, her father, Francis Taylor, suffered a stroke at the age of sixty-seven. Elizabeth flew to California and rushed to his bedside, staying a week to comfort her mother before returning to Dublin. Her father survived, though he would never fully recover. Elizabeth always rose to the occasion when disaster struck; it was when she was bored and feeling neglected that tensions arose.

Burton resumed his heavy drinking on the set. "He had a bottle of scotch in his raincoat pocket," observed John Le Carré, "possibly another in the other pocket." Once, during a nighttime shoot in a Dublin street, dreary enough to substitute for a Berlin location, Elizabeth suddenly turned up on the set. "It was the biggest free show in Dublin—the fire brigade, the police, crowds," Le Carré remembered, "but it was under control. When all of a sudden—the white Rolls-Royce appeared with Gaston . . . and Elizabeth, looking like a million dollars. She drove onto the set! The crowd was out of control and surged up to her." Burton was upstaged and his concentration broken. He yelled at the crowd, "My God, there's my little girl!" and then scrambled toward the car, insisting that Elizabeth leave the set. She did so, and Burton finished the night's shooting. Still, she had made her point. "No one makes an entrance like Elizabeth Taylor," Sammy Davis Jr. once said, and she would prove that time and again.

Elizabeth and Claire met only once during the three months of filming, when the Burtons invited the actress and Le Carré to a dinner at their Gresham Hotel suite. It was a bit of a gunfight between two great raconteurs—Le Carré and Burton—taking turns topping each other's stories. In the middle of dinner, Elizabeth rose from the table and went to her room. Shortly thereafter, her voice could be heard through an intercom, making loud and frequent summonses for Richard to come to bed. She finally appeared, furious at being ignored, and a shouting match ensued.

It wasn't the only time guests were treated to the sight of the Burtons in full battle armor. Earlier on, Le Carré had been summoned to the Burtons' penthouse suite at an early hour because Elizabeth wanted to meet the author of the popular spy novel. He arrived to find Burton alone in a vast sitting room, a pile of books by his chair. As he entered the room, he heard the intercom crackling with Elizabeth's voice.

"Richard?"

"Yes, darling?"

"Who's all here?"

"The writer."

Burton disappeared into the bedroom to fetch Elizabeth and "they had a mother and a father of a row," Le Carré recalled. "Sounds of slapping. All of that. And all coming through on this intercom! Eventually she arrived in this sort of fluffy wraparound dressing gown you send away for, barefooted, rather broad-arsed, but extremely cuddly, extraordinarily attractive—those beautiful eyes, far more beautiful off-screen than on. And she gave me one of those little-girl handshakes."

As far as Le Carré was concerned, some of the wind had gone out of Richard Burton's sails. "I had the impression that it wasn't much fun anymore—it had been fun—fighting and fucking his way up, but now it just wasn't anymore." Burton had been Ritt's choice for Alec Leamas all along, but Le Carré had hoped that James Mason or Trevor Howard might fit the bill, because, in his view, they looked more world-weary. But when Le Carré saw Burton a few months later on the beach at Scheveningen in Holland, he was stunned to see how "deteriorated" Burton looked. The case can be made that Burton's dissipated appearance reflected how much he had taken on the role of the beaten-down Alec Leamas. Intended or not, it served him well. And it would serve him even better for his next role, arguably his greatest: the henpecked, eternally disappointed George in Edward Albee's *Who's Afraid of Virginia Woolf?*

In March, near the end of filming, Elizabeth was back in the hospital. Her delicate health and frequent injuries often brought them closer together. He loved taking care of her, being depended upon, and she luxuriated in his attentions. She was grateful, in fact, knowing how much the sickroom terrified Richard. He wrote in his leather-bound journal, his notebooks, "nervous all day worrying about her," and confided how much he wanted to have a child with Elizabeth. A spinal injury that required the fusing of two discs when she was first married to Mike Todd, and complications with her earlier pregnancies, made it inadvisable for her to bear another child, but they apparently hoped another surgery would make a full-term pregnancy possible.

Filming finally behind them, they took their leave of the chronic tensions of the shoot and decamped to the Riviera with their four children. Away from the public and the rigors of filmmaking, it was a blissful time for all of them, as Burton recorded in his notebooks: "Went tramping with Michael, Christopher, Liza, after having watched them at the riding school. Liza and Mike splendid but Christopher started to show panic, and with my usual hatred of watching others humiliated, I left with Maria for a stroll to the river." Elizabeth joined Richard and Maria outside the riding school, not wanting to make Christopher self-conscious. Richard seemed to find genuine solace and pleasure in the company of the children, playing board games for hours, going on long walks. He was delighted to have adopted Maria, to have given her his name, and he felt a special bond with both Maria and Liza. For once, he didn't have to be the brilliant raconteur, the endless entertainer, dazzling with his erudition and wit. He could be himself. Richard, the former rugby player, was equally at home rough-housing with the children and acting out scenes from Shakespearean plays, which they loved.

Elizabeth, too, was grateful for her children's bonding with Richard. Michael and Christopher had inherited their mother's deep blue eyes and dark lashes. Christopher played the flute and looked like the English singer and guitarist Nick Drake. He had begun by being hostile to Richard, but eventually he would "throw himself into Richard's arms and kiss him," Elizabeth remembered. Maria, who would grow into a tall, athletic, and graceful young woman, was particularly close to Richard. Liza, who had her father's stubborn chin and shrewd eyes, shared Elizabeth's love of animals and affinity for horses. Elizabeth called her "an independent tornado" who loved to "take charge of Richard." Though she never knew her father, as she was seven months old when Mike Todd was killed, Liza was very much like him in "her mannerisms, the way she uses her hands, the way she shrugs her shoulders—and the larceny and con of her mind," Elizabeth observed. She would later become an artist known for her sculptures of horses.

In one of the undated notes he wrote to Elizabeth while she slept in the next room, Richard described the blissful evening he'd just spent with Elizabeth and "that lovely and loving Liza of ours," making her "giggle almost . . . to the point of hysterics (*which you asked me to do*)." He went on to describe massaging Elizabeth's foot, adding, "It's equally extraordinary what ugly but nonetheless lovable feet you both have! Don't hit me, but the only beautiful feet are babies' . . ." He ended his note, "The greatest invention I know is a marvelous collection of superbly confected brilliance called E. T. Burton. What great God invented her?" He signed it, "Rich. (In every way.)" Burton's genuine love for Elizabeth's children was one of their deepest bonds.

In April of 1965, Burton was nominated for an Academy Award for his work in *Becket* the previous year. It was his third nomination, but he would lose the Oscar to Rex Harrison for *My Fair Lady*, Marc Antony overshadowed once again by Julius Caesar. Disappointing, but there were more heights to scale as he confronted his looming fortieth birthday. He had already surpassed Elizabeth at the box office, though she remained more famous—more beloved—than he could ever hope to be. Now the unasked question was, did their alliance help or hinder his career? His best and most rewarding film work—*Becket*, *The Night of the Iguana*, and now *The Spy Who Came in from the Cold*—were all made without Elizabeth costarring. In fact, the dramatic climax of *Spy* can be read as emblematic of where Burton was, psychically, in his relationship with Elizabeth. As his character, Leamas, scales the Berlin Wall in his final dash for safety, he reaches back to help his lover, Nan, over the wall. Suddenly, she's shot by a German soldier. Burton hesitates for a long moment, his rough face caught in the glare of the East German searchlight: should he leave her behind and make his escape into freedom, or try to rescue his beloved, thus sealing his own doom?

Leamas—Burton—climbs back down the wall.

6
WHO'S AFRAID OF ELIZABETH TAYLOR?

"I *am* George."
—RICHARD BURTON

"Let's face it—a lot of my life has lacked dignity."
—ELIZABETH TAYLOR

urton reacted with good grace to losing his third Academy Award, for *Becket*. After all, he had been nominated for his work in *My Cousin Rachel* and *The Robe*, and he was likely to be nominated as well for *The Spy Who Came in from the Cold*. With his unrivaled success as Hamlet on Broadway, and toning down his film-acting technique, how could he not be nominated again—and win? He would bide his time.

Burton had mixed emotions, however, when he got word in June of 1965 that Sybil Burton, at thirty-six, had married the twenty-four-year-old rock musician Jordan Christopher. He was pleased to see Sybil moving on with her life, but it was a blow to his ego—to be supplanted in the marriage bed by a twenty-four-year-old rocker was unsettling. Burton himself was fond of pointing out that the Welsh were among the most brilliant tribes in the world, but they possessed a talent for everything except being middle-aged. He was turning forty. His youthful roguish charm had been replaced by a kind of gravitas, a heaviness that sometimes made him seem haunted by ghosts from his past, an inability to enjoy the enormous personal and professional successes he had torn out of the world.

For her part, Sybil was having a renaissance. She opened a night-club in Manhattan called Arthur (the name inspired by an ad-libbed line in *A Hard Day's Night*, when Ringo tells a clueless reporter that he calls his haircut "Arthur"). The group Jordan Christopher fronted, The Wild Ones, was the house band. It became the most popular disco-theque in New York in the 1960s. Andy Warhol described it as "all dark brightness. It was Sybil Burton Christopher's club, of course, and Sybil was an upbeat, outgoing woman—everything was fun! witty! a ball!—the energetic English type that wants everybody to have fun. I met so many stars at Arthur—Sophia Loren, Bette Davis— everybody but Liz Taylor Burton." (Warhol was an early worshipper of Elizabeth—he'd been enamored of her since his sickly childhood in Pittsburgh, reading movie magazines in bed. He would write her fan letters, and his early silk screens made in The Factory in 1962 further apotheosized Elizabeth, from giant blow-ups of the "Eddie Fisher– Elizabeth Taylor Break-Up" headline to the gorgeous silk screens of Elizabeth at the height of her youthful beauty.)

So Sybil had survived the humiliation of her public breakup with Burton, after all. She not only survived, she flourished, once she'd moved to Manhattan and the Hamptons and remarried. She had always had a gift for friendship. Sybil had maintained the loyalty of many of Burton's old pals—Robert Hardy, Emlyn Williams, Philip Burton, the Stanley Bakers, Rex Harrison, and friends such as Dirk Bogarde, Lord Snowdon, Princess Margaret, and even Elizabeth Taylor's childhood friend Roddy McDowall. Burton, in contrast, was becoming increasingly cut off from his former friends as the Taylor entourage became more and more difficult to penetrate. Robert

Hardy remembered being unable to break through in the years following *The Spy Who Came in from the Cold*, sending messages that never reached Burton, as his once close friend became increasingly isolated in his gilded life. "A terrifying position, isn't it, to be totally, helplessly in love with this amazing star," he acknowledged.

> Of course, he drifted, to some extent, away from most of his friends. Because, from the Elizabeth time onward, he traveled round with a court. It was very difficult. He always rang me up when he came to London and said, "come around the Dorchester tomorrow." I would always say, "How many people are going to be there?" There was going to be a big party on Wednesday, and on Thursday, but on Friday . . . "alright, come on Friday, just the family." There were 150 people there! And more caviar than you can imagine.

His male vanity notwithstanding, Burton was pleased that he would no longer be paying Sybil alimony, and—more important—he felt he would be able to spend more time with his adored eldest daughter, Kate. Jessica, meanwhile, was being cared for in an institution on Long Island, visited rarely—if ever—by Burton, who still carried grief and guilt over her condition.

In 1965, thirty-two-year-old Elizabeth was still stunningly beautiful, but her much-commented-upon weight fluctuations sometimes gave her a matronly look. She did not carry weight well. Tiny in stature—barely five foot two—with short legs and a bosomy hourglass figure, she had a hard time finding clothes that fit her well and flattered her Gibson Girl figure, especially when 1960s fashion got into full sway and favored the young, the long-legged, and the small-breasted. This new look was embodied by London's Carnaby Street models such as Twiggy, Jean Shrimpton, and Penelope Tree, miniskirted gamines ten to fifteen years younger than Elizabeth. By 1965, stars who had become household names in the 1950s—Elizabeth Taylor, Sophia

Loren, Doris Day—were being supplanted by younger actresses: John Schlesinger's *Darling* won Julie Christie an Academy Award in 1963; Richard Lester's *A Hard Day's Night* the following year introduced a bevy of teenage mod chicks led by Pattie Boyd; a young, tomboyish Jane Fonda dazzled in *Cat Ballou* in 1965.

It wasn't meant to change so quickly. Just two years earlier, Warhol noticed how "the girls . . . in Brooklyn looked really great. It was the summer of the Liz-Taylor-in-*Cleopatra*-look—long, straight, dark, shiny hair with bangs and Egyptian-looking eye makeup." *The V.I.P.s* that same year had been launched with a fashion tie-in with Pierre Cardin, which popularized the white mink hat Taylor had worn so fetchingly in the film. But by 1965, Elizabeth would no longer launch fashion trends. She just wasn't convincing as a bohemian artist in *The Sandpiper* despite her Irene Sharaff poncho. Her look was becoming passé to a younger audience, though older women still admired and envied her, and the public maintained its insatiable curiosity about all things relating to the Burtons.

It was a kind of genius that instead of trying to compete with her younger, more nubile competition, Elizabeth appeared in her next role as the blowsy, middle-aged, overripe faculty spouse, Martha, in Edward Albee's *Who's Afraid of Virginia Woolf?*, a scathing drama about a self-destructive academic couple at a small New England college. Instead of dieting, she added twenty-five pounds to her diminutive frame, and she covered her black glossy hair with a salt-and-pepper wig. She took a liability and turned it into a virtue, even appearing on the cover of *Life* magazine in her middle-age guise, throwing down the gauntlet to all who questioned her devotion to her craft. She was Mrs. Richard Burton, yes, but she was still, after all, an actress.

If Elizabeth was losing a younger generation of moviegoers, she endeared herself even more to her lifelong fans, especially the women who had loved her as Velvet Brown and had grown up with her. As Martha in Edward Albee's blistering drama, she would play a forty-five-year-old woman entering menopause, graying, overweight, and full of regrets. *Who's Afraid of Virginia Woolf?* would shake to the core women in their thirties, forties, and fifties who had grown up with *National Velvet* and *Father of the Bride*. Here was Elizabeth, suddenly older, heavier, disappointed, disillusioned, and drunk. Elizabeth herself would later observe that women identified with her in a way they did not identify with that other larger-than-life movie star, Marilyn Monroe, because Marilyn never went through menopause. Marilyn had died two years earlier, in 1963, at the age of thirty-six, still beautiful and young. She'd never had children. She seemed to have had no attachments, no family around her; she seemed always in need of someone to take care of her. Elizabeth was someone her fans knew as a girl, as an ingénue, as a young wife, and now, as Martha, as a grown woman fighting the gravities of middle age, trapped in a disappointing marriage, her angers unleashed by too much alcohol. "She's discontent," her character says in Act I of the drama, a line with which many suburban housewives in the mid-1960s could identify.

Ernest Lehman had already made a big reputation for himself in Hollywood as a preeminent screenwriter specializing in adapting Broadway hits for the movies, such as *The Sound of Music* and *West Side Story*. He had written *North by Northwest* for Alfred Hitchcock, having earlier launched his career by writing, with help from the great Clifford Odets, the adaptation of Lehman's own novella (or "novel-ette"), *Sweet Smell of Success*.

Lehman had first approached Elizabeth while she was filming interiors in Paris for *The Sandpiper*, to ask if she'd be interested in playing Martha in *Who's Afraid of Virginia Woolf?* Albee's play had won five Tony Awards and was a *succès de scandale* on Broadway, given its blistering vocabulary and frank sexual content. Lehman was writing the adaptation as well as producing the movie for Warner Bros. He wanted Elizabeth to play Martha, the harridan who goads two un-witting guests into helping her humiliate George, her long-suffering husband, in a night of raucous drinking. Uta Hagen and Arthur Hill had embodied the roles on Broadway, and Albee himself wanted Bette Davis and James Mason to play George and Martha onscreen. Patricia Neal was also seriously considered for the role, but, as Lehman later recalled, "When I saw the lines around the block for [The] Night of the Iguana, which was just Burton, I thought to myself, 'Imagine the lines around the block in every city of the world if Elizabeth Taylor and Richard Burton were to star together.'"

No one else in Hollywood could see the glamorous star in the role of a middle-aged, gone-to-seed Martha. At first, not even Elizabeth, who had "taken an abiding dislike" to the shrewish character when she first read the play. However, Burton was impressed with the language of Albee's tragicomedy. "You've only to read the first lines and you know this is a great play," he said. Richard agreed that Elizabeth was too young and too beautiful for the part, but they both sensed that this could be her Hamlet. He told Elizabeth, "You'd better play it to stop anyone else from doing it and causing a sensation."

Curiously, given Lehman's appreciation of Burton's box-office draw, he wasn't the producer's first choice to play George. Names were bandied about—Peter O'Toole and Arthur Hill (who had originated the role). Lehman had offered the part to Jack Lemmon and Glenn Ford, who passed on it, because they felt the role of the henpecked, emasculated college professor would ruin their images. When Taylor nudged Lehman toward Burton, the producer at first turned him down with a compliment, saying Burton was too masculine for the role. But Elizabeth made it clear that Richard was her first choice as costar, and Lehman gave him a screen test. After looking at the results, he still wasn't sure the actor was right for the part. He told Burton that, just as he feared, he "looked all wrong; much too strong . . . As I told him later, he looked as if he had four balls. . . ."

Burton shot back, "Only four?"

Lehman concluded that they were "going to have to do a lot of work on him." Nonetheless, the producer conferred with his boss Jack Warner, the tyrannical head of Warner Bros., and they made the deal:

$1.1 million and 10 percent of the gross for Taylor, plus director approval, and a flat fee of $750,000 for Burton. By now, Elizabeth had so warmed to the idea of playing Martha—especially with Richard as her costar—that she told Lehman, "Ernie, I'd have done this role for nothing, you know. But Hugh French [her agent] told me to say a million wasn't enough. We took you, we really took you!" she said with a delicious cackle.

The role of Nick, the young biology professor Martha seduces, was first offered to Robert Redford, who turned it down. George Segal and Sandy Dennis, two acclaimed Broadway actors, were then cast as Nick and Honey, the mismatched couple trapped in a night of fun and games, whose own shaky union, like a comic subplot, reflects the lies and illusions of George and Martha's marriage.

While still in Paris filming interiors for *The Sandpiper*, Taylor, Burton, and Lehman had discussed possible directors over dinner at La Méditerranée. Fred Zinnemann's name came up, but Lehman said he had already declined, choosing instead to direct Paul Scofield in *A Man for All Seasons*. Burton next suggested Henri-Georges Clouzot, noted for suspense films like *The Wages of Fear* with Yves Montand and *Diabolique* with Simone Signoret.

"You don't know anything about anything!" Elizabeth teased her husband, with a sharp punch to the shoulder. "You made *Ice Palace*!" (referring to the rather awful 1960 adaptation of an Edna Ferber novel about the founding of Alaska). Then John Frankenheimer's name came up. He had been riding high since directing a string of hits: *The Manchurian Candidate*, *The Birdman of Alcatraz*, and *Seven Days in May*. But Lehman said he had already been to see Frankenheimer, and the director insisted that his name appear above the title.

"Fuck him!" was Elizabeth's response. Then she asked, "But you know who's a genius?"

"Who?" asked Lehman.

"Mike Nichols."

"But he's never directed a picture," Lehman said.

"I'm in awe of him," Richard admitted. They had been friends since *Camelot*.

It was a daring choice. Nichols had been such a good friend to the couple in Rome. At thirty-three, he had gone from a long, popular engagement on Broadway as half of the hip, satirical comedy duo in *An Evening with Mike Nichols and Elaine May* to directing three wildly successful Broadway plays (*Barefoot in the Park*, *The Odd Couple*, and *Luv*), but he had never directed a film before—and certainly not a searing drama, though the play is laced with black comedy as well. Now he would be getting into the cage with two personalities—unleashed tigers—for a film whose graphic language, psychosexual content, and scalding harangues were far beyond anything American movie audiences were used to. "A movie is like a person," Nichols would later say. "Either you trust it or you don't."

The Burtons trusted Nichols, and all the principals involved trusted the power of Albee's play. Burton commented that after John Osborne's Jimmy Porter in *Look Back in Anger*, the role of George was "the most brilliantly written role" he'd ever undertaken in a film. The work was so challenging and so emotionally raw that Elizabeth requested the soundstage at Warner Bros. Studios be closed to the press.

Mike Nichols—born Michael Igor Peschkowsky—was very much the man about town, New York's most eligible bachelor. He was squiring around both Gloria Steinem and Jacqueline Kennedy at the time, and, in fact, Mrs. Kennedy reportedly called on the first day of shooting to wish him well. (It wouldn't be the first time Jackie's path would cross the Burtons', ever since she adopted the charmed metaphor of Camelot to describe her husband's all-too-brief tenure as president.) One Warner Bros. executive was quoted as saying, "In fact, we later lost an entire day of shooting—twenty-four hours—just so Mike could fly to New York to have lunch with Jackie."

Nichols brought cinematographer Haskell Wexler onboard to film in black-and-white, to underscore the dark realities explored in the movie (and to make Elizabeth's aging makeup look more believable). Burton was not happy about that, fearing the harsh lighting would make his acne scars look like craters on the moon, but Nichols and Wexler prevailed.

The cast and crew would later film exteriors on the Smith College campus in Northampton, Massachusetts, but most of the movie was shot in Studio 8 at Warner Bros. The set was designed by Richard Sylbert, who visited eighteen campuses and faculty homes to get just the right look, down to the warped floorboards, old copies of the *Kenyon Review*, and groaning bookshelves in George and Martha's slightly down-at-the-heels, two-story house.

On the first day of rehearsal, the Burtons arrived at the Warner Bros. Studios and inspected their expansive dressing rooms, replete with Lehman's gifts—bouquets of white roses and lilies of the valley, buckets of Veuve Clicquot, and bottles of scotch. Elizabeth was thrilled with the flowers—"somebody knows what I like," she said to Lehman, kissing him lightly on the cheek. Then, like the stateroom scene in the Marx Brothers' *A Night at the Opera*, their dressing rooms quickly filled up with agents, valets, and the usual suspects— their publicist John Springer, their agent Hugh French and his son Robin, their dressers, Bob and Sally Wilson, and Elizabeth's favorite costumer, Irene Sharaff. Meanwhile, Mike Nichols waited on the soundstage to begin rehearsal.

Nichols, whose entire directing career so far had been on the stage, started by holding lengthy rehearsals as if he were putting on a play. Studio-trained Elizabeth had never worked that way before. She always learned her lines and professionally hit her marks and did what the director asked of her, waiting for him to shout "Action" before she slipped into character and showed any emotion. Now she had to perform in rehearsals, but it helped that Elizabeth trusted her director, though for the first time, actress and director were virtually the same age (Nichols was now thirty-four); however, she far outdistanced him in experience. *Who's Afraid of Virginia Woolf?* would be her thirty-fifth film; it was Nichols's first—choosing Nichols was certainly a brave and inspired choice.

What was scheduled to be a two-month shoot became six months, lasting from July through December of 1965. Like *Cleopatra*, the film went over budget; as in *Cleopatra*, there were expensive delays caused by Elizabeth's health issues. This time she suffered an eye injury playing with one of her nephews. (By now, her brother, Howard Taylor, had moved to Hawaii, where he was living in privacy: an oceanographer, married, with five kids.) It was a painstaking, difficult experience for Elizabeth, as the highly emotional role called on her to express bitterness and rage, even at one point spitting into Richard's/George's face. Nichols often made her do repeated takes; one day she collapsed, weeping from exhaustion and frustration. Lehman felt that Nichols "was especially tough on her because he wanted the picture to be good and she needed the most help. We were all under a lot of pressure, but Elizabeth was really out on a limb. Everyone said she'd make a fool of herself." Nichols had wanted Elizabeth to take lessons to lower the register of her voice, but Elizabeth refused, telling her director that she acted by instinct, and vocal drills would only interfere with that. Nevertheless, she was well aware that of the four cast members, only she had no real stage experience, beyond the poetry reading she and Richard had given in New York.

Somehow, it all worked: Elizabeth would give the greatest performance of her career.

Taylor, Nichols, and Burton flourished in each other's company, playing practical jokes and word games, each trying to one-up the other. Burton described it as indulging in "a little harmless hilarity" to break the emotional intensity on the set, often challenging Nichols to identify the author of poems he quoted at length, such as:

> *Fear no more the heat o' the sun,*
> *Nor the furious winter's rages;*

Thou thy worldly task hast done,
Home art gone, and ta'en thy wages;
Golden lads, and girls all must,
As chimney-sweepers, come to dust.

"A. E. Houseman?" Nichols asked.

Burton shot back: "Shakespeare. *Cymbeline.*"

Burton described his director, tongue-in-cheek, as "a very disturbing man. You cannot charm him—he sees right through you. He's among the most intelligent men I've ever known and I've known most of them. I dislike him intensely—he's cleverer than I am." For Taylor, it was a simple case of adoration. Once, when she fell off the bicycle she used to travel from Studio 8 to her dressing room, Nichols rescued her and carried her back to the studio in his arms. "You have to carry me *every* day," she teased.

"I'll have to get into training," he answered, registering the extra twenty-five pounds Elizabeth had put on for the role.

Lehman kept extensive diary entries during the shoot, speaking them into a tape recorder and having them transcribed by a secretary. They reveal some details of the day-to-day life on the Warner set, where rehearsals had begun. Lehman wrote:

7/6/65 . . . A very exhilarating day. The Burtons and George Segal and Sandy Dennis all arrived at about 10:30 and we went to Stage 2. Bloody Marys, of all things, were served at about noon as we did the reading.

At one o'clock the whole group went to lunch. At my end of the table I was chatting with Sandy and Elizabeth. A good deal of it was woman talk. Elizabeth and Sandy were comparing their bellies. Elizabeth claims she's got a permanent belly from all her cesarean operations. Sandy claims that she has a belly that makes her look like a woman who has been pregnant for 12 months.

Indeed, Elizabeth was concerned about her weight gain, as Lehman recorded. She reminded the producer that he and Mike Nichols had called her when she was in Paris and instructed her to gain "as much weight as she could for the role of Martha." That must have been a pleasurable challenge for Elizabeth, who dined with gusto and loved not only beluga caviar and champagne but American fare like cheese-burgers, French fries, and, of course, chili from Chasen's. She told Lehman that she had been gorging on "a lot of cream and butter and sweets," but when she arrived in Los Angeles, Nichols took one look at her bursting curves and told her to lose ten pounds.

"Listen, Ernie," she said. "You must be sure to tell the press tomor-row that you and Mike have ordered me to get fat for this picture. I don't want them to get the idea that I'm overweight and sloppy simply because I don't know any better."

Lehman's diary also reveals that Elizabeth was taking thyroid pills, possibly as a way to lose those ten pounds. Once, when she showed up having accidentally taken two pills instead of one, she was "hopped up," in Lehman's phrase, and Burton refused to let her have her Bloody Mary for lunch. Burton knew she was having a hard time. He watched over her, using his own considerable skills to help her modulate her performance. When she seemed "a bit nervous" during rehearsals, Lehman noticed, Burton frequently reassured her, going over to her and "giving her a little kiss."

Elizabeth's confidence would be slightly shaken one day when Marlene Dietrich showed up on the set. She watched quietly from the sidelines while all four actors went through their paces. When the scene was over, Dietrich ran up to Richard Burton and fawned over him, telling him he'd surely win an Academy Award for his performance. She then kissed Elizabeth on the cheek and said, "Darling, everyone is so fantastic! You have a lot of guts to perform with real actors."

Elizabeth just smiled. She then said, "Yes, I do. And when I get home, Marlene, Richard and I are going to fuck like bunnies."

Curiously—and Ernest Lehman would notice this as well—the constant domestic battles filmed for the movie had a felicitous effect on the Burtons' own marriage. The role of Martha called for Elizabeth to not only heap contumely on poor George, but to physically pummel him as well. The two actors engaged in frightening violence onscreen—at one point, George slams Martha's head into the side of their car. "Elizabeth loves to fight," Lehman observed. "She was constantly hitting and punching Burton," part of her physicality and her need to have her man stand up to her and fight back. But in real life, heading home in an air-conditioned Cadillac to their rented villa on Carolwood Drive in Bel Air's Holmby Hills, where they would lounge around two swimming pools with their children in the evenings, the Burtons ceased their quarreling. Because much of it was driven by Elizabeth's need for drama, to challenge and be constantly challenged, that need was now being met by the physically and emotionally wrenching role she was playing. The experience of becoming George and Martha, locked in a destructive and complicated marriage, ironically drew the Burtons even closer together. "It was very cathartic," Elizabeth recalled, "because we would get all our shouting and bawling out on the set and go home and cuddle."

Nichols knew that this searing film had to be a labor of love, and with the Burtons, he found that to be the case. "I am just constantly surprised at how good Elizabeth and Richard are," he told the *Saturday Evening Post.* ". . . I love them. Their flexibility and talent and cooperativeness and lovingness is overwhelming. I can't think of one disagreeable thing. I've had more trouble with little people you've never heard of—temper tantrums, upstaging, girls' sobbing—than with the so-called legendary Burtons. The Burtons are on time, they know their lines, and if I make suggestions, Elizabeth can keep in her mind fourteen dialogue changes, twelve floor marks, and ten pauses . . ." Nichols even somehow persuaded Burton to watch the rushes for the first time since he'd appeared in *The Last Days of Dolwyn,* in 1948. Burton normally could not bear to see himself onscreen, nor did he ever read his reviews, good or bad. He nursed a core of self-hatred that no amount of love, lust, or laurels could completely assuage. "I don't run out screaming as I used to," he said after watching himself onscreen as the self-pitying George, whose dreams and hopes have been destroyed by passivity and his all-too-powerful wife.

Emotionally, it was a difficult role for Burton. Long after the film was completed, Nichols recalled how "Richard had black days. It's as simple as that. During the production he had perhaps eight or ten of those days, and they took various forms." In one instance, Richard just walked away, telling Nichols, "I can't act tonight." Later, when they were filming on location in Northampton and Burton was called upon to weep while Martha has sex with Nick in an upstairs bedroom, Burton just couldn't do it. He asked to be excused, claiming he had to leave at four p.m. to spend time with Michael and Christopher, who were about to leave for their schools in Switzerland. He was eventually coaxed into doing the scene—and doing it brilliantly. Nichols recalled, "Looking back now, with my greater knowledge of alcoholic personalities, I think it was somehow connected to the fact that he had either drunk too much, or needed to drink more. He couldn't pull himself away from it and concentrate." But it was Burton's old fear of inadequacy cropping up, his *hiraeth*, his sense of alienation, his longing to feel at home.

Nichols observed that sometimes "it took the form of being abusive to Elizabeth, which was horribly upsetting to us. It was infrequent, but what happens is, when such a day occurs, everyone is constantly afraid another is coming. I wasn't afraid of Richard," Nichols said, "and I'd just tell him he was being a shmuck. But not that night in Northampton, because I saw it as despair and inability. How can you tell him he's a shmuck when he's telling you he's so untalented and hopeless?"

If Nichols noticed Richard occasionally being abusive to Elizabeth, Lehman couldn't help but notice Elizabeth treating Richard as if he truly were George. "She was constantly punching him," Lehman said. In fact, Nichols saw that all of his actors were becoming obsessed with their roles. When Burton showed up on the set costumed as the ineffectual history professor, he told Lehman, "I *am* George. George is me." Burton had long harbored the idea that if he hadn't become an actor, he would have been content to teach English "to grubby boys" at a small school or college. Later, in Northampton, Burton took Nichols and Lehman aside to read them a book review of a new biography of Dylan Thomas, which he had just written for the *New York Herald Tribune.* He told his director and producer that he had written the piece "as though I were George."

Or perhaps Burton identified with George's lacerating secret, his source of shame, cruelly betrayed by Martha when she reveals that as a boy George had accidentally shot his mother and later killed his father in an automobile accident. Again, Burton is sublime in a role full of self-contempt, and in his two revelatory monologues, or "arias," in which he reveals his past, Burton gives perhaps the most affecting performance of his long, extraordinary career. We see a man gripped by both the best and the worst memories of his youth—a day of innocent camaraderie at a roadhouse, when he childishly mispronounces "bergin and soda," to the delight of his friends, and the tragic day, not long after, when, with his driver's permit in his pocket, he accidentally kills his father by swerving to avoid a porcupine on the road. This is a shattering revelation, and Burton is mesmerizing in his delivery of those sacred memories. If you see Burton's repudiation of his father as a kind of metaphorical murder, then Burton *is* George, in a performance that would surely win him his long-delayed recognition from The Academy of Motion Picture Arts and Sciences.

Though Elizabeth still managed to look sexy under her troweled-on makeup, extra pounds, and wig (Nichols had wanted to put putty under her eyes to look like bags, but she refused), she completely nailed the role of Martha. She's terrifying in her diatribes against her husband; screamingly funny in her inventive insults ("I am the Earth

Mother and all men are flops!"); touching when she and George cuddle and he rebuffs her attempt to make love to him; and heart-breaking when she's finally stripped of her illusions and left facing her own loneliness and regret. She has one declaration in which her own personality seems to shine through Albee's words: "I'm loud," she yells at George at the height of their battle, in the parking lot of a roadhouse. "And I'm vulgar. And I wear the pants in the family because somebody has to. But I am not a monster."

In that scene, the parking lot's harsh neon light shines pitilessly on the couple, like a prison searchlight examining every hidden corner of their marriage, sparing no one.

Cast and crew arrived in late August 1965 at Smith College in Northampton (Sylvia Plath's alma mater, incidentally). The college president, Thomas C. Mendenhall, was at first reluctant to turn his campus over to the movie crew, given the unflattering picture of academic life in Albee's play ("Musical beds is the faculty sport here"), but Warner Bros.'s offer of $150,000 went a long way to overcome his reluctance. Smith College, however, preferred not to be mentioned in the film's final credits.

The studio hired seventy security guards, instead of the usual five, to protect the Burtons and maintain privacy during filming, but it didn't help. Despite a torrential rainstorm, four hundred people clamoring for autographs flocked to the lakeside house rented for the Burtons, turning the quiet, woodsy town into Via Veneto. It just wouldn't do—there was no way they could secure their temporary quarters. Elizabeth trotted around to the Victorian homes rented for Lehman and Nichols, and finally decided that Nichols's splendid quarters would suit them perfectly. Nichols, always the gentleman, packed up, and the Burtons moved in for the four-week duration of the shoot.

Filming was done entirely at night, in keeping with the real-time experience of the movie, which begins at night and ends at sunrise.

Even so, villagers stood around the movie set all night, held back by security guards, trying to get a glimpse of the famous couple. It was emotionally draining—working in the dark, unleashing Albee's ravaging dialogue, dodging the inevitable press of fans lurking on the perimeter. One rainy night on a soggy Northampton lawn, as Burton rehearsed his lines, he reminisced about an early review he'd received for his professional debut stage role in *The Druid's Rest*, twenty-two years earlier, when he was just eighteen. "In a wretched part," the critic for the *New Statesman* had written, "Richard Burton showed exceptional ability." Perhaps it was his role as George that brought about another round of regret for the life not lived, as Burton complained, "I would have become a preacher, a poet, a playwright, a scholar, a lawyer or something," had it not been for that favorable review. "I would never have become this strange thing, an actor, sitting in a remote corner of the universe called Northampton, drinking a vodka and tonic and waiting to learn the next line. He's got a bloody lot to answer for, that man."

But the rainy, difficult shoot brought the Burtons even closer together. "I never had a better time in my life," Elizabeth later said about making *Virginia Woolf*. On September 23, the crew returned to Los Angeles to finish five months of filming.

Back in California, Burton turned forty and was treated to a grand celebration on the Warner Bros. soundstage. The stage doors swung open, and there, wrapped in a huge red ribbon, was Elizabeth's gift to her husband: a white Oldsmobile Toronado. He was less happy with his director's playful gift of a puppy, yet another mewling mouth to feed among their growing menagerie. He retaliated by later giving Nichols four mice in a cage, representing George, Martha, Nick, and Honey.

After filming at Studio 8 was finally completed on December 13, 1965, Nichols presented Taylor with a pair of ruby-and-diamond earrings. Extravagant gifts were exchanged all around: the Burtons gave their director a pair of gold David Webb cuff links, and they gave

Lehman a 1633 first edition of Francis Bacon's *The Advancement of Learning.* Their greatest gift to their producer, however, was not charging him overages for the additional two weeks of shooting that had been required, which would have come to more than a million dollars. They knew, perhaps, that in making *Virginia Woolf* they had done something important, and, as Elizabeth had joked earlier, she would have done it for nothing.

Earlier in the shoot—practically from day one—Elizabeth had let it be known that she'd already picked out an $80,000 brooch that she expected from Jack Warner, and a piece of David Webb jewelry that she expected from Lehman. But both men had demurred. Warner had groused, "I'm paying her a million, one hundred thousand, plus 10 percent of the gross. Let her buy her own brooch." And Lehman—who tended to be a bit fussy and timorous in any case—let it be known that his wife would divorce him if he bought Elizabeth Taylor an expensive piece of jewelry. "I did tell her that I had thought of buying her a baby wolf. She squealed with delight," Lehman wrote in his diary. But Burton was put out with him.

"You son of a bitch. You'll say anything to get out of giving Elizabeth a present," he told his nervous producer. What followed was a not-too-subtle bid on Elizabeth's part to remind Lehman what was expected of him. She showed up one day wearing a double rope of 9½-millimeter pearls given to her by Martin Ransohoff, "because *The Sandpiper* was doing so well at the box office." But Lehman would not budge.

Meanwhile, not only Elizabeth had gained extra weight. Sandy Dennis had put on about twenty pounds, and finally revealed that she was pregnant. Lehman worried about how that would affect filming, but when he finally saw the dailies on December 1, 1965, all his fears vanished.

> . . . I finally know what it feels like to cry at the dailies. I saw the
> film alone toward the end of the day. It was the scene of Martha

talking about her "beautiful, beautiful boy." Honey was listening and slowly her eyes were filling with tears and pouring down her cheeks. Finally she cried, "I want a child! I want a child! I want a baby!" That did it for me.

I went down on the set and saw Sandy Dennis and told her how beautiful her performance was. I then called Elizabeth and thanked her for making me weep.

Twelve days later, Lehman presented Elizabeth with a pendant. "She was absolutely thrilled with it," Lehman recorded. But nineteen days later, Sandy Dennis suffered a miscarriage and lost her baby.

Who's Afraid of Virginia Woolf? premiered on June 22, 1966, in Hollywood and opened in New York's Criterion theater with a performance benefiting two of the Burtons' charities: the Richard Burton Fund of the National Hemophilia Foundation and Philip Burton's American Musical and Dramatic Academy. At $7.5 million, it was the most expensive black-and-white film yet made in Hollywood, and its shocking, explicit language flew in the face of Hollywood's decency code. Jack Warner struggled to find a way to open the film despite the complaints of the National Catholic Office of Motion Pictures over language and sexual content. He had come up with the policy that "no one under the age of eighteen will be admitted to a viewing unless accompanied by his parent. Adults also must be advised that the theme of *Virginia Woolf* may prove to be confusing and its language offensive to the casual filmgoer." Exhibitors had to sign a contract agreeing to the policy, and it's been noted that Warner's solution dismantled the old, censorial Production Code and paved the way for the more flexible rating system put into effect soon after.

The film opened to mostly glorious reviews, the Burtons nominated for British Film Academy Awards. Elizabeth also won the New York Film Critics Circle Award for Best Actress. Though it was widely noted that Elizabeth gave the best performance of her career, it was Richard who garnered the most praise from reviewers. *Newsweek* hailed Burton's performance as "a marvel of disciplined compassion . . . With the self-contained authority of a great actor, he plays the part as if no one in the world had ever heard of Richard Burton." The *Village Voice* described his work as possessing "heroic calm," which other actors could use for a textbook. "Burton simply soars . . . with inscrutable ironies flickering across his beautifully ravaged face. Without Burton, the film would have been an intolerably cold experience."

Elizabeth, Richard, George Segal, and Sandy Dennis were all nominated for Academy Awards. Elizabeth's performance scorches the paint off the walls and puts to rest any doubt about her as not just a "movie star" but a serious, first-class film actress. For once, Richard and Elizabeth seemed to have switched places in terms of their on-screen technique: Elizabeth is operatic as Martha, whereas Richard holds back, underplaying George. His reticence was a way of spotlighting Elizabeth and setting the pace for her. In short, it was his gift to his wife.

The public continued its mad adoration of the Burtons. Crowds met them whenever they traveled, sometimes turning dangerous in their infatuation. Elizabeth, as usual, could handle it, but Richard was finding it increasingly intolerable. He was, at heart, a deeply private man who preferred hours spent reading, and now writing in his diary, which occupied him more and more, and trying his hand at a short story and a novel. He traveled with a trunk filled with the complete plays of Shakespeare. He couldn't bear the sound of the telephone and rarely answered it. Elizabeth reminded him that it would be more troublesome if the crowds *stopped* coming, auguring the end of their popularity, but that didn't make the experience any less uncomfortable for Richard.

To fulfill (and continue to stoke) the public's interest, Elizabeth was paid $250,000 for a memoir titled *Elizabeth by Elizabeth*, written with the biographer Richard Meryman, published by Harper & Row in November 1965, and generously excerpted in *Ladies' Home Journal* magazine the same month. Bert Stern's *LHJ* cover photograph of the Burtons, still in their first year of marriage and the third year of their grand passion, show a contentedly smiling Elizabeth in Cleopatra eye makeup with her arms protectively and possessively wrapped around Richard. Her stunning engagement ring and diamond-studded wedding band—Burton's gifts, of course—are also dazzlingly on display. Burton's rugged face is impassive, unreadable.

The book would be criticized as thin, but the *LHJ* excerpt is charming, breezy, self-deprecating, and immensely likeable. It showcases Elizabeth's willingness to stand up for her unconventional choices and admit to her many youthful mistakes and misjudgments. It's impossible not to like her, especially as it was written—or spoken, with Meryman committing her thoughts to print—during the heady months after her marriage to Burton and his triumphant conquering of Broadway in *Hamlet*. How could she not be sublimely happy? After all, she had won the publicity wars, had lived down public outrage at her marriage to Eddie Fisher, the negative reviews for *Cleopatra*, the condemnations from the Vatican and the House of Representatives, the invasive paparazzi, the "Liz and Dick" tabloid stories. With Burton at her side, she had prevailed. What she does reveal is her joie de vivre, her fighting spirit, and above all, her gratitude.

She is surprisingly candid about a number of things—how after the birth of her two children with Michael Wilding, her "career had become only a way of making money. It was very hard to take any great interest in a career of playing the perennial ingénue." A few revelations were omitted from the published book—Eddie Fisher standing over her with a gun at the height of the *Cleopatra* madness, for example, and Burton telling her when they first began their affair that he was tired of acting onstage, that all the excitement of live performance had left him. Elizabeth omitted that because she felt it was an indictment of Sybil's failure to inspire him, and she wanted to spare Sybil. And she edited out of the published book what she'd written about Debbie Reynolds going along with the MGM publicity machine, playing up her role as the wronged wife, when all three had known that the Fisher-Reynolds marriage was, for the most part, a studio-arranged mirage.

Elizabeth does air her misgivings about the gypsy life she and Burton were living. ("We've got to stop moving around so the kids can have one school, one set of friends, a pony and all their dogs and cats. I'm dying to unpack so I can hang all my paintings, so Richard can put out all his books—so I can have a house to take care of.") She also admits to worrying that her movie-star status has been detrimental to her children ("No, we're terribly proud of you" is their answer, Elizabeth tells us).

She takes delight in disparaging her own impressive beauty, especially when quoting Burton as "a perverse tease! He will describe me to a reporter as 'my comfy, nice little girl,' and then throw in something about a double chin and stumpy legs, ending with 'she has breakfast like any normal person. There are times when she is so normal I am tempted to leave her.'" Elizabeth always thought Ava Gardner, Lena Horne, and her own daughter Liza Todd far more beautiful. She'd never stopped considering Jacqueline Kennedy exquisite, her great dignity enhancing her beauty. "I am pretty enough," she writes. "My best feature is my gray hairs. I have them all named; they're all called Burton."

Perhaps most surprisingly to her fans, she offers the possibility that she and Burton will "go into semiretirement in a few years. I think Richard will eventually give up acting to become a serious writer." What follows is a joyful description of her private moments with Burton:

My favorite time is when we're alone at night, giggling and talking about books, world events, poetry, the children, when we first met, problems, daydreams, real dreams. Even our fights are fun. Richard loses his temper with such enjoyment that it's beautiful to watch—he goes off like a bomb—sparks fly, walls shake, floors reverberate. . . . Above all I want very much to please Richard, not to be pleased.

Scandalous love can be forgiven, even by Americans, if, after all, it results in a genuine marriage—intimacy and companionship—which the Burtons seem to have found, so far, four months shy of their first wedding anniversary. Elizabeth goes on to describe a mystical tie she shares with Burton, recalling two Chagall-like, out-of-body experiences:

. . . once, for instance, on shipboard, when he was walking through the dining room toward me; again during a party when he was mesmerizing a bunch of people. I sort of detached myself, as though I were floating upward and looking down with great clarity on the two of us—like in a Chagall painting. Then a shock, a thrill, goes through my entire body. . . . It's almost as if I were seeing him for the first time, falling in love with him again.

MARRIED LOVE

"I can't say it in words like that, but my heart is there."
—ELIZABETH TAYLOR

"We live in a blaze of floodlights all day long."
— RICHARD BURTON

Between filming *The Sandpiper* and *Who's Afraid of Virginia Woolf?*, Elizabeth had talked often with Montgomery Clift over the telephone, trying to keep up Clift's interest in working together, trying to keep up his spirits. By the time Burton was treading the boards in *Hamlet*, Clift's career was nearly over. His struggle with alcohol and barbiturates had made him virtually unemployable. When he'd acted with Marilyn Monroe in *The Misfits* in 1961, Monroe had commented, "Monty has even more problems than I do." In 1964, he was emaciated, down to a hundred pounds, and Elizabeth had been shocked at his appearance.

Clift was one of Elizabeth's dearest friends. Their bond had been forged when the actor had partnered Elizabeth so sublimely in *A Place in the Sun*. MGM had loaned Elizabeth to Paramount to appear in the film, George Stevens's adaptation of Theodore Dreiser's *An American Tragedy*. She believed that it was Monty Clift who had first introduced method acting to the movies, not Marlon Brando or James Dean.

"Though we were linked romantically by the media," she recalled, "I sensed from the beginning that Monty was torn between what he thought he should be and what he actually was." During the shoot, they developed a loving and lasting friendship, which only deepened when the troubled young actor crashed his car into a telephone pole after leaving Elizabeth and Michael Wilding's Benedict Canyon home.

Elizabeth had virtually saved Clift's life that night in 1956, crawling into the crushed vehicle and pulling out two teeth that had lodged in his throat, cradling his head before the ambulance arrived. He survived, but the broodingly handsome actor had suffered devastating facial injuries that left his face stiff and slightly disfigured. By the time he appeared in *Suddenly, Last Summer* with Elizabeth in 1959, he seemed a haunted man.

During the run of *Hamlet*, the Burtons had occasionally dined with Clift at his East 61st Street brownstone, or at Dinty Moore's in the theater district, where an unacknowledged rivalry for Elizabeth's affection often played out. At one such occasion, Richard had turned to Elizabeth and said, "Monty, Elizabeth likes me, but she loves you." Clift never told Elizabeth what he thought of Richard, that he jealously dismissed him as "a phony actor."

Nonetheless, Richard got into the act, suggesting that the three of them costar in a remake of Ernest Hemingway's *The Macomber Affair*, but Clift wasn't too keen on the idea. Elizabeth thought of other projects that she and her friend might do together, such as starring in the film version of *The Owl and the Pussycat*. They could always make each other laugh, and both had longed to do a comedy together.

Robert Lantz, Clift's Austrian-born agent, suggested they consider starring in a film adaptation of a novel written by another one of his clients—Carson McCullers's *Reflections in a Golden Eye*, a Southern gothic tale about desire and sexual repression. Clift would play Major Weldon Penderton, a latent homosexual army officer obsessed with a young private, who, in turn, is obsessed with the major's beautiful wife, Leonora, played by Elizabeth.

Elizabeth had already agreed to play the part of Leonora, but Ray Stark, who was going to produce the film for Seven Arts, was nervous about insuring Clift and insisted that he put up his cherished brownstone as collateral. Desperate for work, he considered doing so, but Elizabeth wouldn't let him. After time spent with Clift in New York, however, Elizabeth had confided to one of her press agents, "If Monty doesn't work soon, he'll die."

Elizabeth was driving this train. And when she took it upon herself to announce to the press that she and Monty were going to costar in another film—their first since *Suddenly, Last Summer* in 1959— she was, in effect, forcing Stark and Seven Arts to accept Clift as her costar. When Stark pleaded with her to reconsider, Elizabeth shot back that "she would pay the bloody insurance," offering to give up her million-dollar fee.

Elizabeth had not just come to the rescue of another close friend; she was trying to give Clift back his career, his reason for living. And unlike Richard, Elizabeth was unfazed by McCullers's subject. It was part of her fearlessness—or, if she did have such fears, they were quickly conquered by her devotion to her gay friends and fellow actors. It is what allowed her, decades later, to step onto the world stage as the first prominent advocate for AIDS research and the compassionate care of HIV and AIDS patients. It is what made her so convincing when she begged Richard to renounce his shame over his hemophilia and epilepsy. (She also reminded him of the great princes of Europe with whom Richard shared these afflictions). None of the books in Richard's vast library had given him the courage with which to embrace those conditions, accept them, and deal with them, the way Elizabeth did. He was grateful to her for it. In fact, his gratitude went so deep that, when he was in his cups, he might even resent her for it. And then the imprecations would begin. And it drove her to tears when he came after her with that beautiful voice saying such ugly things.

Clift read the script of *Reflections in a Golden Eye* and was eager to do it, but when Elizabeth told him that Richard wanted not only to costar but to direct the movie, Clift became upset. He had never cared for Richard's acting (he called it "reciting"), and the macho Welshman made him feel uneasy. He and Roddy McDowall had often discussed "poor Richard," as they called him behind his back. He kept it a secret from Elizabeth—"Bessie Mae"—what he really thought of Richard. It was Elizabeth he loved, not "Liz and Dick," though it must have pained him that Richard's career had surged alongside Elizabeth's, while his own had languished.

When Monty and Elizabeth were together, or had long phone conversations, they would compare injuries and illnesses. Clift thought that was funny, and he would come up with a catalog of Elizabeth's ailments: ruptured spinal disc, bronchitis, phlebitis, ulcerated eye, tracheotomy . . . They could laugh at themselves. It was a trait Elizabeth shared with Richard, but one that Clift was unwilling to share with Elizabeth's husband.

But the two men shared something else: their love of Bessie Mae. Both men took her seriously, appreciated her intelligence. Her emotional life meant something to them, and they cared about her as a person. Clift was, according to his biographer Patricia Bosworth, "the first person to take her seriously as a thinking, feeling human being." Richard was devoted to her in that way as well. But having Elizabeth/Bessie Mae in common did not bring the two men any closer. According to Bosworth, Clift even tried putting his thoughts about Richard into a letter, explaining why it would be impossible for the two men to ever work together. Thanks to Clift's thoughtful secretary, however, the letter was never sent.

In any case, Richard backed away from *Reflections*, deciding not to do it, after all. With Elizabeth's help, he had come a very long way in accepting the homosexual dalliances of his youth. "The world is round, get over it," she had told him. "You chose me, didn't you? It's a choice, and you made yours. I'm the luckier for it." But perhaps McCullers's dark tale made Richard feel uncomfortable in the role. Anyway, hadn't he just torn his heart out as George? Also, in his unacknowledged, maybe even unrecognized, contest for Elizabeth's affections, Richard didn't like the role of Major Penderton, that of "a third banana," as one agent who had read the script described it. So plans were made to film McCullers's novel—which would be the first time a homosexual character would appear in a major motion picture—with Monty Clift slated to play Elizabeth's husband.

The Taming of the Shrew, which would put a positive, sexy spin on their new image as "the Battling Burtons," was filmed in March and April of 1966, in Rome, the city that had first turned them into "Liz and Dick." As they were often influenced by the roles they were playing, it was a blessing—or a stroke of genius—that they were now able to turn their famous fights into near-slapstick in Shakespeare's comedy. *The public likes to see us fight? We'll show them! And show them what marriage really means.*

Approaching their second wedding anniversary, they were well aware that their private lives were going to be lived in public, no matter what. "The truth is," Burton told the *Daily Mirror*, "we live out, for the benefit of the mob, the sort of idiocies they've come to expect. We will often pitch a battle purely for the exercise. I will accuse her of being ugly, she will accuse me of being a talentless son of a bitch, and this sort of frightens people. . . . I love arguing with Elizabeth, except when she is in the nude . . ." They loudly traded all sorts of silly and insulting endearments, like "Mabel" or "Mabes," "Lumpy," "Twit Twaddle," "Snapshot," and "One Take" for Elizabeth; and "Fred," "Charlie Charm," "Old Shoot," "Boozed-up, Burned-out Welshman," and "Pockmarked Welshman" for Richard. And they did it all in public. Elizabeth learned about a couple staying at the Regency Hotel, who took the suite below theirs just so they could eavesdrop on the Burtons' *battles royale*. They reportedly climbed up on chairs, placed empty glasses against the ceiling, and listened in. "Well, they got an earful," said Elizabeth, "but what the poor schmoes didn't know was that it was a vocal exercise."

The Burtons knew each other's vulnerabilities: Richard's sensitivity over Elizabeth's higher earning power and top billing, for example. Elizabeth's sensitivity over her fluctuating weight and her increasing frustration with Richard's drinking. "I think you should go and take a nap, Old Shoot," she'd tell him. "You're drunk again. I mean—the hair of the dog was the whole dog this time!" Often their quarrels were a kind of teasing foreplay, or sheer theatrics meant to entertain themselves and anyone within earshot. But their squabbles could take a darker turn. In the first few months of filming *Virginia Woolf*, Elizabeth had occasionally found it difficult to shake off the iron grip of Martha. At times, "Martha completely took me over," she admitted. Though their off-screen life was less tempestuous during the making of *Virginia Woolf*, there were times when, as Elizabeth recalled, "Richard and I would be out with friends and I'd hear myself saying to him, 'For Chrissakes, shut up. I'm not finished talking.' And then the next morning, I would think, 'That wasn't me, it was Martha.' I had to fight to regain myself."

By the mid-1960s, the institution of marriage was under siege in America, as reflected in movies like *Sweet November*, in which Sandy Dennis played a "liberated" woman who prefers to spend each month living with a different man rather than look for a life mate, and *Guide for the Married Man*, a comedy that exploited the phenomenon of "swinging" (i.e., adulterous) married couples in the suburbs.

But—ever ahead of the curve—the Burtons were making *married* love glamorous and sexy. They had been such notorious, dangerous people in the two years following *Cleopatra* that they had found themselves shunned by longtime friends, like Rex Harrison and Emlyn Williams. But after *Hamlet*, Elizabeth noticed, everything changed. "There is no deodorant like success," she said at the time. She sensed a change in how she and Burton were being regarded. "Richard and I are going through a period now, I feel, in which a lot of people are beginning to realize that we're not monsters. Some may even like us for being honest. Some may even have an inkling of what bloody hell it was . . ."

But the tabloid press remained "more interested in illicit love, rather than married love," she quickly came to realize. With the insatiable hunger for scandal, an addiction that had to be fed, the tabloids and even mainstream publications came out with stories like "Is Liz Legally Wed? (When Richard Touches Me, Nothing Else Matters: Her Own Story)." And when they couldn't find a sexy angle, the press covered their fights ("Liz Confesses: Burton's Ruining Me with Liquor" announced *Photoplay*, and "Richard Burton to Liz: I Love Thee Not" claimed the *Saturday Evening Post*). The press descended to a new low when, in the lounge of the Lancaster Hotel in Paris, the Burtons were bushwhacked by a photographer and two women. While the photographer snapped pictures, the two women exchanged words in German. It immediately dawned on the Burtons what was going on.

"Is that Maria's mother?" Elizabeth and Richard both asked, alarmed that the birth mother of their adopted child had been brought in to confront them.

"Yes. I'm a great friend of hers and I'm going to interpret for her," the younger of the two women said.

"You're no friend of hers!" Elizabeth shouted. "You're a journalist. Get out of here before I kill you!" When Richard's anger boiled over, the woman fled. The Burtons took Maria's mother aside and tried to comfort her, but she spoke only German. Luckily, the Burtons' lawyer, Aaron Frosch, who spoke Yiddish and a little German, came by and interpreted for them. They found out that one of the tabloid newspapers had tricked Maria's mother into coming to Paris, supposedly at the Burtons' invitation, so she could visit her daughter and come away with some money. They'd been in Paris for a week, waiting to ambush the Burtons. The photographer had also tried to take a picture of Maria in the Burtons' Rolls-Royce, with Maria's mother in a tattered coat looking longingly at the daughter she had given up for adoption. "How cruel to use those poor people in that way," Elizabeth said about the ugly incident.

The press also made much of Elizabeth's plans to move permanently to England, the country of her birth. "Elizabeth Taylor Seeks to End U.S. Citizenship" wrote the *Los Angeles Times*; "Liz Can Slash Taxes as Briton" the *Los Angeles Herald Examiner* proclaimed erroneously. The *New York Times*, however, got it right. Elizabeth had dual citizenship and would have had to forswear allegiance to the United States in order to divest herself of her American citizenship. This she declined to do, keeping her American passport (proudly made out in the name of Mrs. Richard Burton). "I love America," she wrote in her memoir. "I want to do nothing that might seem ungrateful or might hinder my returning here. But I don't like living in Hollywood." It's true that they could live a more private life in England, where they could go to pubs unimpeded, and be greeted by friends, not fans or scolds. More important, Elizabeth knew that Britain was Burton's home, and she wanted to be wherever Richard was happiest.

In 1964 and 1965, they continued to inspire a cottage industry of quickly written books about their lives and lifestyle: Ruth Waterbury, former editor of *Photoplay* and founder of *Silver Screen*, brought out two paperbacks—*Elizabeth Taylor, Her Life, Her Loves, Her Future*, followed quickly by *Richard Burton, His Intimate Story*. Taylor's own book helped to set the record straight on a number of things, and Burton was delighted to have his first short story published in 1964— the Dylan Thomas–inspired, highly autobiographical tale of his early childhood in Wales, called *A Christmas Story*. And his charming essay about meeting Elizabeth, "Meeting Mrs. Jenkins," which first appeared in *Vogue* ("Burton Writes of Taylor"), was brought out in a hardcover edition in 1965.

The Taming of the Shrew would be the Burtons' first coproduction, which was made for Columbia Pictures. Actually, perhaps, it was their second, according to Richard: "The marriage," he told a *Life* magazine reporter, "was our first." Also named as coproducer was their film director Franco Zeffirelli, who had made his reputation as a designer of opulent opera sets, especially his lush, oversize productions of *La Bohème* and *La Traviata*. He would also have been known to Burton for directing two memorable Shakespearean productions at the Old Vic—one notable for its artistic achievement and popularity (*Romeo and Juliet*), the other notably misguided (*Othello*, with John Gielgud). Later in his film career, Zeffirelli would direct two more visually stunning, crowd-pleasing film adaptations of Shakespeare, *Romeo and Juliet* and *Hamlet* with Mel Gibson.

While in Dublin, where Richard was filming *The Spy Who Came in from the Cold*, the Burtons met with Zeffirelli, who had flown in to discuss the prospect of casting them as Petruchio and Katharina (Kate). Though he'd originally thought of Sophia Loren and Marcello Mastroianni for the leads, he had heard from an intermediary that Burton was eager to take on another Shakespearean role.

When the Italian director arrived at their hotel in Dublin, he found their household in a not-unusual state of near chaos. Elizabeth had taken in a new pet—a tiny, leaping African primate known as a "bush baby." God knows where she'd picked it up, but it was wreaking havoc in the luxurious suite, ripping up cushions and curtains and overturning lamps. It had retreated to the bathroom, clinging to the hot-water pipes, while Elizabeth yelled at Richard to come immediately to rescue it. But Burton was deep in conversation with Zeffirelli on the proposed Shakespearean production.

"Will you please stop talking about your damned Shakespeare and give me a hand!" Elizabeth shrieked.

Burton, nursing a drink, yelled, "Will you please stop this bloody nonsense with that horrendous little monster and come and talk to this man? He's a superb Shakespearean director and you might be lucky enough to work with him one day. Can't you be more pleasant to him?"

"I don't care what he thinks of me," Elizabeth retorted. "All I want is some help for my bush baby."

Zeffirelli claims that the only reason he was able to get Elizabeth onboard to play Kate was that he was able to go into the bathroom and rescue the little bush baby, which by now was exhausted and allowed itself to be removed from the hot-water pipes and placed in Elizabeth's arms. That did the trick. Later, the Burtons flew Zeffirelli to Elizabeth's home in Gstaad, where they further discussed the film, and Burton suggested that the director contact his old mentor, his adopted father Philip Burton.

"I wondered if I was going to find myself arguing with some sort of dusty Welsh bookworm with petty notions of how the Bard should be preserved," Zeffirelli recalled. Luckily, the director found Philip Burton "a charming, well-informed gentleman, only too happy to listen to my ideas and quite entranced by everything we were planning to do." Plans went ahead despite an apparent lack of interest on Elizabeth's part, fueling more squabbles. Zeffirelli remembered one such spat when Richard referred to Elizabeth as "a Hollywood baby."

"A golden baby," she shot back.

"Well, you certainly like gold and you're as plump as a baby."

"There are countries where they like women with a little meat on them," Elizabeth retorted. "If they hadn't banned my films because I'm pro-Israel, those Arabs would be drooling over me. Just take care I don't meet a rich sheik."

But they decided to take on the film, and coproduce it, waiving their own salaries. ("We had invested $2 million in this venture and I didn't want another *Cleopatra*," Burton confided in his notebooks.) Once the Burton-Zeffirelli production got underway, filmed entirely on created sets in Rome, the Burtons' star magnitude did much to elevate Zeffirelli's status.

The Burtons flew to the Eternal City to begin work on *The Taming of the Shrew*, where, on March 15, 1966, they would celebrate their second wedding anniversary. After the harrowing debacle of filming *Cleopatra*, they had sworn off Rome. Nonetheless, they moved into another luxurious villa, on Via Appia Antica, the Old Appian Way, with full entourage (Dick Hanley and John Lee, Bob and Sally Wilson, Elizabeth's makeup expert Ron Berkeley, their chauffeur Gaston Sanz, their usual bodyguard Bobby LaSalle, plus a tutor, a governess, and a nurse for Maria—all paid for by Burton). They settled in with their family ("four children, dogs, cats, goldfish, tortoises, a rabbit, and a bird"), and, according to one source, eight additional bodyguards. They were living like royalty, and royalty were now their only peers. They socialized with Princess Grace (formerly Grace Kelly, now a *real* princess) and her husband, Prince Rainier of Monaco; Baron and Baroness Guy de Rothschild; the fetching Princess Elizabeth of Yugoslavia; and that other scandalously married couple, now safely past middle-age and beyond scandal—the Duke and Duchess of Windsor.

The Burtons still felt the taste of ashes from *Le Scandale* in their mouths, but the atmosphere had changed. Where once they had been hounded by the paparazzi, the fire had died down—somewhat—now that they were respectably married. They were still followed by photographers, but it was less frenzied. The press still managed to get under Burton's skin by baiting him as "Mr. Taylor No. 5."

A visual genius, the charming, blue-eyed Zeffirelli knew exactly how he wanted his production of *Shrew* to look, down to the opulently dressed extras (many of whom, incidentally, were Zeffirelli's own cousins, uncles, and aunts). In 1958, he had traveled to England to direct Joan Sutherland in *Lucia di Lammermoor* at Covent Garden. When he met the diva, bundled up against the English cold, the first words out of his mouth were, "Where are the bosoms?" And that's how he wanted his actresses—especially Elizabeth—to look: overflowing décolletage in fabulous costumes. And to emphasize Petruchio's manliness and mastery, he wanted his costumes to be outsized, larger than life. But in this he ran into trouble with Irene Sharaff, Elizabeth's friend and preferred costume designer whom she'd hired for the production. Sharaff had something more modest in mind for Burton. Noting Richard's rather large head and narrow shoulders (Claire Bloom had once described him as looking like Caliban), Zeffirelli insisted on doing it his way. Elizabeth wouldn't have Irene fired (she was nothing if not loyal to her friends and employees), so they compromised: Sharaff designed Elizabeth's costumes and Danilo Donati designed Richard's.

As for Burton, he told the director that he "didn't give a damn" about the costume as long as "it's light to wear," but when he showed up on set in Donati's magnificent, capaciously sleeved costume, he roared, "Good! I feel like a lion." Shearing off nearly half of the play's dialogue, Zeffirelli set about to make this the most rollicking, comic, opulent, and enjoyable *Shrew* ever filmed. "It was all very Douglas Fairbanks, with lots of athletic action, yet [we] never lost sight of its classical origins," Zeffirelli wrote in his autobiography. Purists, however, like the veteran stage actor Cyril Cusack, who played Petruchio's servant, Grumio, in the film, would mock the production as "Shakespeare-elli."

This would be Zeffirelli's first film, and Elizabeth's first Shakespearean role, about which she had considerable misgivings. Just as she had been the only actress in *Virginia Woolf* without stage training, she would be taking on the Bard in a company of mostly veteran Shakespearean actors—Burton, of course; Cyril Cusack; Victor Spinetti; young Michael York; and Michael Hordern (who had appeared with them in *The V.I.P.s* and with Burton in *The Spy Who Came in from the Cold*). "Why can't we take on one death-defying risk at a time?" she'd complained, mock-seriously, to Burton.

"Elizabeth was very shy to play Shakespeare to begin with," remembered Zeffirelli, "but she brought a marvelous devotion. On the first day, I remember, she was like a girl coming to her marriage too young; she had extreme concern and humility. That day, she was really enchanting . . . I consider that Elizabeth, with no Shakespearean background, gave the more interesting performance because she invented the part from scratch."

The film was shot at the Dino De Laurentiis Studios just outside of Rome, where four enormous soundstages were transformed into sixteenth-century Padua. The Burtons would be driven each morning in the Rolls-Royce, past the Colosseum, to their suite of palatial dressing rooms, complete with kitchen, offices, and white carpeting throughout. There they would be ministered to by a small battalion of servants—"maids, secretaries, and butlers as well as hairdressers and makeup artists." They often held court there for visiting journalists and columnists, like Sheilah Graham, and famous friends, like Rudolf Nureyev and Edward Albee.

At first, Zeffirelli had to work around their different schedules—Burton showing up promptly at seven thirty a.m. and ready for his first take at nine twenty, but Elizabeth not turning up until nearly eleven a.m. ("[her] morning was given over to her famous face—skin massage, eyebrow-plucking or whatever," the director supposed). Even worse, a long, festive lunch party was held most days in their dressing rooms, lasting from one to four in the afternoon. Impossible to work after that! Zeffirelli got them to agree to adhere to "French hours"—starting at noon and working straight through till eight p.m., with a break for tea. But that didn't work either—it meant the whole crew had to stay on set all day—so they ended up working from eight in the morning till three in the afternoon, without a break, despite Elizabeth's dislike of starting so early. For all the problems her habits initially caused, the director was impressed by how well she understood the camera. "She is not called 'one-shot Liz' for nothing," he recalled. Of course, as the Burtons were producing the film, they had an added incentive to bring it in on time.

There would be little late-night carousing: Richard rehearsed with Elizabeth every evening, helping her master Shakespearean verse. Despite the pressures on the Burtons, now responsible for the entire production, the set was surprisingly convivial, with everyone pitching in. There were spontaneous poetry readings (Burton reciting Dylan Thomas, of course), and Victor Spinetti, who played Hortensio in the film (and who was in the first flush of his movie fame after appearing in *A Hard Day's Night* and *Help!*), recalled how

Elizabeth pitched in where needed. When Zeffirelli realized that he required fifty extras onscreen for a scene to be shot the next day, the makeup department rebelled—"We'll have to start at five thirty!" they wailed. Elizabeth immediately told her director, "Don't worry. I'll do it." And she did, starting early the next morning, applying makeup to fifty extras, and doing Spinetti's makeup, as well. "May I give you a beauty tip?" she'd asked the actor, who was Welsh despite his Italian name. "Always extend the eyebrows. They set your eyes farther apart . . . Oh, and don't use an eyebrow pencil. Use an ordinary lead one."

Even though the frenzy had died down considerably since *Cleopatra* days, the Burtons still found themselves tailed by paparazzi on their occasional forays into Rome's nightlife, or on rare jaunts outside the city. When they managed to get away to Positano on a short break from filming, Burton took their poodle, E'en So, for a walk outside their hotel. His very presence caused an enormous traffic jam. Somehow they had found him out. Burton, who was essentially solitary, even antisocial when sober, found the attention nightmarish. Hounded by the shouts of the public and the exploding flashcubes of paparazzi, Burton fled back to the hotel. He confided in his diary: "I never gaped at anybody in my life and much as I admire certain famed people, Churchill, and various writers . . . Dylan Thomas, T. S. Eliot . . . etc., etc., I have never asked them for an autograph. I actually feel as embarrassed seeing a public figure as being one."

After an evening in Rome when the Burtons had dined with Zeffirelli and a visiting Edward Albee, Burton recorded:

Albee was very flattering, especially to E. about *V. Woolf* and, for him, was very talkative . . . we had a hair-raising drive, pursued by paparazzi all the way. I think Mario the driver takes too much notice of these butterflies of the gutter. They risk their lives, too . . . why don't they go where there's real risk. Like a war. Like Viet Nam. Like anywhere.

So when Zeffirelli wanted to arrange an outing with the Burtons to see the famed Villa D'Este fountains, they had to plan a bus trip on a Sunday night, when the grounds were closed to tourists.

"Wonderful! A bus trip," Burton said, rather wistfully. "I haven't been on one of those since I was a boy."

Elizabeth was just as keen on the idea. "We'll make an evening of it," she said, according to Spinetti. "Everybody come up to the villa first. I'll order in hamburgers and hot dogs from Nathan's and we'll eat them before we set off." And so she did—grilling all afternoon and serving them with lots of yellow mustard and cold beer. The trip to the Villa D'Este, however, was canceled when Cyril Cusack suffered a mild heart attack, ending their plans and postponing the shoot for two days. Still, the night of grilling hamburgers and hot dogs was just the kind of simple pleasure that Elizabeth loved—the camaraderie, playing mama to a crew of actors, the homey, unbeatable American food.

There were other simple pleasures. Between takes on the set, Richard would finish the crossword puzzles from the London newspapers, and Elizabeth would playfully spill her drinks over his pages. Burton also enjoyed taking Liza and Maria to school in the morning, while their two brothers, Michael and Christopher, appeared as extras in crowd scenes in the movie. Richard also loved buying books— twenty or thirty paperbacks in one haul—at a favorite bookshop on Via Veneto. In the evenings, he dined alone with Elizabeth; they often read favorite passages to each other during their meals. And then— to bed, where Richard worshipped at "the exquisite softness of the inside of your thighs . . . the half hostile look in your eyes when you're deep in rut with your little Welsh stallion," as he would later write in a heartsick letter to his beloved.

Michael York, who made his film debut as a greatly appealing Lucentio, has remained forever grateful to the Burtons for signing off on him for the role and thus launching his long, distinguished career in film. He shared Burton's love of antiquarian books. "I would sometimes find books in marketplaces," he recalled, "and show them to Richard. I would pick up these old rare books, and we would talk about them on the set." Actually, the young actor would show Burton his finds, and Burton would just assume they were gifts. "They were like gods to be showered with offerings, they strode the world like two Colossi," according to York. When he found a book of bawdy lyrics that he showed to Richard, Burton said, "Thank you," and greedily pocketed it. The same thing happened to the photographer David Bailey when he appeared on the set and demonstrated a new camera— within minutes, it belonged to the Burtons. And, as usual, Elizabeth expected her tribute from her director, letting Zeffirelli know about a little shop on Via Condotti that held a bauble she wanted. That shop was Bulgari's, and Zeffirelli bought it for her: a gold bracelet that had once belonged to Napoleon's sister.

York was impressed with how good Elizabeth was, tackling Shakespeare for the first time, noticing that even her biggest liability— her thin, sometimes shrill voice—"was well suited" for the role of Katharina the shrew. He also took great pleasure in watching Burton's Petruchio evolve, and indeed it's a pleasure to witness Burton's masculine swagger and braggadocio, as he goes from lion-tamer to the one being tamed.

York also noticed how each brought something to the relationship that the other lacked, "Richard bringing Elizabeth culture with a capital K," and Elizabeth "revving up his courage, making him realize his potential. That was her gift to him." When he saw *Virginia Woolf* a few months later (it was released in June of that year), he was deeply impressed by their performances. "I loved it," he recalled. "I thought about them a lot after having seen the movie, because there's that undertow of sadness. But they were wonderful to me, and I owe them a great deal. They gave me my chance."

If their evenings were becoming more bookish, by day the set was something of a moveable feast, with old and new friends stopping by to visit the Burtons. In early April, Mike Nichols visited, with Mia Farrow on his arm. ("That M. Nichols really gets the girls,"

Burton recorded in his diary on April 5. "I wish Farrow would put on 15 pounds and grow her hair.") The Burtons always enjoyed being around Nichols, though he had put them through their paces in *Virginia Woolf.* Elizabeth considered him "one of the most brilliant and nicest people I've ever known." They had also been impressed that of all the many directors they'd worked with, together and separately, he was the only one who had memorized Lehman's entire script (which was virtually Albee's play, with one additional location and only two words changed).

Nichols, a German Jew who had emigrated to America as a boy on the eve of World War II, had a wry, self-deprecating manner that appealed to Burton far more than the florid personality of their Italian director. After Nichols left, Burton wrote in his diary,

> I'm not sure I like Zeffirelli. As a mind and a personality, he's not a patch on M. Nichols. But he has flair, shall we say. He has a sense of the spectacular. He will succeed. Yesterday he was worried again about his billing. I told him for the umpty-ninth time to fix it with Columbia, and that whatever was mutually agreeable to them was also so to us.

One of Elizabeth Taylor's biographers, Brenda Maddox, made the rather surprising discovery that Sigmund Freud's Welsh biographer, Ernest Jones, had referred to the Welsh as "the Jews of Britain," a comment on their self-identity as the underdogs and outsiders of the United Kingdom. In that light, Maddox rather playfully remarked, "Burton was [Taylor's] third Jewish husband."

Elizabeth had completely embraced Judaism after her conversion to marry Mike Todd, an identity that had roots in her childhood. "During the war, as a kid," she wrote, "I had Walter Mitty dreams about being Jewish and wishing I was . . . after Mike and I were married, I had told him that I wanted to be a Jewess." When Todd died so suddenly, she'd found true comfort in Judaism. "I am absolutely

Jewish now in my beliefs and feelings," she later wrote, taking as her Jewish name Elisheba Rachel. For Elizabeth, increasingly a citizen of the world, it gave her an identity beyond that of actress, adulterer, wife, and mother. It was as necessary to her as Burton's Welshness, as a way to stay rooted in their gypsy life.

But her Jewishness was one of the things Burton loved to tease her about, and sometimes they'd have real fights over it. "My great-grand-father," Burton told a reporter, "was a Polish Jew named Jan Ysar, and that was the family name until they changed it to Jenkins. It's true. I'm one-eighth Jewish. Elizabeth hasn't a drop of Jewish blood. I've told her so. It makes her furious." Earlier, during the making of *The Night of the Iguana*, in a thatched roof bar in Puerto Vallarta, a drunken Burton had announced, "I was born a Jew. I am perhaps the very oldest of the really ancient Jews."

"You're not Jewish at all," he told Elizabeth in one of their very public fights—which members of their staff had taken to timing. "If there's any Jew in this family, it's me!"

"I *am* Jewish," she answered. "And you can fuck off!"

But in a few years he would begin to pour out his heart to her in a series of intimate letters, sometimes addressing her as "Dear Sheba," a version of her Jewish name, or, playfully, "Shebes," as in an undated letter: "All my love. Never think of anything but you for very long. I fancy you a very lot, Shebes.—Rich."

In June, the Burtons and Zeffirelli were invited to Princess Pigna-telli's home, where they saw Robert and Ethel Kennedy, whom they'd met during their *Hamlet* year. They dined out and ended up at a night-club, and on the way back to the Hotel Eden, where the Kennedys were staying, Burton and Bobby Kennedy got into a poetry competi-tion, each trying to outdo the other in reciting Shakespeare's sonnets from memory. In the hotel lobby, Richard won the contest by throw-ing back his head and roaring out Shakespeare's 15th Sonnet ("When I Consider Everything That Grows") *backward*, without missing a syllable. Elizabeth, beaming with pride, said, "Isn't it awful to have to tolerate this monster?"

The Burtons adored Robert Kennedy. It's interesting to note that two years later, in June 1968, when the senator was assassinated in the kitchen of the Ambassador Hotel in Los Angeles, just after winning the California primary for the Democratic presidential nomination, Elizabeth spent $50,000 on a full-page advertisement in the *New York Times* pleading for gun control.

The Burtons' five months in Rome—unlike their first experience there—were idyllic, alternately sacred and profane, like the city itself. There were more visits to Bulgari's "money room," resplendent with antiques and silver-and-gold samovars, where the Burtons would examine the "crème de la crème pieces" that were reserved for special patrons.

One evening after sharing a peasant meal of cheese, kidney beans, and *vin du pays* in a trattoria near the Church of the Madonna of Divine Love, they heard the celestial strains of a boy's choir emanating from the church. Burton wrote tenderly in his diary: "It was one of those moments which are nostalgia before they're over." Again, the familiar refrain about wanting to stop making films—"Both Eliz. and I agreed solemnly that we never want to work again, but simply loll our lives away in a sort of eternal Sunday. Quite right, too. We are both bone-lazy and enjoy it."

But the truth about idylls is that idylls must end. Elizabeth's contentment was shattered by the sudden death on July 22 of Montgomery Clift, and it fell to Richard to give her the grim news.

Clift had died in his New York City brownstone. His secretary, Lorenzo James, had discovered him sprawled across his bed, having apparently suffered a heart attack after years of alcohol abuse.

Richard took Elizabeth's loss very seriously. He later recorded in his diary:

Sept. 24. [Monty's] companion, nurse, and major domo very kindly sent E. his (Monty's) handkerchiefs, which he had only recently bought in Paris, and which he loved, delicate white on white. And to me—Monty's favorite soap! Should I use it or keep it? E. was very upset and still cannot believe he's dead. A little Monty Clift cult has started since his death. It would have been more useful when he was alive. He couldn't get a decent job for the last 5 yrs of his life. Poor sod. I didn't know him very well, but he seemed a good man. E. has received a couple of lovely letters from his mother.

Elizabeth was devastated. Unwilling to stop production for a few days, however, she did not attend Monty's funeral, instead sending two huge bouquets of white chrysanthemums, which were placed near the casket. Her accompanying card read, "Rest, perturbed spirit— Elizabeth and Richard." But she broke down and wept on the set. Then, pulling herself together, she gave one of her best, and funniest, performances on the day of her friend's funeral.

Now she would have to find another actor to replace Clift in *Reflections in a Golden Eye*, which would be filmed that year, also in Rome, at the De Laurentiis Studios.

Four months earlier, in April, Burton received another slight from the Academy of Motion Picture Arts and Sciences. He'd been nominated for Best Actor for his work in *The Spy Who Came in from the Cold*—his fourth nomination—but it was Lee Marvin who won, for his comic portrayal of a sloshed gunfighter in *Cat Ballou*. "What do you think they're trying to tell me? That Lee Marvin is a better class of drunk?" Burton quipped, but as his nominations and his losses piled up, it was beginning to trouble him. (He was in good company, though, as Lee Marvin's hilarious but lightweight performance beat out Laurence Olivier's *Othello*, Rod Steiger's star role in *The Pawnbroker*, and Oskar Werner—who had also appeared in *Spy* with Burton—in *Ship of Fools*.) Though Burton was often cavalier about acting, dismissing it as an unmanly profession, it bothered him that

Taylor had her Oscar for *BUtterfield 8*, and despite four nominations now, the prize continued to elude him.

Two months later, on June 29, 1966, *Who's Afraid of Virginia Woolf?* was released in New York to mostly ecstatic reviews, later garnering thirteen Academy Award nominations. Both Richard and Elizabeth were nominated for Best Actor and Best Actress awards. Maybe this time he would win.

In October 1966, *LOOK* magazine, in yet another opulently illustrated cover story on the Burtons, asked the question: "Does Burton Tame the Shrew, as Shakespeare Intended?" The press was still infatuated with the couple, blurring the lines between the actors and the roles they embodied. *LOOK* even asked, in describing the Zeffirelli movie, "What other young couple would go to such lengths to make home movies for their fans?" In a flattering preview of the film, Elizabeth vividly graces the cover of the magazine in full Elizabethan dress, her black hair tumbling down her shoulders and décolletage. "Between scenes," the magazine enthused, "he spouted sonnets while she poured champagne and fed him quail eggs—just the way Liz & Dick fans would have wanted it."

On February 28, 1967, *The Taming of the Shrew* premiered in London, selected for the Royal Command Performance for a screening at the Odeon, in Leicester Square. The Burtons checked into the Dorchester on Park Lane for the premiere, and Richard reserved fourteen suites for the weekend, to house his entire Welsh clan, whom he brought in by train from Port Talbot, South Wales. They all came—Burton's six brothers and his three surviving sisters. It was the first time they had come together since the death of Edith "Edie" Jenkins, who had died a few months earlier, at the age of forty-three, the first of Burton's grown siblings to pass away. She had been the youngest, and the most playful, of all of Burton's sisters. The rest of the Jenkins clan arrived with spouses and children, plus a handful of aunts and uncles, many of the women going to the premiere in gowns from the trunkfuls of cast-off clothes Elizabeth had sent to them. (Hilda Owen wore a fuchsia-and-yellow caftan from Robinson's of Beverly Hills.) Rolls-Royces picked them up at Paddington Station and drove them to the Dorchester. The luxury was far beyond anything the Jenkinses could imagine—sumptuous flowers in every room, room service at their disposal.

For Burton, it was a triumph and a vindication. Four years earlier, he had slunk back from visiting his wife and children in Hampstead to take up his Dorchester penthouse suite to be with Elizabeth, to his family's utter disapproval. Now they were forgiven and embraced by all the living Jenkinses, and Burton savored the ability to shower his riches on his entire clan. On top of it all, it was Elizabeth's thirty-fifth birthday on February 27, adding to the mad festivities. Burton gave her—what else?—a diamond-and-emerald bracelet he'd bought at Bulgari for $320,000. The following night, he transported his family in chauffeured Daimlers to the Odeon, where he had set aside 150 premier seats for family and friends such as Emlyn Williams, Stanley Baker, Elizabeth's friend and costar in *BUtterfield 8,* Laurence Harvey, and royalty in the form of Princess Margaret and Lord Snowdon.

Before the curtain rose, Burton addressed the audience. "My real name, of course, is Richard Jenkins, and therefore my wife is Lizzie Jenkins," acknowledging his Welsh family and bringing Elizabeth into the very heart of it.

After the crowd-pleasing premiere, all the Jenkinses returned to the Dorchester for a glittering ball celebrating Elizabeth's birthday. While champagne was passed around, Verdun Jenkins held forth with family stories, to Burton's great delight. At one point during the night, Richard and his six brothers found themselves standing next to each other at the marble urinals in the Dorchester's perfumed men's room. Elizabeth later shrieked with laughter when she heard Richard's description of the Jenkins men so arrayed, all "holding their Welsh cocks."

Christopher Plummer, fresh from his success as Captain Von Trapp in *The Sound of Music* and ripely drunk, sang and played the piano while Hilda Owen offered up Welsh songs from their childhood. Graham Jenkins sang his signature piece, "Sorrento," in three languages. When Verdun was asked to join in, he yelled out, "As soon as that bloody Captain Von Trapp shuts his trap, I'll conduct the Jenkinses' hundred-voice choir, brought at enormous expense from South Wales, in a selection of hymns." Several of the Jenkins men had vied for singing prizes in their youth, their gift for music nurtured by the vibrant tradition of Welsh choral societies, in which miners' sons fought for preference and attention in the highly competitive choirs throughout the dells and valleys of Wales. Cis raised her exquisite soprano voice; Verdun and Hilda sang, with Elizabeth and Richard joining in. They all rose to sing a song for their lost sister, Edie.

They stayed on, celebrating till the first shafts of light peered through the windows of the ballroom. By now, Elizabeth was dancing with the waiters, who'd peeled off their tuxedo jackets and were down to their suspenders. Hilda and her sisters, along with Richard, took turns serving the rest of the exhausted waitstaff, while Laurence Harvey, Christopher Plummer, and other guests stood behind the bar, serving drinks to the kitchen staff and washing glasses.

By morning, Elizabeth noticed, Richard didn't want them to leave. Bags were packed and limousines were lined up in Park Lane to whisk them back to Paddington Station. "They can take a later train," he said, wanting to prolong the drinking, the reminiscing, the camaraderie. For the Burtons, such extravagant evenings would become almost routine. For the Jenkinses of Port Talbot and Pontrhydyfen, it was the celebration of a lifetime. But eventually, Richard had to let them go.

Richard never mentioned it, but his sister Hilda noted another absence among the clan that weekend. "We were only sad for one thing: my father would have been tickled pink to have been there," she later said. It was the last time Richard would see his entire family brought together.

The next day, the Burtons left the Dorchester and headed for the South of France, for a well-earned vacation. By the summer, they would find themselves in Sardinia. In September, they flew into Paris—Burton's favorite city—where they had a quiet dinner with the Duke and Duchess of Windsor and the Rothschilds before attending the European premiere of *The Taming of the Shrew*. Once again, they took up residence in the beautiful Lancaster Hotel off the Champs-Élysées. Nothing could have prepared them for the premiere at the Paris Opera House, however. "We had as much, if not more, attention as we used to have in Rome, Paris, etc., during *Le Scandale*," Burton wrote in his diary. Police barricades were set up to keep several thousand fans from storming the Opera House. Many had arrived the night before, just to stake out a spot from which to catch a glimpse of the Burtons as they emerged from their limousine. The evening turned out to be "sweet revenge," Burton wrote, "for the social ostracism we endured such a relatively little time ago." The film, and the gala that followed, was an enormous success, and the European press was out in full force. "E. wore a diadem," Burton recorded, "specially created for her by the De Beers Company of Van Cleef and Arpels, designed by Alexandre, which cost $1,200,000. With her other jewelry, she wore a total of roughly $1,500,000." When the Burtons left their hotel, it was with eight bodyguards parting the waves of hotel guests in the lobby on their way to the waiting limousine, while scores of flashcubes exploded all around them. And that was just getting into their car.

At the Opera House, another excited crowd awaited them. One of the government ministers in attendance presented Richard and Elizabeth with congratulations from President de Gaulle himself. Among the many luminaries present, "E. was unquestionably the queen of the evening," Burton wrote proudly of his wife. "They hardly photographed anybody else." Being Welsh and being Burton, the miner's son had to pinch himself until it hurt, on such magical evenings: "[T]he flattery we were subjected to was very rich and heady. It, however, I hope, has not gone to our heads." Earlier that day, Burton bought Elizabeth the jet plane that had brought them to Paris, for $960,000. "Elizabeth was not displeased," he recorded.

When the reviews came out for *The Taming of the Shrew*, there was some caviling about Zeffirelli's commedia dell'arte treatment of the Bard and the cutting and transposing of Shakespeare's dialogue. But most reviewers noticed how well-suited the material was for the famous couple, a theme picked by the movie's trailer, which announced, "Elizabeth Taylor. Richard Burton. Need we say more? . . . The world's most celebrated movie couple in the movie they were made for." A certain grudging respect was given to Elizabeth for acquitting herself well as Katharina. Hollis Alpert, who would publish a biography of Burton in 1986, wrote in *Time* magazine, "In one of her better performances, Taylor makes Kate seem the ideal bawd of Avon—a creature of beauty with a voice shrieking howls and imprecations." Burton, he writes, "catches the cadences of iambic pentameter with inborn ease . . . An inspired chase across the rooftops and into piles of fleece establishe[s] him as a kind of King Leer, the supreme embodiment of a raffish comic hero."

Indeed, that "leer" was genuine. There's a delicious sexiness to their rooftop chase, in which they begin in her parlor, continue through a wine cellar, leap over the roof tiles, fall through a trap door, and collapse into a bed of fleece, where Elizabeth all but bursts out of her low-cut bodice. She then bonks Richard on the head with a board—her own embellishment on the script—before he plants "his first whiskery kiss" on her reluctant lips. The scene in which Petruchio and Kate start to undress on their wedding night is also provocative, Kate shyly disrobing and getting into bed, only to fend off Petruchio's oafish approach by striking him with a copper bed-warmer. But in real life, Elizabeth recalled the five-month shoot as "one long honeymoon."

The final scene of reconciliation, in which Petruchio presents his tamed wife to Paduan society, was directed by Richard Burton, because Zeffirelli had left to stage a production at New York's new Metropolitan Opera. Under Richard's direction, Elizabeth gives Kate's speech glorifying female subservience:

Thy husband is thy lord, thy life, thy keeper,
Thy head, thy sovereign; one that cares for thee,
. . .

And when she is forward, peevish, sullen, sour,
And not obedient to his honest will,
What is she but a foul contending rebel,
And graceless traitor to her loving lord?

That sentiment does not go down well with modern women, but Elizabeth truly believed those words. Zeffirelli noted that most actresses deliver that speech with a wink at the audience, but Elizabeth "played it straight." Though her actions had arguably helped usher in the sexual revolution, though she would always be more famous, more powerful, and richer than her husbands, she still wanted the kind of marriage that Kate comes to prize at the conclusion of *The Taming of the Shrew.*

After the speech was given and the cameras stopped rolling, Elizabeth looked around the crowded banquet set, then at Richard, who was "deeply moved" by her delivery of Shakespeare's speech, telling her, "All right, my girl, I wish you'd put that into practice."

Elizabeth responded, "I can't say it in words like that, but my heart is there."

In that transformative scene, Kate/Elizabeth embellishes the lines with loving glances at a knot of children playing with a dog under the banquet table, followed by a meaningful look at Petruchio, as if to say, it's the presence of children that make a true marriage. As if to say, we will bring children into the world. Following the speech, Kate and Petruchio finally indulge in a long, deep kiss, then Petruchio's line, "Come, Kate, we'll to bed"—as if the entire film were foreplay to that moment.

In reality, however, Elizabeth and Richard had entered into their marriage knowing that Elizabeth would be unable to conceive a fourth time. Her deeply held desire to have a child with Richard would remain unfulfilled, which is one reason why they had been so intent on adopting and raising Maria Burton. But they wanted to give Maria another sibling, and they would later try again for another adoption. A confidante of Elizabeth's observed, "If she could have, Elizabeth would have been like Josephine Baker with her 'rainbow tribe.'" (The celebrated cabaret performer adopted twelve multi-ethnic orphans.) The loving glance from frolicking children to Richard's face was a true reflection of her emotional state, and hopes for the future, at the time.

After the scene was completed, Elizabeth suffered another health crisis. Burton wrote in his diary on April 6: "E. very ill from that bloody bleeding. We have sent for a doctor from London. I went to bed in a huge depression and nightmares of her dying." Though he doesn't describe the cause of her spontaneous bleeding in his published diary, it was probably bleeding hemorrhoids, an affliction that would recur over the next few years and would require repeated hospitalizations. The amount of blood loss was horrifying to Richard. On April 8, he wrote, "E. has blood pressure of 90—very low apparently, from loss of blood." Four days later: "E. to go into hosp. tomorrow for curettage. Came to lunch with me and felt sick and faint. On arriving home, bled. [Dr.] Price flying in from London to knock her out. Poor little thing. I shouted and bawled at her for being 'unfit' for lack of discipline, for taking too much booze. I think I was talking about myself—out of fear for her." On April 13, "Then the blower [telephone] blew and joy of joys, it was herself on the other end and the operation was over, and she was in pain but alive and will live to be shouted at another day."

Burton finished work that afternoon, removed his makeup and showered, fixed himself a vodka and tonic, and was driven to the hospital. On the way home, he had his driver, Mario, stop at St. Peter's Basilica. Burton stared at "the whole huge thing" and muttered a prayer of thanks under his breath.

8

SEDUCED BY FAUST

"I am madly in love with her at the moment,
as distinct from always loving her, and want
to make love to her every minute . . ."
—RICHARD BURTON

"I'm just a broad, but Richard is a great actor."
—ELIZABETH TAYLOR

The Burtons' $2 million investment in *The Taming of the Shrew* would net a handsome profit of $12 million, but one of the real rewards for Burton was that he was able to reconcile his two worlds: the Shakespeare he loved and many felt he was born for, and the movies he made with Elizabeth. He was now prouder of his film successes—*Becket, Iguana, Spy, Woolf*—than his stage triumphs, but he had never meant to turn his back entirely on his theatrical roots. In this, Elizabeth was his fiercest supporter. After making thirty-six films, she hoped to do the impossible—play second fiddle to Richard's career. And so: *Doctor Faustus*, which would reduce Taylor to a non-speaking role in a production dear to Burton's heart.

It seemed like a good idea at the time.

Before filming *The Taming of the Shrew* in Rome, the Burtons had traveled to Oxford in February 1966 to pay homage to Nevill Coghill,

Richard's former mentor during the six months he was in residence at Exeter College in Oxford, as part of his RAF training. Coghill, like Richard's previous mentor, Philip Burton, was probably in love with his former protégé. "This boy . . . will be a great actor. He is outstandingly handsome and robust," Coghill had written on Richard's report card when the latter was his drama student twenty years earlier; he's "very masculine and with deep inward fire . . ." Coghill invited Sir John Gielgud, Noël Coward's producer Hugh "Binkie" Beaumont, and other luminaries of British theater to take their measure of his new discovery, men who would smooth Richard's way to his theatrical career in London.

In 1944, Coghill had directed Burton in his first Shakespearean role, Angelo in *Measure for Measure*, and had famously said about his former pupil, "I have had many students of very great gifts, and many of very little. But I have had only two men of genius to teach— W. H. Auden and Richard Burton. When they happen, one cannot mistake them." Those now-idealized six months at Oxford had begun roughly for Burton. As a Welshman, older and not of the same class as most of the undergraduates, Burton had had to "bloody a few noses." He recalled, "I was fairly ruthless when I arrived at Oxford, fresh from South Wales, with a powerful Welsh accent, and determined to play the leading part in whatever Oxford University Dramatic Society (OUDS) production was coming up." But Coghill and Robert Hardy, Richard's classmate and fellow RAF trainee, were struck by Burton's sheer presence and force of personality.

"When he came to Oxford as an undergraduate in 1944," Hardy recalled, "he had an astounding beauty—a blend of classic Greek serenity and smoldering Celtic fires, emanating from mysteries and humor. And above all, the fires of enormous laughter. His laughs have always been infectious, outrageous, and terrifying. Behind it all, there is an element of Welsh magic or mystery."

Burton agreed to take the starring role in an OUDS production of Christopher Marlowe's sixteenth-century play *The Tragical History* of *Doctor Faustus*, for a charity performance that would raise nearly $40,000 to build the Oxford University Theatre. Elizabeth would appear briefly as—who else?—Helen of Troy. They looked forward to their Oxford hiatus, what life might have offered had they not stepped through the looking glass of world fame.

It was a sentimental return. Richard indulged in a fantasy of becoming an Oxford don—the road not taken, or even offered—with Elizabeth at his side, serving undergraduates cake in a low-cut dress. Elizabeth sensed in her husband a need to go back and replenish that part of his life, and she, too, fantasized about buying a house in Oxfordshire, raising show horses while Burton taught poetry and she, perhaps, taught a course on Tennessee Williams—one of her many fleeting dreams of what a "normal" life might be like.

The Burtons checked into the Randolph Hotel, a stone's throw from the Oxford Playhouse, for a three-week stay—ten days of rehearsal and a week of performances. They held court at their hotel for the student actors, who were thrilled with the Burtons' presence in Oxford and with how friendly and down-to-earth the two mega-stars were. While Elizabeth made drinks for the eager drama students, Burton regaled them with stories about his days at the Old Vic and gossip about Gielgud and Olivier and Coghill, when he first knew the latter twenty-two years ago. Coghill, in his final year as a Merton College Professor at Oxford, immediately warmed to Elizabeth, and to Burton's dresser, Bob Wilson. The tall, slim, distinguished-looking, African-American was always waiting just offstage with a glass of scotch to hand to Burton when he exited a scene, to the delight of the student actors.

For Burton, *Doctor Faustus* was a very personal play. He first read it at the age of twelve and had fallen in love with Marlowe's thrilling speeches. Now he had a chance to play the quintessential role of the scholar who sells his soul to the devil—for knowledge, for wealth, and for the world's most beautiful woman. Burton identified with Faustus on all three counts, and he attacked the role as if it were an exorcism.

It was a gargantuan role, and Burton was, perhaps, asking too much of himself to perform it after only ten days of rehearsals. But it was something he needed to do.

During rehearsals, Coghill and the student actors were impressed with Burton's performance. "I remember the shock of thrill that went through the entire cast when for the first time he let us hear the voice and see the gesture of his 'Earth, GAPE!' in the play's final scene. So the performance grew gradually through a fortnight to something tremendous in the old sense of that word—something that makes you tremble." The show, not surprisingly, sold out, with students standing in long lines in the freezing rain to see the play. Coghill noted the hush that descended on the audience when Elizabeth appeared in her brief, nonspeaking role of Helen of Troy and made "her slow walk around the stage."

Sadly, despite Coghill's assessment and Burton's good intentions, most of the critics thoroughly panned the student production. When Coghill saw how they had come down upon them "with thunder and slaughter," he felt he should have been forewarned. The critics were already in a bad mood: to raise as much money as possible, OUDS had limited the number of tickets to reviewers (one apiece) and did not give them a chance to meet the stars. The London *Times* called the production "a sad example of university drama at its worst. Mr. Burton seems to be walking through the part," cruelly complaining that Burton's performance was "as embarrassing as those of the undergraduate actors."

A few of the Oxford dons, however, loyally praised the production, such as Professor of Poetry Edmund Blunden, who wrote in his review in the undergraduate student newspaper, *Cherwell*: "To praise most cordially all whom we watch would be just. The gusto and swiftness of the performance was one of the finest efforts that an amateur company, even assisted by two actors of genius, could ever make." Wolf Mankowitz, in a letter to the *Guardian*, praised the Burtons for their artistic philanthropy and called for the queen to reward

Burton with, at the very least, a Cross of the British Empire. (But then, Mankowitz had written the adaptation of the Marlowe play for Coghill's production.)

As soon as *Doctor Faustus*'s brief run was over, the Burtons left for the De Laurentiis Studio in Rome. After the five-month shoot was completed for *The Taming of the Shrew*, Richard brought the student cast of *Doctor Faustus* to Rome to film the play, coaxed Columbia Pictures to produce and distribute the film, and invested $1 million of his own funds in the production. He and Elizabeth agreed to be paid just the union minimum of $45 per week for their appearances in the film to be codirected by Burton and Coghill. It was almost as if they wanted to throw down the gauntlet to the reviewers who had gleefully panned the Oxford performance.

And then, of course, there was Burton's obsession with the Faust legend. Years later, Mike Nichols would say, "Richard seemed to be the prisoner of a fantasy of having sold his soul to the devil," always keenly aware of what his former rivals and companions were accomplishing on the stage. Whether it was a fantasy or not, it was part of the story Richard told himself about his extraordinary life and the opportunities he had seized for himself, and the ones Elizabeth had made possible. "Why me?" he would ask later—"why me?"

Elizabeth must have known what a risk it was to lend their names to what was virtually a student production of a noncommercial work, but she went along with it as a gift to Richard, and to give him another opportunity he had wanted for some time: to direct. She knew her happiness depended upon Richard's happiness.

In October 1966, also in Rome, Elizabeth began work with director John Huston on *Reflections in a Golden Eye*, with Marlon Brando replacing Montgomery Clift. It was an ironic replacement, perhaps, because the two men had had a special bond as rivals and fellow acolytes of Lee Strasberg's Actors Studio, the New York school of method acting (which Burton, and many other British actors, disdained).

The film would be shot mostly in Italy, despite the fact that the

movie was set on an army base in the American South. Warner Bros.–
Seven Arts settled on Rome as an accommodation to Elizabeth, though
it wasn't lost on Jack Warner that the Italian crew would mean far
lower production costs. So the De Laurentiis studio in Rome would
again play host to the Burtons. Richard would be there, but it was now
his turn to be idle, much as Elizabeth was during the making of *The
Night of the Iguana*. He didn't like it; though he had declined to play
Major Penderton, this was the first time since their affair and marriage that Elizabeth was making a movie without him.

His crankiness, perhaps, was vented on Kenneth Tynan, when the
drama critic showed up at the spacious villa they'd rented in Rome to
interview Burton for BBC TV. Tynan later noted in his published diaries that Burton had polished off about five bottles of wine during the
day. Burton then invited Tynan to join him, Elizabeth, and a number
of other guests to dine that night at the villa.

More libations were poured at dinner. Afterward, lingering in the
villa's grand hall, Burton turned to him and, with a "wolfish grin,"
asked, "How do you think Elizabeth is looking, Ken?"

"Fine," he answered, immediately on his guard.

"How would you like to go to bed with her?" he goaded.

At this point, Tynan didn't know how to answer. If he said yes, that
would betray lusting after the host's wife. If he demurred, was that
not insulting to Elizabeth's allure? He answered, diplomatically, "To
be quite candid, Richard, I doubt whether I'd be capable of making
it with Elizabeth."

"You mean you couldn't get it up?"

"Something like that."

At which point, Richard shouted across the room to Elizabeth that
Ken "doesn't think he'd be able to get it up for you in bed."

Elizabeth's eyes blazed, Tynan recalled. "*That* is the most *insulting*
thing that has ever been said to me. *Leave my house!*"

But after throwing him out, Elizabeth called the unfortunate critic
the next morning to offer a "hungover apology." She also had flowers

delivered to his hotel room, realizing no doubt that not everyone shared the Burtons' sense of humor.

But one who did was Marlon Brando.

Reflections gave Brando the chance to spend more time with Elizabeth and Richard. Often during the ten-week shoot, Richard would come to the studio to pick up his wife and the three would set out for dinner. As a kind of mute tribute, Richard would sometimes appear early enough to watch Marlon in a scene. It didn't take long before rumors appeared in print, particularly in movie magazines in the States, that Richard was showing up to "keep an eye on Elizabeth," that he was jealous of Brando, both personally and professionally, and that this "would be a repeat of *Cleopatra*" only with Richard in the Eddie Fisher role.

But that was ridiculous. It was just "feeding time for the press," Elizabeth said. The public's appetite for scandal had only deepened over the last six years.

Burton, as astute about human nature as ever, wrote in his diary on November 3, 1966, "Marlon's immorality, his attitude to it, is honest and clean. He is a genuinely good man, I suspect, and he is intelligent. He has depth. It's no accident he is such a compelling actor. He puts on acts, of course, and pretends to be vaguer than he is. Very little misses him, as I've noticed."

Brando's biographer Peter Manso observed a "tacit connection between Burton and Brando. Both men had been criticized for their choice of film material, and both had been criticized for abandoning the stage for movies, which Brando had been more guilty of than Burton." Richard, Manso noted, "had heard that song before, and would never, not even when they were drinking together, would ever bring it up to Brando. The plaint had been used on him too often, he had been goaded by that question too often to turn around and torture a fellow actor with it, especially an actor with such remarkable gifts as Marlon's." They spent a great deal of time together, often joined by Christian Marquand, a charming, jovial Frenchman who was making his way as a producer and director. Marquand was Brando's friend from the early 1950s, and they were both out to seduce Richard into appearing in *Candy*, Marquand's doomed-to-disaster film adaptation of Terry Southern and Mason Hoffenberg's underground classic, which was an exercise in sexual reassignment of Voltaire's *Candide*. Their Saturday evenings together, "everybody became sloshed to the gills . . . A thoroughly forgettable time was had by all," Richard wrote in his diary, but forgettable in the sense that no one could remember, afterward, what happened. And indeed, the small role Burton would take in *Candy* the following autumn as a favor to Brando would prove forgettable as well.

The Burtons enjoyed Brando's playfulness, and Richard especially enjoyed Brando's eclectic knowledge (Native American history, the biology of electric eels). They would have good-natured arguments about what was the easiest language to learn—Richard insisted that it was English, while Marlon insisted that Spanish was unquestionably easier. Most of these dorm-room jaw sessions took place over vodkas before and after dinner, Marlon wondering how many "misguided people" would be waiting for him outside his hotel room. Brando actually felt sorry for his fans. He felt they were wasting their lives. Elizabeth was far less gloomy about the whole thing. She saw her fans as a part of her job; she didn't live for their approval—hardly!—but she didn't pity them either. It could be worse, she told them. "We could be the Beatles."

Burton wrote in his diary that he didn't find Brando boring or pretentious, qualities that Richard loathed, and that he often fretted he had been guilty of himself. That's one reason for the drink, the stories, all those anecdotes that flooded out of him, because he felt he had to be "interesting." Some people, like their lawyer, Aaron Frosch, always felt badly around Richard, no matter how much Elizabeth tried reassuring them ("Richard likes you, he thinks you're absolutely brilliant."). Frosch worried that Richard was bored with his company.

"What do you have to do to be friends with him," Frosch asked Dick Hanley, "memorize poetry?"

John Huston himself was trying to make a comeback after directing a string of flops, including *The Bible*, which Richard and Elizabeth had first seen together in Rome (Richard saying that his favorite part was "Creation"). Huston was an important director to Burton. It was in *The Night of the Iguana* that Richard began to take film acting with the same kind of seriousness as Elizabeth. And it was in Puerto Vallarta, a place Huston loved as well, that Richard and Elizabeth had felt relaxed, comfortable enough to completely indulge their sexual desire for each other. It had been a powerful combination, acting under Huston's direction and spending nights with Elizabeth. Richard thought that sex with Elizabeth had brought him even greater strength as an actor, and he had marveled that he could be that enthralled by one woman over such a long period of time. For someone who prided himself on moving on, acquiring "another notch on his gun belt," in Elizabeth's words, this was seemingly the last notch. It surprised him and delighted her. He admitted to Huston (himself a notorious womanizer) that Elizabeth was the only woman he thought he could kill someone over, out of jealousy. Her body still excited him, and when she was ill, he counted the days before they could be together again.

So, both Burtons associated Huston with Mexico and their passion for each other. And Huston repaid the compliment by praising Elizabeth's theatrical gifts, describing her in his memoir as a "supremely fine actress." Always impressed with physical courage, Huston marveled at Elizabeth's horsemanship. In spite of nearly constant back pain, she rode a white stallion in the film, and rode it well.

Over the next decade, the Burtons would earn approximately $88 million (about $616 million today), and spend three-fourths of it on furs, diamonds, paintings, designer clothes, travel, food, liquor, a yacht, and a jet. The production company they'd formed to produce

The Taming of the Shrew, named Taybur (for Taylor-Burton), became the holding company for their wealth, though *Shrew* would be the first and last film they produced. When the Burtons contemplated taking a three-month hiatus from making films, the movie industry shuddered, because, as one observer noticed, "nearly half of the U.S. film industry's income . . . came from pictures starring one or both of them." The year 1967 alone would see the release of three Burton-Taylor films: *The Taming of the Shrew*, *Doctor Faustus*, and *The Comedians*—and, for Elizabeth, the release of *Reflections in a Golden Eye*. "They say we generate more business activity than one of the smaller African nations," Burton admitted, shaking his head in wonder.

They invested $50,000 in the Vicky Tiel Boutique in Paris, bought a ten-passenger, twin-engine de Havilland jet for $1 million (named *Elizabeth*) and paintings by Utrillo, Monet, Picasso, Van Gogh, Renoir, Rouault, Pissarro, Degas, Augustus John, and Rembrandt (Elizabeth very much her father's daughter in her eye for ever-appreciating works of art). They bought a fleet of Rolls-Royces and invested in real estate: 685 acres on Tenerife in the Canary Islands (where they grew bananas), 10 acres of land in County Wicklow, Ireland (where they bred horses), in addition to Casa Kimberly in México, with its spectacular view of the Banderas Bay, replete with pre-Columbian art given to them by the Mexican government (for putting Puerto Vallarta on the map as a tourist destination). And, of course, they held on to their three homes—his in Céligny and Hampshire, and hers in Gstaad.

Despite their vast real estate holdings, they continued to live mostly in hotels, booking entire floors to house their entourage and their children. When they ordered room service, they often ordered it from another country: in Rome, it was chili flown in from Chasen's in Los Angeles; in Paris, pork sausages flown in from Fortnum & Mason in London.

And then there was the entourage they supported. One of them, Emlyn Williams's son Brook, estimated that Burton was supporting forty-two people at one time, including his brothers and sisters, whose houses and cars he bought and whose retirement pensions he funded. And they kept bodyguards on the payroll for each of their five children—Michael, Christopher, Liza, Maria, and, ever more frequently, nine-year-old Kate Burton, who began spending more time with her father and Elizabeth. Jessica, whom Richard rarely saw, was still institutionalized. Richard paid for that, too. But Richard and Elizabeth loved having Kate around. Now that Sybil was remarried and the mother of a son, Kate was allowed to spend more time in the Burtons' fantastical menagerie.

"Kate came to stay with us from London, with Ifor and Gwen as guardians," Burton wrote in his diary on September 27, 1966. "She looked bonny and long-legged and freckled and slightly pigeon-toed. She is so far physically so like us that she takes my breath away. There's no sign of Syb in her at all . . ." Richard was pleased to see how Kate took to Elizabeth. ("[S]he is loving and quite clearly loves E., and E. her.") When both Kate and Elizabeth came down with the flu, they spent the day recovering in bed together, gossiping and taking each other's temperatures. Richard carried Kate to her bed when she fell asleep, "because cunningly, she thought, perhaps, that she could sleep the whole night with E. . . . but I was firm and took her away."

As their entourage grew, Elizabeth and especially Richard became increasingly isolated from their old friends. Just to get past security, guests would often have to wear badges before being ushered into the Burtons' presence on movie sets. The Burtons often sat, isolated in their luxurious hotel suite, wondering why they never heard from anyone. Robert Hardy had watched this happen, as it became increasingly impossible for him to see his old friend from their Oxford days.

John Gielgud recalled that the Burtons never carried any money, like the royal family, so they relied upon members of their entourage to take care of everything. He remembered having lunch with Richard in a New York City restaurant during the run of *Hamlet*. Gielgud was pleased to see that Richard had apparently slipped out of the clutch of his handlers and assistants, but when it came time to pay the bill, Burton waved his hand and said, "Oh don't worry. They'll pay." Gielgud looked around and realized that all the neighboring tables were taken by the Burton entourage, like extras on a set, waiting to be summoned.

By the end of 1966, despite their tremendous wealth, the Burtons' expenses were so high that at times they found themselves short of funds. Besides their constant travel and gift-giving, Burton was sending big annual Christmas checks to his many brothers and sisters. That's one reason they agreed to appear in MGM's screen version of *The Comedians*, Graham Greene's jaded political drama set in François "Papa Doc" Duvalier's Haiti: they needed the money. For the first time, Richard's salary ($750,000) eclipsed Elizabeth's ($500,000), and, also for the first time, Richard Burton was given top billing over Elizabeth Taylor. Peter Glenville, the film's producer and director, had not especially wanted Elizabeth to play Richard's love interest in the movie—the ambassador's wife, Martha Pineda—but Burton insisted. She reportedly accepted the role just to accompany Richard to Africa. "I'm just a broad, but Richard is a great actor," she told Glenville, and that's why she'd asked for only half of her usual salary.

Expectations were high for the film, which combined an important political cause, a top-flight cast and crew, and a renowned writer. Burton, who was in awe of writers, greatly admired Graham Greene, who was adapting *The Comedians* for the screen even before the book was published. The Burtons also admired Glenville, who had so ably directed Burton in *Becket*, and their fellow cast members, especially Sir Alec Guinness, who played the bogus commando Major Jones. They were also fond of Peter Ustinov (Burton thought Ustinov one of the best conversationalists he'd ever met), appearing as the ambassador in the film. The cast was rounded out by silent-screen actress Lillian Gish, veteran comedic actor Paul Ford, and some of the most notable black actors of the day, including James Earl Jones, Roscoe Lee Browne, Raymond St. Jacques, and a young

Cicely Tyson in her second film appearance. (The year before, Tyson had debuted in *A Man Called Adam* with the Burtons' good friend Sammy Davis Jr.)

Guinness was apprehensive about seeing Burton again, because over the last few years he had made several calls on the Burtons, leaving unanswered messages at the Dorchester, and had even sent gifts that had been returned. Richard was surprised to hear that—he'd had no idea. Apparently, their entourage was doing more than just keeping their household safe and functioning; they were keeping the Burtons from their oldest friends.

During the filming of *The Comedians*, the Burtons added another person to their entourage: Gianni Bozzacchi, a photographer and retoucher still in his teens, whom Elizabeth hired to make sure all the photographs of her that went out into the world were as beautiful as humanly possible. "I used to be considered the number one retoucher in Italy," Bozzacchi recalled, "and not only in Italy, because they used to send me stuff to retouch from the United States." He learned his skills from his father, Bruno Bozzacchi, a famous restorer of priceless manuscripts and photographs in Italy at a kind of "hospital for books," called Patologia del Libro. (Among other things, Gianni's father worked on such treasures as the letters of Machiavelli and Leonardo da Vinci.) But Gianni decided early on that he did not want to live his life in a darkroom. He now works primarily as a film producer and photographer. ("I don't have to retouch anymore," he says, "because I know how to retouch with light.")

Elizabeth had approval of any pictures published of her, so when the film company decamped to Africa, Glenville hired the famous photographer Pierluigi Praturlon, for whom Bozzacchi worked at the time, to fly to Dahomey with their portable lab. (Pierluigi was both Frank Sinatra's and Federico Fellini's favorite photographer.) "Richard was not that vain," Bozzacchi recalled, and he didn't require the approval that Elizabeth insisted upon. After all, her face truly was her fortune, and she knew that she had to look beautiful from every angle.

Elizabeth was at first angry when Bozzacchi took candid photographs of her when the production company moved to Nice. She summoned him and said, "You're really good, Gianni, but you're an asshole to have taken these pictures without my consent." But she liked the shots so much that she invited him to join their moveable feast and chronicle their adventures in photographs. She appreciated the fact that he could do so unobtrusively. "When I take pictures of people, I disappear," Bozzacchi says. "They don't feel the camera. Even Elizabeth, and she's such an expert. For Elizabeth, it's important the dress is right, and the makeup is right, and that she looks wonderful. As a photographer, you are basically the curator of her image. And the relationship to the camera, you see—if the makeup doesn't work, the hair doesn't work, you see all that. You establish that relationship in communication, you don't even have to talk. And that is a special relationship."

Bozzacchi, like Peter Medak before him on the set of *The V.I.P.s*, noticed that Elizabeth was even more beautiful in person than on camera. "That's what the world sees: the beauty, the dress, the makeup—but without makeup she glows! With makeup she doesn't. I photographed her without makeup—my God! There's a sensuality always present." He was struck by the fact that her left and right profiles were equally symmetrical, and he later wrote about her, "If Botticelli were living today, he would be inspired by Elizabeth."

The tall, curly-haired teenager didn't yet speak English. He felt young and ignorant, and he stayed away from Richard, who could be intimidating. Just seeing the good-looking youth hovering around Elizabeth, taking her pictures, made Richard jealous. "When you get injected into that world, it's a little bit scary. I'd do my work and that was it," he recalled. But the Burtons treated him like family. He would stay with the couple as their friend and official photographer for seven years. In fact, he met his first wife through the Burtons. Claudye Ettori was working for Elizabeth as her hairdresser on the set of *The Comedians*. Richard would be the best man and Elizabeth the matron of honor at Gianni and Claudye's June 1968 wedding, which was held at the country home of Alexandre de Paris, Elizabeth's exalted hairdresser (who also counted among his clients the Queen of England; Farah Diba Pahlavi, the wife of the Shah of Iran; and Grace Kelly, Princess of Monaco). Because of the Burtons, at least a hundred photographers surrounded the estate, waiting to photograph the wedding party.

Another gifted photographer was Elizabeth's close friend Roddy McDowall, who photographed her over the decades of their friendship. McDowall remembered that he had been so struck by her beauty when they were child stars appearing together in *Lassie Come Home* that at his first sight of her, he burst out laughing. (That had been Burton's response when he first saw her at Stewart Granger's house, reading a book by the pool.) He thought she was "perfect, an exquisite little doll . . . the most perfectly beautiful creature I ever saw." Throughout their friendship, McDowall was always on hand to prop up her ego when she needed it. He believed that "being beautiful" was an art form in itself—great beauties were great artists, in their way. He told Elizabeth, "Some beautiful people don't know how to carry it, and so they shrug away from it. Others"—like Elizabeth— "wear their beauty with enormous ease." McDowall long marveled at Elizabeth's composure, which he considered a necessary element of true beauty. As someone who photographed her often, and had acted with her in front of the camera, McDowall saw her ability to be absolutely still as the secret to her iconic image.

They began filming *The Comedians*, their seventh movie together, in January 1967, soon after completing *The Taming of the Shrew* and *Doctor Faustus* in Rome. MGM and Peter Glenville had planned to make the film in Haiti before the book was even released, before Duvalier and his murderous enforcers known as the Tonton Macoutes could take their revenge, but they feared word would leak out before the film was completed. Instead, the entire cast and 115-member crew were flown into Dahomey (now Benin), on the West African coast, which would stand in for Haiti, the capital city of Cotonou, a close fit for Port-au-Prince. Dahomey had a historical, cultural, and geographical resemblance to Haiti—the newly independent country had been colonized by the French and had a history of slavery. In fact, the Dahomeans were the descendants of Africans who were enslaved and sent to the Caribbean, and many of the cultural elements had remained the same, including ritual voodoo. When a voodoo priest was brought in from Haiti for a scene in which voodoo rites were shown for the first time on camera, the Dahomean locals, hired as extras in the film, didn't need to be instructed in the rituals.

There were rumors that Duvalier had voodoo witch doctors place a hex on the entire production. Indeed, accidents plagued the shoot— several near drownings, various illnesses that required leaving the country for treatment, and, incredibly, a mysterious rash in the shape of Africa that appeared on Alec Guinness's chest for four days. ("I was glad to leave Dahomey," Guinness wrote from Africa to a friend when filming was over. "I couldn't help feeling it was sinister . . . ideas of voodoo are never absent from one's mind there. Peter Glenville, an intimate friend, very nearly drowned under my eyes.")

The Burtons arrived in Africa with their entourage, including Alexandre de Paris; the ever-faithful Bob Wilson, Burton's right-hand man; and Dick Hanley and John Lee. Three hundred people greeted the Burtons when they arrived in Cotonou. Actors are often well-received when they arrive on location to make a film, but the Burtons were met by President Soglo and given use of the presidential compound at Cotonou. Richard and Elizabeth were led through the presidential palace by the former general, who had helped win his country's independence from the French ten years earlier. The palace could barely hold a candle, however, to the luxurious hotels the Burtons were used to. When "Mon Général" showed them his wife's clothes closet with great fanfare, Elizabeth was touched to see "a perfectly ordinary rack of shoes." When Elizabeth was invited to step onto a mat that automatically switched on a couple of lights, she feigned delight. Outside the sprawling palace, the Burtons noticed washing hanging on lines strung up in the presidential courtyards. It was not lost on them that their considerable assets were in excess of many African countries' annual gross national product, certainly including Dahomey's.

The Burtons were enchanted with the country and with the Dahomeans, especially the children who flocked to the sets. For the first time since *Cleopatra*, they were able to walk into a restaurant without being gawked at. One local journalist popped up to interview Richard, but didn't recognize Elizabeth, mistaking her for Burton's assistant. That delighted her. Another local newspaperman mistook Burton for a cameraman, further endearing the Dahomeans to the couple. That they were treated more as curiosities than as royalty was a needed change. Glenville noticed that the lack of outside stress helped them relax in front of the camera, and Burton particularly gives a believable and affecting performance in the role of a troubled hotel proprietor who tries to stay politically neutral, a kind of Rick in *Casablanca* who finds his conscience at the end of the film, deciding to lead an insurgence against the corrupt regime.

LOOK magazine covered the shoot, putting the Burtons on the cover of their June 27, 1967 issue. "On Location with Richard and Liz: Why They're Never Dull." The public still could not get enough of the Burtons, and they're beautifully photographed in color by Otto Storch, looking vibrant and relaxed, strolling along the beach or surrounded by African children. "Elizabeth and I love children," Burton told *LOOK*. "We would adore having some together, but the doctor said Elizabeth can't have any more." Clearly the idea of having a child of their own was still very much with them after Elizabeth's hospitalization in Rome. They look genuinely happy surrounded by a half dozen children, Richard kissing a small boy he's holding in his arms. Children, at least, did not know or care who the Burtons were, and they did not fawn over them or judge them.

They spent their evenings reading, Taylor discovering a genuine interest in poetry under Burton's influence, and Burton absorbed in Alex Haley's *The Autobiography of Malcolm X*. But the relentless African heat, and both Richard's and Elizabeth's prodigious alcohol intake, soon took their toll. On some days, the temperature reached as high as 110 degrees. "You took your life in your hands if you went out in the midday sun," Burton said, evoking Noël Coward's song "Only Mad Dogs and Englishmen (go out in the midday sun)." Richard discovered that under the movie lights, the temperature reached 138 degrees. So everyone did what they could to reduce the number of takes required—never a problem for "Quicktake" Elizabeth, or Lillian Gish, then seventy-four years old, who was particularly bothered by the heat.

Despite the heat—or because of it—Burton's drinking seemed to increase exponentially. Graham Greene, also known for his high capacity for alcohol, noticed, "[W]hen they are both off, they knock it down in their little trailer—he beer and she pastis. How can [they], in this heat . . ."

Guinness was also somewhat alarmed. In Richard's early years in the theater, back in 1949, he had occasionally dined with the Guinnesses at their house in St. Peter's Square in London, where Richard had introduced Alec Guinness to the poetry of Dylan Thomas. (Guinness later portrayed the Welsh poet in a one-man show in London.) Now, eighteen years later, Alec wrote in a letter to his son about his reunion with Richard: "I hardly find him the same person. Although he's a bit dour at the moment, he can be amusing and is highly intelligent and not uninteresting. But drink has taken a bit of a toll, I fear."

And, in the usual way that the Burtons' films so often reflected or commented upon their private lives, there's a throwaway line delivered by Paul Ford, playing an eccentric American idealist who travels to Haiti with his wife (played by Lillian Gish), which could have been written for Burton himself. When Burton, as Mr. Brown, the proprietor of a hotel imperiled under the Duvalier regime, tells Mr. Smith

(Paul Ford) that he's putting him and his wife up in the John Barrymore Suite, Mrs. Smith asks if John Barrymore really stayed there.

"I can show you his liquor bills," Mr. Brown answers.

"A great talent ruined," Mr. Smith remarks.

Elizabeth blamed Richard's excessive drinking on his "Welsh hours," his recurring bouts of depression that seemed to require more and more alcohol. But both were drinking heavily. Once, as a result, they failed to show up for a state dinner in their honor, to which two hundred guests had been invited. But it was Richard who was usually the worse for wear. Sometimes he would disappear for hours. Elizabeth would call out his name in their air-conditioned presidential compound, but there would be no answer. She would have to leave the comfort of their villa and make the rounds of the back alleys and streets in Cotonou, searching the small hotels and African bars for him, where the most famous woman in the world had trouble making herself understood.

"Have you seen Richard Burton?" she'd ask in the local bars.

"Who?"

"Richard Burton!"

"Is he black or white, madame?"

Could he have been kidnapped? There were rumors of kidnapping by Duvalier's henchmen swirling around the set, sometimes two or three threats a week. Eventually, she would find him having wandered off with a few members of the crew. Once, Alec Guinness stumbled onto Elizabeth in his dressing room; she had been weeping throughout the afternoon because Burton, in his cups, had been so nasty to her. But, as usual, they patched up their quarrel and things went on as before. When there wasn't acting, there was drinking. When there wasn't drinking, there was fighting. And when there wasn't fighting, there was lovemaking.

Burton noticed how, despite it all, Elizabeth seemed to grow even more beautiful in Africa. "E. is looking gorgeous—she blooms in hot climates," Burton wrote in his diary in January. And later, "I am madly in love with her at the moment, as distinct from always loving her, and want to make love to her every minute. But alas it is not possible for a couple of days."

The more he drank on location in West Africa, the more he became a Dr.-Jekyll-and-Mr.-Hyde figure, and it was Elizabeth who suffered most when Burton turned mean. Though she was playing another Martha in *The Comedians*, Elizabeth didn't want to be turned into Albee's Martha. He could be so loving toward her, so devoted, but with too much drink in him, he turned on her and on the world she had brought him into. Everyone was a "bore" or "a poor bastard." He lashed out and she felt the lash. Cursing was a sport to Elizabeth, a release—it was fun to curse—but Richard's profanity when he was drunk had a scorpion's sting in it. And it pained her to hear it, and on those occasions when he'd reject her, she would be inconsolable when the teasing turned to taunting. It was their seventh film together, the fifth year of the floating island of this strange life they shared, a marriage with an international audience. The public, the "yellow journals" as Elizabeth called them, wanted to see "Liz and Dick," nicknames they both hated. They wanted to be Elizabeth and Richard.

It was heartbreaking to see "Liz and Dick" win that fight. There were, in fact, two marriages: the public and private. She thought that having a top billing and a larger salary—that male obsession with being on top—would please Richard. But, at least in Africa, and under those hot movie lights, nothing seemed to please him. Drinking was what you did. What Richard did.

Once filming was over in Dahomey, the cast and crew were transported to soundstages in Nice and Paris to complete the shoot. In an elegant hotel in the Maritime Alps above Saint-Raphael, an hour from Nice, *LOOK* continued its interview. On their hotel balcony, where one could see the Mediterranean, and the sweet air was redolent of umbrella pines that grew in the scrubby hills, Burton was asked if the "American viewing public" had changed over the years. Burton thought that it had, given the popular success of such challenging productions as *The Spy Who Came in from the Cold*, *Who's Afraid of Virginia Woolf?*, and *The Taming of the Shrew*. As for the roles of Leamas and George, Richard admitted that they were quite different from his previous fare. "I would never have dreamed of myself portraying such seedy, famished men . . . it was immensely challenging, but it was such agony. Playing everything down, down, holding myself in all the time." When asked why he made so many movies, he answered that, among other things, being with Elizabeth had given him much more respect for filmmaking. And again, that old bugaboo—did he feel he had forsaken the stage? It's a good thing Elizabeth wasn't sitting on the terrace with them. "Oh, no. I haven't given it up by any means," he answered. "I always have a great ache in me for the stage, a sort of duty, you might say."

And finally, no interview could be complete until it touched on *Le Scandale*. "Well, I must say that everyone seems to have quieted down," Richard said. "Good lord, the reputations we had! I mean, I was a bestial wife-stealer, and Elizabeth was a scheming home-breaker . . . We've been through a lot of fire together, Elizabeth and I. You'd think we were out to destroy Western Civilization or something."

This time, Richard really wanted to win. On April 10, 1967, the Academy of Motion Picture Arts and Sciences held its annual Oscar celebration. Word had already reached them at Saint-Jean-Cap-Ferrat in Nice that Elizabeth had won the New York Film Critics Circle Award for *Virginia Woolf*, but that Richard had lost to Paul Scofield. As the NYFCCA was often an augur for how the Academy voted, Burton was somewhat shaken. He and Elizabeth had both been nominated for Oscars for *Who's Afraid of Virginia Woolf?*—Burton's fifth nomination—and he deserved to win. But his competition was the Shakespearean actor Scofield in *A Man for All Seasons*. This was the Oscar that Richard really wanted to win, *needed* to win—his George had been a quiet triumph, perhaps his best performance in his long, celebrated career. But he had never felt accepted in Hollywood, par-

ticularly by the older crowd who tended to vote conservatively for
Academy Award nominees. That crowd had not been comfortable
with Albee's graphic language, and had not liked the terrible headlines coming out of Rome only five years earlier, when Richard and
Elizabeth had found themselves shunned by an industry waiting to
see how the *Cleopatra* debacle would play out. If they both won their
awards, it would be a sign of complete acceptance by the entertainment industry.

Elizabeth wanted to attend the awards ceremony, and Jack Warner,
head of Warner Bros., wanted her there. He had even sent a telegram
to her in Nice, begging, "Do not burn the bridges you have built."
Elizabeth, of course, had already won her Oscar for *BUtterfield 8*, but
she held out hope that there would be a double win for husband and
wife—a first in the history of the award.

Elizabeth was urged to attend, knowing it would be a great triumph for her. She was a sure bet to beat out her competition: Vanessa
Redgrave in a small but scintillating role in *Morgan*, Lynn Redgrave in
Georgy Girl, Anouk Aimée in the very adult *A Man and a Woman*, and
the older Russian actress Ida Kaminska for *The Shop on Main Street*.
Richard, some felt, couldn't bear the fact that Elizabeth might win
and he might lose. He decided not to attend.

Perhaps in a bid to dissuade her from attending, Richard told Elizabeth that he had dreamed her plane had crashed returning to California,
and that it was he who found her body. So Elizabeth stepped out of
her hotel bedroom in Nice and announced to her entourage that she
had decided to stay with Richard. Her official excuse was that Richard
was still shooting *The Comedians*, so neither one of them could leave.
Just the idea that Richard might lose—and lose in front of 150 million
people—was more than either one of them could bear.

And, in fact, Richard did lose. Paul Scofield won, as did his director, Fred Zinnemann, as did *A Man for All Seasons*, taking the Oscar
for Best Picture. To deepen the loss, Scofield—whom Burton liked

and admired—was often pointed out to him as the Shakespearean actor who did *not* abandon the stage for movies. Scofield had made but a handful of films—*A Man for All Seasons* was only his fourth—but his performance had earned him a Golden Globe as well as the New York Film Critics Circle Award. Of the two roles—the sainted, historical figure, Sir Thomas More, versus Albee's wounded and cuckolded history professor, George—there was no contest for sentimental favorite. It didn't matter that Scofield had ably and nobly recreated his stage role for film, whereas Burton had created George wholly from his own psyche, a more emotionally challenging feat. If Shirley MacLaine had lost her Academy Award to a tracheotomy back in 1961, then Richard Burton had lost to a saint.

Mike Nichols—who lost his Best Director nomination to Fred Zinnemann—understood how Burton felt. "He was always very aware of what the other guys were doing that he wasn't," he later said. "The plays of Olivier, the plays of Scofield—what he felt he should be doing, and what he feared he was doing instead."

Although Burton sent Scofield a congratulatory telegram (and Scofield sent an appeasing cable to Burton), Richard wrote in his diary, " . . . we heard that E. had won the Oscar and I hadn't! Bloody cheek. But P. Scofield won, so that's alright." Indeed, he was proud of Elizabeth's much-deserved win, and he was gentlemanly and almost cavalier about his loss, but it hurt him. As for Elizabeth, it probably hurt her in Hollywood that she'd chosen not to show up for their most important ceremony. She had been their darling, and this was her fourth nomination and her second win, and the Hollywood community was really behind her this time—this wasn't a sympathy win. She had earned the award. It wasn't a good thing that she'd stayed away.

Sammy Davis Jr. had known Elizabeth since her *National Velvet* days and was often Elizabeth's guest when Richard was onstage in *Hamlet*, seeing it fifteen times "and never tiring of it." Davis had even been in Rome with his then-wife May Britt when *Le Scandale* broke. He knew that "Richard's name was mud with 20th Century-Fox" in 1963, because the studio saw the love affair as a threat to their multimillion-dollar investment in Elizabeth Taylor. "Richard has to be accepted back in the fold," Sammy Davis Jr. would later write; "he needs the respect of his peers. He needs that Oscar."

Burton handled his disappointments by continuing to drink, and he confided in his diary the ill effects that alcohol was having on him. "I drank steadily all day long yesterday," he wrote on May 10, 1967. "Today I shall not drink at all while working. I don't know why I drink so much. I'm not unhappy and I really don't like it very much—I mean the booze itself." Elizabeth tried valiantly to bring him out of his dark mood. "Elizabeth joined us for lunch," he wrote on May 30. "She was gay and sweet but nothing could drag me out of my tantrum."

In June of that year, Burton had taken part in a race at Maria's grade school. They were concerned that Maria, after numerous operations, might feel vulnerable competing with her schoolmates in physical contests, such as beanbag throwing, sack races, and obstacle races. Burton signed up for "the father's race," but after having consumed three Bloody Marys, he came in twentieth. It bothered him enough that he described it in his diary, vowing to go into training for it the next time. Richard loved his and Elizabeth's children. They were truly a family now, and when Eddie Fisher made one last-ditch effort to win custody of Liza Todd later that year, Burton threw down the gauntlet. "Over my dead body," he roared, and Fisher backed off.

Four months later, Richard went on the wagon for a while, but Elizabeth continued to drink, making it more difficult for him to remain sober. By November, a few days before his forty-first birthday, Burton went on a two-day bender. He insulted Bob Wilson, and made a pass at Maria's nurse, Karen. He immediately felt guilty and apologized profusely to Elizabeth the next morning. She laughed it off, more concerned that it had embarrassed the nurse than that it was a sign that Burton's eye was beginning to wander.

Despite these gathering clouds, the Burtons had had a spectacular five years that saw the release of six money-making films, four Academy Award nominations, and Elizabeth's win for *Virginia Woolf*. When Richard had told the *LOOK* reporter that he thought American tastes were changing in their acceptance of more difficult, challenging films, he could take credit for helping to bring about that change. But the tide was beginning to turn on the Burton-Taylor juggernaut, just as Richard was losing control of his deadly dance with alcohol. *Doctor Faustus*, *The Comedians*, and now *Reflections in a Golden Eye*—three ambitious and grown-up films—would be sent packing by the critics and the general public. Little did they know what lay in store for them: a roadside bomb called *Boom!*, which would dramatically alter the landscape.

9

BOOM!

"[We are] a lovely charming decadent hopeless couple."
—RICHARD BURTON

"People don't like sustained success."
—ELIZABETH TAYLOR

Soaring high on the accolades heaped upon them for *Who's Afraid of Virginia Woolf?*, the Burtons next took on another artistic, and therefore risky, project—*Boom!*, based on Tennessee Williams's play *The Milk Train Doesn't Stop Here Anymore*. It would be directed by Joseph Losey and filmed on a craggy mountaintop set in Sardinia, surrounded by the sparkling Mediterranean, from a screenplay adaptation written by Tennessee himself. It was to the Burtons' credit that they used their star power to make literary, not especially commercial, films—*The Taming of the Shrew, Doctor Faustus, Reflections in a Golden Eye*—and now a somewhat cryptic, highly eccentric movie based on a Broadway play that had flopped twice—first with Hermione Baddeley, then with Tallulah Bankhead in the lead role. But given Elizabeth's unforgettable performances in *Cat on a Hot Tin Roof* and *Suddenly, Last Summer*, and Richard's in *The Night of the Iguana*, the Burtons had always had great luck with Tennessee Williams.

However, it took a little persuasion on all sides. Tennessee had wanted Simone Signoret to play Flora "Cissy" Goforth, the ailing, seventy-three-year-old reclusive millionaire who's buried six husbands and who rules an island in the Mediterranean, and Sean Connery to play Chris Flanders, the poetry-spouting "Angelo del Morte" (played previously by Tab Hunter on Broadway), known to seduce and dispatch elderly ladies.

Losey wanted to pair Ingrid Bergman with the English actor James Fox, but Bergman had turned down the role as too vulgar ("I can't say the word 'bugger' without blushing," she'd told the director). Losey needed the Burtons because he needed the money.

An American expatriate living abroad after being blacklisted in the States in the 1950s, Losey had refashioned a career in Europe as the auteur of psychologically brooding films. Losey had directed several well-regarded movies, such as *The Boy with Green Hair* in 1948, *The Servant* in 1963, and the pop-art, spy parody *Modesty Blaise* in 1966, but he was having trouble raising the $1.4 million he needed to make *Boom!*

The Burtons were already spending the summer in the Mediterranean aboard a chartered luxury yacht, the *Odysseia*. In port, they visited frequently with Rex Harrison and his Welsh wife, Rachel Roberts, at the Harrisons' home in Portofino, where Richard and Elizabeth had once hidden away during the height of *Le Scandale*. The Burtons' involvement in *Boom!* was born at the Harrisons' home, and later, over drinks and dinner at La Gritta Bar in Santa Margherita Ligure with their agent Hugh French and producer John Heyman. Heyman also advised the Burtons on tax shelters; and his wife, Norma, would become one of Elizabeth's closest friends.

Losey flew to Portofino to meet with the Burtons, but, to his chagrin, he was sitting on his hotel balcony having breakfast when he saw the *Odysseia* leave port. He finally caught up with them aboard their yacht, where Losey was immediately ushered to the bar. Richard showed off a check he'd received for $1.25 million, the Burtons' first-quarter profit from *The Taming of the Shrew*, which he'd plucked out of a script. He was using it as a bookmark.

Losey next showed up at the Harrisons' villa, bemoaning the fact that he was unable to raise the funds to make *The Milk Train Doesn't Stop Here Anymore*, as it was still being called at the time. Later, at dinner portside, Tennessee Williams arrived with his companion Billy Barnes, very drunk and fresh from a recent suicide attempt, his words an angry blur. Elizabeth begged Tennessee to lower his voice, as people were beginning to stare. "Call me Tom," he insisted, suddenly requiring everyone to call him by his given name, which he had abandoned decades ago.

The next night they moved their traveling feast to the yacht's bar, where Rachel Roberts became "stupendously drunk" and "uncontrollable." It would turn out to be an evening that even Tennessee Williams would have had a hard time imagining. When she began abusing her husband, Rex Harrison—"sexually, morally, physically, and in every other way," Burton recorded—Tennessee, certainly no prude, asked to leave.

Suddenly, Rachel dropped to the floor of the bar and started barking like a dog, exciting the real dogs—Elizabeth's Pekingese and Rachel's basset hound. Thoroughly drunk, Rachel began masturbating her dog, "a lovely, sloppy old dog called Omar," Burton wrote. (Every living thing seemed to be in a high state of arousal that summer in Sardinia, as Burton noted in his diary that their two dogs "have been making love now since last Sunday, at least three times a day. Who would have thought that dogs in heat went on so long? . . . O'Fie's penis is beginning to look the worse for wear.") Elizabeth and Richard tried talking sense to the intoxicated woman; she answered them by again turning on her husband and cursing his three former wives.

At some point during the three-day bacchanal, Elizabeth agreed to star in *Boom!* as long as Richard would be cast opposite her as Chris Flanders. Elizabeth was much too young and gorgeous to play the seventy-three-year-old dying millionairess, and Richard was too old to play the gigolo-poet, in a love duet similar to the December-May romances of Tennessee's *Orpheus Descending* and *Sweet Bird of Youth*. No matter. The roles would be changed to accommodate the Burtons. Losey was pleased, because it meant he could now raise the money, although once Richard and Elizabeth came onboard, the budget jumped to $4.5 million, which included $1.25 million for each of them.

There was another slight problem—or not so slight. Losey thought both of his stars had put on too much weight. He managed to sneak in an expensive French salt substitute into the meals for his "overweight stars." It worked, or perhaps it was Elizabeth's tendency to "bloom in hot climates," because she is, again, stunning on film. Dressed mostly in white caftans, she seems to catch the light, which gives her skin a preternatural glow. Burton, too, looks golden, dashing about in Goforth's dead husband's samurai robe, though a tad world-weary to play the young gigolo.

The Goforth villa was built entirely on location, with blindingly whitewashed walls, a vast terrace, and open archways where pale muslin curtains lifted seductively on the breeze. The travertine marble used to construct the $500,000 set came from the same quarry that had been used for the Colosseum in AD 80. Stark and stunning, the villa looks both ancient and futuristic, surrounded by Easter Island heads. It took fifty-six workmen to bring up the travertine and cement to construct the set. (After work, covered in cement dust and plaster, the workmen would dive into the Mediterranean to wash themselves clean.) In the middle of filming, a huge gale came out of the sea and wreaked havoc, nearly destroying the white villa, which had to be rebuilt.

Despite the remoteness of the setting, the international press flocked to Sardinia to cover the shoot. The public was still hungry for any news of the Burtons, even in their third year of marriage. Their status as worldwide celebrities—"superstars"—showed no signs of abating. Any distinction between their on- and off-screen love life didn't exist; they had become who they were portraying. That was part of their power, but it would also prove dangerous. They could no longer disappear into their characters: they *overwhelmed* them. Elizabeth, after all, had already been dubbed too spectacular to play the quiet librarian in *The Spy Who Came in from the Cold*. Audiences were finding it too difficult to suspend disbelief, unless she played a character as larger-than-life as she was. Or played herself.

Right from the opening scene of *Boom!*, we're in that strange territory where art imitates life, as Burton/Chris Flanders jumps into a boat hired by journalists circling Cissy Goforth's island. (The boat, incidentally, is piloted by Elizabeth's brother, Howard Taylor.) Inside her villa, Goforth's wealth is conveyed in the film by a huge entourage— servants, two Indian musicians playing sitars, guards, a masseuse, a manicurist, a hairdresser, a personal physician, and "Blackie," a private secretary engaged to help her write her memoirs. As she dictates her book, we learn she's had six husbands (to Elizabeth's five), the last of whom died horribly in a tragic accident (as had Mike Todd). Playing "the richest woman in the world," in one scene, Elizabeth wears a Kabuki-style robe that weighed forty-two pounds and was festooned with over 21,000 beads hand-stitched by Italian seamstresses. She also wears some of her own jewels in the film, most notably, the spectacular, 29.4-carat diamond ring given to her by Todd (which she liked to call her "ice-skating rink"). Like Elizabeth, Cissy Goforth suffers from debilitating back pain, for which she receives injections and massages. And the Burtons' real-life friend, Noël Coward, plays Goforth's friend, "The Witch of Capri," an *artiste* who is first seen being carried aloft on a chair up the craggy rocks to Goforth's villa, for a *dinner-à-deux*. When he arrives, Cissy Goforth—bedecked in a shimmering white caftan and a Las-Vegas-showgirl-style headdress—serves him a monstrous baked fish that repulses him. It was an added attraction for Elizabeth to work with Noël Coward, and between scenes, they gossiped wickedly about the other actors.

The parallel universe of the movie, not surprisingly, was made much of in the promotional materials for the film, circulated to theater managers by Universal–World Film Services. "SHE OUTLIVED SIX RICH MEN," it proclaimed in boldface. " . . . HE WAS A TAKER ALL HIS LIFE . . . *they do things you've never seen before!*" More modestly, however, the promotional booklet reveals, "Elizabeth Taylor is seriously considering going into semiretirement within a few years. The superstar . . . at the zenith of her career, declares that she would be quite content simply as Mrs. Richard Burton." After all, this was her third Tennessee Williams film adaptation, her eighth movie with Burton, and the fortieth movie of her long career. She'd had enough, and her private life was now far more interesting to her than her film career—that is, if she could separate them. "Once you're up there on that last rung, you can only go down," she's quoted as saying. "I don't want to be pushed off. I want to walk down with all the dignity I can summon—and not with crutches."

The Witch of Capri was originally written as a female character. In fact, Losey had first asked Katharine Hepburn if she wanted the role; far from being interested, she was insulted (by the role's campiness or its brevity?) and she turned him down. He then offered it to Dirk Bogarde, who had costarred in Losey's *The Servant* and *Modesty Blaise.* "No thank you," he said. But Coward, the witty, insouciant playwright, actor, and entertainer, was delighted by the opportunity to work with his friends the Burtons, and in that beautiful setting. He loved the hotel he was housed in, the Capo Cacchio, which was perched high above "a picture-postcard sea." When he wasn't filming a scene, he investigated the little coves and beaches nearby, baking under the hot sun, then plunging into the bracing waters of the Mediterranean. And he had been flattered when Tennessee Williams left a note for him at his hotel: "[P]lease feel completely free to alter any part of the dialogue you see fit," a profound compliment from one great writer to another.

Rounding out the cast is Joanna Shimkus, a lovely, lithe former cover girl making her film debut as Goforth's secretary, and Michael Dunn, the diminutive actor who had been nominated for an Academy

Award for his supporting role in *Ship of Fools*, playing the sadistic guard of Goforth Island, the keeper of the dogs who attack Burton/ Chris when he arrives on the island.

Sardinia's natural setting—the blazing blue sky, the hot sun, the baked cliffs—was so starkly beautiful the Burtons thought about buying land there. In fact, their $250,000 investment in Tenerife two years earlier had already doubled in value. They invited Losey to come in on a land deal with them, but, ultimately, nothing ever came of it. The Burtons' yacht was moored in the rocks just under the constructed villa, and they didn't need the money.

Losey loved the Burtons' spectacular wealth and high consumption— he loved the drinking, the rows, the delight they took in their food. He noticed that each morning, when they arrived with their entourage, they began their day with large Bloody Marys. One morning during filming, the Burtons' trailer tipped over and tumbled down the steep hillside. Losey was aghast to see red liquid oozing over the rocks, until he discovered it was the tomato juice for their Bloody Marys.

Elizabeth would be the first to admit that she adored food and drink. "Our credo might have been 'Eat, drink and be merry, for tomorrow we report to work,'" she wrote in her 1987 memoir-cum-diet-book, *Elizabeth Takes Off*. But for Elizabeth, that kind of indulgence was dangerous to her profession. While Richard seldom gained an ounce, nor did his prodigious alcohol intake seem to damage his amazing memory, Elizabeth gained weight easily and had to work at taking it off—and she hated exercise. Even as early as 1959, when, at twenty-seven, she appeared in that revealing white bathing suit in *Suddenly, Last Summer*, Joe Mankiewicz had told her to lose weight and "tighten up those muscles. It looks like you've got bags of dead mice under your arms." It seems hard to believe that someone whose reputation and livelihood depended on flawless beauty would risk it all by sheer overindulgence. Yet it's possible that Elizabeth had a love-hate relationship with her beauty: it was part of her identity and a source of her enormous success, but it was also what had stolen her childhood and imprisoned her in an unreal life. She was a freak of nature, constantly being gawked at, lusted after, envied, and subjected to extreme scrutiny. It's not surprising that a part of her would want to destroy it. So she would eat and eat and eat—pâté de foie gras, heaping helpings of chili, fried chicken and mashed potatoes with gravy, hamburgers and French fries, malted milkshakes—and still she was beautiful. She would drink to excess—Bloody Marys for breakfast, straight vodka, beer, and champagne—and still she was beautiful. She purposely gained twenty-five pounds to play Martha in *Who's Afraid of Virginia Woolf?* and appeared on camera in too-tight clothes and graying hair—and still she was beautiful.

Besides that, the sensual delights of her time with Burton were much more enjoyable than mere moviemaking. "Creating a life with him," she later wrote, "was far more interesting than interpreting somebody else's life on the screen, but then I've always lived my life with too much relish to be a mere interpreter of dreams."

Despite being enamored of the Burtons, Losey later complained that it was a struggle working with Elizabeth, who was "belligerent" and didn't understand what he was after. "My working relationship with Elizabeth had begun with absolute hell." Taylor didn't like her clothes, couldn't sleep, shooting was delayed by three days, Losey had to shoot her first scene thirteen times, unusual for "Quicktake." She "was belligerent with me from the start . . . she didn't know what I was doing and it was a struggle."

But Noël Coward loved working with Elizabeth in their scenes together. When Coward, then sixty-eight and an inveterate traveler, first arrived in Sardinia, Burton thought he looked "very old and slightly sloshed and proceeded to get more sloshed." With his heavy-lidded eyes, Coward was fond of calling himself "the oldest Chinese character actor in the world." Burton wrote, "He embraced us both and lavished compliments on E. about her beauty and her brilliance as an actress. Occasionally he threw a bone to me." The next day, he wrote, "E. and N. Coward are madly in love with each other, particularly he with her. He thinks her most beautiful, which she is, and a magnificent actress, which she also is." Burton had known Coward since 1951; like the Burtons, Coward owned a home in Switzerland, and, in fact, the two men had once invested money in the film of Harold Pinter's *The Caretaker.* As the oldest and most experienced member of the cast and crew of *Boom!*, Coward admired Elizabeth's professionalism, the way she "never lost his eye" in their scenes together, and just how considerate she was, for Coward was not in the best of health at the time. In fact, he would have only five more years to live. He saw how her cheerfulness lifted the spirits of the cast and crew, especially during the long night shoots. Elizabeth would stay up half the night with Coward for deep-dish gossip sessions.

While on location, Coward asked the Burtons to think about starring in his signature play, the bittersweet comedy *Private Lives*, as the once-married couple now wedded to other partners, who meet on their honeymoons and discover they are still in love with each other. Coward said cryptically that they should play those roles "before it's too late," but the Burtons were not ready for those roles, often taken by stars at the end of their careers, as a sentimental journey or a last comeback. (He astonished Burton, the aspiring writer, by mentioning that he dashed off *Blithe Spirit* in five days, *Hay Fever* in six, but *Private Lives* took an entire week.)

Burton found it hard to clamber on the steep crags surrounding the villa, overlooking a deep, two-hundred-foot plunge into the Mediterranean below. "I'm supposed to leap up there on that parapet with the wind tugging at my kimono and walk along it," he told Losey and the film crew. "I can't. It's no good. What's the name of the phobia I suffer from? Acrophobia? I'll look it up in my little book later on." After such harrowing scenes, Richard would calm his shaky nerves with whiskey and a game of dominoes.

When their scenes were over, the Burtons would meet for drinks at the bar in Capo Cacchio. But on one occasion, Richard failed to show up. As in Dahomey, kidnappings were frequent in Sardinia at the time, so everyone was especially concerned. Alarmed, Elizabeth contacted the police and had all the hospitals searched. Hours later, he was found in a small, seedy bar described by the chief of police as "a den of thieves," where Burton had gotten up on a table to declaim Shakespeare. He'd promised a round of drinks to anyone present who could name the speech he recited from *Titus Andronicus*. His valet, Bob Wilson, was with him, and he'd pleaded with Burton to get down off the table. The police chief and Wilson managed to return Richard to the hotel and to Elizabeth.

It wasn't just the press and the public who were obsessed with the Burtons—the Burtons were obsessed with the Burtons. Despite their continued public squabbling—sometimes playful, sometimes explosive—they were still obviously in love and in lust with each other. Burton was driven wild by Taylor that summer. She was "looking infinitely sexy" in white mesh leotards and "the shortest miniskirt I've ever seen," Richard wrote in his diary. "It barely, and when she moved it didn't, covered her crotch."

He noticed that she was also driving the local boys wild, the young men loitering on the beach, who, Richard thought, appeared to be stoned. When she and Richard left the beach, the young men shouted "sundry offers of fornication" at her, hungry as the ragamuffin boys circling her in *Suddenly, Last Summer*.

Filming completed, Richard felt that *Boom!* would prove a financial success, and he looked forward to the release of *The Comedians*, which he thought would bring them critical esteem, given the subject matter and the pedigree of the film.

That, however, was not to be.

Filming *Boom!* in Sardinia in the summer of 1967 had brought many pleasures. One of them was the Burtons' decision to buy the *Odysseia* and turn it into their floating home, now that they were too famous to live on land.

Richard and Elizabeth rechristened the 130-foot, sixty-year-old yacht *Kalizma*, an amalgam of Kate's, Liza's, and Maria's names. Elizabeth had fallen in love with it. It boasted seven bedrooms and three bathrooms, with the capacity to sleep fourteen passengers. A crew of eight—including a maid and a waiter—was required to keep it afloat, and Burton estimated it was going to take close to $30,000 a year to run it. "Not too bad," he wrote in his diary, "when one considers our last house (rented) costs ten thousand a month plus approx. one thousand dollars a week for food and staff, etc.! Then, if we can use it as much as possible instead of hotels, we can actually save money." The provenance of the yacht appealed to Burton's dramatic sense: the previous owner loved to head out into the stormiest seas where he would proceed to play Bach on the organ he'd had installed. Nonetheless, Burton had the instrument removed and replaced Bach with a bar.

They bought the boat for $192,000 that summer and spent another $200,000 to refurbish it. Elizabeth hired a designer named Arthur Barbosa to refit the interior with Chippendale mirrors, Louis XIV chairs, English tapestries, Regency sofas, transforming it into what one observer described as an Edwardian palace, albeit one with a movie screen. (Barbosa had decorated Rex Harrison's Portofino home, and the Burtons had admired the décor.) They brought in an enormous, hand-carved bed for the master suite, painted the walls "canary, and not mustard," and had bookshelves built in for Burton's ever-expanding, floating library. He loved the fact that he could now have his beloved books with him when he traveled. The yacht was fitted with radar equipment, and Graham Jenkins thought that the sound system they had installed cost more than his house. Elizabeth would end up spending nearly $1,000 every six months to replace the Super Peerless Wilton carpeting, spoiled by her menagerie of untrained cats and dogs, who relieved themselves all over the rugs.

This is how they lived: on the world stage. By 1967, the private marriage of Richard and Elizabeth was increasingly held hostage to the public marriage of "Liz and Dick." Theirs was the first reality show, a marriage with an audience, and, to escape that, they spent months aboard the *Kalizma* as the world's richest vagabonds, where they would cruise the fashionable Mediterranean ports, making their way to the Riviera and then to Paris. The mad premiere of *Doctor Faustus* in Paris had reminded them of how popular they were in the City of Lights, how they were practically held captive by French aristocrats. The Rothschilds, Guy and Marie-Hélène, were the Burtons' great friends and hosts in Paris. Their favorite house in all their travels was Ferrières, the Rothschilds' country estate outside Paris. Their vagabond life in the summer and early autumn of 1967 became a blur of barons and baronesses: "We are lunching with somebody called Alex or Alexis who is Baron de Redee. There must have been a hundred people for the lunch. I had a Madame Debreu, American, on my right, and Marie-Hélène Rothschild on my left, and a Count de something or other, and a Monsieur de X and astonishingly a lady with a distinct London-Provincial accent. . . . Two devastating wars & crippling taxes, and the moneyed Aristocracy still live like Aristos," Burton confided in his diary. Despite his wealth, Richard was still very much the working-class hero among the "Aristos," the only one who drained his glass of wine before leaving the table, the man who would go on to play Leon Trotsky for Joseph Losey.

Elizabeth loved him for that. She was never impressed by titles. She was the biggest and most famous movie star in the world, and she and Richard were Hollywood royalty. It was the barons and dukes, the lords and ladies who wanted to meet *them*, to bask, if only for an evening, in the blinding light of the Burtons' celebrity.

At the Prix de l'Arc de Triomphe, walking from the paddock to the loge with the Rothschilds, Richard watched as thousands of people applauded Elizabeth on her way to her seat to watch the race. "Not bad for an old woman of thirty-six," Richard wrote admiringly. "I am always pleased and surprised by that sort of thing. We have been expecting it to stop for years but it hasn't." Afterward, a party at the French equivalent of the Kentucky Derby, with the Rothschilds and "La Callas"—Maria Callas, the tempestuous soprano from Queens, New York, who had conquered the Metropolitan Opera House and

La Scala and the world with her brilliance and personality. "And possibly Ari Onassis. Aren't we posh."

The Greek shipping tycoon Aristotle Onassis was a kind of bête noir for Richard. He prided himself on spending more money on Elizabeth than Onassis spent on Callas, his inamorata for many years, pulling up alongside the Onassis yacht with the *Kalizma* and, later, outbidding him on important jewels. The Burtons were in Paris when headlines began appearing throughout the world that Jacqueline Kennedy would marry Onassis. At sixty-nine, he was twice the age of the former first lady, who had lost her husband to an assassin's bullet just five years earlier. Elizabeth and Richard consoled Maria Callas, who had been unceremoniously thrown over for the grieving American widow.

Elizabeth and Richard had been through that before—the abandonment of so-called friends, the harsh words and long knives. Richard embraced the Divine Callas, as her legions of devoted opera lovers called her, and whispered in her ear that Ari was a son of a bitch. Richard later told Elizabeth that it wasn't out of some moral indignation over Ari's desertion of his long-time mistress, but because of the way she learned about his engagement to Jacqueline Kennedy— through the newspapers. What was even more unforgivable to the generous Burtons was that, despite all of his millions, Onassis had left Callas, then at the end of her career, without a cent. After ten years together, he had left her completely broke.

Callas was grateful to them for their moral support. The Burtons, however, could be harsh in private, even about the people they publicly supported and whose work they admired. When Callas told Richard over dinner one night "how beautiful his eyes were" and that they revealed a good soul, Elizabeth's ears perked up. She had unerring antennae for women playing up to her husband ("eyes in the back of her bum," Richard liked to say, and "ears on stalks"). And when Callas shyly mentioned to Richard that she'd read in the newspapers that he and Elizabeth were planning to make a film version of *Mac-*

beth, she asked Richard if she might play Lady Macbeth. "I suppose she thought you were going to play Macduff," he told Elizabeth later. They would poke gentle fun at her afterward. "A silly woman, but one can still feel sorry for her," Burton wrote in his diary.

When Elizabeth discovered that Onassis had presented Mrs. Kennedy with "half a million pounds worth of rubies surrounded by diamonds," keeping up with the Onassises became a mild obsession. "Now the battle of the Rubies is on," Richard noted, "I wonder who'll win. It will be a long war, and the idea has already been implanted that I shouldn't let myself be outdone by a bloody Greek. I can be just as vulgar as he can. . . . Well, now to get the money."

Which meant, of course, more movies, which meant more travel, which meant more of their wandering, extravagant life—Dior nightgowns, Savile Row suits, Lafite Rothschild for lunch. It was no different from how many of their friends, such as Noël Coward, liked to live, but the public remained obsessed with how the Burtons were spending their money and their time. It even entered the language in the mid- to late 1960s: "Spending money like the Burtons." They continued to buy extravagant gifts for each other: matching mink coats, a Picasso for him, a Monet for her. (But old habits die hard, and Richard the miner's son would sometimes wander around their chalet at Gstaad, turning off the lights to cut down on the electric bill. Elizabeth teased him about ordering the cheapest wine while admiring the $65,000 sapphire brooch glittering on her dress, his gift to her.) They were the most generous of couples, spending tens of thousands of dollars on people who were virtually strangers but whose personal tales of woe moved them. But to keep this extravagance going, Richard felt he had to keep working, no matter what was being offered. His life with Elizabeth required it.

Such conspicuous consumption was beginning to be suspect in the nascent age of the commune, the blue jeans, the Johnson Administration's War on Poverty. It became harder not to care about where the money was going. As generous as they were, the Burtons were in danger of being seen as out of touch in their spending habits, as they would soon be seen in their choice of film roles. A new generation was gaining on them. While their poodles and Pekingese roamed the luxurious cabins of their yacht, the world was changing. As one of the Burtons' traveling companions would later characterize this period in their life, "*Cleopatra* seemed like ancient history." The Burtons were unaware of the real price they were paying to play Dick and Liz.

As they were constantly on the move, it became hard to have the children continuously with them, which would have been their preference. Michael and Christopher attended a school in Gstaad, when they were not staying in Hawaii with Elizabeth's brother, Howard, his wife, Mara, and their five children. When Kate joined the Burtons on the *Kalizma*, she and Elizabeth would spend pleasant days shopping together in port, but it would be all too brief, as their itinerant life provided no consistent way to raise their combined family. To make matters worse, there were frequent kidnapping threats against the children, and the Burtons had to hire bodyguards to protect each one of them.

So they drifted around the Mediterranean on their fabulous floating island, spending a week in Portofino, then on to Monte Carlo, where Orson Welles was waiting to dine with them. Welles had appeared with the Burtons as the tax-exile, Hungarian director Max Buda in *The V.I.P.s*. Over a sumptuous dinner, Welles complained that he never made any real money from any of his films—if anything, they had cost *him* money. He'd had to dig into his own pocket for the $75,000 to finish *Chimes at Midnight*, his great Falstaff movie. Though it took him a long time to rise from the table, he left the Burtons with the bill. When Welles was safely out of the room, Richard turned to Elizabeth and marveled at Welles's size. "How can he possibly make love?" he wondered.

Then they would fly to Gstaad, to pick up Michael and Christopher from their boarding school. Christopher, the younger boy, was flourishing, but Michael was having a harder time, so the Burtons flew to London on their private jet to try to get Michael into Millfield, another private school. There, the Burtons ran into Ava Gardner. She was with her companion, visiting his nineteen-year-old son, who had yet to graduate from the boarding school.

On a commercial flight back to Sicily to return to the *Kalizma*, the Burtons ran into Peter O'Toole and his wife, Sian. Richard proceeded to get magnificently drunk with his former *Becket* costar, just as they had five years earlier.

"How many nominations have you had?" O'Toole asked Burton.

"Five. And you?"

O'Toole proudly held up four fingers. But he exaggerated—he'd had only two nominations, as Burton knew—Burton kept track of these things.

The yacht was a kind of refuge that kept Richard and Elizabeth from prying eyes, and it brought them both great happiness. For one thing, both Burtons hated to fly. They would stay up till early morning hours walking the deck and wandering its corridors, they were so thrilled with their new purchase. They couldn't stop "touching it and staring at it as if it were a beautiful baby." They took great pride in showing off their sea-borne treasures to guests. It wasn't just Burton's books that they traveled with—the great art went with them, too. The Monet hung in the salon, the Picasso and the Van Gogh hung side by side in the dining room. The Vlaminck was hung in the stairway to the children's cabins (though Burton wanted to rehang it when the rest of the artwork arrived). The Jason Epstein bust of Churchill brooded over it all.

They continued to host a wide array of celebrities—vintage and newly minted—from different phases of their lives. Sir John Gielgud came aboard the *Kalizma* and was surprised to find, instead of quiet and solitude on a boat in the middle of the Mediterranean, the usual whirlwind. "When I got there," he said later, "there were fourteen Portuguese sailors looking after them, and terrible tourists passing by on boats." A tour guide shouted out, "Captain Cook's graveyard on our right, and [there's] Richard Burton's yacht . . ." Burton started swearing, but Elizabeth, always aware of her obligation to her fans, said, "Oh, no, blow them kisses." Gielgud saw that Burton was already in a foul mood, as he had brought along income tax advisors. Elizabeth locked herself in her cabin till lunchtime, when Ringo Starr and his then-wife, Maureen, came aboard the *Kalizma*. "I don't think they'd ever heard of me," Gielgud recalled, "and I'd never heard of them!" That was one lunch aboard the yacht when the sap did not flow.

Sometimes their peripatetic life just got to be too much. When Howard and Mara Taylor and their children spent time with the Burtons, just moving around the extended menagerie required military planning. Like during all family trips—whether on a yacht or in a Winnebago—tempers flared. "A terrible day, frantically disorganized, thousands of bags all over the place, nine children, six adults all on one plane, Howard and Mara's incessant screaming, my and E.'s pre-film nerves," Burton wrote in his diary. To add to the chaos, their chauffeur, Gaston, had fallen in love with Christopher's girlfriend's mother, and they were stranded at the airport, crammed into a tiny room, waiting for the *Kalizma* to be ready for them. By the time they made it to a hotel until they could board the yacht, Richard had had enough. In the middle of the hotel lobby, in that famously mellifluous voice of his, Burton screamed *"Fuck!"* at the top of his lungs. It "was the only possible way to mete the justice of the day," he later wrote.

Still, their love affair smoldered, despite the pressures of their chaotic lives. Burton continued to write in his diaries, which he saw as sketches for an autobiography. Moored in Portofino harbor one evening, Elizabeth challenged him to write a publishable book by Christmas, of at least a hundred pages, wagering $900 (and her makeup expert, Ron Berkeley, came in for $100). She also asked him to sketch her in prose, which he obliged with the following playful, contrary portrait of everything Elizabeth was not, which he read to her aloud:

She is a nice fat girl who loves mosquitoes and hates pustular carbuncular Welshmen, loathes boats, and loves planes, has tiny blackcurrant eyes and minute breasts and has no sense of humor. She is prudish, priggish, and painfully self-conscious.

She loved it.

The Comedians was released in Hollywood on October 9, 1967, six days before the Oxford premiere of *Doctor Faustus*. Both films would prove bellwethers for the now increasingly cynical reception that would meet the Burtons' films.

The reviews for *The Comedians* were mixed. The *London Daily Express* wrote, "The Burtons seem to revel in togetherness as they earn their daily crust . . . they both give faultless performances. . . . Burton kisses Taylor with such passion and devotion that it is easy to imagine a less contented wife complaining that she doesn't get that sort of treatment at home. . . . I'd say these two have something very special going for them to have such a successful life both in public and privately." But the *London Evening Standard* found it "amazing how a couple like the Burtons seldom manage to generate a spark of credible passion when together on the screen."

Even though the movie's trailer would tout Elizabeth as "the world's symbol of ultimate beauty," Graham Greene had thought that Elizabeth was miscast as Madame Pineda, the adulterous wife of the ambassador played by Peter Ustinov, and the movie bears that out. Her German accent is understated and good, though it slips a bit on the upper registers—something her critics loved to point out, especially since it was the first time Elizabeth had taken on a foreign accent for a role.

Whether it was Alexandre de Paris's dowdy, overteased coiffure or the matronly clothes that didn't flatter her figure, Elizabeth's beauty didn't translate fully to the screen. She was always more beautiful off

Richard with his father, Richard "Dic" Jenkins, in the mining town of Pontrhydyfen, South Wales, 1953. [Raymond Kleboe/Getty Images]

A playful moment between Montgomery Clift and Elizabeth Taylor while filming *A Place in the Sun,* 1950. Elizabeth treasured the troubled actor's friendship, though Clift was critical of Richard. [Peter Stackpole/ Time Life Pictures/Getty Images]

The happy marriage here was Elizabeth's to impresario Mike Todd *(far right)*, though it would end tragically with Todd's death in a plane crash fourteen months later. Eddie Fisher *(left)* and his wife, Debbie Reynolds, *(second from left)* were best man and matron of honor. [Ronnie Luster/mptvimages.com]

(Left) Precursor to a scandal: the marriage of Elizabeth to Eddie Fisher, after Todd's death, in May of 1959. [© Bettmann/Corbis]

(Right) Richard and his Welsh wife, Sybil Burton, arriving in London in November of 1954. She tolerated his affairs; he vowed he would never leave her. [Central Press/Getty Images]

(Right) Elizabeth on holiday in Naples in September 1961, just before beginning work on *Cleopatra*. [SSPL/Getty Images]

(Left) Richard and Elizabeth in a love scene from *Cleopatra*, as they began their off-camera romance. Their films would often mirror their private lives. [20th Century Fox/ Courtesy of Neal Peters Collection]

(Right) Richard and Elizabeth in a private moment during *Cleopatra*. What many thought was just another conquest for Richard turned into a world-shaking love affair. [© Elio Sorci/Photomasi/ Camera Press/Retna Ltd.]

This secretly photographed image of Elizabeth and Richard was the shot seen 'round the world, announcing their love to a scandal-hungry public. [Pat Morin/Globe Photos Inc.]

" . . . from those first moments in Rome we were always madly and powerfully in love," Elizabeth later wrote about their relationship. [© Bert Stern]

A happy Elizabeth embraces her son, Michael Wilding, Jr., on the set of *Cleopatra*. *Right to left:* Elizabeth, Michael, Liza Todd *(back to camera)*, Richard costumed as Mark Antony, and Christopher Wilding. [Photofest]

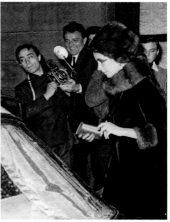

Their affair would usher in modern celebrity culture. Their appearances were feeding frenzies for the paparazzi. [John Frost Newspapers]

Elizabeth and Richard leaving a nightclub in Rome. Her *Cleopatra* eye makeup started a fashion trend in the summer of 1962. [Globe Photos Inc.]

Richard and Elizabeth outside the Tre Scalini restaurant in Piazza Navona, Rome, on July 27, 1962. [Keystone/Getty Images]

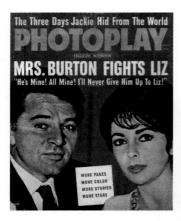

(Left) Richard agonized over leaving Sybil and their two young daughters.

(Right) Richard and Elizabeth "were the most vivid example of a public love affair that I can think of," said columnist Liz Smith. *Life* magazine gets into the act. [Portrait © by Bert Stern]

(Above) The V.I.P.s capitalized on Richard and Elizabeth's notoriety as the world's most famous lovers, 1963. [Photofest]

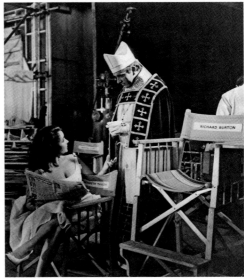

On the set of *Becket,* 1963. Elizabeth encouraged Richard to take the role of Thomas Becket, putting her own film career on hold for two years. "I'm just a broad, but Richard is a great actor," she later said. [Denis Cameron/Rex USA/BEImages]

At the premiere of *Lawrence of Arabia,* starring Richard's friend and *Becket* co-star, Peter O'Toole, at the Theatre des Champs-Elysées in Paris, June 1963. Their school for scandal did not faze the French, who were quick to celebrate the famous couple. [A.P. Images]

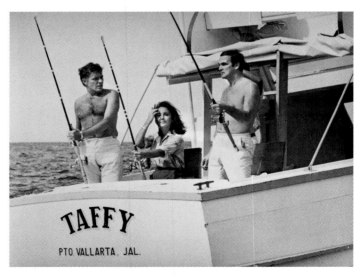

Richard, Elizabeth, and Welsh actor Stanley Baker fishing on Elizabeth's boat, the *Taffy,* christened after one of Elizabeth's pet names for Richard. [from the Private Archives of Dame Elizabeth Taylor]

On location in Mexico for *Night of the Iguana.* They bought Casa Kimberly in Puerto Vallarta, where Elizabeth "bloomed in hot climates," Richard noted. October 1963. [Gjon Mili/Time Life Pictures/Getty Images]

Richard, his dresser, Bob Wilson, Stanley Baker, and Elizabeth. Their presence in Puerto Vallarta changed the sleepy fishing village forever. [from the Private Archives of Dame Elizabeth Taylor]

Richard and Elizabeth enjoying the sea near their villa in Puerto Vallarta. [Courtesy of the University of Wisconsin Press]

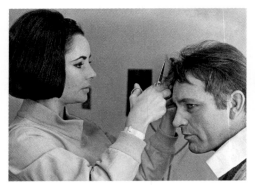

(Left) Elizabeth cutting Richard's hair during the run of Burton's *Hamlet* on Broadway. She loved to fuss over him. [William Lovelace/Express/Getty Images]

(Right) "You're the one they've come to see," Elizabeth teased. "You're the Frank Sinatra of Shakespeare." Burton in stage makeup as Hamlet, in the longest-running production of the play on Broadway. [© Henry Grossman]

Backstage at the Lunt-Fontanne Theater for *Hamlet* on Elizabeth's thirty-second birthday. The cast and crew adored Elizabeth, who attended most of the rehearsals and performances. [© George Silk/Time Life Pictures/ Getty Images/from the Private Archives of Dame Elizabeth Taylor]

(Left) "I love not being me, not being Elizabeth Taylor, but being Richard Burton's wife," Elizabeth said on the occasion of their March 15, 1965, marriage in Montreal. [© The New York Daily News]

(Right) One of Elizabeth's favorite wedding photographs. She's wearing the emerald-and-diamond brooch from Bulgari, Richard's engagement present to her. [William Lovelace/Evening Standard/Getty Images]

(Left) The Burtons in Richard's dressing room in Montreal, playfully getting ready for their wedding reception. [© Henry Grossman/ from the Private Archives of Dame Elizabeth Taylor]

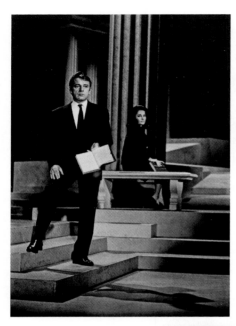

(Left) Richard and Elizabeth onstage. Elizabeth made her first stage appearance in a triumphant poetry reading with Richard, to benefit Philip Burton's drama school in New York. [© Estate of David Gahr]

(Right) Elizabeth on location in Big Sur, California, for *The Sandpiper*. The Vincente Minnelli–directed film capitalized on their adulterous love affair. [© Photos 12/Alamy]

(Above) The most
photographed couple in
the world. On location
for *The Sandpiper,* 1964.
[MGM/courtesy of Neal
Peters Collection]

Liza, Christopher, and Michael pretending to escape over a Berlin
Wall built on location in Dublin, where Richard was filming *The Spy
Who Came in from the Cold.* In real life, the Burtons tried to protect
their children from the public glare. [© Henry Grossman]

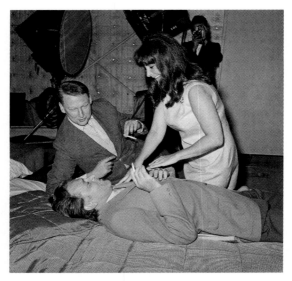

Richard, Elizabeth, and first-time film director Mike Nichols clowning on the set of *Who's Afraid of Virginia Woolf?* in 1966. It was their finest and most challenging film, earning Elizabeth her second Academy Award and Richard his sixth nomination. [© Bettmann/Corbis]

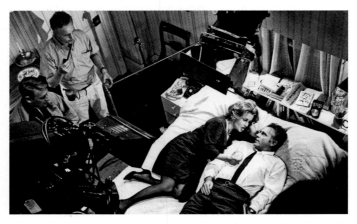

As George and Martha, being directed by Mike Nichols. By now, the Burtons' off-screen battles were reflected in their film roles. [The Everett Collection]

On January 1, 1966, the Burtons were the first guests on *The Sammy Davis, Jr., Show*. [Photofest]

In Gstaad in 1966, near Elizabeth's Chalet Ariel—a tax haven that became a refuge, as did Richard's home in Celigny, Switzerland. A bearded Richard gets ready for his next role, Petruchio in *The Taming of the Shrew*. [Corbis]

(Left) The Burtons watching Cassius Clay knock out Henry Cooper in London in 1966. Elizabeth shared Richard's love of sports, especially rugby and boxing. Sugar Ray Robinson's boxing gloves hang in her office to this day. [Mirrorpix]

Their off-screen fights were lustily parodied in Franco Zeffirelli's rollicking adaptation of Shakespeare's *The Taming of the Shrew.* [Pictorial Press Ltd./Alamy]

the set, in no makeup, her hair loose, than coiffured and couturiered in designer outfits, and it was especially true in *The Comedians*. In an MGM behind-the-scenes publicity reel, she looks youthful and radiant as she clowns and makes faces at the camera, dressed casually in slacks, but that sexy insouciance, for once, just didn't come through on film. It didn't help that, in 1967, Elizabeth was being bested by younger, slimmer, trendier stars such as Vanessa Redgrave and Anouk Aimée, whom she vanquished for the Academy Award, yes, but who embodied the new, bony, androgynous look that Elizabeth would never have. The voluptuous woman as the ultimate film goddess was on her way out.

But Richard—surprising, perhaps, given his high alcohol intake— is again mesmerizing on film. His voice, in fact, is so plangent, you hardly notice James Earl Jones's golden tones in their scenes together. Burton looks soulful, but also virile and unharmed by drink; he more than holds his own with scene-stealers like Alec Guinness, especially in powerful and intimate dialogue in a hillside cemetery where both men pour out the secrets of their souls. As a character who has "lost faith in faith," Burton is playing a familiar role. In a love scene with Elizabeth, Martha playfully calls him a "defrocked priest"—a phrase from *The Night of the Iguana*, and a role he identified with.

Graham Greene was not particularly happy with the movie, but he took the blame for the lackluster reviews. He felt the script he'd written was at fault, and, in fact, it would be the last time Greene adapted one of his own novels for the screen. But he saw that he had hit his target in Duvalier's response to the film. Papa Doc declared war on *The Comedians*, threatened Greene with death, and had his ambassador to the United States condemn the movie as "a character assassination of an entire nation." He also condemned the Burtons, who had lent their star power to the film, making death threats against them as well. He complained through his ambassador that the film portrayed Haiti as "a country of voodoo worshippers and killers," yet he reportedly engaged a voodoo priest to bring harm to the Burtons.

Whether it was the curse of the voodoo priest, or the fact that *The Comedians* was overly long and too somber, or that the Burtons failed to sizzle onscreen, the movie did not make a profit for the first time in the Burtons' entwined careers.

Doctor Faustus was released in Oxford on October 15, 1967, and the Burtons traveled there for the premiere. Upon their arrival, Coghill joined them in an interview with David Lewin, a journalist known for asking provocative questions. The Burtons were both dressed conservatively for the occasion—Richard in a suit and tie, his hair neatly combed, and Elizabeth in a sleeveless black knit dress with a stunning diamond brooch in the shape of a dragon, the symbol of Wales.

Lewin turned to Burton and rather pompously challenged him, "You must at some time have faced the question of whether you should have continued as an imposing and even—in the view of some—great stage actor, or moved into the realm of films, which is perhaps more commercially rewarding, but not as rewarding artistically. Any regrets?"

At that point, Elizabeth jumped in. "Oh, excuse me, Richard, that makes me so angry! Because he has *not* left the stage! That's absolute, bloody rubbish!" She leveled a steely gaze at Lewin. "Last year he just got finished doing a play for Oxford on the stage. The year before that—what was he doing on Broadway? That was the stage! How can you say he left the stage?"

Lewin sniffed, "That is not a *continuous* career," like Paul Scofield's or Laurence Olivier's.

Elizabeth, still fuming, answered that Olivier's career is "not continuous either, on the stage. He does film appearances—for *money*! And so does Paul Scofield!"

When Lewin asked if Burton identified with Faustus, Elizabeth was further incensed. With the camera rolling, she let him have it. (Martha would have been proud.) "You bastard, David! I knew you'd ask that. Would *I* be 'selling out' if I deserted film for the stage?"

She knew what he was driving at: if Richard was Faust, then who was she, and the life she'd made possible for him?

Through it all, Burton sat impassively while Elizabeth defended him. Why wasn't it enough that he and Elizabeth had so vibrantly brought Shakespeare to the screen just nine months earlier? They had waited almost a year before releasing *Doctor Faustus*, not wanting to flood the market with Burton-Taylor films. But Lewin's provocative interview set the stage for what would bring Richard and Elizabeth the worst reviews of their lives and another financial disappointment. The film grossed only $610,000 worldwide (a mere $110,000 from the United States and Canada) against Burton's million-dollar investment.

After the film's New York premiere, Renata Adler, writing in the *New York Times*, sneered, "*Doctor Faustus* is of an awfulness that bends the mind. The Burtons . . . are clearly having a lovely time; at moments one has the feeling that *Faustus* was shot mainly as a home movie . . ." Pauline Kael griped in the *New Yorker*, "*Doctor Faustus* becomes the dullest episode yet in the great-lovers-of-history series that started with *Cleopatra* . . . it is clear that Faustus and Helen of Troy are not characters from Marlowe or actors playing them; they are Liz and Dick, Dick and Liz—the king and queen of a porny comic strip." The viciousness of that review reveals how in certain quarters critics were licking their chops for the chance to skewer the Burtons, as much for the ostentatious way they were living now as for their artistic over-reaching. Instead of seeing the film as a charity production—which is essentially what it was—they saw it as an indulgence.

In one of the few favorable reviews, the *Los Angeles Times* commends Burton's voice as "absolutely the right organ on which to play Marlowe's mighty lines, and Burton runs through all the changes from quavery whisper to stentorian roar." But he describes "Mrs. Burton" as the film's principal weakness, not for her performance but because by now, her presence overwhelms the part. "Her vivid personal imagery—solo and in tandem with Richard" distorts the mood of the film. The Burtons, not the roles they were playing, were now the main characters under review. It was so bad that Elizabeth's private secretary, Raymond Vignale, would rise early, collect all the newspapers, and weed out the worst of the reviews.

The glamour of the Burtons, and Richard's genius for speaking Elizabethan verse, could not lift up the low-budget, amateur nature of the movie—the minimal sets, the psychedelic effects (the purple haze of smoke, the fiery lights of hell), and the fact that most of the actors were students who had never before set foot on a soundstage (some of them quaking in their boots when the cameras rolled). Like most actors, Burton flourished under good directors; unfortunately, his and Coghill's direction tended toward the literal (as Kael complained, "if Faustus says 'gold' or 'pearls,' the screen shows gold or pearls"). Coghill just wasn't a filmmaker—he was a theater director and a teacher, and it showed. And just as no defendant should hire himself as a lawyer, there are few actors who can credibly direct themselves. Imagine the material, and Burton in it, if Zeffirelli—or John Huston, or Mike Nichols—had gotten their hands on it. "No one sets out to make a bad movie," Graham Jenkins later said about his brother's first directorial effort; "those reviews had to have set him back."

Unfortunately, the withering reviews scuttled Burton's hope to direct himself and Elizabeth in a film version of *Macbeth*. He'd felt that Elizabeth, at thirty-six, was the perfect age to play Lady Macbeth. But the goodwill generated by the box office success of *The Taming of the Shrew* was negated by the lukewarm reviews for *The Comedians* and the howls of protest over *Doctor Faustus*, so there would be no more Shakespeare for Richard or Elizabeth.

Nonetheless, the public still could not get enough of the Burtons. At the movie's New York premiere in February 1968, it was like *Hamlet* all over again. Crowds overwhelmed the couple, crashing through police barriers at the Rendezvous Theatre, nearly starting a riot. After the premiere, the Burtons hosted a gala to raise money for Philip Burton's American Musical and Dramatic Academy (perennially in need of a boost, it seems), with guests such as Robert and Ethel

Kennedy, Peter Lawford and Patricia Kennedy Lawford, Spyros Skouras, and even one of Lyndon Johnson's two daughters.

The film, actually, does bear a number of treasures—Burton's performance evokes terror, and Marlowe's rich verse rolls beautifully off his tongue. And there is one moment that sends shivers down the spine of those who know, in retrospect, what fate awaited Burton: when Faustus tries to lift up his arms to pray to Christ to save his immortal soul at the end of the film, he finds he cannot. "I would lift up my arms, but, see, they hold them—Mephistopheles and Lucifer!" he wails. Burton's neck and shoulder troubles would lead to a botched surgery, making him, in the last year of his life, unable to lift up his arms.

But the Burtons had more immediate problems. As far as the critics were concerned, just nine months after the predominantly warm reception of *The Taming of the Shrew*, for which Burton won the British Film Institute's Best Actor award, there were whiffs of blood in the water. What the press giveth, the press taketh away.

After two box office disappointments, *Reflections in a Golden Eye* was released in November 1967. It, too, was coolly received. Once again, the critics were not kind to "the greatest film actress in the world." Bosley Crowther, who had so adored Elizabeth in *Cleopatra*, described the film in the *New York Times* as "anticlimactic and banal." Both Brando and Taylor would be given poor marks for what would later be seen as powerful work. Burton thought that both Marlon's and Elizabeth's sheer physical beauty were so great that they could have "got[ten] away with murder" onscreen, but he disliked what he called Brando's "under-articulation." He blamed Elia Kazan and the Actors Studio for that, and he longed to "take him in my teeth and shake enthusiasm into him." However, Burton confided portentously in his diaries, "deep down in his desperate bowels he knows that like Elizabeth and myself, it is all a farce. All three of us, in our disparate ways, know that we are cosmic jokes."

Not surprisingly, given the poor reviews, *Reflections* was a serious failure at the box office, with producer Ray Stark eventually blaming the subject matter of homosexuality for the movie's rejection by the public. (Curiously, the public had not rejected Tennessee Williams's florid *Suddenly, Last Summer*, which had homosexuality *and* cannibalism at its center, but Gore Vidal, who adapted the one-act play for the screen, thought it was because its 1959 audiences didn't really understand what the movie was all about.)

Despite the churlish reviews, Huston went to his grave proud of *Reflections*, which he considered one of his best pictures. "Scene by scene," he would write fourteen years later, "in my humble estimation—it is hard to fault." If Elizabeth was disappointed with the poor reviews, she didn't show it. She had gotten used to the barbs of the press and had developed a much tougher skin than Richard, who still seemed to need the esteem of the world.

The year 1967 had begun with filming *The Comedians* and, for Burton, ended with *Candy*, the Terry Southern parody in which Richard had a small role, along with Marlon Brando and Ringo Starr. The year 1968, however, would see a palpable shift in the twin careers of Elizabeth and Richard. Roles continued to come Richard's way, but to appear singly, without his famous partner. What ushered in this sea change for Elizabeth was a long time coming: competition from younger and more nubile actresses as Elizabeth approached forty, and the financial disappointments of *The Comedians*, *Doctor Faustus*, and *Reflections in a Golden Eye*. Also, between the flattery and the overprotection of their entourage, they were losing touch with reality and would make poor choices in their next three films together.

10

THE ONLY GAME IN TOWN

"I introduced Elizabeth to beer; she introduced me to Bulgari."
—RICHARD BURTON

"With Richard Burton, I was living
my own fabulous, passionate fantasy."
—ELIZABETH TAYLOR

lizabeth called it "money for old rope." That was her expression for the kind of heroic movie Burton was shivering atop a five-thousand-foot mountain in Austria to finish. He'd decided to make *Where Eagles Dare*, an adventure story for MGM his children could enjoy seeing him in. The World War II espionage thriller with Clint Eastwood was based on an Alistair MacLean story about a group of commandos making a high-risk raid on the mountaintop fortress of the German Secret Service. There was so much derring-do performed by stunt doubles in the film that Eastwood took to calling it *Where Doubles Dare*. Thankfully, filming would be completed on a soundstage in London.

They had other reasons to return to England in 1968. Elizabeth would be working with Joseph Losey again, after Richard finished shooting *Where Eagles Dare* from the safety of a London set. Richard was also offered the lead role in *Laughter in the Dark*, to be directed by

Tony Richardson (who was nearing the end of his marriage to Vanessa Redgrave). Richardson had earlier directed Burton as Jimmy Porter in *Look Back in Anger*, one of Burton's greatest roles, and after the fair-to-horrible reviews of their last three films, Burton was pleased to have the work. He was amazed when *Where Eagles Dare* turned out to be MGM's biggest money-maker after its release the following year, and the most financially successful movie of his career. As it was fairly scoffed at by the London press during an early screening, and *Time* magazine complained, "It is a little melancholy to see Richard Burton reduced to playing cardboard parts like this one, but he at least manages to look as if he's having a good time," the movie's financial success surprised Richard and Elizabeth. More importantly, it helped to restore Burton's sagging box office appeal.

The writing was on the wall—their movies were now more successful when they appeared separately.

Now Elizabeth would have to play catch-up after the bad reviews of *Reflections in a Golden Eye*, and she had hopes that the new Losey film might boost her own ratings. But in the meantime, she was having too grand a time with Richard to be overly concerned with her career. "With Richard Burton, I was living my own fabulous, passionate fantasy," she later wrote about this time in their lives together.

When they arrived in London in January, the *Kalizma* was being refitted, so the Burtons leased another yacht, the *Beatrice and Bolivia*, moored at Tower Pier on the Thames, at a cost of $21,600 a month. As the British press was quick to point out, the yacht was primarily leased for the Burtons' five dogs, including their two Pekingese, O'fie and E'en So. British law required a six-month quarantine for all dogs brought into the country. By keeping their beloved pets on a boat, they could avoid quarantine. It was a gift to the British tabloids, who called it "the most expensive dog kennel in the world," and it brought the Burtons unasked-for publicity as the most decadent dog-owners since the French Revolution. The story became simply that the Burtons had rented a yacht solely for their dogs because Elizabeth couldn't bear the idea of her beloved pets being "locked up" for such an unconscionably long time. It seemed inhumane to her. The fuss would follow the Burtons into biography, where it still sits as an example of their extravagance. But it was of a piece with how money was there to be used, and if it could save the pets from their imprisonment, she was going to do it. Money simply didn't mean that much to them; it was a means to an end; they spent it on themselves—and their dogs—as freely as they spent it on both their families, and on their ever-expanding circle of helpers and business associates. They did it because they could.

By the late 1960s, reporters and magazine editors competed like pearl divers for stories about the Burtons' "extravagant lifestyle." The Burtons played a coy game with the press, particularly Richard, who, if he wasn't talking to someone he truly respected, like Kenneth Tynan, was just as happy to make remarks like "Yes, luv, we did spend $21,600 a month to keep the dogs on board, but what could we do? Elizabeth wouldn't be separated from her pets!"

To the delight of the international press, Burton topped even himself on May 17, 1968, when he flew to New York and bought at auction the Krupp diamond for Elizabeth, for $307,000 (nearly $2 million today). He had already gifted her with several stunning pieces—the beautiful emerald-and-diamond brooch from Bulgari that she had worn at their wedding in Montreal. It had matched the emerald-and-diamond ring he had given her the year before, in Puerto Vallarta, when he was filming *The Night of the Iguana*. He would later add two emerald-and-diamond bracelets to the set (sometimes called "The Grand Duchess Vladimir Suite"), also from Bulgari, whose shop they had discovered in Rome at the beginning of their great affair.

The 33.19-carat, oblong Krupp diamond took Elizabeth's breath away. It had been owned by Vera Krupp, wife of the German arms manufacturer. Elizabeth took special delight in that, saying, "I thought how perfect it would be if a nice Jewish girl like me were to own it." Richard presented it to her on the *Kalizma*, now refitted and moored in the Thames, where they had a small plaque installed to commemorate the occasion. Elizabeth was overjoyed—she later described the stone's "deep Asscher cuts—which are so complete and so ravishing"—as steps leading "into eternity and beyond . . . it sort of hums with its own beatific life." It brought Richard an equal amount of pleasure. As a miner's son, he knew the value of coal and he knew the value of diamonds. He took great pleasure in adorning Elizabeth.

Elizabeth took Richard's extravagant tokens as her due, but she also had an enlightened view of her ownership of some of the world's most expensive and fabled jewels. "I adore wearing gems, but not because they are mine. You can't possess radiance, you can only admire it," she later wrote. Which is why she was often pleased to slip off the magnificent ring and offer it to admirers to try on, as when she famously showed it off to Princess Margaret while attending a wedding in London.

"Is that the famous diamond?" Princess Margaret had asked her.

"Yes," she said, lifting up her hand so that it would catch the light.

"It's so large! How very vulgar!" the princess remarked.

"Yes," Elizabeth answered. "Ain't it great!"

"Would you mind if I tried it on?"

"Not at all!" Elizabeth slipped the ring onto Princess Margaret's finger, and noted that the princess didn't think the jewel so vulgar when *she* was wearing it. Elizabeth loved telling that story, imitating Margaret's plummy tones. She and Richard were not enthralled by royalty and knew that that story pointed up the hypocrisy and envy of the titled class.

Elizabeth and Richard's delight was short-lived, however, when *Boom!* was released on May 26, 1968, to devastating reviews. Again, the critics couldn't help commenting on the Burtons' off-camera lives, adding a dash of schadenfreude when they seemed to stumble. The *Chicago Sun-Times* wrote, "Elizabeth Taylor and Richard Burton remain the nearest thing we have in the movies to a reigning royal family . . . we know so much about them—or think we do—that there is a gruesome satisfaction at the sight of them bogged down in Tennessee Williams's belabored script, especially since its broad lines seem to resemble the Burton and Taylor private lives." *Life* magazine accused the Burtons of "a kind of arrogance . . . they don't so much act as deign to appear before us, and there is neither discipline nor dignity in what they do . . . Perhaps the Burtons are doing the very best that they can, laden as they are by their celebrity." Tennessee Williams couldn't help but feel that his movie had been derailed by what was essentially miscasting: "Dick [Burton] was too old for Chris and Liz was too young for Goforth," he wrote in his memoirs. "Despite its miscasting, I feel that *Boom!* was an artistic success and that eventually it will be received with acclaim," he added, ever hopeful. A number of reviewers attacked Elizabeth as looking fat in those billowing caftans, but in retrospect, she looks voluptuous but fit. Burton was right in one sense—Elizabeth blooms in hot climates—and in Sardinia she has that preternatural glow. Unfortunately, however, former model Joanna Shimkus's tall, willowy figure makes Elizabeth look short and plump in comparison, and Shimkus represented the new ideal in women's bodies. After the bad reviews came out, Burton wrote to Losey that he didn't care about the critics, "we'll all be proud of [*Boom!*] one day. It contains what I consider to be—though I may be alone—a magical combination of words and vision." It's worth noting that over forty years later, *Boom!* has become a somewhat guilty pleasure, enjoyed for its gorgeous setting and style, its archly poetic language, its sometimes unintentional humor. A favorite moment oft cited among the movie's fans is when, after Elizabeth paces up and down, delivering a long, highly poetic aria about the nature of time, Noël Coward remarks cattily, "You're just wrought up, dear." *Boom!*, for example, is a favorite movie of director John Waters, who describes Cissy Goforth in her fabulous outfits as "the ultimate drag queen role." He described it as "beyond bad, the other side of camp—a film so genuinely beautiful and awful that there is only one word to describe it: perfect." And it remained Tennessee Williams's favorite adaptation among all his works. With *Boom!*, the Burtons—and especially Elizabeth—entered the realm of camp.

Burton was never really happy in London—the press had been so relentlessly prying, and he preferred seeing his wife in lush, warm climates like Sardinia and Dahomey and Puerto Vallarta, where they could make love without having to keep their socks on. London taxed not only his income but his patience. And London reminded him of Hampstead and Sybil and Jessica and Kate, and what he had left behind to be with Elizabeth. (In his diary, Burton had described his dilemma as a choice between Kate—not Sybil—and Elizabeth, a choice he did not regret but that had never stopped haunting him.) If Rome had brought him Elizabeth, and the storm that followed, London punished him for it, or so he felt. It was London where a new round of troubles lay in wait.

Licking their wounds from the bad reviews for *Boom!*, in July the Burtons dragged themselves through their separate films—*Secret Ceremony* for Elizabeth and *Laughter in the Dark*, based on Vladimir Nabokov's 1932 novel, for Richard. In his film, Burton played an art dealer. While on location at Sotheby's, he used the occasion to buy a Degas drawing for £58,000 ($140,000), and Elizabeth, attending an auction at Sotheby's with a new friend, Princess Elizabeth of Yugoslavia, won her bid of £50,000 ($120,000) for Monet's "Le Val de la Falaise." There were rumors that the purchase of the two paintings had annoyed Tony Richardson, who considered it showboating— "The Dick and Liz Show" on flagrant display. Richardson seemed to be annoyed with Burton even before filming began.

Burton's respect for Nabokov had attracted him to the project, but it would turn out to be another humiliation. About two weeks into the filming of *Laughter*, Richard showed up thirty minutes late on the set. It was a Sunday, and he had brought Liza with him, thinking she would enjoy the outing with the man who had very much become her father. Richardson was furious at Burton's late arrival, and he dressed him down in front of Liza and the crew. Richard answered back and was fired on the spot.

Woodfall Film Productions announced, "Richard Burton would be leaving the set of *Laughter in the Dark*, to be replaced by Nicol Williamson," fired for being "unpunctual and unprofessional." Richard had never been fired from a film before. The actor Robert Beatty, who had been on that Austrian mountain with Burton filming *Where Eagles Dare*, came to his defense, telling the British press that the movie's producers were behaving "like an immature bride with a brilliant husband who divorces him because he arrived a bit late for dinner."

The firing would mark the beginning of a series of disasters that began the summer of 1968. It harmed Burton's relationship with the former stage director, though the ill feelings were mostly on Burton's part. Richardson would ask Burton to appear in a film adaptation of Robert Graves's *I, Claudius*, and, later, would ask him to play opposite Vanessa Redgrave in a new film of Shakespeare's *Antony and Cleopatra*. Burton, still nursing his wounds, turned down both offers. "One would think," Richard told Elizabeth, "that he'd be scared to even ask me to play Scrabble. But not our Tony." The taste of ashes in Burton's mouth would deprive the world of two performances that might have been wonderful: imagine Richard as the stuttering, reluctant Roman emperor Claudius, and Richard as Shakespeare's Antony.

Richard was shaken by the firing, and his nerves were on edge from continual drinking. He sought to calm his nerves and his mind by faithfully writing in his diary. Nerves were never Elizabeth's problem. She wasn't one to keep things inside. She spoke her mind and didn't require the secret self of a journal. She didn't require confession. Richard admired her candor in the world—he nearly envied her for it. They had both been through so much. The movie-making part of their life had taken them to Africa, London, France, Italy, Sardinia, New York, Austria, and back to London all within a year. Their nomadic life and the social whirl that went with it—to say nothing of their grueling work schedule—finally caught up with them. They had been in England long enough; another few weeks and Britain would slap them with taxes on income for the entire year. Richard was keenly aware of that, but mostly it was Elizabeth who concerned him. Something was terribly wrong. She was, in fact, often in severe pain, and Richard was worried about her.

Her pain went deep and it frightened both of them. Tamping down his own health fears, Richard was terrified that he might lose Elizabeth. He was outwardly tough and rough-hewn, but emotionally, Richard was sensitive, even shy, with the easily wounded soul of a poet. Elizabeth, on the other hand, looked delicate—and her health was delicate—but she was made of very strong stuff. She would have to be, to get through the howling reviews of *Boom!* and to work with Losey again, and endure her now-constant pain.

In *Secret Ceremony*, a disturbing psychological drama about incest and obsession, Elizabeth would be working with Losey again, but this time without Burton. In hopes of capitalizing on the recent success of *Rosemary's Baby*, no doubt, Losey cast Mia Farrow as Elizabeth's costar, and the gruff, sleepy-eyed Robert Mitchum as Albert, a louche professor in love with his stepdaughter. Elizabeth plays Leonora, a woman fallen on hard times, including prostitution, whose only child drowned years earlier due to her own negligence. Farrow's character, Cenci, a disturbed young woman being pursued by her besotted stepfather, takes Leonora into her home because she resembles her recently deceased mother. It's a Harold Pinteresque movie of brooding silences, cryptic dialogue, shocking revelations, and an all-too-believable performance by Mia Farrow as a young woman traumatized back into childhood.

The movie flirts with lesbianism (by now a trendy theme in European films) in a scene in which both women share a bath. It brought out an uncharacteristic shyness in Elizabeth. When it came time to film the scene, she emerged from her dressing room and stood just out of range of the glaring studio lights. There were too many stagehands on the set and all of them seemed to be looking at her—at Elizabeth Taylor, at Gloria Wandrous, at Maggie the Cat, at Cleopatra, at Helen of Troy—as she was about to slip into her bath. With all those eyes upon her, Elizabeth suddenly froze. Losey approached her and whispered something in her ear, and with a wave of his hand behind Elizabeth's back, he gestured for everyone to clear the floor.

When Burton heard about the shoot and Losey's uncharacteristic solicitude, he found himself jealous. "My wife and Joe Losey are having a professional love affair," he told a visiting journalist from the *Evening Standard*. It didn't really threaten them as a couple, but they were both still capable of feeling left out. (Later, Elizabeth would send Losey's wife armfuls of flowers and a Mexican dress from Puerto Vallarta, to remind Richard that Losey was happily married.) Perhaps to keep an eye on Losey, and because he didn't like being parted from his wife, Burton started spending a lot of time on the set at Elstree Studios. When Mitchum expressed displeasure with his role in the film—he'd taken the distasteful part just for the money ($150,000 for two weeks of shooting)—Burton approached Losey and offered to replace Mitchum when the production moved to Noordwijk, a seaside town in Holland, for a week of location shooting. Despite its unsavory quality, the role of the louche, tweedy professor would have suited Richard. But it didn't happen, which was perhaps just as well, as the movie already contained conscious or unconscious reminders of *Who's Afraid of Virginia Woolf?* (including an imaginary pregnancy).

Losey sometimes photographed Elizabeth in poses reminiscent of *Suddenly, Last Summer* and *The Sandpiper*—her dark, loosened hair framing her face and shoulders, camera angles that showed off her lush cleavage—even more lush, now, in 1968, as Elizabeth had noticeably gained weight, a fact not lost on her director. He parodied it, in an earlier scene in which she greedily wolfs down a meal and then belches. Later, looking at herself in the mirror in what might have been an ad-libbed moment, she exclaims, "I'm getting *so* fat!" Elizabeth was nothing if not a game gal.

Back in London, the Burtons stayed at the Dorchester, their usual haunt, where Mitchum was also in residence. Curiously, given their similar, hardscrabble backgrounds, the two men did not forge a bond. Both had lost a parent at an early age, both had known poverty, both were legendary lovers of drink and women, and both had literary aspirations. Both men loved poetry and had a love-hate relationship with their profession. Neither considered acting a manly pursuit. But they seemed to have little to say to each other—perhaps they were too much alike, or were beyond the age of forging new friendships. Or Burton may simply have been jealous of the macho actor's proximity to Elizabeth, another reason for making himself present on the shoot. He was just the kind of rough, masculine character that Elizabeth liked, and neither one of them was above sexual possessiveness—Burton in particular, ever self-conscious about his ravaged skin.

Halfway through filming, Elizabeth could no longer work through her constant visceral pain. After a series of tests, Elizabeth was admitted to a London hospital for a hysterectomy. "Elizabeth had her uterus removed on Sunday morning. The operation began at 9:30 and ended at 1:00," Burton wrote in his diary, marking some of the most awful days of his life. He read Michael Holroyd's *Life of Lytton Strachey* to distract himself during the hours of surgery, and afterward admitted that he didn't remember having read a single word. "There was nothing before," he wrote when she was finally out of danger and recovering at home, "no shame inflicted or received, no injustice done to me, no disappointment professional or private that I could not think away . . . But this is the first time where I've seen a loved one in screaming agony for two days, hallucinated by drugs, sometimes knowing who I was and sometimes not, a virago one minute, an angel the next, and felt completely helpless."

He took the hospital room next to hers to stay overnight after the surgery, but it turned out to be *Walpurgis Nacht*. Through paper-thin walls, he heard her groaning until dawn. There were complications, and, to ease the pain, Elizabeth was given drugs that unnerved Richard with their side effects: "lurid hallucinations" alternating with moments of "extraordinary shafts of clarity," as he described them. Richard had seen mightily drunken men in his day—including his own father—but nothing that filled him with terror like this. "She thinks she is on the *Kalizma*," he recorded, "and when flowers arrive in her hospital room she demands that they be put downstairs in Liza's room." Richard tried to distract her with a book by Muriel Spark, but Elizabeth suddenly looked up from its pages and admonished Richard for shouting at the steward on their yacht. "Hush, he'll hear you," she said, putting her fingers to her lips. She imagined that *Doctor Faustus* was playing on the turned-off television set.

The ordeal brought out the George and Martha in them both. When she suddenly left her bed, Richard tried leading her back to her room, calling her "a naughty girl" for disobeying her doctor's orders. She told him to "fuck off." When he offered to sit with her in her room, she commanded him to sit in a chair in the hall as she couldn't stand the sight of his face. But five minutes later, she cried out for him. To make matters worse, the press filled the hospital lobby, crowding out patients in the emergency room. Elizabeth's hospitalization was headline news every day, and each day more lurid. In her drugged state, Elizabeth wondered if Richard was still with her in the hospital, or if he'd abandoned her.

"She is still asleep and it's half past midday. I'm longing to see her," Richard wrote in his journal. But what haunted him was what the drugs did to her, how they affected the way she acted toward him—those baleful, malevolent looks, her invective. At least he hadn't lost her, though it hit them both when they left the hospital that, now, they would never have their own child.

This was the final verdict. "A child with Richard. I would have wanted that above everything in the world," Elizabeth would later say.

That door had closed. But they still had their fabulous life together, and their family. And they had each other. That had been the most important thing. To give birth to "Elizabeth and Richard"—"Liz and Dick"—had been no easy task. They couldn't take another loss. But another loss would come.

When *Secret Ceremony* was released at the end of 1968, the reviews were, again, so bad that Elizabeth slipped from sixth place to tenth place in box office rankings. A mere two years before, in 1966, she had been ranked third, behind Julie Andrews and Sean Connery. Even her hospitalization and hysterectomy—though it restored her slimmer, more youthful figure—didn't lift the fortunes of this film, as her illnesses had on previous occasions. Judith Crist decried the film as "truly terrible" and Rex Reed lamented, "Her disintegration is a very sad thing to stand by helplessly and watch, but something ghastly has happened over the course of her last four or five films . . . Taylor has become a hideous parody of herself."

In retrospect, Elizabeth is quite convincing in *Secret Ceremony*, and is genuinely moving as the grieving mother who hopes for a chance to replace the child she lost. The *Guardian*'s critic, practically alone among reviewers, described the movie as "quite beautifully made." But the fact that she was willing to play the vulgarian, and to stand by while Mitchum, as Albert, heaps insults upon her, calling her a cow "famous for her mammalia," tilted the movie into parody.

Despite the bad reviews for her two Losey films, and the fact that they both lost money, it was to Elizabeth's credit that she was willing to take on edgier fare. She saw a new direction for her career in European art-house films. She was willing to age gracefully, to become a figure like Jeanne Moreau or Simone Signoret. Unfortunately, Elizabeth was now too famous to disappear into the roles she was playing, a dilemma for any serious actress. There was now more public interest in her private life and her extravagances than in her films. The paparazzi seemed more eager to photograph Elizabeth in unflattering poses, looking heavy, or eating and drinking. Her friend and in-house photographer, Gianni Bozzacchi, noticed this unfortunate trend. "The paparazzi were now getting more money for bad shots of Elizabeth than for beautiful ones," he said. They lay in wait to surprise her looking at her worst.

Elizabeth's hysterectomy in July was followed by more bad news. Two days after Elizabeth's operation, Andrew Besançon, Richard's longtime gardener at Pays de Galle, his Swiss home in Céligny, was found dead in the estate's garage. He had hanged himself. Burton made plans to fly to Geneva for the funeral, bringing with him Kate and Liza, his brother and sister-in-law Ifor and Gwen, and Brook Williams, by now an ever-present member of Burton's entourage. Elizabeth didn't want him to go, but relented if Richard promised to stay in her chalet in Gstaad rather than in the house in Céligny, which had been closed up for two years.

"I remember that he had suffered from a nervous breakdown some twelve or thirteen years ago after the death of his wife," Burton confided in his diary about the death of his gardener. He had known the man since 1957—eleven years—and Besançon was apparently about to go into a nursing home the night before he committed suicide. "He killed himself last night. I feel such a bloody fool for not even suspecting it."

Burton hadn't set foot in the house in Céligny for two years, and it still seemed haunted by its former life, and now by Besançon's suicide. Nonetheless, they decided to spend the night there rather than drive back to Gstaad. Once in Céligny, the three men—Richard, Ifor, and Brook—stopped in at Café de la Gare, situated on a railway bridge just across the tracks from Burton's house. While rain poured outside, the three Welshmen dined on fish and drank heavily, polishing off thirty-seven half-liters of white wine. Around three in the morning, Ifor left the café to go and open up the house, little used since Burton's divorce from Sybil five years earlier.

Stumbling around in the dark, searching for the switch to turn on the outside light, Ifor apparently slipped on a grill or a boot-scrape and fell against a windowsill, breaking his neck. "He literally missed his footing in the dark," recalled Brook Williams. "It left him completely paralyzed."

Richard was shattered.

He had once told his younger brother, Graham, "After Cis, I loved Ifor the best. He was the nearest to a father to me." Indeed, Richard had hero-worshipped his robust and stalwart brother since he was a boy. Ifor used to carry him piggy-back, running over the hills of Pontrhydyfen. Later Ifor would cheer Rich in swimming contests as he fought the rough waves, or kicking up enormous clouds of dust playing Welsh rugby. Ifor was his "hero, brother, father, confessor, and best friend." Once, after Burton's early success, when he brought Ifor out to Hollywood, he was delighted when his towering brother had lifted Humphrey Bogart off the floor by his lapels, angry over some remark at a party, as if the famous actor were nothing more than a drunk in a Welsh pub. When Ifor had protested Richard's treatment of Sybil, it was a blow greater than all the condemnation Richard had received from the Vatican and the international press. Now, this man among men—this force of nature—would be confined to a wheelchair for the rest of his life, paralyzed from the neck down. It was more than Richard could bear, and—as he always had—he blamed himself.

In September, the couple flew to Paris and checked into the Plaza Athénée, so Burton could begin filming an unconventional movie called *Staircase*, directed by Stanley Donen. In this movie, Burton and his good friend Rex Harrison played a pair of aging homosexuals. It seemed an unusual choice to take on such challenging fare, after the twin horrors of Ifor's paralysis and Elizabeth's hysterectomy, and he found himself having to explain it to the press. Like a man going through customs, Richard had to publicly declare that he wasn't homosexual—"I tried it once," he admitted with remarkable candor at the time.

When he was sixteen, Richard had been taken by Emlyn Williams to a party where he quickly noticed that all the guests were gay men, some of whom made passes at him. "What could I say? What could I do? I mean, these were some of the greatest actors in the English theater. I wasn't gay, but it was hard to say no," he wrote about the incident. Later, when he was receiving his six-month course of Royal Air Force (RAF) training at Exeter College, Oxford, he was the only RAF officer trainee who finagled a single room for himself, possibly arranged by Philip Burton (who, as commanding officer of Port Talbot Squadron 499, had gotten Burton the opportunity to begin with). One day, when the RAF trainees were parading in formation on the Oxford grounds, Richard was commanded to step forward. He was pulled out of line and reprimanded for "entertaining an officer in his room." That he wasn't drummed out of the corps was probably due to the influence of his commanding officer—Philip Burton—but Richard recalled it as a particularly humiliating incident, especially for the son of a Welsh miner.

Elizabeth, though, had helped him overcome any shame he might have still harbored. Now, here was a chance to portray the pathos of a gay man living in England at a time when homosexuality was considered a crime. It also offered him a chance to confront his past, and Elizabeth gave him the courage to do so.

Burton announced to the press that he'd accepted the part because Rex Harrison had said, "I will if you will." Elizabeth had urged him to take on the role, given her affection for her many gay friends— Roddy McDowall, Dick Hanley, John Lee, Montgomery Clift, Rock Hudson, Vincente Minnelli, Franco Zeffirelli—and her belief in the film's affirmation of the healing power of love, no matter the orientation. With Elizabeth's help, Richard had become more able to accept his early sexual experiences, and appearing as a gay barber—although sometimes slipping into parody—reflected that self-acceptance. One would have a hard time imagining other actors of his stature at the time—John Wayne, Frank Sinatra, Paul Newman, George C. Scott—taking on an overtly gay role.

Even after a string of poorly performing films, the Burtons still had the clout to demand their highest salaries to date—$1.25 million each—for Burton to appear in *Staircase* and, for Elizabeth, *The Only Game in Town*, both for 20th Century-Fox. ("They must be out of their tiny Chinese minds," Elizabeth had quipped when the producers agreed to their demands.) They also asked that they not be made to work more than an hour's distance apart when they weren't working together, which is why both films were shot in Paris, instead of on location in London's East End or in Las Vegas, where the stories were set. (They had had the same arrangement on their last two films, *Where Eagles Dare* and *Secret Ceremony*, both filmed at Elstree Studios.) Elaborate sets had to be constructed at the Boulogne-sur-Seine studio, but 20th Century-Fox was convinced that the Burton magic was still viable enough to recoup their huge salaries.

The Only Game in Town came about because Frank Sinatra had wanted to know the name of a dog. Sinatra had called the Burtons to ask about the breed of O'Fie, because he wanted to buy a similar dog for his new wife, Mia Farrow. He got their agent, Hugh French, on the phone, and French was suddenly hit by the idea of pairing Elizabeth with Sinatra. They had, surprisingly, never appeared together in a movie. French found the screenplay for *The Only Game in Town*, set in Sinatra-friendly Las Vegas, and Elizabeth agreed to do it. The story is about a piano-playing compulsive gambler—Sinatra, of course—and his Las Vegas–dancer girlfriend, played by Elizabeth. Frank D. Gilroy (author of *The Subject Was Roses)* wrote the screenplay, adapted from his own Broadway play. Elizabeth's first great director, George Stevens, who had catapulted her to true movie stardom in *A Place in the Sun* and *Giant*, was signed to direct. Though working with Stevens, particularly in *Giant*, had been hard on Elizabeth, she had never looked more luminous than in those films, and she trusted that he would again work his magic.

However, before filming began in Paris, Sinatra backed out, to be replaced by Warren Beatty, fresh from his stunning success as both producer and star of *Bonnie and Clyde*. But it wasn't a good match. With his boyish good looks, Beatty seemed to belong to another generation, and the cinematic love affair between him and Taylor just wasn't believable. He wasn't convincing as a jaded Las Vegas denizen, and Elizabeth's womanly figure wasn't suited to the miniskirts and stretch pants of the era. Despite Beatty and Taylor's on-camera mismatch, Burton became jealous of the actor—already well known as catnip to women—whom he described in his diary as "her young & attractive man who obviously adores her." He dealt with his jealousy in the usual way—drinking heavily by five p.m., martinis this time. "I felt desperate all day long . . . I was so drunk & tired that I fell asleep almost before I'd managed to get my clothes off," he confided in his diary. Richard knew it was important for Elizabeth to appear in her own films, but, he admitted, "I don't like Elizabeth working without me."

When Darryl Zanuck viewed the rushes for the two back-to-back films, he was convinced that the studio had two hits on their hands. But once again, both films would lose money. Buckets of it. *The Only Game in Town* lost $8 million, and *Staircase* lost $5.8 million. Zanuck, it appeared, was just as out of touch with what contemporary audiences wanted as the Burtons now appeared to be. The success of lower-budget films like *Easy Rider* and *The Graduate*—Mike Nichols's second movie—would usher in a change in Hollywood, in a world where the Burtons increasingly seemed throwbacks to another era. Elizabeth now had three flops in a row, and she wouldn't make another movie for two years.

The family business was in trouble.

To console himself, Burton found great comfort in tallying up their combined assets, with a mind toward possible retirement. "I have worked out that with average luck, we should, at the end of 1969, be worth about $12 million between us. About $3 million of that is in diamonds, emeralds, property, paintings, so our annual income will be in the region of $1.2 million. That is, God willing, and no wars, and no '29." Burton, however, was still bankable, because *Where Eagles Dare* would turn out to be the biggest money-maker of the year, earning $21 million domestically. But their next joint picture, *Anne of the Thousand Days*, would mark the beginning of the end of Elizabeth's career as a leading lady.

While in Paris, the Burtons continued their round of socializing with the aristocracy, spending time with the Duke and Duchess of Windsor, who visited Elizabeth on the set of *The Only Game in Town*, and Richard, a half mile away, on the set of *Staircase*. The Duke and Duchess were, in a way, the Burtons' only equivalents. Before *Le Scandale*, theirs had been the most notorious, damaging, and publicized marriage of the century, which ended King Edward VIII's reign so that he could marry the Baltimore divorcée Wallis Simpson. England wept at the king's abdication, and the press excoriated the couple—particularly the stylish, aloof American for whom he had thrown over his kingdom. "The beating *they* took by the press," Elizabeth later noted, "made us look like chopped chicken liver." The duke saw himself exiled to Jamaica and ostracized by the royal family, as he and his bride reigned over a diminished shadow empire of millionaires, fashion plates, social climbers, playboys, and movie people. Their story had special poignancy for Richard, as the duke was also the Prince of Wales. To honor the connection, the duchess often wore her stunning "Prince of Wales" brooch—three feathers and a crown, the insignia of Wales in white and yellow diamonds. Over dinner at the duke and duchess's house in Paris, the duchess told Elizabeth that it was one of the few pieces of jewelry that Lord Mountbatten had overlooked when he came to take back all of the royal jewels upon the duke's abdication. (Elizabeth would end up owning the brooch after the duchess's death in 1986, when she bid on it at a Sotheby's auction the following year for an AIDS fund-raising event, paying $623,000. She had phoned in the bid sitting by her pool in Los Angeles. "All along I knew my friend the duchess wanted me to have it," she believed.) Elizabeth loved spending time at their exquisite Paris house with its beautiful gardens that the duke had himself designed and had planted with his own hands.

Burton was less sanguine about spending time with "marred royalty." He was bored at the duke and duchess's soirees. He described the couple as resembling "Two tiny figures like Toto and Nanette that you keep on the mantelpiece. Chipped around the edges. Something you keep in the front room for Sundays only." At one such soiree, on November 13, 1968, he picked up the duchess and swung her around the room "like a dancing singing dervish." Elizabeth was horrified. Of course, it didn't help that Richard was now, on occasion, capable of downing three bottles of vodka a day. Furious with him, Elizabeth locked him in the spare bedroom that night, at the Plaza Athénée. Richard tried to kick the door down, shattering the plaster, and had to spend the next morning picking up the pieces. He later expressed remorse in his diary when he wrote, "I'd better be off to work because I behaved with a fair amount of disgrace yesterday . . . it is not a good idea to drink so much. I shall miss all the marriages of all my various children . . ."

And, on November 15, they set off for a weekend getaway at the Château de Ferrières, the beautiful country house of Guy and Marie-Hélène Rothschild. Richard didn't want to go. "I'd like to be alone with E. for about two hundred years but can't even get two days," he complained.

Elizabeth was still suffering back pain and still feeling weak after her hysterectomy. In October, she complained to Burton that she sometimes had no feeling in her feet and that she feared she might one day become crippled. "She asked if I would stop loving her if she had to spend the rest of her life in a wheelchair. I told her that I didn't care if her legs, bum, and bosoms fell off, and her teeth turned yellow and she went bald. I love that woman so much sometimes that I cannot believe my luck. She has given me so much." And then, in late November, Elizabeth again received sad news.

As it had with the death of Montgomery Clift, it fell to Richard to break the news of Elizabeth's father's passing away on November 20, 1968, a month shy of his seventy-first birthday. After Francis Taylor's stroke three years earlier, his death wasn't unexpected, but Elizabeth was devastated, in part, perhaps, because there had always been some distance between her and her father, unlike her extremely close relationship with her mother, Sara. She would never be close to him now.

Elizabeth was inconsolable in her grief; "like a wild animal," Burton recorded. Though Francis Taylor had disliked his daughter's childhood acting career, and Sara's devotion to it had caused a rift in their marriage, he was, in some ways, responsible for bringing it about. First, he had made his wife abandon her successful stage career (though they were both from Arkansas City, Kansas, he had courted her when she was appearing in a play in London's West End), so Sara had poured all of her frustrated theatrical impulses into Elizabeth. And when he was an air-raid warden in Los Angeles during World War II, he had crossed paths with fellow air-raid warden Sam Marx. Then a story editor at MGM, Marx had told Elizabeth's father that the studio was desperately looking for a little English girl to appear in a movie then in production, *Lassie Come Home*. Francis casually mentioned it to Sara that evening. The rest is history, and Francis didn't like how it turned out. Elizabeth recalled, "He had made my mother quit the stage when she was twenty-nine, and she lived her life vicariously and very strongly through me, and of course, my dad resented that." When Elizabeth started earning more money than her father, their idyllic family life ended. "That's when it fell apart," Elizabeth believed.

The Burtons flew back to Los Angeles to attend the funeral and to console Sara Taylor. Six days later, they were back in Paris, and Elizabeth, ever the trouper, returned to work.

In December 1968, *Candy* was released. As a favor to Marlon Brando, Burton had taken a small novelty role as a Dylan Thomas–like poet making the rounds of college campuses and seducing girls, so it couldn't have been pleasant to read the lousy reviews. *Variety* was alone in lauding Burton for succeeding "by lampooning his own style. He gives an outstanding comedy performance." Practically everywhere else, he was accused of having no gift for comedy. Despite its trainload of fascinating stars and personalities—Brando, John Huston, James Coburn, Walter Matthau, the French singer Charles Aznavour, Ringo Starr, even boxing champion Sugar Ray Robinson and ex–Rolling Stone girlfriend Anita Pallenberg—the spoof was dismissed by most critics as a "frenzied, formless, and almost entirely witless adaptation." That's what you get for hanging out with Marlon Brando and agreeing, while drunk, to appear in movies made by your friends.

In many respects, 1968 had been a terrible year. Though it had begun with filming *Where Eagles Dare*, giving Richard's film career a needed jolt and changing its direction (from dramatic actor to action star), and it brought Elizabeth the fabulous and fabled Krupp diamond, it had ended with the death of Francis Taylor and had seen the paralyzing accident of Burton's beloved brother Ifor.

Through it all, however, their grand passion continued. Burton wrote at the end of the year, "She is a wildly exciting love-mistress, she is shy and witty, she is nobody's fool, she is a brilliant actress, she is beautiful beyond the dreams of pornography, she can be arrogant and willful, she is clement and loving . . . she tolerates my impossibilities and my drunkenness, she is an ache in the stomach when I am away from her, *and she loves me!* . . . And I'll love her till I die."

11

"RINGS AND FARTHINGALES"

"It's just a present for Liz."
—RICHARD BURTON, ON THE PURCHASE OF THE
CARTIER DIAMOND FOR $1.1 MILLION

"Sometimes his joy was perverse and he would become dark."
—ELIZABETH TAYLOR

In December 1968, Richard returned to London to complete filming on *Staircase* while Elizabeth stayed behind in Paris with her mother. Elizabeth grew even closer to Sara following her father's death, cherishing her remaining parent. Even though 20th Century-Fox had given Elizabeth some time off to rest, her health had never fully improved after her hysterectomy. Her constant back pain troubled her, and she had to wear a brace just to get through a day of shooting. Richard worried that she might end up in a wheelchair. He was angry that she didn't take better care of herself, and noted that the doctors had wanted her to remain in bed for at least a month. She didn't do it. Richard thought it was odd that her doctors didn't forbid her to drink while she was also taking powerful prescription painkillers. He had always distrusted doctors, blaming their "sheer neglect" for his mother's death while she was giving birth to her thirteenth child. But he wished that Elizabeth would heed their advice. "So I'll

have my two favorite people in the world, E. and Ifor, tottering about
on crutches," Richard wrote gloomily. But he was actually fooling
himself when it came to Ifor: there would be a slight improvement in
his condition, allowing him to stand up on a few occasions and even
swim, but he would remain paralyzed from the waist down, reduced
to living in a motorized wheelchair.

On the last day of the year, Burton wrote,

> My chief worry . . . is E.'s health. It is getting no better and she
> does maddingly little to help it. . . . I stayed in bed all day yester-
> day, for instance, while she spent the entire day until well after
> midnight sitting in the main room, gossiping, etc. And, of course,
> inevitably sipping away at the drinks. I dreaded at night when she
> has had her shots, etc., . . . and is only semiarticulate. . . . What
> is more frightening is that she has become bored with everything
> in life. She never reads a book, at least not more than a couple of
> pages at a time. . . . I have always been a heavy drinker but now
> as a result of this half-life we've been leading I am drinking twice
> as much. The upshot will be that I'll die of drink while she'll go
> blithely on in her half-world.

The prescription drugs, combined with the alcohol Elizabeth continued to imbibe, had a terrible effect on her. Some days she went to
bed in a "stoned daze," totally disoriented and incoherent. It frightened Richard so much that he stopped drinking temporarily, though
he considered alcohol one of life's few pleasures in "a murderous
world." He saw his own behavior mirrored in Elizabeth, and he didn't
like what he saw.

In January 1969, the Burtons managed to fly to Las Vegas for the final
ten days of filming *The Only Game in Town*. To help distract Elizabeth
from her pain—and because it also captured his imagination—Burton
bid on another fabled jewel at Sotheby's. "La Peregrina" was an ex-

traordinary, pear-shaped pearl that had been given to Mary Tudor, first daughter of Henry VIII, by King Philip of Spain in 1554. The pearl's provenance was so distinguished it came with its own biography, beginning with its discovery by a slave in the Gulf of Panama (which won him his freedom). It made an appearance in two paintings by Velàzquez, the great painter of the Spanish court: worn as a brooch by Queen Margarita (the wife of Philip III), and suspended from a long necklace around the throat of her daughter-in-law, Queen Isabel. The next famous owners of La Peregrina were the Bonapartes in the early 1800s. Burton won his $37,000 bid at Sotheby's, beating out Prince Alfonso de Bourbon Asturias, who had wanted to return the pearl to Spain, which many considered its rightful home. But La Peregrina continued to wander: Sotheby's had the pearl couriered to Las Vegas, to the top floor of Caesars Palace, where the Burtons were then in residence.

When Elizabeth lifted the pearl out of its case, she gasped. She lovingly put it around her neck. She couldn't stop touching it, "like a talisman," and she walked through her hotel suite, "dreaming and glowing and wanting to scream with joy," as she would later write. She wanted to share her joy with Richard, but she saw that he was in one of his Welsh moods. "Sometimes his joy was perverse and he would become dark." She knew Richard, and she knew better than to throw herself at him and cover him with kisses, which was what she wanted to do. Incredibly, there was no one around to share her joy.

Suddenly, when she reached up to touch the pearl, she noticed it was gone. She was horrified—she ran into her bedroom and threw herself on the bed, where she screamed into the pillow. How could she have lost it? She got up and slowly retraced her steps, searching for the pearl before Richard learned that it was missing. Richard loved the pearl as much as she did, mostly for its unique, noble provenance—he loved anything historical. She even removed her shoes so she could feel it underfoot, and she got down on her hands and knees to search every inch of the carpet. It wasn't there.

So she went into the living room, tiptoeing around Burton, pretending nonchalance while she continued to hunt for the pearl. Out of the corner of her eye, she noticed their two Pekingese puppies at their feeding bowls. One of them was apparently gnawing on a bone, which was odd, because they never gave the puppies bones to chew on. When she investigated, she nearly shrieked with delight when she opened the puppy's mouth to find La Peregrina—intact and unscratched. It would be at least a week before she could bring herself to tell Richard what had happened.

For Elizabeth, her pleasure in La Peregrina was another expression of her almost mystical connection to jewels. It had arrived dangling on a lovely little pearl-and-platinum chain necklace, but, three years later, with the help of a designer from Cartier, Elizabeth created an exquisite design to showcase it, inspired by a sixteenth-century portrait of Mary, Queen of Scots, wearing the pearl. The new setting was a stunning double-stranded pearl-and-ruby choker, made with fifty-six "exquisitely matched oriental pearls." And Richard was so inspired by its history that he planned to write a historical novel based on the peregrinations of the luminous pearl.

Their pleasure in La Peregrina did not last long, however. They had been fighting so much that by March, Richard wondered if they would be able to stay together. "The last six or eight months have been a nightmare," Burton wrote. "I created one half and Elizabeth the other. We grated on each other to the point of separation." Burton even contemplated running off to live alone in a shack in a tropical forest, and Elizabeth thought about going to live with her brother in Hawaii. "It is, of course, quite impossible. We are bound together. Whither thou goest . . ."

How fitting, perhaps, that a few months after giving Elizabeth La Peregrina, Richard himself would become Henry VIII, father of Mary I of England, in Hal Wallis's film *Anne of the Thousand Days*. Elizabeth wanted desperately to play Anne Boleyn opposite Richard, but for once, the thing she most desired was denied her. Wallis informed

Richard became close to Elizabeth's children, and they adopted Maria Burton in 1964. *Left to right:* Liza Todd, Michael Wilding, Jr., Christopher Wilding, and Maria Burton. [Bob Penn/Camera Press/Retna Ltd.]

A scene from Graham Greene's *The Comedians,* again playing illicit lovers. For the first time, Richard was paid more than Elizabeth to appear in a film. [Collection Pele/Stills/Gamma-Rapho]

(Above) The Burtons and children at the Nice Airport in 1967. "We've lived like gypsies," Elizabeth later said. They would soon invest in their own plane. [Globe Photos Inc.]

(Left) Elizabeth and Richard in *Doctor Faustus,* 1966, staged for his beloved Oxford University Drama Society (OUDS). The poor reviews of the filmed play scuttled his plans to direct himself and Elizabeth in *Macbeth.* [Terrance Spencer/ Time Life Pictures/Getty Images]

(Right) At the Save Venice Costume Ball in 1967. Elizabeth's elaborate headdress was created by Alexandre of Paris. It would inspire her fabulous costume in the Burtons' next film, Joseph Losey's *Boom!* [SSPL/Getty Images]

(Left) Relaxing in Sardinia on the set of *Boom!*, based on Tennessee Williams's play, *The Milk Train Doesn't Stop Here Anymore.* [© Henry Grossman]

(Above) Richard's drinking increased after the death of his beloved brother Ifor. Elizabeth would be one of the first celebrities to seek treatment at the Betty Ford Clinic. Pictured here in 1967. [A.P. Images]

(Above) Richard and Elizabeth at the Paris Opera House, September 29, 1967. [Keystone/ Gamma-Rapho]

Richard, Elizabeth, and eleven-year-old Kate Burton braving the crowds outside the Winter Garden Theater in New York, to attend a matinee performance of *Mame* on November 11, 1967. This was their first visit to America in nearly two years. [Corbis]

Richard and Elizabeth on a yacht on the Thames, rented to house their Pekinese and Yorkshire terriers to avoid British quarantine. The British roundly criticized their extravagance. February 1968. [Bob Aylott/ Keystone/Getty Images]

(Above) Elizabeth showing off the 33.19-carat Krupp Diamond, a gift from Richard, May 20, 1968. "I thought, how perfect it would be if a nice Jewish girl like me were to own it," she later said. [Express/Hulton Archive/Getty Images]

(Right) Richard with the French-Canadian actress Geneviève Bujold, in *Anne of the Thousand Days.* Elizabeth was deemed too old to play the young Anne Boleyn, but she dazzled as an extra. Richard was nominated for another Oscar for his role as Henry VIII. May 1969. [© Trinity Mirror/Mirrorpix/Alamy]

(Left) If Elizabeth was jealous of Bujold in *Anne of the Thousand Days,* Richard kept a sharp eye on Warren Beatty, her co-star in *The Only Game in Town.* [20th Century Fox/mptvimages.com]

(*Above*) "She is like the tide, she comes and she goes, she runs to me/ as in this stupendous photographic image./In my poor and tormented youth, I had always dreamed of this/woman. And now, when this dream occasionally returns, I extend/ my arm, and she is here . . . by my side. If you have not met or known her, you have lost much in life," Richard wrote on this photograph of Elizabeth, c. 1970. [Courtesy of the University of Wisconsin Press]

(*Right*) Richard and Elizabeth at her mother Sara Taylor's home in Bel Air, March 13, 1970, on a break from an interview for *60 Minutes*. [Photofest]

(Left) Elizabeth's expensive mink coat and her million-dollar Cartier ("Burton-Taylor") diamond inspired disapproval for their extravagance.

(Below) Home at last, aboard their private luxury yacht, *The Kalizma,* purchased for $192,000 and rechristened for their three daughters, Kate, Liza, and Maria. It included fourteen bedrooms and carried a crew of nine.

(Left) Elizabeth, Richard, and their chauffeur, Gaston Sanz, with the Duke and Duchess of Windsor. "The beating *they* took by the press made us look like chopped chicken liver," Elizabeth said about the Windsors. [from the Private Archives of Dame Elizabeth Taylor]

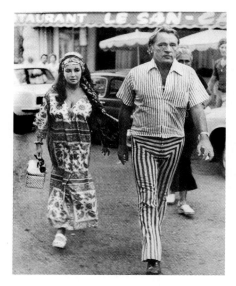

(Left) Elizabeth and Richard on shore leave in Monte Carlo. In the early 1970s, the Burtons sailed the Mediterranean aboard the *Kalizma*. [Keystone/Gamma-Rapho]

Richard, Lucille Ball, and Elizabeth in "Lucy Meets the Burtons," an episode of *Here's Lucy* on CBS. Richard hated working with the comedienne, considering it the nadir of his acting career. September 14, 1970. [CBS/Landov]

(Above) Elizabeth and Richard with Peter O'Toole *(left)* in Dylan Thomas's *Under Milk Wood,* a labor of love for Richard, who greatly admired his fellow Welshman and poet, and a loving gesture from Elizabeth. [Rex USA/BEImages]

(Below) Hollywood royalty: Richard flanked by Elizabeth and Princess Grace of Monaco, at a Red Cross gala in Monaco, August 1971. [Keystone/Hulton/ Getty Images]

(Above) Elizabeth and Richard costumed for the Proust Ball, given by Baron and Baroness Guy de Rothschild at the Chateau de Ferrières, Seine-et-Marne, 1972. [Courtesy of the Cecil Beaton Studio Archive at Sotheby's]

"Get that woman out of my bed!" Elizabeth demanded when she suspected Richard was having a fling with one of his *Bluebeard* co-stars, Nathalie Delon. Photographed on the set of *Bluebeard,* filmed in Budapest in 1972. [© Odile Montserrat/Sygma/Corbis]

Richard made amends with the Taj Mahal diamond, a gift for Elizabeth's fortieth birthday, which he showed off in a press conference in Budapest. Elizabeth celebrated her birthday with a gala at the Hotel Duna International. [A.P. Images]

The Burtons separated after filming *Bluebeard* and Elizabeth took up with Henry Wynberg, Beverly Hills roué. Richard could never get his name quite right. [Friedrich Rauch/Camera Press/Retna Ltd.]

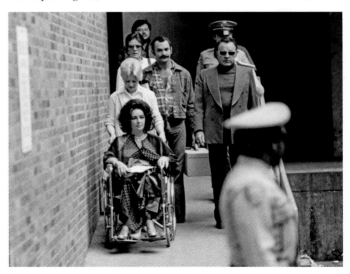

Richard flew from Rome to Los Angeles, where Elizabeth was being treated at University Hospital in December 1973, to replace Henry Wynberg at her bedside. The Burtons photographed leaving the hospital in December 1973. [© Tony Korody/Sygma/Corbis]

Elizabeth and Richard in *Divorce His Divorce Hers,* their first made-for-television movie and their last movie together. Like many of their films, it mirrored their private lives. November 1972. [Courtesy of the University of Wisconsin Press]

(Below) Headline news as Elizabeth and Richard announce their remarriage in August 1975. [John Frost Newspapers]

(Above) Richard with Sophia Loren, his co-star in the 1974 television remake of *Brief Encounter.* Elizabeth feared that Richard was "misbehaving" with the beautiful Italian film star. [Steve Wood/Express/Getty Images]

Elizabeth and Richard in Botswana, where they remarried on October 10, 1975. Their second marriage lasted less than ten months, ending on July 29, 1976. [Argus/A.P. Images]

After the couple's second divorce, Richard married former model Suzy Hunt in August of 1976. Suzy kept him sober, but she also kept him from his friends. They divorced five years later. [Popperfoto/Getty Images]

(Right) Elizabeth's marriage to U.S. Senator from Virginia John Warner lasted six years. She stayed in close touch with Burton by telephone throughout the marriage, her seventh. *Pictured here:* Warner, former U.S. President Gerald Ford, and Elizabeth. [John Full/UPI/Landov]

(Above) A brief encounter with Richard on Elizabeth's fiftieth birthday celebration, arriving at Legends nightclub in London on February 28, 1982. [© Alan Davidson]

(Left) Elizabeth enticed Richard to co-star with her in Noel Coward's *Private Lives* in 1983, a financial success but a critical disaster. "Everyone bought tickets to watch high camp Liz and Dick," Elizabeth said, "and we gave them what they wanted." [John Frost Newspapers]

Richard married his young assistant, Sally Hay *(second from left)*, during the run of *Private Lives*. Elizabeth announced her engagement to lawyer Victor Luna *(far right)*, though the two would not marry. [© David McGough/Time Life Pictures/Getty Images]

(Right) The two women Richard most loved in his life: the sister who raised him, Cecilia "Cissy" James *(left)* and Elizabeth, attending Richard Burton's memorial service in August 1984. "And I'll love her till I die," Richard wrote about Elizabeth. [Mirrorpix]

Elizabeth visiting Richard's grave in Geneva, Switzerland, on August 14, 1984, shielded by umbrellas from photographers camping at the gravesite. [Graham Wood/Daily Mail/Rex/BEImages]

(Right) Elizabeth and Richard leaving the theater in Montreal after a performance of *Hamlet* to attend their wedding reception, March 1965. [© Henry Grossman/from the Private Archives of Dame Elizabeth Taylor]

her that at thirty-seven, she was just too old to play twenty-two-year-old Anne Boleyn. It was a bitter pill for Elizabeth, who had to watch the fresh, beautiful French-Canadian actress Geneviève Bujold pursued on camera by Richard in a role she felt should have belonged to her. Three years shy of forty—the age Joe Mankiewicz had warned all actresses about—she was still beautiful, still idolized by the public, but she had to confront what so many actresses face: the beginning of the end of their careers as "leading ladies." After all, in an industry dominated by men, it was still considered business as usual to pair leading men in their forties and fifties with actresses in their twenties (as in *Love in the Afternoon*, with fifty-six-year-old Gary Cooper romantically paired with twenty-eight-year-old Audrey Hepburn).

Burton, out of loyalty to Taylor, tried to get out of playing the role, but he was threatened with a lawsuit by Universal Pictures. ("I was never sued when I was poor," he complained in his diary.) So before debarking to dreary London where the movie would be filmed, the Burtons returned to the paradise of Puerto Vallarta, a place where they had been enormously happy, a place that seemed to have the power to restore them to sanity and to health, and to remind them why they were still together.

Like everything else, Puerto Vallarta had changed since their discovery of the enchanting village five years earlier. It had grown from a sleepy seaside town of barely a thousand souls to a bustling city of over 25,000 and a tourist attraction, thanks to the Burtons, who became the town's unofficial mayor and first lady whenever they were in residence. After settling into Casa Kimberly, they took a day off and toured the village by jeep, dropping in at the new resort hotels, favorite restaurants and bars. Wherever they went, crowds miraculously appeared, snapping their picture and angling to get a good look at them. Celebrities and writers, such as James Baldwin, visited.

Sometimes the attention became unbearable when photographers and television trucks, parked outside Casa Kimberly, made it nearly impossible for them to leave the house. Richard, trying to grow a beard worthy of Henry VIII, took to his bed and his books while Elizabeth busied herself in her corner of their spacious bedroom. On one such occasion, Richard called out in his best Hamlet voice, "What are you doing, Lumpy?"

"Playing with my jewels," Elizabeth answered, pleased as a little girl.

Elizabeth—as she always had—flourished in Puerto Vallarta. She swam and she relaxed in the sun, reading *Portnoy's Complaint* and *The Godfather*, so her skin was bronzed, her health improved, and Burton's ardor was kindled anew. Their sexual energy cut through all the alcohol and dark moods and ill health, and he again marveled at her beauty, writing in his diary, "Elizabeth is now looking ravishingly suntanned though the lazy little bugger ought to lose a few pounds or so to look at her absolute best," he wrote. "I could detect no sign of aging in her at all," with the exception of quite a few gray hairs at her temples. "But the skin is as smooth and youthful and unwrinkled as ever it was." After six and a half years together, he still took incredible delight in her body. With Elizabeth, he never had to pretend that she was someone else in the dark—he preferred to see her in the light so he could admire her skin, her breasts, her derriere, which he describes as "firm and round." And later, Burton—who was never comfortable writing about sex as he was easily embarrassed—couldn't help but describe Elizabeth as "an eternal one-night stand . . . and lascivious . . . E. is a receiver, a perpetual returner of the ball!"

During this hiatus from the rest of their lives, Richard's need for Elizabeth was so great that it poured out of him not only in his diaries but in notes and letters to Elizabeth, sometimes written when she was sleeping in the next room, sometimes when she left him alone for an afternoon. On May 10, 1969, he wrote in Puerto Vallarta, "You will never, of course, because you are too young, understand the idea of loneliness. I love you better than buckets of brine poured over a boiling body, than ice cream laved on a parched mouth, than sanity smoothed over madness . . . What a strange thing it was to see you drive away."

Like Henry VIII and his court sailing up the Thames toward Windsor Castle, in May 1969 the Burtons arrived in London on the *Kalizma* and dropped anchor just outside the Houses of Parliament. Members of Parliament and their secretaries filled the windows to gawk at the Burtons' arrival in London. But it nearly didn't happen. Back in Puerto Vallarta, Elizabeth had had to make Richard memorize his lines. It was the threat of another lawsuit rather than the script, which he considered "a lot of mediocre rubbish," that forced Richard to don the royal robes of Henry VIII for *Anne of the Thousand Days.*

He insisted that Elizabeth be present with him on the set, and even appear as an extra in the film, which she was happy to do—in part to keep an eye on Richard and his brilliant little costar, the tiny, doll-like Bujold. ("The girl is very small in every way, in height, in weight, and vocally," Burton described her. "I could out-project her with a whisper.") Elizabeth always kept things lively on the set; she knew how to get the crew to fall in love with her. He remembered when she shoveled snow off the walk outside of Elstree Studios during the making of *The V.I.P.s*, and the makeup she applied to all the extras during *The Taming of the Shrew*. It was in his contract that she could visit the set whenever she felt like it, a canvas-backed chair with the initials "ETB" waiting for her when she chose to watch Richard in his beard and kingly robes breathe life into the film, which he tried valiantly to do through the long, hot English summer.

Burton complained in his diary about the obviousness of the dialogue: "I must have a son to rule England when I am dead! Find a way, Cromwell! Find a way. The pope. The cardinal. Orvieto, my lord bishops. Divorce Katharine. Divorce Anne. Marry Jane Seymour!" He uses every actor's trick to vary the lines, but, he wrote, "it's a losing battle." He was impatient, much more so than Elizabeth, with dialogue that didn't measure up to the writers he loved and admired. If he was going to play Henry, then why not Falstaff? If a spy, what could be better than one created by John Le Carré? If he wanted to be seen saying something clever, why not have Graham Greene or Edward Albee or Tennessee Williams write it for him? He didn't understand the movies the way Elizabeth did—Elizabeth, who would have been a brilliant silent film star.

More to the point, perhaps, Burton was made uncomfortable by the content of the dialogue, not the quality (the lucid and eloquent screenplay, after all, was nominated for an Academy Award). Once again, he was forced to relive the central incident in his life: his abandonment of his much-admired wife, Sybil, to marry Elizabeth, the woman to whom he was hopelessly in thrall. When he speaks the words "I will have Anne if it split the earth in two like an apple and fling the two halves into the void!" how could he help but think of the time when he, himself, split the world in two, to divest himself of one wife in order to marry another? And in case he could forget, the script was full of reminders: Henry calls his first wife, Queen Katharine of Aragon, Kate—the name of his treasured elder daughter whom he had left to marry Elizabeth, and the role Elizabeth played to perfection in *The Taming of the Shrew* three years earlier. And there are two Elizabeths in the film: Anne Boleyn's mother, and, of course, Boleyn's child with Henry: Elizabeth I, England's great queen. And there was his own Elizabeth, showing up as an extra, bedecked with La Peregrina and looking more splendid than any queen. He left Shepperton Studios each day for the two-hour drive back to London, to the *Kalizma*, feeling dispirited about the work.

At least Richard was back acting with the great pros of his past—Anthony Quayle appearing as Cardinal Wolsey and Michael Hordern as Anne Boleyn's father (whom he described as "no rubbish and cunning as snakes"). He still had enough respect for acting to be knocked out by their tricks and cunning, the pieces of business that Quayle, with his measured precision, and Hordern, in his sly way, brought to their roles. "They have every shrug, nod, beck, sideways glance and shifting of eyes ever invented," Burton observed. All Michael Hordern had to say was "Yes, Your Grace," and those three words uttered in Hordern's unmistakable way became "slightly longer than Hamlet," Burton thought. But he was bored with his own performance. One day during filming he'd asked, "What's the shot?" and was told it was just going to be a close-up. So he kept his street clothes on—his chinos and loafers—and just showed up with the top half of his costume. To the surprise of the director, cameraman, and the rest of the crew, he played Henry VIII in the clothes he had just worn in the pub across from Shepperton Studios earlier that day.

Unfortunately for Elizabeth, Geneviève Bujold—who is miraculous in the role—summoned up the green-eyed monster, the jealousy that occasionally took both Burtons by surprise. This was the first film since *The Spy Who Came in from the Cold* in which Burton played opposite a love interest other than Elizabeth—and there had been reason to be wary of Claire Bloom. When Richard playfully christened Geneviève with the nickname "Gin," something that, back in his salad days, he did only with actresses he had bedded, Elizabeth suspected the worst. The British press got into the act, speculating that Burton and Bujold were indeed having an affair.

Throughout the shoot, the Burtons were having a rough time of it. About to make love one afternoon, Elizabeth began bleeding profusely, from a recurrence of the unglamorous affliction of hemorrhoids. Richard tried reassuring her, but their afternoon idyll was ruined, and it made the presence of the petite young "Anne" more of a thorn in their side than she might otherwise have been. Elizabeth was already angry that Richard had compared Bujold to Vivien Leigh, an actress that Elizabeth had often been compared to, and whom she had replaced in *Elephant Walk* over a decade earlier because of their physical resemblance. Was she going to be replaced by a younger version of herself, as so many women approaching middle age had been, by straying husbands?

Burton seemed oblivious to Elizabeth's fears. He spent his long drives back to London trying to make the role interesting to himself.

He decided to play Henry as "a demonic charmer . . . capable of stupendous outbursts of rage all co–mixed up with a brilliant cynical intelligence." He does so—compellingly—but there's a lot of Richard in the part as well, at least the Richard who bedded every woman he could, before meeting Elizabeth. "When I've wanted them, I've had them. When I've had them, I've been cured of them," Henry barks to a courtier in the film. And later, while listening to one of his poems set to music, Henry declares, "true verse and music grow from suffering," a variation of an idea Burton had once expressed to Ernie Lehman on the set of *Who's Afraid of Virginia Woolf?* As art continues to imitate life, we watch the great king, the philanderer, wounded and bested—at least temporarily—by a woman he cannot help but love. Through it all, Henry suffers magnificently, because he knows he has transgressed. Though at times monstrous, he manages to inspire our pity.

Although Bujold more than holds her own against the bullying Henry, Richard can't stop thinking of "how marvelous E. would be and how much better." Richard suffered from insomnia while filming *Anne of the Thousand Days.* Concerns about Elizabeth's health kept him up late, and when he did finally sleep, he had nightmares about her, about the blood, about her well-being. Though it deeply troubled him, according to many around the Burtons, Elizabeth's health crises usually brought out the best in Richard. That's when they were often closest—when their fights cooled, when the world went away, when he could nurse her back to health in the intimate privacy of her bedroom.

For his part, Burton nursed a kind of generalized jealousy of Elizabeth, as if their mutual jealousy was a sign of their love for each other. "I am very jealous of E.," Burton confessed in his diary. "I'm even jealous of her affection for Dick Hanley, a sixty-year-old homosexual, and anybody she has lunch with. Girls, dogs—I'm even jealous of her kitten because her adoration of it is so paramount. They'll all die before me, though, so I'll win in the end."

With Elizabeth left out of *Anne of the Thousand Days*, both Burtons were unhappy about the state of their careers. Elizabeth's last two films had been torture to complete, given her hysterectomy and ongoing back pain. They had both been beaten up by negative—even scornful—reviews. Calling in their lawyer, Aaron Frosch, they discussed whether they could afford to retire from the movies. By 1969, Frosch was struggling with the onset of multiple sclerosis, but nonetheless he flew to their side to advise them. He told Richard that he had nearly $5 million, and Elizabeth a little less than that, in ready cash, not including their homes in Mexico and Switzerland and the paintings and jewelry and the *Kalizma*, which came to another $4 million. If they stopped acting and kept their assets invested, Frosch told them they would have at least a half a million dollars a year, in interest, to live on. But they would have to "make do" with half that amount, after continuing to pay the salaries of Dick Hanley, Bob Wilson, Richard's secretary Jim Benton, plus supporting "all the godsons, goddaughters, nephews, nieces," as well as Sara Taylor, and gifts to Elizabeth's brother, Howard. But, Frosch reassured them, because they paid next to no taxes due to their peripatetic lives, they actually had a greater annual gross income than their friends the Rothschilds.

Again, Burton warmed to the idea of retiring, as he often expressed boredom with acting. "There is no question," he writes in his notebook, "but that I must stop acting . . . It is all so perfectly boring. Anybody can play Henry the 8th." He felt that he and Elizabeth were at the zenith of their careers, and that before the critics "start tearing us apart again" (which had already begun), perhaps they should take their final bows. "If E. and I have the strength of mind to give up being famous," he later wrote, "we can at least live in more than lavish comfort. I might even be able to buy her the odd jewel or two."

Elizabeth, after forty-two films and the insult of being passed over for *Anne of the Thousand Days*, seemed eager to "pack it in." Perhaps she feared a future in which Richard continued to work while she became increasingly marginalized—the wife of the internationally sought-after actor. So they imagined a different kind of life together, dividing their time among their homes in Gstaad and Puerto Vallarta, and the *Kalizma*. Burton mused in his diary, "We'll nip over to Paris occasionally and give a party for the Rothschilds. We'll take the Trans-Siberian Express across Russia from Moscow to Vladivostok. We'll go to the hill stations in Kashmir. We'll muck around the Greek islands. . . . We'll revisit Dahomey again," where they could walk down the dusty lanes unrecognized and unmolested, "and look at the washing on the line at the [presidential] palace." Now he warmed to the idea of a life of continuous travel, a future in which he would finally become the full-time writer he wanted to be:

> We can slide down the coast there, in the *Kalizma*. And Spain. And the West Indies. And Ecuador. And Paraguay. And Patagonia. And go up the Amazon. We'll take a month and do a Michelin guide to France. There are many worlds elsewhere, Coriolanus. I can write pretty books with photos by E.

After all, what would they lose by retiring from movie-making altogether, giving up "Dick and Liz" for "Richard and Elizabeth"? The point was brought home by Liza Todd, who was curious, perhaps for the first time, about her parents' profession. She had recently watched *Becket* and now asked them about their other movies. Were they all as good? Elizabeth was never a movie star to her children. They never begrudged their parents the status of the most famous couple in the world and the fact that they made movies for a living. They forgave them for it. But Liza's question—"were they all as good?"—made the grown-ups think about their long list of films, made together and apart.

Richard told his stepdaughter that most of their movies were "rubbish and not even worth seeing," and that Liza was better off reading a book. But Elizabeth said some of them she was damned proud of.

And so it was Elizabeth's idea for her and Richard to sit down, like children taking a test, and write down what they thought their best work in the movies had been. It was overdue, this taking stock, and with Aaron Frosch having just been there to tell them how they might live without working constantly, it made them take a deep breath and evaluate what they'd been doing these last six years of nearly constant work, on top of the decades of films made before they'd even set eyes on each other.

When finished, Elizabeth handed her paper to Professor Burton: the list began with *National Velvet*, followed by *A Place in the Sun*, *Cat on a Hot Tin Roof*, *BUtterfield 8* (which she had hated while filming and for a long time after), *Suddenly, Last Summer*, *Who's Afraid of Virginia Woolf?*, *Boom!*, *Secret Ceremony*, *The Taming of the Shrew*, and *Doctor Faustus*. Burton's list led with *Becket*, followed by *Who's Afraid of Virginia Woolf?*, *The Spy Who Came in from the Cold*, *The Taming of the Shrew*, *Boom!*, *The Night of the Iguana*, *Doctor Faustus*, and the yet-to-be-released *Staircase*.

It dawned on them how their best films were made outside the studios to which they had belonged—MGM for Elizabeth, and 20th Century-Fox and Warner Bros. for Richard. He typed up their lists and pasted them into his diary, commenting, "not a bad record for two people who happen to be in love, and compete with each other . . . I think we should revert to being splendid amateurs."

The list they made opened their eyes to something—the fun and daring of it all had gone out of the work. Somehow it had been better when they were out to prove themselves, when they wanted to show the world that their artistry would sanctify the scandal of their love affair. Elizabeth and Richard were the artists, and "Liz and Dick" the movie stars, and their best films were made when Elizabeth and Richard made them. The sad truth was that they would not be given too many more chances to act together onscreen. After her brief appearance as an extra in *Anne of the Thousand Days*, Elizabeth would not work again for two years.

Their only true pleasure, it seemed, was on the *Kalizma*, after filming was done for the day. Burton described the river "imitating a blue-gray ghost" in the evenings, with all the houses along the Thames looking as if they were asleep. Watching over Elizabeth, he wrote, "No woman sleeps with such childish beauty as my adorable difficult fractious intolerant wife."

But their tempers continued to flare up out of this tranquil setting—Elizabeth's jealousy of Bujold, Burton's own unfounded jealousies and his unhappiness with himself, their drinking and the furies unleashed when the cork came out of the bottle. Columnist Liz Smith, who had visited the Burtons in Paris the previous year, knew that their fights had always been a big part of their relationship. "They fought right from the beginning," Smith recalled. "I think Elizabeth associated it with what love and marriage were all about. Look, if you're a movie star, there's an element of exhibitionism, and I think that was there in her. And her man's attentions—whether it was giving her presents or abuse—was proof of her being. Come in and see how much we're connected—we're fighting—look at this."

After a week of their "running rows," after he insulted Elizabeth and then mumbled a few apologies and started in on her again, it hit him like a bolt of lightning: "I am so much my father's son that I give myself occasional creeps." He remembered how his father had "the same gift for damaging with the tongue . . . the same tipping over into 'violence' "; the same fidelity to his mother that Richard had to Elizabeth, the same "smattering of scholarship," the same tendency to attack the innocent when ridden by guilt. He wrote in his journal that if he was so much like his father while sober, he would simply return to the bottle until it killed him. But then, it was when he was drunk that he was most like Dic Jenkins, père. As Liz Smith observed, "the drinking fed the jealousy, the jealousy fed the drinking. I learned early on that if I was on a movie set with them, I'd better get what I wanted in the morning because after lunch, he, in particular, could just be so mean."

With *Anne of the Thousand Days* nearly completed, Richard and Elizabeth took time off to visit Ifor, Richard clinging to the idea that his brother was improving, regaining some mobility in his limbs. They checked into The Bell Inn, near Aston Clinton, where Ifor was being looked after. Elizabeth bought dozens of the most expensive bedsheets and towels for Ifor's room, but when they were delivered, Richard suddenly became enraged. Elizabeth leaped at Richard and started striking his head with her ringed fingers. He threw her off, stomped out of the hotel, and went for a long walk through some of the neighboring farms. "If any man had done that I would have killed him . . ." he wrote later. "I had sufficient sense to stop myself or I most surely would have put her in hospital for a long long time or even into the synagogue cemetery for an even longer time." The tirade was probably brought on by his own sense of guilt at the sight of Ifor in a wheelchair, unable to move. After all, he had brought Ifor into *his* world, had brought him to Céligny. Just as Henry VIII described Queen Katharine's stillborn sons as God's punishment, was this Richard's punishment for divorcing Sybil and seizing for himself "the most beautiful woman in the world"?

Whatever the cause, the pot had boiled over. Before, their fights were more like foreplay, the making-up afterward being the best part of it. But this didn't feel like *The Taming of the Shrew*, this was starting to feel like *Who's Afraid of Virginia Woolf?* "We are fighting," Richard wrote, "& have been fighting for a year now over everything and anything. I have always been a heavy drinker but during the last 15 months I've nearly killed myself with the stuff, and so has Elizabeth. Neither of us will give in and if one of us doesn't something is going to snap." He started blaming Elizabeth's presence for making his hands shake, forgetting that it was she, that first day on the set of *Cleopatra*, who had brought the cup to his lips because his hands were shaking so badly. "At the moment I am in despair. If we cannot understand each other or, what is worst, not stand each other we'd go our separate ways pretty soon . . ."

Staircase was released that August, to mixed reviews. The movie had been adapted by Charles Dyer from his well-received 1966 play, but some critics complained that the subject matter had been "cleaned up a little for popular consumption." *Variety*, however, praised both Rex Harrison and Richard Burton for having "dared risky roles and . . . triumphed." Burton had cared about *Staircase* and *Boom!* He thought they were good. Audiences didn't. The public apparently didn't want to see two masculine actors portraying gay men, and the movie disappointed at the box office. *Where Eagles Dare* was always going to be more popular with mainstream audiences. It had stormed the box office and had overtaken every other film that year, earning more than $20 million. Now Burton waited for the verdict on *Anne of the Thousand Days*, a film he had not enjoyed making, but one that had the potential to be a critical as well as financial success, like *The Taming of the Shrew.* Secretly, Burton hoped for a blockbuster, because he had "rings and farthingales and things" to pay for.

That September, the Burtons returned to Gstaad. Elizabeth completed the acquisition of a remarkable gift for Richard: the entire one thousand volumes of the Everyman Library. Richard had begun reading those books, one by one, at the age of twelve, leaving them behind in houses in Pontrhydyfen and Port Talbot, in London, in Céligny, in Oxford when he was an RAF officer during the war and used to steal them from Foyle's bookstore in Charing Cross Road. The thousand "numbered, gleaming" volumes, in Burton's description, were carted to Gstaad and lovingly unpacked and shelved. "I shall browse in that place for the rest of my life. They will take up one wall of the room . . . a fantastic reference library with the index in my head," he later wrote. For a man who worshipped the written word, it was the perfect gift.

Later that month, the Burtons looked into possibly moving Ifor out of the clinic and into their Swiss chalet for a long visit. They consulted with Dr. Rossier, who ran the paraplegic ward of the local hospital, about what kind of bed and other special equipment Ifor would require. Unbeknownst to Richard and Elizabeth, Ifor had suffered a stroke in his sleep. Gwen Jenkins had kept this new setback a secret from the Burtons. When the orderlies had come to check up on him in the morning, they discovered that Ifor had lost the one thing he had had left: his beautiful Welsh voice.

Ifor's tragedy would haunt Richard for the rest of his life. "He'd have lived until he was 90 were it not for that trip in the dark at Céligny," he wrote grimly in his notebook. Again, he took out his fury over Ifor's condition on Elizabeth, the person he was closest to, the one who was there and the only one who could possibly absorb the terrible blow of Ifor's paralysis, along with him.

After one of their visits to Dr. Rossier, the Burtons decided to dash into an Italian restaurant for an early dinner. Burton recalled the meal as one of "long silences and deadly insults," with Elizabeth trying to break his mood. At one point, knowing that Richard was "in a state of nastiness," she reached out to him across the table.

"Come on Richard, hold my hand."

"I do not wish to touch your hands," he answered cruelly. "They are large and ugly and red and masculine." Elizabeth withdrew her bejeweled hand.

Richard himself was aghast, horrified by his own malignant remark. He wrote in his diary, as an act of contrition, "[W]hat the hell's the matter with me? I love milady more than my life . . . one of these days it's going to be too late."

But Elizabeth, not one to wallow in her own or anyone else's bitterness, quickly turned Richard's nasty remark to her advantage, making her husband pay dearly for his thoughtless insult. She insisted that now he must really go after the diamond they had both been eyeing, the one owned by Mrs. Paul (Harriet) Ames, the sister of Walter Annenberg, the billionaire founder of *TV Guide* and former U.S. ambassador to the Court of St. James. The 69.42-karat, 1½"-long stone was considered the largest and most expensive diamond in the world. It was set in a platinum ring between two smaller side diamonds. "It will make my ugly, big hands look smaller and less ugly!" Elizabeth teased. "That insult . . ." Burton would write in his diary the following day, "is going to cost me. Betcha!"

There was naturally a great deal of interest in the spectacular jewel. It was going to be auctioned on October 23, 1969 (identified as Lot 133), by the Parke-Bernet Galleries on New York's Madison Avenue. Elizabeth had learned that Aristotle Onassis, the man who had brought out Richard's competitive streak more than any other, had paid a visit to Parke-Bernet to view the diamond, igniting speculation that he intended to buy it for Jacqueline Kennedy. It was then that Richard and Elizabeth asked the jewel be sent to them in Gstaad for their inspection. As soon as she saw it, Elizabeth knew she had to have it. Richard gave Aaron Frosch, who would be bidding by phone from London, a ceiling price of $1 million.

But Cartier outbid Richard Burton, winning the jewel for $1,050,000, the highest amount ever paid for a diamond at that time.

Jim Benton, Richard's secretary, called to give Richard the bad news. Richard and Elizabeth had returned to The Bell Inn, where they had gone to visit Ifor, and where Richard was now standing by a pay telephone in the pub, not ready to admit defeat. He shouted at Benton to get Aaron Frosch on the line, immediately! Elizabeth tried to mollify Richard, telling him that she didn't really care if she had the diamond or not, that "there was much more to life than baubles," adding that she was "completely capable of making do with what she had" (which included Mike Todd's diamond tiara and 29.7-carat diamond ring; La Peregrina; the Bulgari emerald-and-diamond suite; the Krupp diamond, etc.). But this made Richard even more determined.

"I was going to get that diamond," he resolved, "if it cost me my life or $2 million, whichever was greater." After railing at poor Mr. Frosch, he instructed the lawyer to buy the diamond directly from Cartier, and to do so regardless of the price. Like Henry VIII in his pursuit of Anne Boleyn, he would have the jewel.

It would take another agonizing twenty-four hours of living by the telephone in the Inn's small passageway. Richard kept reversing phone charges, as the Inn was running out of coins. Some of the locals sipping their pints at the bar eyed the actor as he paced nervously in the doorway of the pub, waiting for a call back from New York. Would Richard be able to snatch the diamond from Cartier, winning it back for Elizabeth? Some enterprising bookie in the village began taking bets.

The next day, Frosch called. The diamond was theirs.

For $1.1 million, Richard had carried the day. "Liz Gets That Peachy Pear," trumpeted the *New York Daily News*. It gave Richard even greater satisfaction when he learned that two of his rivals for the diamond had been the Sultan of Brunei and—more importantly—Ari Onassis. The Greek tycoon had "chickened at 700,000" dollars.

But it was really all about Elizabeth, as it had always been. "I wanted that diamond because it is incomparably lovely," Burton wrote. "And it should be on the loveliest woman in the world. I would have had a fit if it went to Jackie Kennedy or Sophia Loren or Mrs. Huntingdon Misfit of Dallas, Texas." From then on, the briefly named "Cartier diamond" would be known as the "Taylor-Burton diamond," and it would be placed on exhibit in Cartier's main gallery in New York, and then brought to Chicago, where it was the star attraction at the opening of Cartier's new store. As many as ten thousand people a day came to view it. The jeweler ran a large display ad in the *New York Times*:

CARTIER
cordially invites you to view
THE CARTIER DIAMOND
on display
today through Saturday, November first
from nine thirty a.m. to five thirty p.m.
in our Gallery, Main Floor
at Cartier, Fifth Avenue & Fifty-Second Street
The Cartier Diamond has now been acquired by
Elizabeth Taylor Burton.

The jewel even appeared on *The Ed Sullivan Show* on CBS, as a "guest."

When Elizabeth finally received her prize, she found it too heavy and awkward to wear as a ring, so she spent an additional $80,000 to have a diamond necklace made, from which the heavy, pear-shaped jewel could be hung. A jeweler flew in from New York to measure her neck so that the diamond would hang just right, covering what remained of Elizabeth's old tracheotomy scar.

It would take three couriers (two of them decoys) and three weeks for the diamond necklace to reach the Burtons, who were by then back on the *Kalizma*, anchored in Monaco. Three men carrying identical briefcases, only one of which contained the Taylor-Burton diamond, left New York by plane for Nice, escorted by an armed security guard. From Nice they crossed the frontier of Monaco, where the *Kalizma* was berthed in Monte Carlo Harbor. Once in Monte Carlo, another armed guard (complete with submachine gun) was hired to protect the jewel.

Once again, Elizabeth held her breath when the stunning, heavy-laden necklace was removed from its red leather case and placed around her neck for the first time. She then peeked into the briefcase that had brought the Taylor-Burton diamond to her, as if something was missing. She scooped a small package out of the case. Three 50-cent pairs of hose had been sent over from New York alongside the diamond, because they were stockings Elizabeth liked and couldn't get anywhere else. Like Robert Browning's Duchess Ferrara in "My Last Duchess," Elizabeth's heart was "too soon made glad/ . . . she liked whate'er/She looked on," and she was as delighted to receive the inexpensive stockings as she was the most expensive diamond in the world.

The Burtons were in Monaco to celebrate Princess Grace's fortieth birthday at the Scorpio Ball, to be held at the Hermitage Hotel in Monte Carlo. It was a lavish affair by any standard. Elizabeth chose the party to debut the Taylor-Burton diamond, accidentally (or not) upstaging the event. With the dazzling necklace, wearing a stunning, black velvet cape with two glittering scorpions brocaded across the front, and accompanied by Richard and a pair of security guards carrying machine guns (as stipulated by the $1 million insurance policy with Lloyd's of London), how could she not?

As a little joke between the Burtons, Elizabeth wore her largest diamonds—the Taylor-Burton and the Krupp—alongside one of her smallest, the "Ping-Pong" diamond, to the gala affair. She had won the Ping-Pong diamond—⅛ of a carat costing a mere $14—from Richard after he bet her a perfect diamond if she beat him by ten points at Ping-Pong one day at their chalet in Gstaad. "Well, that's not the sort of thing a woman walks away from," Elizabeth recalled. "He lost. I won. Time to go shopping!" At the Scorpio Ball, whenever anyone said, "Oh, my God, what a magnificent diamond!" Elizabeth would raise her right hand and wiggle her little finger with the tiny Ping-Pong diamond. "Isn't it beautiful! The setting is lovely and the diamond is absolutely perfect." Only the Burtons could afford to joke about jewelry.

But along with its dazzling beauty, the Taylor-Burton diamond came with a heavy responsibility—it further restricted Elizabeth's freedom of movement. Lloyd's of London insisted that the diamond be kept in a vault, that it be worn in public for only thirty days in any given year, and that armed guards must be in attendance whenever Elizabeth appeared in public wearing it. "It was more of a millstone around her neck than an ornament," one British writer observed. Eventually, Elizabeth had to have a replica made at a cost of $2,800, and was often suspected of wearing the fake jewel in public.

There was another negative effect of owning the jewel. The long lines outside Cartier had caught the attention of the *New York Times*, inspiring an editorial excoriating the Burtons for what the *Times* felt were their extravagant indulgences in an age of want. The editorial held up the Burtons as exemplars of "the Age of Vulgarity":

The peasants have been lining up outside Cartier's this week to gawk at a diamond as big as the Ritz that costs well over a million dollars. It is destined to hang around the neck of Mrs. Richard Burton. . . . It won't seem out of place on the yacht parked in the Bahamas or the Mediterranean where the Beautiful People spend much time, not to mention money, impressing each other.

In this Age of Vulgarity marked by such minor matters as war and poverty, it gets harder every day to scale the heights of true vulgarity. But given some loose millions, it can be done—and worse, admired.

As Brenda Maddox wittily remarked in her biography of Elizabeth Taylor, "How many women have been criticized by both the *Times* and the Vatican?"

Besides giving them both enormous pleasure, the Taylor-Burton diamond would prove to be a wise investment. Even careful Aaron Frosch, and Richard's secretary Jim Benton, saw that the wealthy everywhere were protecting their fortunes in the late 1960s by investing in "durables." Maddox, writing in 1977, noted, "The Cartier diamond alone has increased in value to $2.5 million since Burton bought it." She also hypothesized that Elizabeth was attracted to large, fabled jewels because they "ensured that just as through her entire life, all eyes instantly and instinctively turned to her when she entered a room." At this point in their careers, the jewels were a way to continue to shine brilliantly on the world stage.

Though the year had virtually begun and ended with the acquisition of two fabulous jewels, and it had brought Richard his beloved, completed Everyman Library, it had been a grim year in many respects. So, the December 10, 1969, release of *Anne of the Thousand Days* must have warmed Richard's heart, with critics praising his performance as Henry VIII as superior to Scofield's turn as Thomas More in that other costume drama, *A Man for All Seasons*, two years earlier. (That was high praise indeed, as Scofield had sitting on his mantelpiece the

Oscar that might have gone to Richard for *Who's Afraid of Virginia Woolf?*) Richard's Welsh mood lifted—for a moment, anyway—when he received a cable from Hollywood that he had just received his sixth Academy Award nomination, for appearing in that "mediocre piece of rubbish" during those sleepless summer months. No one was happier for him than Elizabeth, and no one wanted him to win more than she did. Unlike Anne Boleyn, Elizabeth had kept her head.

12
FALLEN STARS

"Nobody but nobody will pay us a million
dollars a picture again for a long time."
—RICHARD BURTON

"We've lived like gypsies."
—ELIZABETH TAYLOR

T hank God it was over. In many ways, 1969 had been a dreadful
year—the fighting, the drinking, the ill health, the trials of making
Anne of the Thousand Days. After nine years of being together
in the public eye, and six years of marriage, the Burtons desperately
wanted to get off the merry-go-round. The stress fractures were beginning to widen, with Richard's increased drinking and Elizabeth's
continued health woes. With the new year, Richard was thinking
more and more about retirement—and what would be better than to
retire after finally winning his Academy Award? Elizabeth had two
Oscars, and though his career seemed to be marching along while hers
was in limbo, he needed to catch up before calling it quits. He loved
her, he needed her, but he still, at times, felt competitive with her.

They retreated to Puerto Vallarta, where Burton turned his
thoughts to writing, mining his diaries to begin work on an autobiographical novel, writing two or three hours each day. He had been

offered a teaching position as a don at St. Peter's, Oxford—a long-cherished dream of Burton's. ("How funny it will be to be lecturing at Oxford without a degree!" he confided in his diary.) And there was talk that Queen Elizabeth—the *other* Queen Elizabeth—might bestow upon him the honor of a knighthood, as she had upon Sir John Gielgud and Sir Laurence Olivier. While he and Elizabeth continued their dance of drinking, fighting, and lavishly making up, Burton remained hopeful about a different kind of future, one in which he wrote and taught and led a much quieter life. He carried his portable typewriter with him throughout Casa Kimberly, from the lower of the two tiled, whitewashed villas, up to the top balcony, back to the main house, which looked out over the ocean and the mountains that soared above it. After many fits and starts, he managed to write twenty thousand words toward his novel.

Eager to keep his connection to Oxford, the Burtons hired John David Morley, a former student of Neville Coghill, as a tutor for Liza and Maria. Morley noticed how Elizabeth loved to play with her children as if she were one of them, and how the Burtons relished being together as a family in Puerto Vallarta, relieved that some of the madness around them as a couple had finally abated. If they now occasionally bored each other—Elizabeth with her detailed descriptions of her ailments and her surgeries, Richard often retelling his favorite stories of his Welsh youth again and again—they found renewed strength in being a family. "None of the children think of him as their stepfather," Elizabeth told a visiting journalist, "he is their *father*. He's great with all of them."

But by March, Elizabeth was concerned about Richard's continual drinking, and she tried to get him to see a doctor—something Richard had always refused to do. He simply hated doctors, and it was hard enough on him when Elizabeth underwent so many treatments at the hands of a profession he considered deadly. "If you're a bad actor," he was fond of saying, "you don't get hired. But if you're a bad doctor, you can still practice medicine." Nonetheless, Elizabeth insisted that he check into Presbyterian Hospital in Hollywood for some tests, so they flew to Los Angeles. They were met at the hospital by one of Elizabeth's old friends and trusted doctors, Rex Kenemer, who, a lifetime ago, had been the one to inform her of Mike Todd's death.

Dr. Kenemer examined Richard and could tell just by touch that his liver was enlarged. He checked him into the hospital for further tests, which meant an overnight stay—agonizing for Richard, who couldn't bear the cold, clinical rooms and the monotony of waiting. Elizabeth took the room next to his.

The following day, Dr. Kenemer informed Burton that it was a matter of life or death: he had to stop drinking. He informed his patient that he would have cirrhosis of the liver within five years, and by then his liver would continue to deteriorate whether or not he continued to drink. He had to stop, now.

When Kenemer gave him the news, Burton replied, "Very well. I shall stop drinking. Totally."

They returned to Puerto Vallarta, where Burton managed to stop drinking for two weeks, the longest time he'd been on the wagon since starring in *Camelot*. He found he could stay sober if he took Valium, though he wished he could "break the back of this old pit-pony"—his drinking—without it. In the mornings, he'd pull on his khaki slacks, slip into a V-neck sweater and Italian loafers, and don a sombrero to keep the brutal sun off his face. Climbing to the top balcony of Casa Kimberly, he'd sit for two or three hours and pound away at his typewriter. Unfortunately for Elizabeth, his withdrawal from alcohol brought on his Welsh moods. "The sun is bright," he wrote on March 28, 1970, "the people around me in the house are all engaging, but today at least I don't want to see any of them." Without alcohol, Burton fell into a funk, losing his usual conviviality, his love of storytelling. Sober, he could be cynical and silent, but at least, he reflected, he spared Elizabeth the endless retelling of his stories. But she preferred his stories to his brooding silences. And there was something more basic she missed about Burton now that he'd stopped drinking—his sexual energy. While sober, Richard lost all desire to make love to his wife.

This was a great concern to a legendary lover like Richard, and very frustrating to Elizabeth, who complained to her close friend, Norma Heyman, when she visited, "[H]e hasn't fucked me for weeks!"

When Norma showed up for lunch one day, the Burtons fell into a nasty spat. Norma had split from John Heyman during the making of *Boom!* (John had taken up with Joanna Shimkus shortly after), but had remained close to Elizabeth.

It was a compliment that started it all. When Richard told her that he'd stopped drinking and thus had lost some weight, Norma gushed, "You look marvelous!"

Richard then pointed across the table at Elizabeth and said, "There's someone who could never give up drink."

That's when Norma blurted out, "She hates your guts, I'm afraid." And like some misguided marriage counselor, Norma turned to Elizabeth and said, "But you do love him, don't you?"

"No. And I wish to Christ he'd get out of my life!" Elizabeth declared. And to Richard, "Piss off out of my sight."

Burton got up and left the table, and later recorded the whole incident in his diary. For Richard, this was a watershed in the relationship. They had exchanged those kinds of words before—but never while sober, and never in front of close friends. "I have to face the fact that E. may be going to take off one of these days, and perhaps sooner than I expect. I've known it deep down for some time. . . . a good shouting match is sometimes good for the soul, cathartic, emetic, but I can't be bothered to shout back when I'm sober."

Elizabeth missed the shouting back, just as she missed the old passion. "When he stopped drinking and strangely, for a while, stopped making love to me," she later confessed, "I complained bitterly. I shouldn't have. He needed to find a way out, and I wasn't making things easier for him. We got through it. And we found each other again. Our bed was where the fighting stopped."

It had been Elizabeth who'd insisted that Richard see Dr. Kenemer, but now she found it hard to adjust to a sober husband. Their drinking had been a kind of third partner in their marriage, and when Burton gave it up, even for just a couple of weeks, a gaping hole appeared. Drinking with Richard had kept them in the same house of the spirits, cocooned from the sometimes unbearable pressures of their celebrity. It was, quite simply, something they could do together. And it was a strange kind of comfort during months of idleness; when they weren't working, the day could be built around the drinking. Of course, Richard had seen the light when Dr. Kenemer told him that he had to stop if he wanted to go on living. But by then it was harder for Elizabeth to apply the brakes to her own alcohol consumption. Richard, sober, now had to deal with Elizabeth's drinking, and looming ahead of them was Hollywood during the Academy Awards, when the town would be awash in champagne. For Richard, walking across the lobby of the Beverly Hills Hotel would be like crossing a minefield.

As Oscar night drew closer, they vowed to stop quarreling and finding fault with each other. They both desperately wanted Richard to win his Oscar, and they knew they'd have to present a united front to campaign for the award.

One of Elizabeth's gifts to Richard had always been her stardom. Now, she would summon up her greatest role—Movie Star—if it would help him win the award for Best Actor in *Anne of the Thousand Days*. They would campaign for it all together: Elizabeth, Richard, and the Taylor-Burton diamond, all on display.

Hollywood couldn't resist that much glamour, that much talent, that much money. If Richard's artistry couldn't carry the day, as perhaps it should have, Elizabeth's incomparable star power would dazzle the statuette into Richard's hands, where it belonged. And the Academy of Motion Picture Arts and Sciences still liked Elizabeth, though she'd chosen not to appear when she'd won for *Who's Afraid of Virginia Woolf?* In fact, the Academy had asked her to be one of the main presenters at the Awards.

Burton prepared for his reemergence at the ceremony—for his sixth nomination—by going on a health regimen. Besides giving up alcohol, he went on a low-carbohydrate diet and lost eighteen pounds in two weeks, losing the puffiness in his face that he thought made him look like a bored Mandarin. He would look good for the Oscars. And Elizabeth called on her friend, the prolific costume designer Edith Head, to design her gown for the Oscar night.

They had first met in the fitting room for *A Place in the Sun*, where the legendary designer created Taylor's costumes for the film, influencing fashion with the strapless white-chiffon party dress with its white daisy–embroidered bodice, which Elizabeth wore as the young socialite Angela Vickers. Knockoffs of that gown became the favorite prom dress for teenage girls all over America. The two women wouldn't work again professionally until 1972, but they maintained a close friendship throughout the years. Edith Head "was like a second mother to me," Elizabeth later recalled about their four-decade-long friendship. "Whenever I was in trouble, whenever I wanted a place to hide out and avoid socializing, I would go to Edith Head's house." Edith and her husband, Bill, were childless and they treated Elizabeth like a daughter. Given how hard it had been to be with Richard lately, and the pressure building up over his Oscar nomination, Elizabeth needed some extra looking after.

The diminutive costume designer was known for her short bangs, tightly pulled-back bun, and trademark dark glasses—the blue-tinted lenses helped her see how her creations would look on camera. She always wore a necklace that Elizabeth admired, made up of gold-and-ivory Victorian theater tickets. Edith Head would later leave that necklace to Elizabeth in her will.

On April 3, 1970, the Burtons returned to Los Angeles to attend the Academy Awards ceremony on April 7. Frank Sinatra flew them in from Puerto Vallarta in his Gulfstream jet, in a smooth ride that took them only two and a half hours. They checked into their favorite bungalow at the Beverly Hills Hotel. But they were in for a shock—while they were working and playing among the titled heads of Europe, Hollywood had changed.

MGM, Elizabeth's old studio, was on the auction block, selling off props from its three thousand movies—Johnny Weissmuller's loincloth, Judy Garland's ruby slippers, Gene Kelly's umbrella. Meanwhile, 20th Century-Fox (which *Cleopatra* had nearly torpedoed) had cut its overhead by 40 percent. The year that Richard was making the tony, literate *Anne of the Thousand Days*, a twenty-two-year-old California State University student named Steven Spielberg was making his first film, a short that would win him a contract with Universal. The old movie moguls were being replaced by young businessmen, as conglomerates took over the studios, forcing out the streetwise studio chiefs who had made decisions by their gut instincts. Twenty percent of the population was now under thirty, and that group made up 73 percent of the moviegoing public. For the first time, the actors onscreen were beginning to look more like the people sitting in the audience. Expensive epics were out. It was the low-budget movies by new kids on the block that were making money: *Bonnie and Clyde*, *The Graduate*, *Midnight Cowboy*, *Easy Rider*. Unconventionally attractive "ethnic" actors like Al Pacino, Dustin Hoffman, and Elliott Gould were playing romantic leads—a far cry from the old swoon-inducers like David Niven, Cary Grant, Burt Lancaster, or Stewart Granger. Despite Warren Beatty as Elizabeth's youthful costar, *The Only Game in Town* had "a musty feel to it," and Beatty's young fans stayed far away; the movie grossed less than $2 million.

The very idea of the movie star was changing. "We can't make a picture with Burt Lancaster and Deborah Kerr groping each other anymore," MGM's chief executive James Aubrey remarked at the time. "Thank God," thought Elizabeth, "he didn't mention us." No one seemed safe, though. The scythe of youth seemed to be cutting the movie industry into ribbons. Faye Dunaway, Dustin Hoffman, Al Pacino, Robert De Niro, Jack Nicholson, Dennis Hopper, and Jane Fonda replaced the more familiar faces that the Burtons knew from their three decades of moviemaking. For the first time at Hollywood parties and restaurants like Chasen's, Richard and Elizabeth did not recognize everyone in the room. Perhaps they had stayed away too long, making movies in Europe and England and living on the *Kalizma*.

"The world has changed," Burton wrote in his diary. "I mean our world. Nobody but *nobody* will pay us a million dollars a picture again for a long time. I've had two financial disasters, *Staircase* and *Boom!*, and Elizabeth, *Boom!* and *Secret Ceremony*. . . . I'm afraid we are temporarily out in the cold, and fallen stars. What is remarkable is that we have stayed up there for so long."

As if to protect them from the cold, Richard bought Elizabeth a fur coat for $125,000. The coat was made from the fur of forty-two specially bred Kojah minks, each one three times the girth of an ordinary mink. It was with this coat that *LOOK* magazine—which had in the past published adoring articles and glamorous photographs of the Burtons—ran them into the ground. Describing the mink as "the world's costliest coat for a fading movie queen who has much and wants more," *LOOK* ran a photograph of Elizabeth wearing her new fur over a bikini, the Pacific Ocean sparkling like diamonds behind her. Their skewering further harmed the Burtons' image, in a town where the hottest stars now wore blue jeans instead of Bulgari.

Oscar week began at the Golden Globe Awards, where Richard heard Geneviève Bujold accept her Best Actress award for the role of Anne Boleyn by saying she "owed her performance to Richard Burton. He was generous, kind, helpful, and witty. And generosity was the one great quality." (Bujold was also nominated for, but did not win, an Academy Award for Best Actress, and *Anne of the Thousand Days* was nominated for, but did not win, the Best Picture Award.) If that made Elizabeth uncomfortable—after all, Bujold had made love to her husband onscreen and had bested her for the role Elizabeth had wanted—at least there was hope that Bujold's award prefigured an Oscar for Richard. But he didn't think about it much, distracting himself by watching golf on television, by trying to perfect his billiard game, even by trying to learn Spanish. It was an effort to stay away from the bottle. Surviving nights without drinking became the only thing that took his mind off the Oscar.

"The whole world makes fun of it," Richard wrote, "but every actor wants to win." With his Welsh sense of the looming grave, he noted, "it's the thing that gets mentioned in every actor's obituary . . . the summit of their achievements." For someone who was trying not to brood about his chances, Richard examined the field of nominees like a man in a betting parlor. He knew John Wayne was the sentimental favorite, for his role as a crusty, washed-up gunslinger in *True Grit*. Also vying for Best Actor were Jon Voight and Dustin Hoffman for *Midnight Cowboy* and Peter O'Toole for *Goodbye, Mr. Chips*. He knew that sentimentality played a big role in the Academy's final decision, noting that Liza Minnelli would probably win for *The Sterile Cuckoo* because her mother, the legendary Judy Garland, had died the previous year. "My only chance is that I am a Kennedy–Adlai Stevenson associate and a 'Dove,'" he wrote, "while Wayne is a Republican, 'My country right or wrong' Birchite Hawk, and the 'artistic' Hollywood fraternity is usually very liberal." The Burtons' trusted publicist, John Springer, kept his ear to the ground, reporting back that it could well go Richard's way because so many people thought Richard was robbed when he'd lost to Paul Scofield.

Finally, the day arrived.

When they showed up at the Dorothy Chandler Pavilion, Richard looked sleek at 169 pounds in his dinner jacket with its brocaded waistcoat, Elizabeth beside him in her Edith Head gown—a deep blue-violet chiffon dress with a plunging neckline and a ruffled, slit skirt. The ceremony dragged on in its usual way, saving Best Actor for the next-to-last announcement. While the names of the nominees were finally read out loud, Burton slouched in his seat, studying a piece of paper, silently moving his lips as he read. Those seated around him thought that perhaps he was keeping score of *Anne of the Thousand*

Days' wins, or memorizing his acceptance speech, when, in fact, he was trying to memorize a list of Spanish irregular verbs.

And then John Wayne's name was called.

Wayne had won his first Oscar after forty-two years in the movie business. In Hollywood that night, a drunken, one-eyed cowboy had bested the king of England. Four years earlier, another cowboy with a drinking problem had defeated Richard at the Oscars, when he'd lost his bid for Best Actor in *The Spy Who Came in from the Cold* to Lee Marvin in *Cat Ballou.*

To make the evening more excruciating for the Burtons, Elizabeth had to follow Richard's defeat by appearing onstage to present the award for Best Picture. You can see the disappointment in her face, her genuine heartache when she came out, to great applause, to present the award to *Midnight Cowboy,* just the kind of antiheroic movie that represented how much Hollywood and the movie business had changed since *Cleopatra.* (It was also the first Hollywood film with an X rating to win the Best Picture Award.)

Now the rounds of post-Oscar parties would have to be endured, and the Burtons would have to put on their best game faces. Burton found that he could abstain from drinking if he could substitute Valium for alcohol. At one party, Elizabeth and Richard sat with the grown-ups—director George Cukor, the Gregory Pecks, and the Otis Chandlers, who owned the *Los Angeles Times.* Since he couldn't wash away his disappointment with a stiff drink, Richard turned to Elizabeth and asked her for some of her "pink pills," the Seconals she often took for back pain, which he tossed back at dinner. It seemed to do the trick, getting him through the toughest part of the evening. (Richard later wrote, "They certainly eased the boredom. I shall try them again instead of Valium when I'm surrounded by drunks.")

And then the atmosphere in the room changed. It lit up with flash-bulbs as scores of photographers surrounded the Burtons, snapping them, and Elizabeth's diamond, from every angle. Even Richard was impressed with the attention, secretly delighted with how the evening's big winners were being virtually ignored. "Barbra Streisand who fancies herself a big star was completely eclipsed." Hundreds of people made their way to the Burtons' table to gawk at Elizabeth and commiserate with Richard that he had been "robbed."

Elizabeth whispered into Richard's ear that with all these people coming by to say they voted for him, "Who the hell voted for Wayne?"

When the night finally came to a close, it was nearly impossible for them to leave the room. They had to pay their respects to the winners and run a gauntlet of photographers who wanted one last image of the Burtons. Their stardom, their fame, their glamour, their fabled history seemed to wash away the taint of losing the Oscar race. The winners' circle seemed to be wherever the Burtons were. Their movie stardom had won back the night for them.

Nonetheless, losing the Oscar had been a bitter disappointment. "In some ways, *Anne of the Thousand Days* was the final blow," columnist Liz Smith believed. "They both came to Hollywood, they worked the circuit, they attended the Golden Globes luncheon. Elizabeth has her new big ring. They did everything possible to campaign to get him that Award. They attended the Oscars. She agreed to be a presenter for Best Picture. Edith Head dresses her. But what happens? John Wayne is the winner. And she has to go up after that and give the Best Picture Award to *Midnight Cowboy*. You could just see that not only was she furious, God knows what waited for her back in the hotel suite."

At the Beverly Hills Hotel, their bungalow began filling up with friends and well-wishers. Brook Williams was there, of course, and Norma Heyman, who showed up in tears because she said everyone had left without her. Even John Wayne made an appearance at the Burtons' bungalow, showing up drunk and offering an apology to Richard for besting him. "You son of a bitch, you should have this, not me," he said, shoving the Oscar under Richard's nose. Burton, who had fought the urge to drink all evening, gagged at the smell of alcohol on Wayne's breath. They couldn't wait for him to leave.

"I lost again," Burton later wrote in his notebook, "and am now the most nominated leading actor in the history of the Academy Awards who has never won." Richard sourly wrote that he at least will be known for something, having carved his own niche in the history of the Academy Awards. As Liz Smith observed, "If he had won the Oscar that year, there would have been some parity in his mind, and hers. She would have been able to relax and say, 'Okay, he's got his Oscar now. I've done my duty.' I've always felt that that night, she knew it was the end of her marriage."

The Burtons were now caught in the middle of a great generational shift. The older, more established citizens of the film community in Hollywood—the same people who had rewarded John Wayne—still resented the black eye that Elizabeth and Richard had given to Hollywood from as far away as Rome, during *Cleopatra*. *Le Scandale* had, in fact, scandalized Hollywood as well as the rest of the country. For Old Hollywood, Richard Burton was still tainted by that escapade in Rome, no matter that they had married and had made a go of it, and that between 1962 and 1966, the seven films they'd appeared in had grossed over $200 million. Nonetheless, Richard and Elizabeth had broken up two marriages, and their antics during the making of *Cleopatra* had nearly sunk 20th Century-Fox. These were unpardonable sins to the old guard. And to the younger members of the Academy, the Burtons just didn't seem to matter that much. Their conspicuous consumption seemed suspect in the hippie era. The way the Burtons lived and dressed reminded them of their parents. Hadn't Charlie Chaplin's son Michael just written a book called *I Couldn't Smoke the Grass on My Father's Lawn*? Old Hollywood was unforgiving, and new Hollywood didn't seem to care. No wonder a newspaper headline would say, "The Million-Dollar Era for the Fabulous Burtons Is Over."

Perhaps as a way to connect with the new crop of Hollywood players, Elizabeth shrewdly decided to throw a party for the Oscar losers. After all, she told Richard, there were "more of them than us."

He always liked her sense of humor, how it cut through so much of the bullshit—the reverence of the press, and the nastiness of the press. So they would all come—no winners allowed. It was a gala night, and everyone but Richard was drinking. Jane Fonda arrived and made a beeline for the Burtons, talking to them for over an hour about Eldridge Cleaver, Bobby Seale, and the Black Panthers and coming away with a donation of $6,000. It was close to eleven in the evening when Richard and Elizabeth finally made it back to their pink-and-yellow bungalow beneath the giant palmettos bowing in the early spring air. But the quiet would not last for long.

Elizabeth had been drinking since the party began. She had also been feuding with her mother over the telephone and was not in the mood to be told what to do by Richard, who discouraged her from speaking with her mother after the party. Through the bungalow's walls, Richard could hear Elizabeth arguing with Sara Taylor, and then the usual follow-up phone call, which meant reconciliation was not far off.

Suddenly, Elizabeth began bleeding again. She insisted that Dr. Kenemer come to the hotel, and so the good doctor came shuffling into the Burtons' bungalow in the middle of the night, but by then most of the bleeding had subsided. Nonetheless, Kenemer "put a bandage around her arse, stayed for half an hour," wrote Burton in his journal. But Richard's tender concern for Elizabeth was missing that night. Something had indeed changed. Elizabeth's medical crises, which were very real and often very serious, were garnering less sympathy from her husband. Richard was upset with himself that Elizabeth's cries for his attention seemed to leave him by turns either frightened or frustrated. They were entering dangerous territory as a couple. And because Elizabeth's many illnesses and injuries had become so public, Richard became concerned that she would become unemployable.

Richard was in another kind of pain, the pain of seeing in Elizabeth a kind of mirror image of himself while drunk. He was still on the wagon, but Elizabeth did not join him in his sobriety. For now, he was there all by himself. They couldn't wait to get back to Puerto Vallarta, where they could have a semblance of a normal life. Richard and Elizabeth were still paying the price for being "Liz and Dick," and that legend was burying them. Nothing would make the point more obvious than their next public venture, on an episode of *Here's Lucy*.

On May 10, 1970, the Burtons flew back to Los Angeles to rehearse Lucille Ball's television show. The episode's premise was to take advantage of the flurry of eye-popping purchases that had made recent headlines—the Krupp and Taylor-Burton diamonds. Burton was actually excited about appearing on the comedy show, turning over in his mind the idea that doing episodic television might be a safe and good way to make a living, now that they weren't being offered million-dollar salaries to make movies anymore. And if it meant lampooning their "Liz and Dick" image, so be it. Richard was, however, apprehensive about working with the driven, monomaniacal comedienne. By now, Burton had been sober for ten weeks, and this would be the first time he'd worked without a drink since the age of sixteen. Smoking furiously—as much as a hundred cigarettes a day—Richard had dropped down to 160 pounds. He was so thin that Elizabeth jokingly called him "Mia," saying that sleeping with him was like sleeping with Mia Farrow.

Elizabeth went along with the plan, though she was still in pain and had scheduled surgery on her hemorrhoids for May 18.

The simple plot was to have Richard escape a crush of fans by posing as a plumber. Lucy, unaware of the disguise, gets him to fix her faucet. When she finds him out after he's left his plumbing coverall behind, she discovers the Krupp diamond in a pocket. Lucy tries on the ring, but because she is Lucy, the ring gets stuck on her finger and she can't remove it. Burton returns and discovers her plight, just before Elizabeth is supposed to show off the ring at a press conference that evening. When the ring can't be removed, Elizabeth ends up making her appearance with Lucy standing behind her, behind a curtain, thrusting her hand out to the admiring journalists. Taking advantage of the Burtons' star power, the press conference was stocked with real members of the Hollywood press corps, including veterans Army Archerd, James Bacon (who had visited them on location in Puerto Vallarta), and Joyce Haber.

Unfortunately, Burton's apprehensions about working with Lucille Ball proved true. For an actor who was bored doing *Hamlet* night after night, he couldn't fathom Lucy's lockstep approach, week after week, for nineteen years. After one rehearsal, Burton was appalled when Lucy tapped him and two fellow actors on the forehead, summoning them to her dressing room where she instructed them on how they should play the scene. Burton warned the director that if Lucy attempted to direct his wife in that way, she "would see, in person, what a thousand-megaton hydrogen bomb does when the warhead is attached and exploded." But Elizabeth managed to keep her serenity and was, as usual, a complete pro. Again, Burton marveled at Elizabeth's powerful stage presence. The audience adored her, and her every move, every gesture, found its mark. He'd witnessed her effect on a live audience twice before—when they did *Doctor Faustus* together at Oxford, "she held the audience like a vice," and when she'd read poetry alongside Richard six years earlier, on Broadway, she had dazzled.

Despite the horrors of rehearsal and Richard's resentment of working with Lucille Ball, the episode was something of a triumph, showing that both Burtons had genuine comedy chops. The episode's ratings were the highest in *Here's Lucy*'s long run, proving that the public was still fascinated by the Burtons. Elizabeth and Richard even considered a return to live theater—possibly *Macbeth*, which had long been on Richard's mind.

On May 18, 1970, Elizabeth entered Cedars-Sinai hospital for what would be her twenty-eighth operation in her relatively young life. Dr. Kenemer and her surgeon, Dr. Swerdlow, were concerned about the number of Seconals Elizabeth was already taking for continual back pain. They were all hoping that this surgery would be the last one she would need. The operation was actually a success, but her recovery would prove a problem, as her doctors tried to cure her of her pain-killer habit. She would have to suffer her postoperative pain without the help of strong narcotics, scaling back from 2½ cc's of Demerol to a fraction of that amount. They quickly moved her from Demerol to a mild tranquilizer, hoping to wean her off painkillers. It was distressing for Burton to learn from Taylor's doctors that they weren't managing her pain so much as treating her for the side effects of withdrawal.

Adding to the surreal discomfort of being in the hospital—which Richard could barely stand under any conditions—Elizabeth's privacy was constantly being invaded by strangers. Given a lack of tight security at the time, people would wander into her room, sometimes just to gawk at her. A woman who claimed to represent "The Ministry of Love" was apprehended as she approached Elizabeth's bed. When a "hippie" entered her room, saying that he just wanted "to have a look" at Elizabeth, Richard threw him out. Later, when Richard was napping on a couch in Elizabeth's room, two other characters walked in with a bird's nest, and hung it on the wall as a tribute to Elizabeth. This was all unnerving, as the Charles Manson Family murders had just taken place in Los Angeles the year before and were still very much on people's minds. Dr. Kenemer added to the Grand Guignol atmosphere by joking that rapes were not uncommon in the hospital's vast corridors. Since Elizabeth was no longer being given injections, Burton convinced the doctors to let her recover at home, and plans were made to sneak her out of the hospital, away from prying eyes, and particularly photographers. With the film industry undergoing a sea change and production money drying up, a front-page photograph of Elizabeth in a wheelchair would have had a chilling effect on any future projects.

They recovered from the ordeal at Frank Sinatra's home in Palm Springs, which Burton described as "a kind of super motel, in shape and idea." Elizabeth adored the rakish singer, and there had always been speculation—never proved—that the two had had an affair years earlier. She had been disappointed when he'd pulled out of *The Only Game in Town*, and, in fact, they would never appear together in a film. The last time they were all in one room, back in March, Richard became jealous when Elizabeth had made "sheep's eyes" at Sinatra. He was equally mad at Sinatra for *not* making a pass at his wife. He noted, with a slight sense of superiority, that Sinatra's library consisted of books that had been chosen by the restaurateur "Prince" Mike Romanov.

Three weeks later, in 120-degree heat, one of Elizabeth's stitches broke and blood soon covered the bathroom floor. Burton rushed her to Desert Hospital, and Dr. Swerdlow drove in from Los Angeles. "I aged another ten years," Burton wrote in his diary. As she was being wheeled down the hospital corridor for yet another surgery, she called out to him, "I love you, Richard."

"I love you too, baby," he answered. It dawned on him that she would have to remain in Palm Springs, recovering from her two surgeries, while he embarked on his next film, already set up to begin shooting that summer in the Mexican desert.

He had now been sober for three months.

Richard had decided to take on another macho, historical adventure story, the war epic *Raid on Rommel* for Universal Pictures. If those were going to be the only movies that made money, and if he were to continue to be snubbed by the Academy, why take on risky, artistic properties, why take on Shakespeare or Marlowe or even Tennessee Williams? So he agreed to appear in the Harry Tatelman production, which was originally intended for television, using footage left over from an earlier film, Arthur Hiller's *Tobruk*, released four years earlier. Veteran director Henry Hathaway added clout to the movie, which otherwise boasted no other stars even close to Burton's stature. (Ironically, the tough, take-no-prisoners director had just steered John Wayne through his Oscar-winning performance in *True*

Grit.) Because he could, Burton got his protégé Brook Williams a small part in the film (after securing him a part in the *Here's Lucy* episode they had taped the previous month, before a live audience). With *Where Eagles Dare* and *Raid on Rommel*, Burton was becoming more of an action star, but, given his worsening arthritis and neck pain, an action star who sometimes had trouble moving.

Raid on Rommel was filmed in San Felipe in the Mexican desert, over a twenty-one-day schedule. It was the longest time that Elizabeth and Richard had been separated and the longest that Richard had gone without alcohol. After her two harrowing surgeries, Richard missed Elizabeth dreadfully, and he poured out his longing for her in a series of sometimes playful, sometimes mournful letters.

On June 30, he wrote to Elizabeth, describing the desert's rocky outcrops and mentioning the fact that their good friend Mike Nichols was nearby, filming *Catch-22*, his third film since *Who's Afraid of Virginia Woolf?*, in the same stretch of desert. As both movies were about war, he noted that some of the local Mexicans were stealing guns and prop ammunition and shooting them off. "Dearest Scrupelshrumpilstilskin," he typed in a three-page, double-space letter on Beverly Crest Hotel stationery, using one of his many doting nicknames for her. He urges her to visit him in Mexico, where "the air is like wine."

> . . . I love you and miss you more than you can believe . . . we are, after all, only about 100 miles from Palm Springs. . . . The motel I'm staying in is completely roped off and has police on permanent guard. Once the few tourists have begged off you should be left entirely alone . . .
>
> It is 7:00 in the morn and I have had 2 cups of Nescafé and I love your bruised bumsy . . .
>
> I wouldn't mind building a house on one or the other [rocky outcrops] and living here—that's how startlingly beautiful it is.

A climate like Palm Springs but with the sea to boot . . . so why don't you come down and visit me? I'll show you a good time. . . . I love you. Very very very odd curious strange bizarre unattractive without you.

Millions of kisses and hug. *The bed is huge!*

What he doesn't tell her is that the town of San Felipe, comprising eight hundred souls, had a mean temperature of 113 degrees, only two decent restaurants, not more than two or three dozen beds for visitors in the entire town, and shark-infested waters. And it was hurricane season. After talking on one of the few telephones available in the desert, Richard was thrilled to hear that Elizabeth felt well enough to visit him and that she'd missed him so terribly that she mooned over the sight of a pair of his socks.

On July 9, Elizabeth flew to San Felipe. She arrived while Burton was still shooting, lying in the desert while sand blew into his mouth, looking up at the sky. He opened his squinting eyes and saw Elizabeth's plane flying overhead, buzzing the set. The plane carried not just Elizabeth but Norma Heyman and Liza, Maria, and Kate as well. Later, at their hotel suite, Richard was disappointed by Kate's nonchalant greeting, and by finding the hotel rooms blazingly hot, as no one had turned on the air conditioner. He stood there, dusty and filthy and covered in grease and greasepaint, when Elizabeth danced into the room and fell into his arms. That night, they all went out to dinner at Ruben's, one of the small town's two restaurants. But instead of enjoying a festive reunion, Burton sulked in silence. He had found himself becoming jealous when Elizabeth mentioned earlier that she'd called Marlon Brando and had talked to him on the telephone for an hour. He was angry when she told him that Brando was "keeping tabs" on him.

The next morning, Elizabeth showed up on the set. She stayed with him till well into the afternoon, which proved a tonic to the cast and crew. Everyone—from gruff Henry Hathaway to the lowliest crew member—was delighted she was there, and they all told Richard it had been their best day of shooting. Elizabeth had always shown tremendous warmth toward film crews—the people she relied upon to make her look good—but it was a genuine affection. The good-will lasted all evening, and Richard and Elizabeth finally returned to the hotel to make love. All their old sexual fire returned, despite her recent surgery and the energy-sapping heat. Her presence and her body lifted his Welsh gloom, and it was as if they had just met, as Burton made love to her while completely sober, amazed that all his energy had returned. The desert heat had brought out Richard's old cystic acne, the bane of his existence, but Elizabeth kissed his pustuled back and shoulders and thought nothing of it. Elizabeth always did flour-ish in hot climates, and now she positively glowed, the two of them devouring each other—hands, lips, tongues.

One hundred and forty days without drinking.

Elizabeth and the children returned to Los Angeles on July 13.

Nine days later, horribly missing Elizabeth, Burton typed a one-and-a-half-page letter to her, worrying that he'd get "another attack of gout" after kicking the jeep door while filming ("the foot is still sore but not gouted up . . ."). Elizabeth had just lost one of her tooth caps, and Burton commiserated with her. He closed his letter with "all my love. Never think of anything but you for very long. I fancy you a very lot, Shebes.—Rich."

By now, Richard had decided to appear in a low-budget thriller, *Villain*, to be filmed in London. They planned to take the *Super Chief* to Chicago, then to New York, and then the *QE2* to England. They were also considering making what would be their tenth film together, *Hammersmith Is Out*, a comedic retelling of the Faust myth, set par-tially in a mental hospital. Faust again! The producer, Alex Lucas, brought Burton the script, and they discussed the possibility of film-ing the movie entirely in Mexico, which Richard had come to love. He wrote to Elizabeth on July 25:

Dearest Toothache,

I may come up to see you today but won't know until later . . . Jim tells me that we're on the *Super Chief* on the 1st and the *QE2* on the 6th, so what paperbacks are you going to take with you and will you have breakfast with me and watch Kansas roll by and then Illinois . . .

[Lucas] arrives with scripts. Discuss possibility of filming movie entirely in Mexico. It is very possible if you think about it . . . for the posh house we could use some great house in Acapulco. For the loony bin we could use any large room, fill it with beds and stick some bars on the windows and Gung Ho!

. . .

I love you ghastily and horribly and terribly. See you soon . . .

Four more days . . .

Rich

The next day, on Sunday, July 26, after a morning of frying bacon and then reading, he again wrote to Elizabeth, encouraging her to accept a film offer that had come her way and would be made in London at the same time he filmed *Villain*—an adaptation of Edna O'Brien's novel *Zee & Co.*, for Columbia Pictures. "Dear Long-way-away-one," he wrote,

. . . Very antisocial I am when I don't booze. And no fun when you're not around . . . I hope that girl's teeth are not hurting too much . . . are you going to do the film? Do you love me? Do you want to be a lazy Jane and never work again? Once I stopped boozing I have enjoyed not working. But we can't do it though.

They had another reason to return to London: Elizabeth's first-born son, Michael Wilding Jr., was going to be married to his fiancée, Beth Clutter, in October at Caxton Hall, where Elizabeth had married Michael Wilding in 1952, a mere eighteen years ago.

On the *Super Chief* headed east, Elizabeth and Richard had a rare chance to be alone together, for the first time in over a year. It was idyllic, and they had the pleasure of making love in the swiftly moving train. Elizabeth giggled at what she called Richard's "new technique," which he insisted was simply the movement of the train swaying and rocking as it zoomed down the track. Though her doctor had not wanted Elizabeth to make the trip, she had made a remarkable recovery from her surgery, and they took advantage of it. But the seeds of displeasure were planted on that train—for the first time in four months, Richard took a drink.

"Forgot the momentous news," he confessed in his diary on August 2. "I had a Jack Daniel's and soda and two glasses of Napa Valley red wine last night with dinner. Felt immensely daring and all it did was make me feel very sleepy and not elated or anything like that." A few days later, he polished off a bottle of Burgundy with liver and bacon, and by the time they crossed the Atlantic to England and reclaimed the *Kalizma* and were heading toward Portofino, Burton had slid back into heavy drinking.

Burton's drinking had many sources: it was, apparently, genetic, given his father's alcoholism, but it also represented the model of virility Burton had wholeheartedly embraced. It was like being in the ring with a boxer, as his friend, the columnist Jimmy Breslin, once told him: "Don't forget you're always fighting. The other fellow is booze. You're evading, always evading, but one of these days, unless you're careful, he's going to nail you." It was familial: by several accounts, he was introduced to drink by the age of twelve, and in Elizabeth he found a willing partner. He needed no excuse to start drinking again—"I get a bad notice," Burton wrote, "I'll take a drink. A good notice, I'll take a drink." A period of depression or a period of happiness, a defeat or a triumph, boredom, travel, availability—it didn't matter. Its siren call was always there, waiting for his return.

"Missed yesterday," he wrote in his diary, "as I was more or less stupefied with drink all day long." Along with the alcohol came the awful quarreling—disagreements on every point, constant needling on both sides, surrounded by the *Kalizma*'s crew of eight.

Watching their heavenly train trip turn so quickly into hell, the Burtons realized that they were happiest when they were alone together, out in the world without their staggering entourage. Liz and Dick needed the entourage to survive, but it was suffocating Richard and Elizabeth. Yet being alone together was a difficult feat to pull off—just getting back to Geneva from the *Kalizma* was like a military operation. They had to find a port, and the jet had to be ordered. Once they landed in Gstaad, a helicopter was waiting to take them to a small hotel nestled in a Swiss valley, where they were greeted warmly and fawned over by the chef, who kissed Elizabeth's hand and always knew what they wanted for dinner. After traveling on boat and plane and helicopter to find their refuge, they entered the dining room and all the other guests applauded them. They just couldn't escape who and what they were: the most famous couple in the world.

Back in London at the Dorchester, the Burtons prepared for their seventeen-year-old son's wedding on October 6. Michael was very much a child of his times, and his dark, straight hair hung loose past his shoulders. Looking like hippie royalty, he wore a maroon velvet tunic, bell-bottom trousers, and sandals for the ceremony. Beth Clutter, the daughter of an oceanographer whom Michael had met while staying with his uncle Howard in Hawaii, wore a white muslin dress. As usual, Elizabeth outshone the bride—all eyes were on the star in a white knitted trouser suit and maxi coat, with a very dignified-looking Burton, his hair beginning to gray at the temples, walking beside her through a gauntlet of photographers.

Most parents would object to a seventeen-year-old marrying. As with other parents of their generation, at the end of the turbulent 1960s, there were differences of opinion between Richard and Elizabeth about what was best for the children. Elizabeth was tolerant to the point of indulgence. "They're remarkable," she said, "because God knows, according to all the rules, my life should have been murder for them. Their lives have been up and down. We've lived like gypsies." She indulged them, but she admired them for having come through her public scrutiny and the itinerant lives they had led. The Burtons presented the couple with a Jaguar, a £35,000 check, and a house purchased for £43,700 in Hampstead, next to Squire's Mount, the Georgian house that Burton still owned but rarely used.

Michael, like his younger brother, Christopher, had their mother's arresting eyes and dramatic coloring. As a boy, he'd had a flair for acting, and could recite Puck's speech from *A Midsummer Night's Dream*. Elizabeth thought that of all her children, he would be the most likely to go into the family business. He had attended several exclusive boarding schools, but had ended up living with Howard Taylor's family in Hawaii. Michael had no special plans for his future and seemed to spend a lot of his time smoking cigarettes and reading comic books, all of which concerned Burton, who was baffled that Michael had no desire to further his education. (Later, when Kate Burton attended Brown University to study Russian literature and language, Burton was exceedingly proud, writing to her, "Dearest Ivy League.") To his mind, seventeen was too young to marry, but as Elizabeth was pleased, he would go along with it. Michael Wilding Sr. remained publicly silent on the subject.

A few weeks after the wedding, Beth and Michael Wilding announced that she was pregnant. At the age of thirty-eight, Elizabeth faced the prospect—quite happily, in fact—of becoming a grandmother.

On November 10, 1970, Richard's forty-fifth birthday, Queen Elizabeth honored Burton by making him a Commander of the Most Excellent Order of the British Empire ("CBE"), in a ceremony at Buckingham Palace. He couldn't have been more disappointed. Elizabeth, in fact, had wanted him to turn it down, because they were both holding out for a knighthood. Richard's beloved sister, Cis, attended the ceremony, so Richard had to pretend to be happier about it than he was. After all, the two men whose footsteps Richard had supposedly followed in—Gielgud and Olivier—were already knighted. Their good friend Noël Coward was made both a CBE and, later on, a knight, despite the fact that the playwright had squirreled away his fortune in Swiss banking accounts, as Burton later groused in his diary. He thought the snub was because he, unlike Gielgud and Olivier, had lived outside of England for so long. He did recognize, however, that the CBE was a hell of an honor for one who had not gone after it, and he was "pleased that it means we are no longer notorious but officially posh." He also comforted himself that perhaps a knighthood was not so out of reach, after all.

In early December, the *New York Times* writer Bernard Weintraub visited Richard on location in Bracknell, a suburb thirty miles west of London, where Burton was filming *Villain*, the low-budget gangster movie for which he had waived his usual $1 million salary to work for a percentage of the gross. Elizabeth remained in London, nestled in at the Dorchester, where she planned to meet the Irish novelist Edna O'Brien, author of *Zee & Co.*

When Weintraub met Burton at the pub of the Foresters Hotel in Bracknell, Burton was nursing a cold, and a martini. The journalist noticed that at forty-five, Burton was still a powerful presence, with "an unmistakable aura of stardom." He told Weintraub that the role of a sentimental, sadistic underworld figure in *Villain* was the first "heavy" he had played onscreen, and a far cry from the kings and princes he had played in his earlier years. He noted, too, that the character was homosexual.

Drinking again, Burton was uncensored in his comments to the press, going public with his continual disdain for acting. "It seems fairly ridiculous for someone forty-five or fifty to be learning words written by other people, most of which are bad, to make a few dollars. I'm not dedicated. I never was," he confessed. "I've got to keep acting, though . . . It's compulsive. There are few challenges left, I suppose. I'm forced by ego to play Lear. Macbeth? Yes, I want to do Macbeth."

Later, interviewing Burton in his dressing-room trailer, Weintraub noticed that Burton's hands were shaking as he lit his cigarette, which made the actor seem frail and vulnerable. He continued to rail against acting as a profession, noting, "There aren't that many scripts for people like us," as he sipped another martini.

"It's all so bloody pernicious," he told Weintraub. "Fame is pernicious. So is money. Of course, don't misunderstand—I don't want to be poor. I don't want to repeat *that* performance. Never."

The interview was interrupted by a phone call from Elizabeth, announced by Jim Benton, Burton's trusted secretary. After speaking with her, Burton returned to his interview, sighing loudly.

"She wants me to come back to the Dorchester early because she's meeting Edna O'Brien about a script she's going to do and she's terrified," he told Weintraub. "Bloody terrified. She's always terrified of meeting new people." He added that Elizabeth wanted to go to a Blood, Sweat & Tears concert at the Royal Albert Hall, but he was afraid for her safety.

"How the hell can she go to Royal Albert Hall? She'd need protection. She still hasn't learned," Burton said, shaking his head in dismay. "We used to think maybe some of it would stop, maybe after the marriage was legitimized all the nonsense would end. But it gets worse. And London's not bad. London's probably the best city for us. New York's not bad, either. But Rome. And Boston—Boston, of all places, is the worst for mobs."

Burton washed down a cold tablet and lit another cigarette, confiding in his interviewer how much he feared and dreaded drugs of all kind. "Have you ever smoked marijuana?" he asked. "I think I tried it once. It scared the hell out of me. I keep saying it, but it's *true*. Elizabeth and I are getting to be an old middle-aged married couple."

They talked about how the motion picture business was changing, a fact of which Burton was well aware, and he mused over his now-and-again plans to quit the business. But one thing kept him going—actually, two things. He needed to keep making money to support the entourage and his extended family, and the yacht, and the jet, and his and Elizabeth's extravagant life. And maybe, just maybe, as he told Weintraub, "Perhaps I'm approaching my prime."

13

BLUEBEARD

"All my life, I think I have been secretly
ashamed of being an actor . . ."
—RICHARD BURTON

"No *Bluebeard* broads."
—ELIZABETH TAYLOR

The year 1971 brought the death of Elizabeth's most trusted friend
and confidant, Dick Hanley. Hanley had managed her household
affairs and had lovingly looked after her since she'd hired him
away from Louis B. Mayer when she'd married Mike Todd. It was
a terrible blow, following the death of her father two years earlier,
especially as Hanley had been a father figure to Elizabeth. He was a
bridge to her past, having worked as Mayer's executive secretary and
knowing how the studio system worked, inside and out. Elizabeth was
relieved that Hanley and Burton had accepted each other, though at
times Burton playfully groused about being jealous of Elizabeth's affection for Dick Hanley.

In a favorite photograph of Elizabeth's, taken at a party after *Hamlet*'s final performance in New York City, she is standing between two
surrogate fathers, Philip Burton and Dick Hanley, as she beams at
her then-eleven-year-old son Michael. In the photo, the two sixtyish,

bespectacled men bookend Elizabeth. She had lived to see the demise of the old studio system, and now, more recently, the ushering in of a new generation of filmmakers that threatened to put the Burtons out to pasture. With Hanley's death, her old world was gone. She was in uncharted territory.

After Hanley's funeral, everyone in the entourage moved up a notch. But without his wise overseeing of the Burtons' affairs, it was even more difficult for old, trusted friends to get through to them. They became more isolated. Neville Coghill, unable to get through, despaired reaching his former protégé and colleague: "The Burtons are protected by secretaries who themselves are protected by secretaries, and none of them answer letters . . . I understand now why many ancient emperors were guarded by deaf-mutes."

Elizabeth had just begun filming *Zee and Co.* in London, so was unable to fly back to Los Angeles, but she spared no expense to pay for the funeral and an old-fashioned Irish wake, held at the Beverly Hills Hotel. She sent a magnificent display of flowers with a card that stated simply, "I will love you always—Elizabeth."

Zee and Co. (released as *X, Y, and Zee* in the States) was to be a fourteen-week shoot. Burton accompanied her—a mixed blessing, as Elizabeth found herself watching him like a hawk, especially jealous around Edna O'Brien, who posed a double threat to Elizabeth as she was (and is) a beautiful, redheaded Irishwoman as well as an acclaimed novelist. The movie is about a sexual triangle: Elizabeth plays Zee, a wife trying to keep her husband, played by Michael Caine, out of the arms of a young widow (the blond, waifish Susannah York). She does so by seducing the blonde.

Even when they weren't making a film together, their personal life continued to seep into their films, feeding the imaginations of filmmakers and screenwriters. In the movie, Caine plays a version of Richard Burton, and the screenplay made many allusions to the Burtons' marriage, such as their explosive, George-and-Martha rows.

Zee, Elizabeth's character, is raucous, loud, passionate, and, in Edna O'Brien's words, "a ruthless survivor." Zee and her architect husband go at it hammer and tongs, verbally as well as physically, in graphic and explosive language. In fact, her character was described in the press as another Martha, complete with blowsy wigs and carrying unflattering extra weight (though in stills from the film, you can see that Elizabeth is far from fat; the public, perhaps, had never accepted her as anything but the slim, heartbreaking beauty of her youth, and every weight gain was noticed and commented upon. She was not allowed to age like an ordinary woman). Elizabeth continued to defend her domestic rows in the press. "We both let off steam by bawling at each other," she told a writer from *Ladies' Home Journal*. "But it means *nothing*. And we both feel so much better for it. That's how it should be . . . There's a difference between fighting and being mean."

As usual, Elizabeth showed up at the studio with her entourage. According to Michael Caine, the cast and crew joked that if just the entourage bought tickets to see the movie, it would be a hit. "The people around her," he said later, "make it seem as if you're working with the Statue of Liberty." Her arrival was accompanied by much fanfare, as if the queen herself were deigning to visit the set. Prior to Elizabeth's appearance, messengers dashed in to announce her impending arrival. "She's left the hotel . . . she's in the studio . . . now she's in makeup . . . she's out of makeup . . . she's in hair . . . she's out of hair . . . she's getting dressed . . . she's dressed and on her way!" When she finally arrived on the set, trailing her entourage, she bore a big pitcher of Bloody Marys, which she willingly shared with her costar, handing him a glass and toasting the beginning of the shoot. Nonetheless, Caine was impressed by her professionalism, remembering her as "the only actor I ever worked with who never ever flubbed a line."

Caine was nervous about meeting "a living legend" for the first time, and equally nervous about meeting Richard Burton. He was warned that Burton's presence on the set was his way of keeping an eye on Michael, considered to be a ladies' man—a real-life Alfie—at the time. But Burton, drinking heavily, usually spent the afternoons sleeping on the couch in Elizabeth's dressing room. The tremor in his hands that Weintraub noticed had worsened, and sometimes it was so bad he was afraid of embarrassing Elizabeth; on those days, he stayed away from the studio. A letter he wrote to Elizabeth on the back of a shooting schedule page for *Zee and Co.* read,

> Dear Twit Twaddle etc.,
>   I have the shakes so badly that it would be fatal for me to come out to the studio. There is no power failure here so I am warm but still shaking. So come here tonight. I'm afraid that I had *one* drink but will drink no more until you come home. Try and make it early as we can then see the Cassius Clay fight together . . . also I love you and long to see you but I don't want to shame you. I may even do—with trembling hands—some work. How about that?

He closes the letter with an admonition about her scenes with Michael Caine:

> I love you and miss you and I think you to be the most desirable woman in the world and remember, NO KISSING WITH OPEN MOUTHS or breathless excitement and all that stuff. Otherwise, I will be down at the studio and certain girls will have a very rough time with certain husbands. I love you my little Twitch. —Husbs.

If Elizabeth was alarmed at Richard's tremors, she didn't show it. She herself continued to drink heavily, and they did not as yet consider Richard an "alcoholic." Richard later confided to a friend, "She didn't exactly encourage me not to drink, but then she complained that I wouldn't stop drinking." Elizabeth did have the insight to know, however, that Richard drank because he constantly relived the wounds and grievances of his past, and he gave too much of himself to the public, in interviews and in his work. And Elizabeth had spent years "squelching [her] real feelings for fear they'd become public. All the years of covering up the pain and keeping it quiet had created a lot of scar tissue," so she drank to free her emotions, just as Richard drank to numb his.

Despite their continued drinking, the Burtons embarked on a busy schedule of moviemaking, but none of the next four films they made together or separately would be distinguished, and none would make money. For Richard, there would be a handful of great performances ahead of him, and one more Oscar nomination. But not in the final three films that he and Elizabeth would make together.

Since *Cleopatra*, nothing had changed as much as the film business, and the financing for their next three movies would come from unlikely places. The year 1971 began with a labor of love, as Richard returned to Wales to film *Under Milk Wood*, Dylan Thomas's lyric "play for voices." Burton's homage to his friend and countryman was produced by a small company, Timon/Altra Films International, and by his agent, Hugh French.

It was a small, artistic movie, but it had its advantages: it was filmed on location in the country of his birth. Whenever Burton felt his life was going off the tracks, he returned to Wales.

In January, Burton traveled alone to Wales to meet with the novelist and historian Andrew Sinclair, who had bought the rights to *Under Milk Wood*, the radio play that Burton had taken part in when it was first presented to the world in 1954. The film would be made for a low budget—a mere £300,000—and Sinclair brought in Richard's old friend from his *Becket* days, Peter O'Toole, to play Captain Cat, a blind fisherman who is haunted by the voices of his drowned men. Burton would narrate as the play's First Voice, describing a day in the lives of several villagers in a small fishing town in Wales—Llareggub (which is "bugger all" read backward; a little inside joke that both Richard and Elizabeth loved). Elizabeth was brought in for a small role, that of Rosie Probert, "the most glamorous hooker in the history of Welsh prostitution," as one reviewer cheekily described her. As in *Dr. Faustus,* Elizabeth considered her role as nothing more than a cameo, so she didn't want star billing, but their names together still had magic, so both were listed above the title. The large cast was rounded out by Glynis Johns, Vivien Merchant, Sîan Phillips (married to O'Toole at the time), and Victor Spinetti, their Welsh friend (and Richard's fellow poet) from *The Taming of the Shrew.*

Dylan Thomas was the poet that Richard had long wanted to be. Burton so identified with him that some people thought that Thomas had written the main narrative of *Under Milk Wood* with Richard's plangent voice in mind: "To begin at the beginning: it is a spring, moonless night in the small town, starless and Bible-black . . ." The film flushed out a secret that Richard had carried with him for the past eighteen years. He confessed to Sinclair that in the fall of 1953, Dylan Thomas had asked to borrow £200 from him, to avoid having to go to America to embark on a reading tour, reciting poetry for food and drink. Richard was an actor at the Old Vic at the time, and not rich, but he could have scared up the money. His refusal, he felt, was what forced the Welsh poet to go to America. It was on that trip that Thomas drank himself to death, downing eighteen straight shots of whiskey at the White Horse Tavern in New York City's Greenwich Village. Burton, as he tended to do, blamed himself.

However, being alone in Wales without Elizabeth and the entourage for those first few days was exactly what Burton needed. It was nourishment to him. His whole life he'd made sure he always wore a bit of red to commemorate the Welsh flag, and he never worked on March 1, St. David's Day (St. David being the patron saint of Wales). Visiting one of his sisters, he lounged in the bath with a glass of vodka in hand, looking out the window at laundry hanging on the line, and beyond that, the Welsh hills, where he could hear the calling of owls.

Burton was fond of telling a particular story about his father, Dic Jenkins, and now he thought of it. Jenkins used to sit outside the Miners Arms on Saturday evenings. "After he'd had a few jars," Burton would explain, "he would fix his stupendously stoned eyes on his fellow miners and he would say in Welsh: *'Pwy sy'n fel ni?'* And they would answer, *'Neb.'*

"*'Pwy sy'n fel fi?'*

"*'Neb.'*"

Which translates to "Who is like us? Nobody. Who is like me? Nobody." Elizabeth always liked that story, because the same could certainly have been said about herself and Richard. They were, and would always be, in a class by themselves.

Perhaps one reason Richard needed to return to Wales was to find some connection to his long-lost father, who had died when Richard was still married to Sybil, who now only existed for him in anecdotes, funny stories, and as the butt of jokes. Gianni Bozzacchi, still traveling with the Burtons as their in-house photographer, said that he "never heard Richard talk about his father" in any meaningful way. In Bozzacchi's opinion, Richard "did way too much for his brothers and sisters," but seemed to repress all memory of the man who sired him. It was understandable, Bozzacchi thought. "First of all, his father was drunk all the time. He'd shake, even when he was sober. There must be something that made that transition to Burton, but it was always an untouchable subject. You'd never get anything out of him in that respect. Nothing. It's the cause of why Richard kept the anger inside," Bozzacchi believes. "He had to suppress that. It was something that took an entire life."

Filming the lyric play had been a pleasure for Burton, who took great delight in instructing Peter O'Toole exactly how to say the lines, and marveling at how true was Elizabeth's Welsh accent. Her rendering of Dylan Thomas's verse is immensely appealing, and it must have delighted Richard to see Elizabeth transformed into a "Welsh tart," the subject of his erotic dreams since youth. But when the film was released later that year, few people went to see it. Critics veered from describing it as lugubrious and longwinded, ill-suited to film, to praising Burton's fine and loving rendering of Dylan Thomas's verse. One of the reviewers who praised it was Judith Crist, who had not been generous toward the Burtons in the past. She wrote, "[T]he winning film of the moment is *Under Milk Wood* . . . [Burton's] voice washes over the screen." Even Pauline Kael—also not a fan—described in the *New Yorker* her enjoyment of "just sitting back and listening . . . you feel the affection of the cast and you share in it." Though the movie, not surprisingly, made little money, Burton was glad he had undertaken it, paying his debt, as it were, to Dylan Thomas, to the poetry, and to the country that had made him who he was. And, perhaps, to his father.

If *Under Milk Wood* was a labor of love, the black comedy *Hammersmith Is Out* was another miscalculation that had seemed like a good idea. After all, it was a comedic variation of the Faust legend; it was directed by that most literate and amusing of men, Peter Ustinov; and they were able to film it in Mexico, in Cuernavaca, not far from Puerto Vallarta. Once again, it was strictly a small-budget movie, financed by a manufacturer of mobile homes. A young Beau Bridges played Billy Breedlove, a male nurse in a mental hospital, tempted by Hammersmith, a criminally insane patient who transforms Breedlove into a rich, powerful man. Elizabeth Taylor plays a blond waitress, Jimmie Jean Jackson, a parody of her Helen of Troy role in Marlowe's *Doctor Faustus.* Peter Ustinov plays the institution's head doctor.

Before signing Bridges, the producer had considered Robert Redford, but after watching him in *Butch Cassidy and the Sundance Kid*, Burton was unimpressed. "The man Redford that I'd heard so much about is disappointingly ordinary," he wrote in his diary. "It is just as well that he turned down Hammersmith, as he has a quality of dullness. And I can see quite easily why he has taken so long to become a star."

Redford, who didn't turn out so badly, was wise to have refused the role: the film was a disaster. The reviews noted Burton's unblinking stare and unhealthy appearance. One associate of Richard's thought that he was not only drinking heavily, but was also snorting cocaine, which he'd been introduced to while filming *Villain*. That seems unlikely, however, given Burton's fear of taking drugs, as he admitted to Bernard Weintraub. He hadn't particularly liked the Valium and occasional Seconals he took to try to stay sober, and he would always prefer alcohol to prescription—or nonprescription—drugs.

Elizabeth, approaching her fortieth birthday, often appeared bored and put out with Richard. She didn't show up to watch his scenes, though he always made a point of watching hers. They seemed to be saving their compliments to each other for the press. Melvyn Bragg described them as looking like "two heavyweight champions who had fought each other to exhaustion but cannot quit." This would be their tenth film together and their fifth flop in a row, and—given the nervous state of the movie business—it was questionable that any Hollywood producer would take another chance on the Burtons.

In truth, the Burtons were running an endless marathon. Richard's twenty-one days in the desert without alcohol, during the shoot of *Raid on Rommel*, was followed by drinking with such a vengeance it was taking its toll on everyone around him. But the Burtons were still praising each other, and their marriage, to the press ("The quivering awareness of everyday in my relationship with Richard makes it seem that we're not even married yet," Elizabeth told the *Ladies' Home Journal*), but they weren't speaking those words of love to each other. If anything, Richard was beginning to fear that Elizabeth might leave him.

In May, *Villain* was released, to mostly poor reviews. Vincent Canby in the *New York Times* inquired, "Whatever Became of Richard Burton?"

Calling the film "his latest and least interesting bad movie," Canby dismisses Burton's performance as "drab," then goes on to give a postmortem of Burton's twenty-year career, beginning with the old notion that he had peaked as a Shakespearean actor on the London stage even before coming to America to make movies. It was the tired complaint, to which he added a new charge: that Burton was nothing but an old-fashioned movie star, belonging, with Elizabeth, "more to Walter Winchell's day than to ours." He goes on to dismiss the idea that Burton is a great talent corrupted by wealth and fame, and that a film like *Villain* "is all that Burton ever could have been, that no one has been corrupted, only remarkably lucky, and remarkably lucky for a lot longer than anyone in his right mind could reasonably hope for."

It was a harsh assessment, but, ironically, one with which Burton, on a dark day, would have agreed. One day, after having walked in on Elizabeth and their children all gathered together on the *Kalizma* to watch a print of *Cleopatra*, Richard quickly exited. He still could not stand to watch himself onscreen. "My lack of interest in my own career, past, present, or future, is almost total," he then confided in his diary.

> All my life, I think I have been secretly ashamed of being an actor, and the older I get the more ashamed I get. . . . the press have been sounding the same note for years—ever since I went to Hollywood in the early 1950s . . . that I am or was potentially the greatest actor in the world and the successor to Gielgud, Olivier, etc., but that I had dissipated my genius, etc. and "sold out" to films and booze and women. An interesting reputation to have and by no means dull, but by all means untrue.

Perhaps that's why, when Burton received a letter from Sir Laurence Olivier offering him the chance to take over the running of England's National Theater, he wrote a long letter turning down the offer. "The old Etonians would drive me mad in five months" was his excuse.

Elizabeth had always been more resilient and more realistic about her films and her career. At breakfast the next morning, she said to

Richard about having watched *Cleopatra* for the first time since its premiere in 1963, "You know, it's really not so bad after all."

If drinking, bickering, and making lackluster movies had taken over the Burtons' lives, the only thing that seemed to bring them pleasure was their family. So when Michael and Beth Clutter Wilding brought their first child, Layla, into the world on August 26, 1971, making Elizabeth "the world's most glamorous grandmother," things were—at least temporarily—set right.

The Burtons had escaped the disappointing reception of *Under Milk Wood* and *Villain* by cruising the Mediterranean on the *Kalizma*. When news of the birth reached them in Monte Carlo, they rushed back to London. Elizabeth showed up at Heathrow in an ungrandmotherly outfit of white-lace hot pants and white knee-high boots. She told the handful of reporters how happy she was. "This is the baby Richard and I could never have," she beamed. They took possession of Richard's house in Hampstead next door to the home they'd bought for Michael and Beth, so Elizabeth could lavish gifts and attention on the newborn. She adored Layla and bought the infant Dior baby clothes. She had always been generous and welcoming to Beth as well, but all too soon, there was trouble in paradise.

Not surprisingly, her teenage son was not happy living on his mother's and stepfather's largesse. Elizabeth had already gotten Michael a job as Bozzacchi's assistant on the set of *Zee and Co.*, and she and Richard helped support the young family, but the Burtons—like any set of parents in the early 1970s—were not pleased when Michael turned his London house into something of a crash pad for visiting hippies. The Burtons were spending a fortune on security for their home, but right next door, all kinds of street people were wandering in and out. Soon, Michael ducked out of his life of privilege and headed for the hills, taking Beth and Layla with him. They left London to join a commune in, of all places, Ponterwyd, a small mountain town in Wales not far from Pontrhydyfen. If Richard was touched by his stepson's odd tribute of following in his footsteps—in reverse!—he didn't show it. Instead, it angered him. "I made it *up* and the boy's trying to make it down," he said, utterly bewildered. "I try not to interfere, but I still get goddamned mad. When I think what it took to climb out!"

Burton was hard on Michael, feeling that he didn't quite realize what a gifted actress his mother was, that her success was based only on her beauty. To add to his crankiness, Burton, at forty-five, was beginning to have more health problems—painful recurrences of gout, a tremor, and his old shoulder and neck injuries were starting to affect the use of his arms. In July 1971, he had written: "My left hand and wrist are now completely useless . . . I was so uncomfortable last night that in bed the slightest movement made me groan as if demented." Soon after, a doctor came to attend Elizabeth, and Richard waylaid him to examine his arm. The doctor overcame Burton's fear of taking drugs and prescribed Endocin, a painkiller, which helped for a while, but Burton soon found there were few things he could grasp and pick up with his left hand.

In September, the Burtons traveled to Dubrovnik, Yugoslavia, where Burton would play Marshal Tito in *The Battle of Sutjeska*, a state-sponsored film paid for by the Yugoslav government. One of many fans of Richard's World War II action film *Where Eagles Dare* was the war hero Tito himself, who flattered himself that Richard resembled him when he was a young man fighting the Fascists in World War II.

Again, Richard was warned not to do it. The script was 250 pages long, written entirely in Serbo-Croatian, but Burton was an admirer of the real-life war hero and he wanted to take on the role. He may also have sensed that he would only continue to have a great career— any career—if he played great men of history. But Hollywood was no longer paying.

The producer, Nikola Popovic, wanted to find a cameo role for Elizabeth, but this time she declined. They stopped in Dubrovnik to shop for books for the yacht, and, as usual, Elizabeth's appearance on the streets of the city attracted crowds. They had cruised in on the *Kalizma*, mooring in Cavtat, a harbor town south of Dubrovnik, and each day Burton would be flown by military helicopter to the movie's location in the mountains of Yugoslavia, at the site of the original World War II battle in which Tito and twenty thousand partisans had broken through the German siege.

Marshal Tito invited the Burtons to spend weekends in his palatial home, driving them around his estate in his Lincoln Continental (presented to him by the city of Zagreb). Though Burton admired Tito, he quickly became bored both with the whole production and with Tito's company, and not only because everything had to be filtered through interpreters. They had to listen to Tito's and his wife's long stories before the interpreters could even begin. Perhaps being with a great man was less interesting than playing one. "Were it not, actually, for E.'s delight in the power and the glory of it all, I would do my best to cut and run—so great is the strain of boredom," he wrote in his diary. The production itself was plagued by endless delays, money shortages, and the constant hiring and firing of screenwriters and directors. He spent most of his time sitting around in Tito's hut, drinking Nescafé and trying to get through a Neil Simon script, *The Gingerbread Lady*, which Elizabeth was considering. He wanted out, but it was impossible. To make matters worse, the daily helicopter rides were sometimes harrowing, and at one point he feared he would be killed on his way back to the *Kalizma*. He flashed on an image of Elizabeth lying in her bed on the yacht, reading a book, and he suddenly remembered the words from a poem by the Welsh poet Alun Lewis: "If I should go away,/beloved/do not say,/he has forgotten me./Forever you abide./A singing rib within my dreaming side."

Oddly enough, Elizabeth had her own premonition about Richard. One day she accompanied him to the helicopter pad and watched her husband, his makeup man Ron Berkeley, and another assistant climb on board. "Suddenly, something came over me," she later wrote about the incident.

"Guys, get out of there," she called out.

They looked at her quizzically.

"Richard, get out of there, just get out!"

He didn't argue with her. They climbed into another helicopter. Later, Burton and his makeup man returned, "visibly shaken," Elizabeth recalled. The helicopter they were supposed to have taken had crashed in the mountains, killing everyone onboard.

It wasn't the first time Elizabeth had had premonitions. She *knew*, even before Dick Hanley and Dr. Kemener had walked into her bedroom many years ago with the grim news, that Mike Todd had been killed when the *Liz* crashed into the Zuni Mountains of New Mexico. And the night before the death of her good friend, the actor Gary Cooper, she'd dreamed of his death from cancer, waking up to write down the time on a Kleenex box beside her bed: 12:25 a.m., which was indeed the exact time of his death the following night.

Throughout the shoot, the Burtons, Bozzacchi and his wife, Claudye, and Elizabeth's secretary, Raymond Vignale, stayed at Marshal Tito's house, though Burton usually preferred to hole up on the *Kalizma*, with Maria and Liza. Among the five adults, Richard noted, only Elizabeth was drinking. He had once again attempted to go on the wagon, drinking Nescafé and tea by the gallon. But ever the frugal Welshman, Richard noticed how huge their liquor bills were, amazed that it was even possible when they brought most of their alcohol from the yacht—Smirnoff and Jack Daniel's, which weren't even available in Yugoslavia. Of the five of them, "only Elizabeth drinks, but she drinks *only* booze brought from the boat," he recorded. "I have in my time and at my best put away I'm sure the occasional three bottles of vodka a day . . . but not for two or three days in a row. And not for a week or a fortnight. Otherwise, it would be Dead Dad."

Trying to stay away from drinking was difficult around Elizabeth. He was feeling the strain of sobriety, the boredom of the shoot, and noticing with concern how Elizabeth seemed to give in to a deep lassitude now that she wasn't working. One day, he just snapped when fourteen-year-old Liza asked him if they could keep the dog they were using in the film. Burton said no, because it would whine for its owner all through the night.

Liza persisted, saying, "But he's *your* dog."

"Don't be bloody stupid," he shot back. "He's no more my dog than you are my daughter."

Liza was stunned, but bravely answered, "That was very nice." Elizabeth, overhearing, was horrified. Richard reproached himself endlessly, afterward. "I wanted to cry or slit my jugular," he later wrote, because he really did love his and Elizabeth's children, taking great delight in what a canny little charmer Liza could be. But the damage had been done, and he realized it.

The most frightening part of it, for Richard, was that those cruel, unthinking words had been uttered when he was sober. Adding a new terror to his struggle with alcohol was the fear that drink had already distorted his personality.

For a man who so often expressed contempt for his profession, Burton never stopped working. Elizabeth continued to glide through 1971, making two films (a small role in *Under Milk Wood* and her co-starring role in *Hammersmith Is Out*) to Richard's three (*Milk Wood*, *Hammersmith*, and *The Battle of Sutjeska*). In October, he would appear in a fourth film, playing Leon Trotsky in *The Assassination of Trotsky*, another Joseph Losey–directed film, and another box office disappointment. In fact, the movie's reception was so bad (it was actually booed at the New York Film Festival in Alice Tully Hall when it was shown the following year) that it left sixty-three-year-old Losey a nervous wreck, pacing his suite at the Algonquin Hotel on West 44th Street, asthmatically puffing on his inhaler and longing for a drink. Burton had actually been Losey's third choice, after Dirk Bogarde and Marlon Brando had both turned him down. Losey's blend of Harold Pinteresque silences and stylized, arty set pieces sometimes tipped his films into unintentional parody, and the critics had a field day (*Monthly Film Bulletin* compared it to *Boom!*). Despite the bad reception of the Losey-Burton collaborations, the three remained good friends, and Richard always defended what he considered Losey's genius as a director.

A few scenes were shot on location in Mexico, but most were filmed in a replica of Trotsky's villa on a soundstage in Rome. After a difficult shoot, Burton would return to the *Kalizma*, where Michael, Beth, and Layla Wilding had joined Richard and Elizabeth for a visit. Both Burtons had stopped drinking for a brief time, and Richard remarked in his diary how beautiful Elizabeth looked—newly slim and healthy—and what a pleasure it was to have Michael and his family with them. "The virtual cessation of drink has made a terrific difference to E.," he wrote. "She is more active, more spirited, and at the same time more relaxed. And she looks even more beautiful than before." He and Elizabeth took great delight in Layla, a sweet and happy infant whom Elizabeth absolutely doted upon.

But by November 10, their sober idyll was over. To celebrate his forty-sixth birthday, Burton fixed himself and Elizabeth a couple of large martinis in the early afternoon. And a few days later, Richard wrote, "E. is trying to press me to having a martini before lunch because she wants one and doesn't like drinking alone . . . as I've explained to E. ad nauseam, I find one drink simply not enough. I guess two or three stiff ones are what I find satisfactory, but that means slowly reverting to being a drunkard again, and I simply will not tolerate returning to that. . . ." As for Elizabeth, she didn't seem to show the ill effects of alcohol as much as Richard. She could brawl with Richard and shout obscenities, but she never turned cruel.

The Burtons returned to London in time to attend two great social events that would further test Richard's tenuous grasp on sobriety. The first was the Proust Ball, given on December 2 by the

Rothschilds at their splendid estate, the Château de Ferrières, Seine-et-Marne, in which all the guests were asked to appear as characters from Marcel Proust's *A la recherche du temps perdu*. Touting it as "the Ball of the Century," the engraved invitations requested that women wear jewels in their hair, as befitting *la Belle Époque*, so, of course, Elizabeth needed Alexandre de Paris to accompany her. She came as the Duchesse de Guermantes, one of the rulers of Parisian society in Proust's novel, wearing borrowed jewels from Van Cleef & Arpels in addition to her emerald-and-diamond brooch from Bulgari, which Alexandre had skillfully woven into her elaborate coif. Among the glittering guests were the former French president Georges Pompidou, Princess Grace of Monaco, the Duchess of Windsor, Audrey Hepburn, Andy Warhol, the late President Kennedy's press secretary Pierre Salinger, producer Sam Spiegel, and the celebrated photographer Cecil Beaton, who wandered the vast dining room taking photographs of the guests, including a stunning one of Elizabeth in costume, resplendent in diamonds and emeralds. There were so many jewels entwined in coiffures that dozens of French policemen stood guard outside the château.

Richard, who was seated at dinner next to the sultry Anne-Marie Deschodt, ex-wife of French film director Louis Malle, and across the table from Andy Warhol, would attempt to get through the entire affair sober. Elizabeth, seated at the first table with Guy de Rothschild, Grace Kelly (Her Serene Highness Princess of Monaco), and the Duchess of Windsor (already "slightly gaga"), would have a grand time.

The Burtons had traveled by car from Paris to the French countryside with Grace Kelly, and took possession of two guest bedrooms at the sumptuous estate. The two-hour drive, delayed by traffic and the inconvenience of having to pick up Grace at 32 Avenue Foch, was spent listening to Her Serene Highness extolling the virtues of the Shah of Iran. Richard, miner's son by birth and aristocrat by talent, usually felt awkward around Princess Grace, whom he described as rather dull and in the class of people who are "in a somewhat false position and know it," having ditched her Hollywood career to marry royalty.

They were to descend from their guest rooms at nine ten for a nine thirty dinner, and Richard, ever punctual, found himself waiting for "my girls" to join him—"the Duchess of Windsor and the Princess of Monaco and of course my very own 'girl,'" Elizabeth. But Elizabeth was, as usual, late (problems with Alexandre de Paris), so they didn't descend until ten thirty p.m. As they were guests of honor, dinner was delayed for them.

Once seated, Burton described "an hour or more of absolute agony" as he passed all the wines poured for him to his dinner partner, Mme. Malle, including champagne, a Lafite white wine, and a second white wine (Château d'Yquem). He found himself fascinated by the "cadaverous" man across the table from him, with snow-white hair but no visible eyelashes or eyebrows. The odd-looking man leaned across the table to Richard and asked, "Where's my Elizabeth?" Richard nodded toward Guy de Rothschild's table. The man sighed, clearly disappointed to be stuck with Richard and not Elizabeth. After all, the guest was Andy Warhol, who had burnished Elizabeth's icon status with his stunning silk-screen portraits, who would one day declare that he would like to be reincarnated as a diamond on the hand of Elizabeth Taylor.

Seated across the room, Elizabeth tried to stifle her hilarity at the Duchess of Windsor, who wore an outsized feather in her hair that kept dipping into the soup, the wine, the ice cream, and smacking her host in the face. The duke was apparently not well enough to attend the grand ball, but the duchess invited Elizabeth and Richard to come see him before they left for Gstaad.

After the dinner, Guy de Rothschild asked Elizabeth to help him remove his glued-on mustache, which had become bothersome. They ducked into one of the many bathrooms near the dining hall, with a

Rothschild servant standing guard, while guests wondered if Guy and Elizabeth were, in fact, "making out" in the powder room.

Richard took great pride in noticing how the high-born and fabulously rich guests, as they reveled throughout the night, sneaked glances at Elizabeth and Princess Grace, surreptitiously gawking at their beauty. Curiously, Elizabeth didn't consider herself—nor Grace Kelly, for that matter—truly beautiful. She felt that being too impeccable, too groomed, too studied—"so that you can feel the vanity behind it"— made beauty boring. Her ideals of feminine beauty were women like Lena Horne and Ava Gardner, earthier women ablaze with life and heart.

The music finally stopped at seven in the morning, when the costumed revelers, many of them hungover, drifted to their cars and faced the morning traffic back to Paris.

Four days later, the Burtons visited the Duke and Duchess of Windsor for a dinner party "with half a dozen of the most consummate bores in Paris," as Burton later described them. He found the Windsors quite faded, the duke in ill health and walking with a cane, and the duchess's memory flickering in and out. The most touching part of the evening was when the duke and duchess kept reminiscing how Edward had once been the king of England. The aging lovers who had risked all, had become world-famous, and had lost so much, were now seeing their shadow empire fade.

The Burtons' reign as Hollywood's royalty was beginning to fade, as well. But there was always Europe.

In January of the new year, 1972, Richard and Elizabeth flew to Budapest in their private jet and checked into the Presidential Suite of the Inter-Continental Hotel. Richard would begin work on his fortieth movie, *Bluebeard*, a black comedy-melodrama about a mythical Baron von Sepper, a serial murderer of seven women. As before, he waived his salary for a percentage of the profits (if any), but received $80,000 in living expenses. Elizabeth had fallen to the last place on the top ten box office list in 1968, and appeared neither on the list for 1969 nor on the one for 1970. Burton had begun accepting movie roles without even reading the scripts beforehand. *Bluebeard* fell into that category.

Whenever the Burtons took up residence for a new film, they would rev up their bedtime exercises, to help get into shape for the work ahead and to establish a routine. For Richard, it was hard to keep a straight face watching Elizabeth solemnly go through her exercises, holding her breasts in each hand while she ran in place. ("[F]irm as they are," Richard recorded, "really like a 30 yr old's more than a nearly 40 year old's, they are pretty big and the resultant wiggle-waggle would be pretty odd as well as bad for her. It's a very fetching sight.")

Like his previous three films, *Bluebeard* was a cobbled-together affair, a European coproduction from four different countries, and it was directed by Edward Dmytryk, one of the "Hollywood Ten," who had been blacklisted, had served six months in prison, and had been forced to recant in front of the House Un-American Activities Committee. The director once had a long, respectable career in Hollywood, having made song-and-dance man Dick Powell into hardboiled detective Philip Marlowe in *Murder, My Sweet*; directed Humphrey Bogart in *The Caine Mutiny;* and Marlon Brando and Montgomery Clift in *The Young Lions.* He had directed Elizabeth and Clift in *Raintree County* in 1957, when he had been forced to shoot around the actor after the devastating accident that nearly destroyed his face. But after almost fifty years in the movie business, he was reduced to what would have been deemed B-pictures under the old studio system. Burton felt pity for the downward trajectory of Dmytryk's career, but the director was in awe of Richard and Elizabeth.

Bluebeard would have its own set of problems. First of all, Budapest in winter did not have the romantic, gypsy atmosphere the Burtons had expected; it was a grim, dark, cold, proletarian city. They were used to the warmth and light of the Mediterranean. Secondly—and more importantly—Burton played opposite a "cast of international beauties" appearing as his wives and mistresses, including the new sex symbol Raquel Welch, as well as Virna Lisi, Nathalie Delon, and even the kittenish Joey Heatherton, an unlikely Burton costar. Elizabeth was on her guard. She was sure Richard had been faithful to her throughout the nine years of their relationship, and, in fact, he had. And not only because they were glued to each other's sides, as they made sure to spend time on the sets and locations of each other's movies when they weren't acting in the same film. Elizabeth was possessive, and she accompanied Richard to his movie sets for the last two years because she didn't want to lose him. She knew his effect on women (she sometimes sarcastically called him "Charlie Charm"). Philip Burton had noted that even as young as fifteen, Richard had been surrounded by girls, who hung around him "like cats after cream." The stage actress Tammy Grimes, who had been smitten with Richard before the "Elizabethan era," had described him as "a genius" who "makes women feel beautiful. His acting has such a tragic quality . . . he is a vodka man with a quicksilver mind and a violent temper. He's moody, completely unpredictable, always fascinating, very frugal, extremely shrewd, a tremendous snob, and a beautiful man."

Burton's lady-killer reputation made him particularly well suited to playing Baron von Sepper, literally a lady-killer. It was a campy role in a campy movie: the baron murders each of his wives in imaginative ways when they discover he's impotent, and he keeps their frozen bodies in a secret refrigerated chamber of his villa. Burton knew the role had "to be done with immense tongue-in-cheek. I tried to remember how the master—whassisname—Vincent Price plays that kind of thing. Must be funny serious." In the mock-gothic atmosphere of the movie, Burton "plays the organ, a falcon flies around, a kitten will be killed" (which upset Elizabeth). Vincent Price would have been quite at home. But no matter how bad the script was, Burton was always professional. "If he sold himself, he gave full money's worth," observed Dmytryk.

The backers of the movie asked Dmytryk to introduce nudity into the film, to heighten its box office appeal, and he did so (trying to keep it "tasteful"). Many of the onscreen beauties bared their breasts, and even Richard was asked to disrobe, which he refused to do. For the first time since *The Spy Who Came in from the Cold*, Elizabeth became intensely jealous of two of Richard's costars—not the voluptuous Raquel Welch or the blond, gamine Joey Heatherton, but Sybil Danning, a *Playboy* model who played a half-naked prostitute in the movie. Elizabeth, who came to the set every day, was convinced that the former model played her love scene with Richard with too much enthusiasm. Elizabeth was so incensed that she reportedly reeled back and slapped Danning's face after one such performance. But her real jealousy would be reserved for Nathalie Delon, the ex-wife of heart-throb French actor Alain Delon.

As early as 1964, Elizabeth had recognized that she and Richard were "both mercurial, jealous people." She admitted to being jealous of Richard's past conquests—and they were legion—and she realized that Richard may not always be faithful to her, that even "in happy marriages, during a sort of middle-aged change of life, men do flit around with young, pretty girls." She felt then that if—*when*—Richard began to stray, she would "have the guts and compassion" to do whatever was necessary to hold their marriage together. "I would love him enough to love the hurt he might give me," she wrote rather masochistically, adding, "I really, profoundly believe that no such thing will ever happen." But now, for the first time in their marriage, it *was* about to happen.

Adding to Elizabeth's insecurity, she would turn forty on February 27. The great English fashion photographer Norman Parkinson came to photograph Elizabeth for the cataclysmic event: the hitting of the wall for Hollywood actresses, the point of no return, the beginning of middle age with menopause in sight. For the legions of Elizabeth's female fans, who had grown up with the beautiful child star, it meant a final farewell to youth. For Elizabeth, it meant a farewell to screen-goddess roles. Elizabeth had once said that she welcomed the lines and gray hairs of middle age, but now that it was on the horizon, there had to be some qualms about keeping her notoriously attractive and flirtatious husband by her side.

When Richard pored through the photographic proofs, he was struck anew by Elizabeth's beauty, remembering how he "fell in love with her at once . . . like the pull of gravity." But he disliked his own appearance. "He didn't make me look very fetching," he wrote on Valentine's Day, noting with distaste his thinning hair. "I've never been—at least not for 20 yrs or so—and am never likely to be the pin-up type." Norman Parkinson's photograph, published to commemorate Elizabeth's fortieth birthday, showed Elizabeth and Richard in a somber mood, in matching black furs, Elizabeth's Krupp diamond glinting dully on her finger, the ethereal lights of Budapest flickering behind them. It is indeed a wintry view of the couple, bundled against the cold, yet it's haunting, and it remains one of Elizabeth's favorite photographs, hanging in a glittering oval frame in her bedroom till this day.

Burton was struggling hard to maintain his sobriety throughout the shoot, despite the gloom of the city, the banality of the script, the temptations of his costars, and Elizabeth's vigilant jealousy on the set. He would be especially tested when he threw a lavish birthday party to celebrate Elizabeth's turning forty.

Like a repeat of the gala thrown in the Dorchester for the premiere of *The Taming of the Shrew*, Burton flew in the vast Jenkins clan from Wales. The invitation, sent out as a telegram under Elizabeth's name, stated:

We would love you to come to Budapest, as our guest, for the weekend of 26 and 27 February to help me celebrate my being 40 birthday STOP The hotel is very Hilton but there are some fun places to go STOP. Dress slacks for Saturday night in some dark cellar and something gay and pretty for Sunday night STOP Dark glass for languorous in between STOP Lot of love Elizabeth and Richard STOP P.S. Could you RSVP as soon as possible to Inter-Continental Hotel Budapest so I know how many rooms to book.

It went out to two hundred guests in Monaco, London, Paris, and Los Angeles, including Princess Grace; Ringo Starr and his wife, Barbara Bach; Michael Caine and his fiancée, Shakira Baksh; Joseph and Patricia Losey; the Cartiers; the Bulgaris; and Alexandre de Paris. Elizabeth's ex-husband Michael Wilding and his new wife, actress Margaret Leighton, were invited, as was David Niven, and, to please Richard, the English poet Stephen Spender.

Ambassadors from seven countries arrived to celebrate Elizabeth. Elizabeth's mother, Sara, and brother, Howard, were flown in. Also present were Neville Coghill and Francis Warner, another Oxford don, who took the occasion to offer Richard an honorary fellowship to teach at St. Peter's, Oxford. (Burton was thrilled: "It cld be a step toward a D.Litt., which is the only honour I really covet.") The children were there—Chris Wilding and Liza and Maria, of course, but Michael Wilding Jr., who still rejected his parents' conspicuous consumption, stayed away. As did six of the seven "Bluebeard broads," whom Elizabeth disinvited when the guest list grew too long (Raquel Welch managed to show up anyway).

The party was Richard's way of renewing his vows to Elizabeth, and perhaps of assuring her that rumors of infidelity brewing on the set were just rumors. Others thought the extravagant event was Elizabeth's way of reminding the world that she could still command international publicity, now that her film career had cooled. She took great delight in planning the gala, visiting private homes with the designer Larry Barcher, brought over from Paris, to get ideas on how to redecorate the InterContinental Hotel (The Duma), transforming it with borrowed paintings and silver into the kind of luxury dwelling in which her more distinguished guests would feel at home.

Journalists flocked to Budapest. They came from everywhere—Japan, India, Sri Lanka, Europe, the States. Burton found it necessary to appease them with a press conference, which he did, showing off his new gift to Taylor: the 50-carat, heart-shaped "Taj Mahal" diamond, on a gold-and-ruby chain, bought for £350,000.

Elizabeth knew what she was getting. She'd already fallen in love with the byzantine story behind the diamond necklace, which had been fashioned in 1627 and given as a gift to the Empress of the Mughal Empire, Nur Jahan, by her husband, Shah Jahangir, the Emperor of the Mughal Empire. She then gave it to his son, Shah Jahan, the emperor who built the Taj Mahal as a monument to Queen Mumtaz, his favorite wife. The yellow-tinted diamond bore an inscription in Parsi: "Love Is Everlasting." Curiously, the jewel had been purchased in advance of Elizabeth's birthday, during a layover at Kennedy Airport. Cartier accommodated the Burtons by bringing a king's ransom of jewelry to the airport for them to consider while they waited for their next plane. The Taj Mahal necklace was among the selections. Richard further pleased Elizabeth by telling her that he would have bought her the Taj Mahal if there had been a way to transport it to Gstaad.

At the press conference, which he attended alone, Richard playfully draped the jeweled necklace on his forehead; he later hung it around the neck of a Hungarian boy who had wandered into the press conference.

The gala lasted two days. At the cocktail party the first night, Richard took great delight in introducing Maria, now a willowy eleven-year-old, to her Welsh aunts and uncles, all of whom were happily chattering away in Welsh. The relatives were struck by how much cherubic-faced Maria resembled Richard's daughter, Kate. Richard had brought them in on a chartered British Airways Trident. Some of Burton's relatives, like his brother Verdun, had never flown in an airplane before. They were bowled over by the flight, and by the view of the Danube from their hotel bedrooms, and by meeting Princess Grace.

(The second night, Her Serene Highness led a conga line around the ballroom.) The Jenkins brothers brought with them a 16-mm reel of highlights of the British Lions, the Welsh rugby team's victorious tour of New Zealand, which they all took turns watching and cheering, Burton among them ("by God, they're really good . . .").

For the dinner-dance on the second night, Burton showed up in a dark jacket and white turtleneck, while Elizabeth—down to 128 pounds— was dressed in a white Grecian gown, her hair regally arranged with white cyclamen blossoms, the Taj Mahal diamond around her neck, and her Krupp diamond proudly on display on her left ring finger. At Richard's table were his sister Cis and Princess Grace, as well as Stephen Spender and the British envoy to Hungary. Thousands of gold, helium-filled balloons floated above the glittering crowd as they dined on Chicken Kiev, fruit salad, and a chocolate cake that had been brought in ablaze with forty candles. The ballroom was fes- tooned with white lilacs and red tulips. Champagne everywhere, for everyone, but not for Richard, who still struggled to remain sober.

Seated between Michael Caine and the American ambassador to Hungary, across from Ringo and his wife, Elizabeth held court while guests lined up to see the ring. But it was the Taj Mahal necklace that drew the most admiring stares. To her credit, Elizabeth always con- sidered herself a "custodian" of her fabulous jewels, to be looked after and cared for until their next owners claimed them, and she always took great delight in showing them off, even letting anyone who asked try them on. "One day somebody else will have them," she later wrote, "and I hope that new person will love the jewelry and respect it as much as I do . . . I've never, never thought of my jewelry as trophies. I'm here to take care of them and to love them."

But not everyone celebrated.

Emlyn Williams's son Alan (Brook's brother) attended the "cellar dance" on the first night. It was held in the wine cellar of the old part of Hotel Duma, and Richard had brought in *Bluebeard*'s set designer to add cobwebs and musty bottles and crates (Cis, at one point, tried to clean them up). But Alan Williams was appalled by the lavish display of wealth for the two-day extravaganza, especially in a Communist country. A novelist and student of the Hungarian Revolution of 1956, he drove Elizabeth to tears by his condemnation of the Burtons' lack of sensitivity to being in a proletarian country. He made himself so unpleasant that Gaston Sanz, their black-belt-holding chauffeur and bodyguard, gave him the heave-ho.

There was considerable grumbling in the Hungarian press as well, beginning with their amazement when the Burtons first arrived in Budapest and it took over an hour to unload all of their luggage and caseloads of vodka and bourbon off the plane. What they didn't realize was that the money, and how it was spent, almost didn't matter to Burton anymore. As he grew increasingly jaded about *acting*, he grew increasingly cavalier about the wealth it brought him. Nonetheless, after the two-day party, Richard shrewdly neutralized the criticism of the press by pledging to donate the cost of the gala, $45,000, to UNICEF.

Elizabeth loved every minute of it. She adored parties, she adored gifts, she was used to being the center of attention, and she needed to take the focus off Burton's "bevy of international beauties" and the rumors of his possible infidelity. Privately, she often said she'd be just as happy living in a shack with Richard and her children, but the world demanded "Liz and Dick," and Liz and Dick they got.

Finally, the long-dreaded news came a few weeks after Elizabeth's gala: Ifor Jenkins died on March 21, 1972.

Richard was devastated. The last time he'd visited his worshipped brother, the sight of his diminished life had made Richard wish for Ifor's death. Richard had written in his diary in July of the previous year, "Ifor is very near the end. Death is written all over his face. He did not know me when I saw him yesterday. He can barely speak. He is already dead. I wish he were." Elizabeth had sobbed all the way back to the Dorchester that day after visiting Ifor. Now his wish had come true, and Burton was again awash with guilt. After recording his brother's death, Burton put away his diary and did not take it down again for eight years.

They flew back to England and then Wales, to bury his brother and attend the funeral. Ifor had been the one to hold the Jenkins clan together; "he was the nearest to a father to me," Richard often told his brother Graham.

With Ifor gone, Burton's hard-won sobriety was over. Back in Budapest to finish his work on *Bluebeard*, he began drinking again, with renewed abandon, bent finally on destroying himself, his life with Elizabeth, his deteriorating health, and the gifts the gods had given him: his voice, his talent, his fire.

DIVORCE HIS DIVORCE HERS

"I shall miss you with passion and wild regret."
—RICHARD BURTON

"Maybe we loved each other too much. . . . Pray for us."
—ELIZABETH TAYLOR

When Richard returned to Budapest after a three-day leave to bury his brother, Dmytryk thought him a changed man. Burton's day would now begin with a large vodka-and-orange-juice, and by the time he showed up on the set, Bob Wilson and Gaston Sanz would have to carry him upright between them, from the Rolls-Royce to his dressing room. He could only manage to work for a few hours; then he'd return to the hotel and drink for the rest of the day. Dmytryk, who was genuinely fond of both Burtons, lamented the effect it had on Richard. He noticed that he now went everywhere in the company of Wilson and Sanz. "Richard needed their protection," he said, "because when drunk he became nasty, and in the wrong places might have been killed without them."

Richard's dissolution became especially apparent at an official dinner given by the British ambassador. The evening began well enough, with Richard reciting Dylan Thomas to the ambassador's teenage sons. But by the time the Burtons sat down to dinner, however, Richard became eerily quiet, refusing to touch his food. He continued to drink throughout the evening. At one point, he looked over at his dinner companion, the wife of the Swiss ambassador, and blurted out, "You remind me quite distinctly of a hungry vulture." When the ambassador tried to smooth things over, Burton turned on him, saying, "You Swiss are a very bad lot."

"Richard!" Elizabeth said sharply, having had enough of this. Burton allowed Gaston to drive him back to their hotel, while Elizabeth gamely stayed on, trying to save the evening with gracious small talk. The next morning, she sent around flowers and apologies.

At one point, Richard tried to take himself in hand, aware that Elizabeth was fed up with his behavior, on and off the set. He often left little notes and letters for Elizabeth, even when they were together, and on April 18, 1972, he wrote:

Hey Lumps,

I think I'm over the hump—not that kind, giggler—my kind! All I've had are three cups of tea and I'm sorry about the two cold bangers which I've ravaged as if they were you. I had one whole Valium and half a pinkers—I will take one of each to work with me. Stay for me here. I will not fail to join thee. . . . I feel very odd. Possibly because I'm sober. Though odd, it's a nice sensation. Can you believe your husbs coming home sober? I can hardly believe it myself, but I will. This time I mean it. That sod inside me has decided to give in and cry "uncle." Then read my diary. There's a little bit in it about you. I thought you might like to know what it feels like to fuck you.

Hastily, Husbs.

But his attempts at sobriety didn't last long, and soon he was at it again. Dmytryk had worked with other alcoholics in his long career, certainly Monty Clift on *Raintree County*. "[Spencer] Tracy's drunks were periodic," he recalled, "sometimes months of abstinence followed by a week or two in which he'd get mean and wild. [Clark] Gable didn't start his drinking until five thirty in the afternoon, so you could get a day's work in." As for Burton, his director "could see him getting older week by week. We covered it up with the usual lighting tricks."

One day, Burton's two fourteen-year-old daughters, Liza and Kate, showed up at his dressing room and confronted their father about his drinking. They pleaded with him to stop, and Kate later complained to members of her father's entourage. They had always been there, it seemed, waiting backstage and on movie sets with Bloody Marys or vodka martinis at the ready. "You're so tough on your father," she was told by one of the entourage. But she had to be. She told her father that if he didn't stop drinking, she never wanted to see him again.

And still, he could not stop.

In retrospect, Dmytryk thought that Elizabeth drank as much or almost as much as Richard at the time, but it didn't seem to affect her as it affected him. "She was stronger than Richard in every way," he felt. They both, however, seemed well under the influence when David Frost came to Budapest to interview the Burtons for *The David Frost Show*. The interview was set up on the *Bluebeard* soundstage, and it lasted for two hours. Richard talked about his adopted father, Philip Burton, and recited passages from the Old Testament—amazingly, his memory wasn't affected by the amount of alcohol he was consuming. Elizabeth wore her stunning Taylor-Burton diamond and her tiny Ping-Pong diamond as well, and talked about both jewels.

Frost aired the interview in its entirety on two successive nights, March 20 and 21, 1972, showcasing clearly inebriated Richard and Elizabeth. Frost had been someone they'd trusted, having appeared with him in *The V.I.P.s*, where the boyish television host had played himself, but he didn't bother to edit out Elizabeth's long silences and slowed speech, as she drank off-camera from a constantly refilled glass of Jack Daniel's throughout the interview. Elizabeth later admitted that she had made a fool of herself. But Burton didn't care.

It was just too much. The grief and guilt over Ifor's death were unbearable, and he knew only one way to handle it—by dissolving his torment in alcohol. Ifor had come to represent the true father, the only one he'd really known, the one who embodied all the masculine and native virtues Burton hoped to possess. He felt that he, Richard, had carelessly contributed to Ifor's paralysis and death. Unlike Elizabeth, he had never learned how to be private in public, and he wore his private grief on his sleeve. It was the one thing she couldn't teach him about this business of fame. She had already explained in her 1965 autobiography, *Elizabeth Taylor*, "I owe the public who pays to see me on the screen the best performance I can give. As to how I live my personal life, my responsibility is to the people directly involved with me." But Burton was unable to separate his private life from his public life, and he finally cracked from the pressure.

And, for him, the presence of seven stunning, half-naked women making love to him throughout the schedule of *Bluebeard* was an almost comic temptation. When the film was released in August of that year, Richard looked like an automaton onscreen, stoically resisting their writhing charms. But off-camera, he flirted with his costars, and Taylor had already delivered a resounding smack to Sybil Danning for putting too much of herself into her sex scene with Burton.

To assuage her suspicions of a possible affair, Richard wrote her a soul-rending letter with, perhaps, an eerie presentiment of his death:

Hotel Duma Budapest:
My Darling,

I think I'd better go and wrestle myself in the little bedroom. Try and rest also. I would be very grateful if so often you'd shove your head—your beautiful head—through the door (opening it first, of course) to make sure that I'm not dead. I know I'm a terrible liar sometimes but please believe that I have never betrayed either in word or deed the physical you or the mental you. I simply love you too much. I flatter and am flattered and both too easily. It's only a question of booze. I behaved like an idiot and quite a lot of people would like to take me away from you, but the only person who can remove me from *you* is *you*. If you leave me, then, beauty, I refuse to be responsible for myself. I will, like Lear, go mad. And Christ help anybody who happens to be around. I might even kill. Good-bye for I hope not more than a few hours. Just check up to make sure that I am not with some dreadful and frightful flatterer. And I don't necessarily mean Raquel Welch or Nathalie Delon . . . Please hang on for another twelve years. If you wish to leave, of course, how could I stop you? I deserve all the injury that you can inflict, and I will take it as long as you stay with me.—Husbs. (I hope)

But during a night shoot, Richard and Nathalie Delon slipped away while rehearsing a scene in which they walk down a street and turn a corner. Once out of sight, they didn't return. Instead, they'd slipped into Burton's idling Rolls-Royce, while Dmytryk and the crew waited interminably for them to reappear. The shoot had to be canceled for the night. The next day, Richard wrote an apology to Dmytryk: "Dear Eddie, please believe that the Richard you saw last night is not the real Richard Burton." But the damage was done.

Elizabeth was incensed when she learned about the incident. She flew to Rome, where she was being fitted for her next film, *Night Watch*. Her first evening there, on May 6, she had an intimate dinner with Richard's old competitor for the Cartier diamond, Aristotle Onassis. Jacqueline was not present. Nearly thirty paparazzi got wind of it and ambushed the couple, turning their dinner à deux into a brawl. Elizabeth escaped to her suite—alone—at the Grand Hotel, but she couldn't sleep. She knew something was up—not only from her own intuition, but from what members of her entourage were reporting back to her. At five a.m., she placed a call to the InterContinental Hotel and demanded of Richard, "Get that woman out of my bed!"

Over the phone, Elizabeth wrested a confession from Richard that he had, for the first time in their eight-year relationship, broken their marriage vows. Richard had always promised himself that the only way to sanctify this marriage born of scandal, betrayal, and adultery, was to be utterly faithful to Elizabeth. And for eight years, he had been. Until now.

Elizabeth returned to London, where filming would soon begin on *Night Watch*, a thriller in which she played a wealthy woman dressed in Valentino and dripping with jewels, being driven mad by her husband, played by Laurence Harvey, her old friend and costar from *BUtterfield 8*. It would be a difficult time for her, not only because of Burton's infidelity and alcoholism, but because Laurence Harvey was visibly ill.

Richard entreated Elizabeth to let him come home. She finally relented, and Burton returned to the Dorchester, where he continued to battle his alcoholism, hoping, as one of his letters suggests, to bring her into a pact to curtail her drinking and overuse of prescription pills, as well. On Hotel Duma stationery, he wrote to Elizabeth,

Dearest Child,

How nice to be home again, and thank you for having me back, but like George Washington, I cannot tell a lie and I was shaking so much I had a beer. It's ghastly stuff, tasting somewhat like piss, but it has actually helped. I advise you to try the same if you feel really diabolical, as I did. And for God's sake, you're not forced to that pact we made last night. Since the demon has yet to turn you into a devil, have a drink but please, please, don't get stoned. I know you will not anyway. Between 3 and 5, when the day seems to refuse to move forward at all, the watched-kettle day that never boils. That's a Dylanesque line if ever I heard one. George Washington Burton never tells a lie and I confess to a second beer, but please comfort yourself. I am not "off again." I was actually unable to shave until I had the beers. Deepest love, Richard.

Husbs.

Anent the shaving: the first time I tried I nearly took off one of my eyebrows.

Elizabeth managed to nurse her wounds with the help of a large sapphire ring given to her by Richard ("This is for Nathalie," she reportedly said when showing it off to a friend). Richard also persuaded Elizabeth to join him for a weekend trip to Vienna, in an attempt to erase the lingering damage of his night with Delon. There they checked into the resplendent Hotel Imperial on the Ring, near the Vienna Opera House. When they learned that the Imperial had been one of Hitler's favorite hotels, Richarad asked for the suite where *der Führer* had stayed. Just as Elizabeth had been tickled that a "Jewish girl" ended up owning the Krupp diamond, Richard kicked off his shoes and leaped into bed, shouting, "It's a triumph of life over death!" With the stern statue of Prince Karl looking in on them from the nearby square, they made, in Richard's phrase, their "lovely love."

When they returned to London, Burton announced his intention to take up the offer to teach literature courses at Oxford, commuting from London while Elizabeth worked on *Night Watch*. For Richard, it was the path he might have taken had not the theater and movies claimed him. It gave him special pleasure to be teaching at Oxford without an advanced degree.

They borrowed a house in Oxfordshire, and Burton taught for a term at St. Peter's College, where he was, not surprisingly, a popular professor. Earlier, in 1968, when Francis Warner had first approached him with the offer, he had written in his diary, "I'm as thrilled by the English language as I am by a lovely woman . . ." He promised himself that he would lecture his students "until iambic pentameter came out of their nostrils. Little do they know how privileged they are to speak and read and think in the greatest language invented by man. I'll learn them." Being in Oxford also gave Richard a chance to try to live without their entourage—Elizabeth's more extensive than Richard's. But

Bob Wilson, Gaston Sanz, and Ron Berkeley had become more like family. Gianni and Claudye Bozzacchi were certainly family, and Dick Hanley had been a father figure for Elizabeth. And Richard needed Jim Benton, who helped with the mountains of correspondence. Their agent, Hugh French, their attorney, Aaron Frosch, their brilliant public relations man, John Springer, were all necessary to have nearby, as long as Elizabeth and Richard were still making movies. So it was harder to give up the entourage than he'd anticipated. Elizabeth, after all, was used to adoring attention her entire life, and she thrived on the bustling activity of a large household. And Burton found that he loved and needed the presence of protective brothers, even more so now that Ifor was gone. Wilson and Sanz filled that role.

In November 1972, the Burtons agreed to appear in another drama that would again resonate with their private lives: *Divorce His Divorce Hers*, a movie in two parts about the dissolution of a marriage. It would premiere on Harlech TV, produced by John Heyman and directed by a thirty-four-year-old Anglo-Indian director, Waris Hussein. Despite his relative youth, Hussein was among the top tier of British television directors at the time (he'd begun his career directing episodes of the popular science-fiction series *Dr. Who*). Being chosen to direct the Burtons was a coup, and he was thrilled to have the opportunity.

Four years earlier, Burton had agreed to be placed on the board of directors of Lord Harlech's nascent television station, the first to be set up in South Wales. Burton's involvement virtually assured the success of the venture. When Harlech Television (HTV) debuted, their first program was an unveiling of the Krupp diamond. Burton contributed funds and agreed to appear in a drama for the fledgling enterprise, but had put it off until now. John Heyman had set up the production as a way of satisfying Burton's obligation, while giving Elizabeth a costarring role. The film was funded mostly by Heyman himself and by the American Broadcasting Company in New York (ABC-TV), which put up more than $1 million. If Elizabeth's and

Richard's films were no longer moneymakers, American television audiences had been eager to see the couple in 1970, as their stint on *Here's Lucy* had proved. Perhaps that would still hold true.

In a *Rashômon*-like fashion, *Divorce His Divorce Hers* chronicles a divorce from alternately the husband's and then the wife's point of view. Set in Rome, it would be filmed in Rome and Munich. (Richard had tried, unsuccessfully, to have the story set in Mexico or the south of France, where he'd have access to Casa Kimberly or the *Kalizma*.) *Divorce His Divorce Hers* is often described as another case of art imitating life, but in actuality, it was more like art *predicting* life, because at the time both Burtons were trying very hard to shore up their marriage.

Burton was clinging to sobriety like a drowning man, and Elizabeth decided that the best way to breathe new life into their relationship was to adopt another child. She made inquiries at various Jewish adoption agencies, to no avail. She even asked Madame Broz, Marshal Tito's formidable wife, to help find her an orphan in Yugoslavia to adopt, but Broz failed to find Elizabeth and Richard a suitable child. There was even talk of traveling to Vietnam to bring home one of the many war orphans born of American servicemen and Vietnamese women, offspring who were often shunned by their communities. That did not work out either.

The first draft of the screenplay for *Divorce His Divorce Hers* was written by John Osborne, whose early play, *Look Back in Anger*, had helped make Burton a star when he'd appeared in the film adaptation, but when the Burtons declared that they hated the script, he was fired. The producers started over with another writer, the playwright-turned-television-dramatist John Hopkins. Hopkins was well known and well regarded in Britain for his literary approach to scriptwriting. He had done some celebrated work for British television, including *Talking to a Stranger*, another *Rashômon*-inspired drama, about an incident seen from the points of view of four different family members, and it starred a young Judi Dench.

The Burtons were not all that enthusiastic about the production, but it was time for Richard to keep his promise to Lord Harlech. The TV station had been after Richard and Elizabeth to participate in a piece written especially for them, which could be shown in Britain on commercial television and then sold everywhere else. *Divorce His Divorce Hers* seemed just the project.

Waris Hussein recalled that the drama was going to be done with four cameras, like traditional television, and they'd planned to film in Bristol—Harlech Television's headquarters—near the romantic, medieval town of Bath, where the Burtons would be housed. HTV made arrangements with all the five-star hotels in Bath to empty out their best rooms to accommodate the Burtons and their entourage. Everything was set.

But first of all, the Burtons wanted to meet their director, so Hussein was summoned to Squires Mount in Hampstead to meet Richard while Elizabeth was in London filming *Night Watch*. It was proving a difficult shoot for Elizabeth, as she had to watch Laurence Harvey slowly succumb to the cancer that would finally kill him. "She had this extraordinary fate in her life," Hussein remembered thinking at the time, "to always be working with dying actors or people who get injured on film. There's a whole side to Elizabeth that is very fatalistic."

When the director appeared at the Burtons' front door in Hampstead, Richard was there to meet him. Hussein was struck by how "charming and sober" he was, and that he "made a great show of drinking Perrier." The two men "got on like a house on fire," Hussein recalled, "he being Welsh and me being Indian, both colonized by England." That Hussein was a Cambridge man, and had directed *The Six Wives of Henry VIII* for BBC-TV, also impressed Burton.

"What can I call you?" Richard had asked. It made it easier for Richard, naturally shy around strangers, if he could use a nickname. "Can I call you 'Waristo'?"

"If you want to."

"But don't ever call me 'Dick.' "

Hussein agreed, and after that, he felt that Richard seemed to approve of him.

His next task, however, would not be as easy. He was to see Elizabeth.

John Heyman drove the director to the London studio where Elizabeth was still completing *Night Watch*, and he was quickly ushered into her dressing room, "a huge area with lots of lavender around," he recalled. But Elizabeth wasn't there and Hussein was kept waiting. "It was like being in a movie, because I'm sitting there terrified. All my faculties were on hold."

Suddenly he heard "that voice," as he later characterized it, and it was not a cheerful one.

"I don't even know what's it about!" the voice complained. "I haven't read it. What's he like?" the voice asked.

The voice was getting closer, and the door opened, and Elizabeth appeared with a big smile on her face. She was wearing a caftan, Hussein recalled, and "looking very Elizabeth Taylor-y."

"Look," she told the director, "I've only got a few minutes. Can you tell me what I'm doing and why I'm doing it?" Hussein began reciting the convoluted plot of *Divorce His Divorce Hers*, but he saw Elizabeth's eyes beginning to glaze over. ("It's a very complex piece," Hussein recalled, "and if you're going to try to explain it in five minutes, it begins to sound like a potential car crash.")

"Stop, stop, stop," Elizabeth interrupted. "Where do I start in this? How old am I?"

"In the script, you're in your early and late twenties, and you go into your forties and fifties."

"Oh, right . . . Okay. Alexandre!"

Suddenly, out of nowhere, the famous Parisian hairdresser appeared.

"Alexandre, did you hear what the guy said? I'm supposed to be twenty. Now look, can you make me look like I did in *A Place in the Sun*?"

Elizabeth went through her list of movies while Alexandre de Paris furiously took notes.

"I have to go now," she told Hussein, "but Alexandre can show you the kind of hairdos he's been designing in your absence." And then she swept out of the room.

When Alexandre showed the director his sketches, they didn't seem to have anything to do with the movie Hussein was about to direct. "They're sort of elaborations of something you might wear to a ball," he remembered. "I don't think she understood a word of what I had said, apart from the fact that it took place over a number of years." Hussein would have similar problems with the costumes designed by Elizabeth's dear friend, Edith Head.

When the immaculate costume designer, in her trademark crisp suits and dark-blue glasses, was hired for the shoot, she warned Hussein, "I'll do the dresses you want, but you do know she has a veto on everything." A week after Head's designs were delivered to Elizabeth at the Dorchester, she took a red pencil and marked through everything she didn't like, which was everything that had a high neck, covering up the breasts that Richard so adored. She told her director that she would wear the dresses she wanted to wear, and the jewels, starting with La Peregrina pearl.

When Hussein explained that her character wouldn't be able to afford something like La Peregrina, Elizabeth answered simply, "Well, I'm going to wear it." She told the director that she knew how the public wanted to see her, and that included the jewels. Hussein jokingly told her that every time she bent down to kiss her children in the movie, she was going to knock them out. She gave a short laugh, but the jewel would be worn.

When Hussein told Elizabeth that they would be shooting the two-part drama in Bristol, "because that's where Harlech TV is,"

Elizabeth asked, "What do you mean, TV?" Hussein felt that by now the whole idea of fulfilling an obligation to Harlech was an imposition. She was doing it as a favor to Richard, but at the moment—after Nathalie Delon—she didn't feel like doing Richard any favors.

"And when are we doing this?" Elizabeth wanted to know. "Has anybody checked out how long I can stay in this country, for taxes? I can't be here if it's going to be getting into my tax area. I'm going to have to talk to somebody." If she exceeded the limited amount of time they could spend in England each year, then she and Richard would owe the British government over £2 million in back taxes.

A short time later, Hussein got a phone call from John Heyman. "We're not going to be shooting in England. Elizabeth is not happy about the tax situation."

There were problems as well with the location shoot planned for Rome, where the estranged lovers meet in Hopkins's drama. The only way that Heyman and his partners were able to get total financing was to make a deal with a German company, which meant filming exteriors in Rome but the rest of the movie would be shot in studios in Munich.

So, in November of 1972, Richard arrived in Rome, alone, as Elizabeth was still finishing *Night Watch*. They shot for a week. Richard hadn't touched a drink the entire time. He was, in Hussein's words, "absolutely civil, very cooperative. He just wanted to know what he could do. I just thought he was wonderful, this man."

By the end of the week, they were filming at night along Via Condotti, which had many memories for the Burtons. Richard was supposed to walk down the street, now brilliantly lit for the night shoot, having just encountered his wife in the movie, and he was lost in thought about what had just happened. It wasn't a difficult scene— just a walk down Via Condotti as the cameras whirred. Elizabeth wasn't due for another couple of days.

Suddenly, there was a commotion in the distance: a great deal of shouting and blaring horns as a crowd appeared, lights flashing. It was Elizabeth. She had arrived two days early. As usual, the paparazzi came out of nowhere, disrupting the shoot.

"Now everybody is, like, 'get a chair,' 'take her coat,' 'would you like a drink?' " Hussein recalled, "so that by the time we've settled down and got her comfortable, she says, 'I'm so sorry to intrude. I just wanted to see how it was going.' "

Hussein and his crew looked around. Where was Richard? He'd disappeared. Hussein sent the assistant director out to look for his actor, now missing in action.

"Is there a problem?" Elizabeth asked.

"We hope not."

"Okay, there's no problem. It's fine." She sat in a chair provided for her, swaddled in her big fur coat, while they searched for Richard. Suddenly, they saw him. "He's coming down the street," Hussein remembered, "walking like a drunken man."

Hussein managed to get his shot and everyone went home, Richard and Elizabeth leaving together. "That was the beginning," Hussein believed. "He just hit the bottle. I'm not going to say why, all I can say is that's what happened. I can't tell you the tragedy of his life, but talk about the Faustian pact!"

Over the course of filming, the Burtons' entourage seemed to break apart into two camps: Richard's and Elizabeth's. "They both had their hangers-on," observed Hussein. "She had her hairdresser and her photographer. He had his hairdresser and his makeup guy, who, by the way, wanted to direct movies, and who used to report back to Richard."

One day, Richard complained to Hussein, "I hear I'm looking onscreen like a fucking volcano, that the marks on my face are like volcanic craters."

"What?"

"In close-up."

"Richard, I don't think so." Hussein was convinced that the Burtons' makeup man, Ron Berkeley, was telling him that.

But far worse, Hussein felt that Elizabeth had made up her mind to sideline him right from the beginning. In retrospect, he realized he didn't quite know how to treat Elizabeth. At one point during the shoot, he asked her, "Could you just give me some indication of a memory that you might have had?" And then he jokingly suggested, "Maybe you could stop and blow your nose or something."

"I've never blown my nose on screen in my life and I'm not going to do it now!" she answered.

"I didn't mean it, Elizabeth! Can you just give me some other thing?"

So, on "Action," Hussein recalled, Elizabeth walked toward the camera, flipped her scarf over her shoulder, kissed the camera lens, said "Bye-bye," and left. "That was my first-day shoot with her, so I knew where I stood."

In retrospect, Hussein admitted he was probably too polite, too deferential, for Elizabeth's tastes. He could tell that she liked "a raunchier, bigger personality" to contend with—a director like George Stevens or Joe Mankiewicz or John Huston—but this "Indian guy with an English accent," as he described himself, was far too reticent for Elizabeth Taylor. "Or if I'd come on in full makeup and drag, it might've opened her up," Hussein suggested, "but as it was, I was too buttoned-up."

Waris Hussein couldn't help but notice how, during the one formal lunch he'd had with the Burtons, the words flashing between them now seemed to be dropped in boiling oil. He'd been summoned to lunch in a long, white dining area with white-gloved waiters serving a four-course meal with a selection of wines. He'd already discovered what other directors had had to deal with: most of the Burtons' movie-set lunches could last from noon till three in the afternoon, and if a lot of drinking took place, no work could be done afterward. "Everybody would be waiting to get on with the shoot, and we couldn't do it," the director recalled.

"If you were summoned to one of their lunches, it was like royalty. One day the phone rang on the set and it was, 'Waris, the Burtons would like you to have lunch with them.' So I dropped everything and went to this area where there was a guard. I had to show my ID, then go upstairs. They're having this lunch at a very long table full of people, Elizabeth with her hair in a towel, looking ravishing."

Hussein, who genuinely admired Richard, sat beside him and told the nearly forty-seven-year-old actor how he had seen his *Hamlet* at the Old Vic. Richard suddenly put down his wineglass and asked, "You saw me?"

"Yes, I did. And I walked around in a daze for a week because I thought you were so wonderful. I just hero-worshipped you."

"That is the nicest thing anyone has ever said to me." Richard then started to tell a few familiar stories about acting at the Old Vic, about how he once drank so much before a performance that he had to relieve himself onstage, in his armor. But then he met Elizabeth's eye and he stopped.

"We shouldn't be talking about this," he said. "After all, we're making a movie, and I'm indebted to that lady over there for what I am doing in the movies. This is my life. She's taught me everything I know." All eyes went to Elizabeth.

"Oh, Richard, please, let's not get too emotional about this," she said sarcastically. "We know what a wonderful actor you were on stage."

"No, no," said Richard. "We're talking about making films."

"Yes, I know, but Waris just told you how wonderful you were as Hamlet. We don't want to hear how I've taught you what to do on film."

From there, recalled Hussein, "It's George and Martha by now. Richard brought up the fact that they had adopted a child who'd been sick, the sickest child in the place. And how Elizabeth chose that child, nursed that child back to normality and health. And there were tears in his eyes. 'She was the most wonderful person one could find,' Richard said, 'our daughter Maria.' But it was clear he was talking about them both, about Elizabeth *and* her daughter," trying to stitch this whole thing together that was in danger of coming apart.

After the Nathalie Delon incident, Elizabeth seemed even more possessive of her husband. "I remember thinking," Hussein said, "she just didn't let him relax." Richard was "all man, I mean he was a hunk in every way. Handsome, charismatic. Every woman in the world wanted him. And she's got him. It had to have been difficult for her. I don't see her as unsympathetic." In one particular scene meant to take place in an Italian hotel, Richard's character goes to the telephone, and right behind him is a group of women speaking English. Just before the scene could be shot, though, Hussein's assistant told him that the women in the scene would have to go. According to Hussein, one of the girls had been invited up to Richard's dressing room, where Elizabeth was hiding behind the sofa. She reportedly jumped up, brandished a broken vodka bottle, and chased the terrified girl out of the room. "There are going to be no more women on the set," the director was told in no uncertain terms.

For Hussein, who hero-worshipped Richard Burton, Richard's drunkenness was nothing short of heartbreaking. Watching the dissolution of someone who was so charismatic, still in control of his gifts, had a deep effect on the director. Among other causes, Richard's drinking had become an endless wake for Ifor. Richard once came on the set of *Divorce His Divorce Hers* incapable of sitting upright in a chair, swaying so much the camera operator could not follow him. On another occasion, during a long dialogue—the kind of scene Richard could do in his sleep—Elizabeth sat patiently waiting for her shot. All of a sudden, Richard let out with "the loudest, screaming, guttural-sounding voice. The whole set shook. The entire crew froze." Richard had to be practically carried home, and he was heard shouting, "I could have been King Lear. I could've played Lear!" A terrified Hussein escaped to his office and stayed there the rest of the day.

As Hussein later observed, the shoot was already fragmenting. But despite the deep troubles on the set, Hussein had compassion for both Elizabeth and Richard. He was aware of the physical pain she had experienced in her life, how often she was surrounded by death, and how her level of fame isolated her. Yet, despite their bickering and Richard's drinking, the sexual energy between them was still evident.

Richard seemed possessed of superhuman stamina. Their love life appeared to flourish in a pool of alcohol. A flash of Elizabeth's leg peeking out of the blanket in "that blue nightie he loved" while she read a book in bed would mean the door would be slammed shut and the two of them would make "lovely love," as he called it. It made them feel like the forbidden lovers they had once been, when they'd lived that "wonderfully nourishing sense of defiance which had given them such outlaw energy in the 1960s."

But they were no longer outlaws, no longer, as one writer described it, "pirates on the main taking booty from the great galleons of studios and governments." Had Richard at last become tired of picking up after the dogs in his $1,000 suits, of being jealously watched, of being called "Mr. Elizabeth Taylor," as Gianni Bozzacchi had once observed? Had Elizabeth finally had enough of Richard's Welsh hours, his alcoholic binges, and the meanness they sometimes unleashed?

And yet, they were still in erotic thrall to each other, as revealed by a handwritten letter from Burton to Taylor, thanking her for the Christmas gift of a fountain pen at the end of that year.

December 27

Continued with the same gifted pen. It's no use pretending that you are an ordinary woman. Quite clearly, like this pen, you are not. I don't mean, for a second, that you are in any way comparable with a pen. And yet you are, like this divine pen you are heavy and light at the same time . . . there is nothing like you. You are heavy like the pen—your ass, your tits, the smooth (sublimity) of your back, bewitch. But they are heavy. Pendulumed [sic] like an infinitely desirable clock. . . . How [to] watch the puritanical face relax into slow lust? How to watch that watch catch its breath and, for a speck of a speck of a millionth of a second, become the animal that all men seek for in their women? And since we're talking of pens and you, how [to] watch the ink splurge out of the pen . . . reach[ing] out from the inner depth of the divine body. Will you, incidentally, permit me to fuck you this after-noon? Yours truly (you have just come into the room), R.B.

Divorce His Divorce Hers was barely finished when John Heyman sold it to ABC Television without a single shot being seen. Even though reduced to the small screen, the Burtons still had it, and people still wanted to see them together, or so the executives at ABC-TV thought. But when Barry Diller, then at ABC, finally viewed the finished prod-uct, according to Waris Hussein, "he hated it."

Meanwhile, Heyman also picked up the Burtons' hotel bill. The damages at the Four Seasons, recalled Heyman, were "astronomical . . . the damage to the carpets, the furniture, mirrors, the clean-up from the animal excrement. It was like a dog's house." The Four Seasons staff celebrated after the Burtons left, toasting the couple's departure at a small party in the basement. "They were so happy when they left. It had been such a strain catering to their every whim," Heyman said.

When *Divorce His Divorce Hers* was finally aired in America on February 6 and 7, 1973, "the critics were waiting with their knives out." The reviews, said Hussein, "were the worst you have ever read in your life." *Time* magazine called the two-part drama "a matched pair of thudding disasters"; the *Hollywood Reporter* described it as "a boring, tedious study of the crumbling marriage of two shallow people"; and *Variety*, usually kind to the Burtons, wrote that viewing the drama "holds all the joy of standing by at an autopsy."

It's hard to assess the drama today, because the available prints suffer from low sound quality, as if *Divorce His Divorce Hers* were a foreign film poorly dubbed. It seems as if the writer, Hopkins, like so many before him, had set out to incorporate facts of the Burtons' lives into his screenplay. Taylor's character, Jane Reynolds, complains of their gypsy life, and how Burton (Martin Reynolds) travels so much "he's never more than ten minutes in the same place." And he complains, "One of my daughters doesn't want to see me." At one point, he says, "Of course, I travel with an enormous entourage." This parallel universe had once been a recipe for box office success; now it was coming dangerously close to parody.

Oddly, given Hussein's admiration of Burton and his difficulties with Taylor, their performances are the opposite of what one would expect. Burton, his voice thickened by drink, walks through the film like a zombie, his back now so stiffened from his old afflictions that he again seems like an automaton. But Elizabeth is the emotional center of the film, making sense out of her melodramatic lines, evoking sympathy for the beautiful, though ordinary, woman she portrays. Through the horrible ordeals of that year, she managed to not only be professional, but genuinely moving as well. And she is still beautiful—as is La Peregrina, resting on her sloping décolletage.

As for Waris Hussein, who had fled to Los Angeles to hide out with friends, his career "just went down the tubes. I couldn't get a job if I'd gone and stood on Sunset Boulevard with my hat out. *Divorce His Divorce Hers* was like a bomb going off, and I was the one who got killed; no one else did." In actuality, Hussein recovered and would go on to a successful career directing movies for television, including the mini-series *Edward and Mrs. Simpson* in 1978; *Little Gloria . . . Happy at Last* in 1982; *Princess Daisy* in 1983; *Onassis, the Richest Man in the World* in 1988, and, in 1998, *Life of the Party: The Pamela Harriman Story*. But working with the Burtons had been an ordeal.

"Years later," he remembered, "I met with Roddy McDowall. He said, 'You mustn't hold this against them.' I said, 'But she never liked me.' And Roddy said, 'No, no, you're wrong. If you were to see her again, it would all be different. You were just caught in the middle of two people who were falling apart.'"

Divorce His Divorce Hers had been the Burtons' eleventh film made as a couple. It was also their last. "If there is one thing for a movie actor worse than failing at the box office, it is failing on television," wrote Brenda Maddox. Failure on TV doomed the Burtons as a couple on the big screen. They would continue to get offers to star alone in mostly European productions—especially Richard—but "The Liz and Dick Show" would now take a backseat to Elizabeth and Richard's struggling marriage.

In January 1973, before the release of *Divorce His Divorce Hers*, the Burtons were in the Eternal City, with Richard signed to play a German SS officer in *Massacre in Rome*, a film produced by Carlo Ponti. Richard was superstitious about Rome, feeling that bad things often happened there—yet it's where he had fallen in love with Elizabeth, and the couple had reclaimed their affection for the city while making *The Taming of the Shrew.*

Playing a Nazi officer, Burton was challenged to humanize his character, Lieutenant Colonel Herbert Kappler, as Marlon Brando had done with his 1958 role of a German officer in *The Young Lions.* His portrayal would later garner good reviews—increasingly rare—but not for two more years, as the film's release was delayed until 1975.

In May, Elizabeth took on the role of Barbara Sawyer in *Ash Wednesday*, a wealthy, fiftyish woman who undergoes plastic surgery to keep her husband, played by Henry Fonda, from divorcing her. An actual face-lift performed on an Elizabeth Taylor look-alike is shown in the film. Having turned forty-one that year, Elizabeth was still too beautiful to play a woman in need of a face-lift, but to make her dilemma believable, heavy makeup was applied to her face to age her, in a process that took two hours to apply and, later, two hours to remove. The makeup was so masklike that she felt compelled to take out a $1 million insurance policy against damage to her famous face.

Produced by Dominick Dunne, *Ash Wednesday* was filmed in Cortina d'Ampezzo, a ski resort in the Italian Alps, and the Burtons were given a spacious ten rooms in the Miramonti Hotel. Dunne recalled later that he had been "spellbound by the couple, even when I was being driven crazy by them." Elizabeth and Richard continued to draw huge, cheering crowds whenever they appeared in public. Dunne, staying on a different floor of the Miramonti, saw Elizabeth every day during the shoot and felt that she was "at the peak of her great beauty." When he met her for the first time on New Year's Eve, he did what he'd promised himself he would not do: he gasped. "Her beauty was even more breathtaking in person than on the screen," he would later write.

But since Burton was not working, he was, as usual, miserable, and he hung around the hotel, reading and drinking. In Dunne's words, he "seethed on the sidelines." At their first meeting at the Burtons' New Year's Eve party, Dunne noticed Burton, dressed in a green velvet dinner jacket, on his hands and knees, picking up with a Kleenex dog droppings left by one of the un-housebroken shih tzus that scampered freely throughout the ten-room suite. He also couldn't help but notice that the Burtons were still surrounded by an enormous entourage, chief among them Elizabeth's Swiss-born secretary Raymond Vignale, who appeared on New Year's Eve in a white mink coat with jeweled buttons and Cartier watch. It was like having Oscar Wilde as a personal secretary. Vignale, who could be charming and campy in five languages, made the trains run on time as the Burtons traveled from hotel to hotel, managing their thirty trunks, Elizabeth's jewels, and even, when necessary, hiding her pills.

Elizabeth's intake of alcohol and prescription pain medication was by now alarming, but she seldom showed any signs of inebriation. The movie's director, Larry Peerce (son of the great Metropolitan Opera star Jan Peerce), noticed that she "drank champagne by the magnum," but, unlike Richard, she never lost her appetite for food. She wasn't looking to kill herself on the installment plan, and the food absorbed the excess alcohol in her system. Though her weight would vary from week to week, she was able to drink without becoming drunk.

Burton again turned his hand to writing magazine pieces and took to referring to himself as a writer, not an actor. He not only resented Elizabeth working while he was idle, he loathed the kind of movie she was making, which was the kind of movie they had both appeared in together: the dilemmas of the rich (*The V.I.P.s*, *Boom!*, *Divorce His Divorce Hers*).

Richard had rediscovered his working-class roots to the extent that he railed against *Ash Wednesday*, telling Elizabeth, "I don't like the thought of you doing that kind of thing, because it represents the worst kind of people." He told Brook Williams, "I really don't like the jet set, you know. They offend me"—ironic, coming from a man who, with Elizabeth, had embodied what it meant to be a member of the jet set in the second half of the twentieth century. What had all those fabulous shopping sprees been about—competing with Onassis for the largest jewels, buying a jet and a yacht and furs and houses? He had done it because he could, because it was a lark for a working-class boy, because it kept Elizabeth happy in the way she was used to being happy. It was part of the adventure of being Liz and Dick, perhaps their greatest roles. But now his old Welsh sentiments surfaced, and he was sheepish about the way he had lived his life for the past ten years.

Gianni Bozzacchi had seen this in Burton. "Richard Jenkins, Richard Burton—they were two people. 'If I had remained Richard Jenkins, I would have done everything different'—that's what Richard would say. I could see that sometimes Richard just needed to be himself, not the person he had become," but the person he was born to be.

When Zeffirelli met with the couple in Rome that year, their former director was surprised at how Richard seemed to chafe at Elizabeth's jealousy. Burton's romp with Nathalie Delon had apparently increased her possessiveness. Now, when she playfully punched him in the arm, it was a punch he could feel, and when Burton was too engrossed in talking with an attractive woman, Elizabeth would yell "Richard!" in a loud voice from across the room. Zeffirelli had worked with the

Burtons at the height of their film success, and at the height of their love for each other—their true honeymoon—and six years later, the dissolution of their relationship was painful to witness.

Dunne believed that Elizabeth was still crazy about Richard, but "they fell out of love" during the making of *Ash Wednesday*. It began with an excruciating, jealous row when Richard accused Elizabeth of having an affair with one of her costars, the handsome Helmut Berger, who played her young lover in the film. Dunne and Peerce were often called in to witness their fights. Elizabeth was in despair, and on at least one occasion Vignale cradled her, weeping, in his arms, trying to console her. When she showed up two hours late for a scene with Henry Fonda, the director tried to reason with her. When she failed to show up at all on another occasion, and then lost a week to the German measles, he feared that *Ash Wednesday* was becoming "a mini-*Cleopatra*," but instead of Richard and Elizabeth coming together, they were breaking apart.

Elizabeth flew to New York when filming was over. This time, Richard did not go with her. He made his way to Los Angeles and checked into the Beverly Hills Hotel, where he wrote Elizabeth a drunken, heartfelt letter on June 25, 1973, marked "Very Private and Personal":

So My Lumps,

You're off, by God! I can barely believe it since I am so unaccustomed to anybody leaving me. But reflectively I wonder why nobody did so before. All I care about—honest to God—is that you are happy and I don't much care who you'll find happiness with. I mean as long as he's a friendly bloke and treats you nice and kind. If he doesn't I'll come at him with a hammer and clinker. God's eye may be on the sparrow but my eye will always be on you.

Never forget your strange virtues. Never forget that underneath that veneer of raucous language is a remarkable and puritanical

LADY. I am a smashing bore and why you've stuck by me so long is an indication of your loyalty. I shall miss you with passion and wild regret.

You know, of course, my angelic one, that everything I (we) have is yours, so you should be fairly comfortable. Don't, however, let your next inamorata [sic] use it, otherwise I might become a trifle testy. I do not like the human race. I do not like his ugly face. And if he takes my former wife and turns her into stress and strife, I'll smash him bash him, laugh or crash him slash him trash him etc. Christ, I am possessed by language. Mostly bad. (Sloshed, d'yer think?) So now, have a good time.

. . .

You may rest assured that I will not have affairs with any other female. Anybody after you is going to be disinteresting [sic]. I shall gloom a lot and stare morosely into unimaginable distances and act a bit—probably on the stage—to keep me in booze and butter, but chiefly and above all I shall *write*. Not about you, I hasten to add. No Millerinski Me, with a double M. There are many other and ludicrous and human comedies to constitute my shroud.

I'll leave it to you to announce the parting of the ways while I shall never say or write one word except this valedictory note to you. Try and look after yourself. Much love.

Don't forget that you are probably the greatest actress in the world. "At this point in time," as they never boringly stop saying on the "Watergate" things, you are the best there can be. I wish I could borrow a minute portion of your passion and commitment, but there you are—cold is cold as ice is ice . . .

. . .

A few days later, Richard holed up in Aaron Frosch's guest cottage in Quogue, Long Island, about seventy-five miles from New York City. Richard felt safe there. Before he worked for the Burtons as a couple, Frosch had been Richard's lawyer, when he was still married to Sybil in the era before Elizabeth. It had been Frosch who'd had the sad duty of depositing a million dollars into Sybil Burton's Swiss bank account, and arranging for her to receive $500,000 annually for ten years, when Richard finally made the decision to divorce her and marry Elizabeth. "They were like brothers," Elizabeth felt. "He was our lawyer forever and took such great care of Richard and me." Now his Long Island house was where Richard was hiding out while he came to terms with their separation.

Still drinking, Richard telephoned Elizabeth and ordered her to meet him there, in one last attempt to patch things up and go on as before. He met her plane at Kennedy Airport, but as soon as she got into the limousine next to her husband, she could tell he was smashed. At one point on the long drive to Frosch's house, he turned to her and said, "Why did you ever bother to come back?" By the time they reached Quogue, they had quarreled so furiously about his drinking that she ordered the limo to take her back to New York. She checked into the Regency Hotel on Park Avenue, where they had once been so happy during their triumphant *Hamlet* year.

Back in New York, she took Richard's suggestion to "announce the parting of the ways," writing a personal statement about separating from Richard that would be issued to the press. That was her training, after all. She belonged as much to the public as she did to herself and to Richard, and she owed them an explanation. She had always understood publicity. On July 4, 1973, Elizabeth issued the following, handwritten statement:

I am convinced it would be a good and constructive idea if Richard and I separated for a while. Maybe we loved each other too much. I never believed such a thing was possible. But we have been in each other's pockets constantly, never being apart but for matters of life and death, and I believe it has caused a temporary breakdown of communication. I believe with all my heart that the separation will ultimately bring us back to where we should be—and that's together. I think in a few days' time I shall return to California, because my mother is there, and I have old and true friends there too. Friends are there to help each other, aren't they? Isn't that what it's all supposed to be about? If anybody reads anything lascivious in that last statement, all I can say is it must be in the eye of the reader, not in mine or my friends' or my husband's. Wish us well during this difficult time. Pray for us.

With Elizabeth gone, for the first time Richard enlisted the help of a doctor to try to detoxify from alcohol. Insisting that he wasn't an alcoholic but merely a "drunk," like his father, who imbibed by choice, he must have known that this was his last chance to save his marriage, and, possibly, his life.

15

MASSACRE IN ROME

" . . . [I]f you leave me, I shall have to kill myself. There
is no life without you, I'm afraid. And I am afraid."
—RICHARD BURTON

"I don't want to be that much in love ever again."
—ELIZABETH TAYLOR

Though he had provoked it, and perhaps had sought it, Richard was
blindsided by Elizabeth's public announcement of their separation.
Three months earlier, in Rome, he had written a revealing letter to
Elizabeth while she slept in the next room. In it, he'd addressed his
own bad behavior (his "usage" and "jealousy"), his cynicism about
the very concept of love, and how Elizabeth had somehow vanquished
that cynicism.

The last day of March
My darling Sleeping Child,

. . .

. . . I am oddly shy about you. I still regard you as an . . . invio-
late presence. You are as secret as the mysterious processes of the
womb. I'm not being fancy . . . I have treated women, generally,
very badly and used them as an exercise for my contempt *except*

in your case. I have fought like a fool to treat you in the same way and failed. One of these days I will wake up—which I think I have done already—and realize to myself that I really do love. I find it very difficult to allow my whole life to rest on the existence of another creature. I find it equally difficult, because of my innate arrogance, to believe in the *idea of love.* There is no such thing, I say to myself. There is lust, of course, and usage, and jealousy, and desire and spent powers, but no such thing as the idiocy of *love.* Who invented that concept? I have wracked my shabby brains and can find no answer. But when people die . . . those who are taken away from us can never come back. Never, never, never, never, never (Lear about Cordelia). We are such doomed fools. Unfortunately, we know it.

So I have decided that for a second or two, the precious potential of you in the next room is the only thing in the world worth living for. After your death there shall only be one other and that will be mine. Or I possibly think, vice versa.

Ravaged love,

And loving Rich

There was no hiding from the press in the wake of Elizabeth's July 4 announcement. Reporters made a beeline to Quogue, congregating on Frosch's driveway, to get Burton's response to the separation. Burton hid in a cottage on the property but was found out by London reporter Nigel Dempster of the *Daily Mail.* With a bottle of vodka in front of him (he had yet to start his detoxification regimen), Burton vented his complaints about marriage with Taylor, blaming everything but his own drinking—their volatile temperaments, her demands upon him. "Perhaps my indifference to Elizabeth's personal problems triggered off this situation," he mused. "I have only twenty-four hours a day. I read and write and film. Elizabeth is constantly seeking problems of one kind or another. She worries about her figure, about her family, about the color of her teeth," he complained defensively.

"She expects that I drop everything to devote myself to these problems." He even tried to make light of the situation, describing himself as "amused" by it, but when asked if a divorce were imminent, he changed his tune, insisting that Elizabeth had not really left him.

"There is no question of our love and devotion to each other," he said solemnly.

"I don't even consider Elizabeth and [me] as separated . . . I even have Elizabeth's passport in my possession. Does that look as if she has left me?" He had, a few days earlier, written a three-page letter to Elizabeth from Quogue, again declaring his need for her, though recognizing their intractable differences:

> I love you, lovely woman. If anybody hurts you, just send me a
> line saying something like "Need" or "Necessary" or just the one
> magic word "Elizabeth," and I will be there somewhat faster than
> sound. You must know, of course, how much I love you. You must
> know, of course, how badly I treat you. But the fundamental and
> most vicious, swinish, murderous, and unchangeable fact is that
> we totally misunderstand each other . . . we operate on alien wave-
> lengths. You are as distant as Venus—planet, I mean—and I am
> tone-deaf to the music of the spheres. But how-so-be-it nevertheless.
> (A cliché among Welsh politicians.) I love you and I always will. . . .
> Come back to me as soon as you can . . .

Realizing that his drinking was out of control, Richard finally sought treatment with a New York internist. Perhaps if he really sobered up, Elizabeth would return to him. And he needed to get in shape for his next film for Carlo Ponti, *The Voyage*, in which he would costar with Sophia Loren, Ponti's wife and an actress whose iconic beauty and sensuality rivaled Elizabeth's. The great Italian Neorealist Vittorio De Sica would direct what would turn out to be his last film. Burton asked if he could stay in the Pontis' guesthouse at their home in Marino, outside of Rome, afraid he would be overrun by the press were he to check into a hotel. They graciously agreed. So on July 12, 1973, Burton traveled to the Ponti estate, a fifty-room, sixteenth-century villa in the Alban Hills outside of Rome, where he would nurse his wounds. He brought with him a reduced entourage: his new doctor and nurse, a secretary, and two bodyguards.

Elizabeth flew to Los Angeles, in part to be near her widowed mother, Sara, but really to put distance between herself and Richard's endless drinking and their endless quarreling. She managed to hide from the press at the 1600 Coldwater Canyon home of her friend, Edith Head, and her husband, Bill. She loved their Spanish-style home, complete with swimming pool and tennis court, and she found it "a haven, where I could get away from everyone and work out my problems on my own." An added attraction to Edith's safe harbor was the fact that both women loved Jack Daniel's. Whenever Edith returned home from her work, they would have "a nice, big glass of Jack Daniel's together," Elizabeth remembered. They were so close that the famous costume designer had a plaque placed on the stairs going up to the guest room that read, ELIZABETH TAYLOR SLEEPS HERE, which completely delighted Elizabeth. So much of her life had been devoted to recreating a sense of home and family, and Edith Head's was yet another of Elizabeth's surrogate homes, even more important now that her true home, with Richard, had foundered.

And so, Elizabeth reentered Hollywood, where she had spent her youthful years and her too-brief marriage to Mike Todd. She began going around town with Peter Lawford, her long-ago costar in *Julia Misbehaves*, filmed when Elizabeth was just an ingénue but had also had a woman-sized crush on the debonair English actor. (He gave Elizabeth her first screen kiss, but had been reluctant to romantically take on the sixteen-year-old.) By now divorced from Pat Kennedy, the late president's sister, Lawford was on a downward slide, indulging in Quaaludes, cocaine, and vodka. Elizabeth also saw Dominick Dunne in Hollywood, and her longtime friend and confidant, Roddy McDowall. She found herself doing things she would never have done with Richard, such as a wild daytime trip, by helicopter, to Disney-land with Dunne and his daughter, Dominique; Lawford and his son, Christopher; and Roddy McDowall. For the first time in its history, a helicopter, which had picked them up at the top of Mulholland Drive, was allowed to land inside Walt Disney's massive amusement park. Once they were inside Disneyland, crowds began to surround Elizabeth and her coterie, and they retreated to the Pirates of the Ca-ribbean ride, where the grownups passed among themselves a flask filled with Jack Daniel's. It was a desperate kind of fun.

But when Roddy McDowall and eighteen-year-old Christopher Lawford brought Elizabeth to meet Mae West in the Ravenswood Apartments, Elizabeth was uncomfortable. The plump eighty-one-year-old former sex goddess greeted them wearing a silver gown that fitted her like a second skin. Her long, platinum-blond hair framed her frozen face like cotton candy. Two muscle-bound bodyguards stood by her side. After fifteen minutes of strained conversation, Eliz-abeth leaned over to Roddy and whispered, "Can we get the hell out of here?" Elizabeth had been asked to appear in *Myra Breckinridge* a few years earlier—the Gore Vidal satire in which Mae West had made a gloriously bizarre screen appearance (her first in twenty-seven years). Elizabeth had turned it down, but the sight of the tiny, preserved-in-aspic diva made Elizabeth wonder if this was her future. Was she on the edge of camp, and would she be unable to come back from that edge, without Richard? Of the many costs of fame, the preservation of endless copies of herself, each one less authentic—like Warhol's brilliant repeating images of her—threatened to trap her in unreality. Were she and Richard becoming like the stiff effigies in Madame Tussaud's Wax Museum in London, which were placed on opposite sides of the room when the Burtons' separation was an-nounced? She beat a hasty retreat.

Elizabeth also reunited with the novelist Truman Capote, whom she had known since *Cleopatra* days. He had been witness to Eliz-abeth and Richard's "affectionate rows" throughout their nine-year marriage. "They really riled each other up," Capote thought, "and I always felt that they did it on purpose so that they could have a big makeup in bed." But Capote had remained skeptical about Burton's motives from the start. He'd always felt that Burton had only married Taylor to boost his career prospects. "She loved him," he believed, "but he didn't love her." In the wake of their separation, people in Hollywood were beginning to tear down Richard—it was really Elizabeth's town, as Hollywood had never embraced Burton—but Elizabeth knew better than anyone that Capote was flat-out wrong. The proof was not just in their lovemaking, his devotion to their children, their thousands of nights together, the magnificent, storied jewels he gave her, but in letter after letter in which he had poured out his love and his need for her. Ten days after she'd announced their separation, she received a telegram from Richard, in Rome:

BELOVED IDIOT. MISS YOU TERRIBLY . . . I AM NOW ONE UP ON YOU HAVING WON THE DONATELLO AWARD FOR MASSACRO IN ROMA SO I SHALL BE GOING.

Like much of Old Hollywood, Lawford had no real fondness for Richard Burton, and he introduced Elizabeth to another man-about-town, the Dutch businessman, photographer, and used-car dealer Henry Wynberg, a swinging bachelor who was cutting a swath among Hollywood women of all ages. Tall, attractive, and divorced, Wynberg spoke in a charming, Dutch-accented English. He was five years younger than Elizabeth, and he seemed to be living out a Hugh Hefner fantasy, with a plush couch and wall-sized aquarium in his apartment where he did his wooing. He was also half-Jewish, and Burton himself had noted in his diary how much Elizabeth was attracted to Jewish men, like Mike Todd, Eddie Fisher, Max Lerner, even the potbellied, out-of-shape writer Wolf Mankowitz, and Joe Mankiewicz as well. (And himself, perhaps, if Burton's claims to a Jewish heritage were true.) "Elizabeth has always fancied Jews," Burton wrote. "She seems to have a rapport with them, which she doesn't have with the ordinary Anglo-Saxon." For now, Wynberg consoled Elizabeth, taking her dancing, squiring her around town, hanging out in nightclubs—all things in which Richard had long ago lost interest (if indeed he ever enjoyed them). "Going out was *life* for Elizabeth then," said Vignale. But that was all Wynberg was to her at the time—an attractive escort— as Elizabeth made plans to return to Rome, where she would begin work on another film, *The Driver's Seat*, her forty-ninth. And to see Richard.

Richard had written Elizabeth again, from Rome, two letters in particular that showed the depth of his despair without her, suggesting that he might kill himself if she did not return:

> Well, first of all, you must realize that I worship you. Second of all, at the expense of seeming repetitive, I love you. Thirdly, and here I go again with my enormous command of language, I can't live without you. Thirdly, I mean fourthly, you have an enormous responsibility because if you leave me I shall have to kill myself. There is no life without you, I'm afraid. And I am afraid. Afeared. In terms of my life, scared. Lost. Alone. Dull. Dumb. (That will be the day.) And fifthly, and I hope I will never repeat myself, I fancy you. I bet that you would be alright if you loved me and stuff like that. Sixthly, I bet if you could persuade me to stop acting, which is a practice I've always deplored, I could work out a way whereby I could stay alive until I'm fifty-five. That rhymes . . .

Curiously, Elizabeth did not seem to answer any of Richard's letters, though she would treasure them for the rest of her life, keeping them private for four decades. "Richard had so much passion for life through words," she later said, whereas she was more invested in living for the moment. And there was that other problem: she had been trained since childhood to control whatever might turn up in the press, which meant being careful about what she wrote, and to whom. A letter from Elizabeth Taylor could easily go astray. It wasn't until she entered the Betty Ford Clinic for the first time, on December 5, 1983, that she realized the price she'd paid for that careful secrecy: she had suppressed some of her deepest emotions.

Meanwhile, letters of condolence and telegrams from old friends and colleagues poured in from around the world, to both sides. Joe Losey, reading about the separation, wrote to Richard from London, "I will not talk about the present situation with Elizabeth . . . I will only say, tragically sad and mistaken."

Later that month, *The Battle of Sutjeska* would win the "Best Anti-Fascist" movie award at the Moscow International Film Festival, a good omen for the "great men" roles Richard would continue to take on—after Tito, Winston Churchill; after Churchill, Richard Wagner. Yet Burton continued to rail against his profession, writing again to Elizabeth,

> I have never quite got over the fact that I thought and I'm afraid I still do think, that "acting" for a man—a really proper man—is sissified and faintly ridiculous. I will do this film with Ponti and Loren out of sheer cupidity—desire for money. I will unquestionably do many more. But my heart, unlike yours, is not in it. The French have a word for what I am and it's called "manqué," meaning a failure of desire . . . I am everything "manqué." An actor manqué, a philosopher manqué, a writer manqué, and consequently an intolerable bore. (Not manqué, I'm afraid.)

Within two weeks of their separation announcement, Richard was able to cable Joe Losey, "You are too old a hand to believe what you read in the papers. Elizabeth returns here to Rome next Friday . . . it was simply a burst of disillusioned inebriation. Am sober, slim and beautiful."

On July 20, 1973, dressed in a red blazer and white cotton pullover, Richard was chauffeured in his Rolls-Royce to the Fiumicino Airport in Rome to meet Elizabeth's plane. Nearly four hundred members of the press surrounded the airport, held back by two hundred policemen. It was *Le Scandale* all over again, or Cleopatra's entry into Rome, or was it a scene out of *The V.I.P.s?*—the limousine idling on the tarmac—as if "Liz and Dick" were condemned to endlessly live out their lives on film. They watched Richard slouched in the back of the Rolls, waiting for Elizabeth to arrive.

So many of the important things in Elizabeth's life seemed to happen in Rome. She had flown over from Los Angeles in a leased jet, with two dogs, a cat, and nine cases of luggage. As she deplaned, dressed in blue jeans, an oversize orange T-shirt, and the Taylor-Burton diamond, Burton still waited in the back of his car, unmoving. Many in the press assumed it was a game they were playing—neither wanted to make the first move.

Elizabeth disappeared into customs.

Burton sat, patiently waiting, in the Rolls.

She finally left the terminal, and policemen made a passageway for Elizabeth through the throng of reporters and paparazzi, as flashbulbs exploded all around her.

Still, Richard sat, unmoving, until the door opened and Elizabeth was practically propelled into the waiting car by a surge of photographers. That's when they finally had the satisfaction of seeing Richard, through the darkened windows of the Rolls, kiss her face and bury his head in her breasts, taking in the smell of her. The Rolls inched through the crush of reporters and made its way to the Pontis' villa thirteen miles away, chased by paparazzi the entire distance.

The Pontis' villa was—thankfully for the Burtons—guarded like Flora Goforth's island in *Boom!* The Rolls passed through electronic gates and armed guards, complete with snarling German shepherds on leashes, till it finally reached the magnificent villa, where Sophia and Carlo greeted the couple with drinks in hand. There, they dined on a splendid lunch of "risotto, roasted Palumbo fish, fruit, and white wine."

Elizabeth had always been wary of Sophia Loren. When the tall, voluptuous Italian movie queen was proposed to star with Richard years ago in *The V.I.P.s*, Elizabeth had commanded, "Let Sophia stay in Rome!" and had taken the role for herself. Sophia was a taller, darker, Mediterranean version of Elizabeth, admired as an actress, worshipped as a sex goddess, loved for her earthiness and warmth. She was tall and regal where Elizabeth was short and flamboyant. Elizabeth had shown up in a cotton T-shirt and jeans that day (after traveling all night), whereas Sophia had greeted them in "a Dior suit, matching handbag, and shoes." They shared, however, a love of and appreciation for jewels. Earlier, Sophia had responded to Elizabeth and Richard's purchase of the Taylor-Burton diamond by telling *Photoplay*, "The stone had been offered to Carlo," but "he appraised it and decided that it was not worth the price. And I assure you, Carlo knows the value of jewelry." Battling divas often slugged it out in the pages of movie magazines, but Elizabeth had too much dignity to catfight in print.

Despite the seclusion and luxury of the Ponti estate, the Burtons' reconciliation lasted only nine days. First of all, Richard was drinking again (having sent his internist packing), which had finally become intolerable to Elizabeth. And Richard had heard about the attentions of Henry Wynberg, whose name he continually, and contemptuously, mangled, calling him "Mr. Wiseborg," or "Weinstein," or, simply, "the used-car salesman." Now, Elizabeth suspected Richard was having an affair with his sultry costar, especially when she happened to see the draft of an article he was writing about her for *Ladies' Home Journal*. He had never written such lavish praise of another woman before— certainly not for public consumption. He praised Sophia as "[t]all and extraordinary. Large-bosomed. Tremendously long legs . . . Beautiful brown eyes set in a marvelously vulpine, almost satanic face . . ." But when he described her as "beautiful as erotic dreams," that phrase was uncomfortably close to his earlier description of Elizabeth as "beautiful beyond the dreams of pornography." She now felt she had proof that the two were more than just friends.

After what had happened in Budapest, during the shoot of *Bluebeard*, Elizabeth was furious. "I knew he was flirting his head off," she recalled, "and she was flirting right back, both of them speaking in Italian, which made me feel ridiculously left out. I thought, I'm not going to sit here and watch this. Screw them both!"

So the Burtons separated again, and Elizabeth checked into a baroque, seven-room suite in the Grand Hotel in Rome, where she was to begin filming *The Driver's Seat* the following day. Miserable, she arrived very late to the set, where she was overwhelmed by a standing ovation by cast and crew. She told her producer, Franco Rossellini, that she never thought she could ever feel as awful as she did on the day of Mike Todd's death, but she was wrong. "Today is the second sad day in my life. I am desolate," she told him. She and Burton both put in a call to Aaron Frosch, to begin divorce proceedings.

Like her lonely character Barbara Sawyer in *Ash Wednesday*, Elizabeth spent days in bed when she wasn't working on her new film. "I don't want to be that much in love ever again," she told a friend. "I don't want to give as much of myself. It hurts. I didn't reserve anything. I gave everything away . . . my soul, my being, everything." She sought consolation with Andy Warhol, who was in Rome to appear in a cameo in *The Driver's Seat*. She poured out her heart to him during a long lunch, over drinks and tears, while she distractedly pulled all the leaves off of a decorative tree near their table. But lunch with Andy did not end well. She discovered that he had been secretly taping her anguish with his state-of-the-art, micro-cassette tape recorder, for use in *Interview* magazine, which Warhol had recently founded. Elizabeth jumped up, furious, and pulled the tape out of the micro-cassette with her long fingernails, destroyed it, and departed, prompting Warhol to later ask the question, "Gee, she has everything—magic, money, beauty, intelligence. Why can't she be happy?"

And so, again like Barbara in *Ash Wednesday*, she took a lover—the ever-ready Henry Wynberg, who quickly flew in from Los Angeles to console Elizabeth in Rome.

On July 31, John Springer announced that Aaron Frosch was drawing up divorce papers for the Burtons. They were, of course, both concerned about the impact of the divorce on their children. Michael was on his own, but seventeen-year-old Christopher was still in school and living with his uncle Howard in Hawaii. Liza, sixteen, and twelve-year-old Maria were in boarding schools in Switzerland. Sixteen-year-old Kate was attending the United Nations School in New York, living with Sybil when she wasn't flying in to be with Richard and Elizabeth. They continued to regard Richard as very much their father, though Richard had often reminded Michael and Christopher to honor Michael Wilding as their true father, and Liza to honor the memory of Mike Todd. The meaning of fatherhood had always been important to Richard. Throughout the Burtons' nine-year marriage, they had done all they could to shelter their brood from the paparazzi and the prying questions of journalists. When not in school, the children had spent fabulous vacations aboard their floating zoo, the *Kalizma*, or chasing lizards and playing in the sun-warmed waves at Busseria, their private beach in Puerto Vallarta. The three eldest had appeared as extras in *The Taming of the Shrew*, and had reveled in their mother's unending, effortless glamour. Whatever emotional costs inflicted upon them by the turmoil of their parents' lives—and their parents' drinking—remained private, except for Kate. Kate would later appear in Tony Palmer's brilliant documentary about Burton, *In from the Cold*, recounting how she told her father to stop drinking or she would never see him again.

As for Elizabeth, the only time she ever cried after reading what had been written about her was when *Life* magazine questioned her devotion as a mother. She loved her children and tried to give them as "normal" a life as she was capable of. "Let's face it, I was a freak,"

Elizabeth later admitted. She didn't see her first baseball game until she was in her mid-fifties. "I never went to a senior prom. I wasn't a normal teenager. I wasn't even doing the things my brother was doing, or the girl across the street."

The only child of Richard's that he kept locked out of his life was Jessica, living in an institution on Long Island, for which Richard paid, and paid, and kept on paying.

A few days after his impending divorce was announced, Richard began filming *The Voyage*, moving between the Pontis' villa and the *Kalizma*, moored off of Palermo. He refused to take Elizabeth's calls. He rattled around the massive yacht, drinking cases of white wine, entertaining journalists onboard, just because he was lonely, though surrounded by the boat's crew and by members of his entourage. He missed the presence of his children, and he missed Elizabeth most of all.

Sophia accepted an invitation to spend a weekend on the yacht, though Burton still denied that they were having an affair. Indeed, an affair seems unlikely, as Sophia was devoted to her husband, and the two of them actually spent most of their time talking about Elizabeth or playing Scrabble (Sophia often beat Richard, to his dismay). It's doubtful that Richard would return Carlo and Sophia Ponti's hospitality by having an affair with his host's wife, even if he were capable. When he wasn't playing Scrabble and flirting with Signora Ponti, he was trying, unsuccessfully, to dry out.

Holed up on the *Kalizma*, Burton would go out drinking at a Palermo hotel with crew members from the yacht, who had to watch him carefully now. Not so long ago, when he was with Elizabeth, he had ended a night of pub crawling with Gianni Bozzacchi and had nearly drowned. Standing at the edge of the marina, Burton had jumped into the water to swim back to the *Kalizma*. Bozzacchi—who was not drinking, and who was not even a swimmer—jumped in after him. The next morning, Richard had asked Bozzacchi how they'd gotten back that night, and Bozzacchi, who'd almost drowned rescuing Burton, angrily replied, "You fuckin' English!"

"Welsh!" Burton corrected.

"English! Welsh! I thought we were gonna die!"

De Sica, too, was concerned about his star actor, who seemed like a man determined to kill himself with drink. "He came onto the set shaking, in a daze. It broke my heart to see him . . ."

In October, the *Ladies' Home Journal* got into the act by analyzing the Burtons' marriage and separation in their popular column, "Can This Marriage Be Saved?" Except they retitled it, for the Burtons, "Why This Marriage Can't Be Saved," listing, among the couple's many challenges, "Public pressure to be always on display, to live up to manufactured identities—to glow and sparkle regardless of fatigue, indigestion, or hangovers"; "too much togetherness"; "too much drinking and partying"; "Elizabeth's severe back trouble and other health problems . . . an emotional strain on any marriage"; and, finally—tactfully stated—"Richard's reported 'drinking problem.'" They were accurate in all their assessments. What the article didn't say, and the author could not have known, was that Richard faced that classic dilemma: he felt he couldn't live without Elizabeth, nor could he live with her.

Richard was still writing to Elizabeth, but if he was hoping to bring about a reunion, his behavior made that impossible. On October 9, he wrote to Elizabeth from Rome:

E. T. Burton

It may very well be that this is [the] last time that your last name be, in my presence I mean, the same as mine, but I bet you the impossible bet that when I am on my last bed and nearing the eternal shore that the words Elizabeth Elizabeth Elizabeth BURTON will be on my lips.

In November, Elizabeth Taylor and Henry Wynberg returned to California, stopping in London to visit Laurence Harvey, who was now near death from lung cancer. Elizabeth cradled her dying friend. She had already survived the deaths of many in her forty-one years of life—Mike Todd, Monty Clift, Francis Taylor, Dick Hanley, Ifor Jenkins. Even Nicky Hilton, her unfortunate first husband, had died at the age of forty-two, alone except for three male nurses in his sixty-four-room Holmby Hills mansion. When his physician had arrived to forcibly take Hilton to Menninger's Psychiatric Hospital, he'd greeted the doctor sitting up in bed, holding a loaded pistol. He would die a few months later of a heart attack.

For the next four months, Richard continued to deteriorate, drinking heavily and taking up with a number of young women. Philip Burton, in touch by telephone, was concerned about him. Though outwardly carousing, Burton was still tortured by the loss of Elizabeth, and he wrote her from Venice just before flying to New York.

Hotel Danieli/Royal Excelsioni/Venice

You asked me to write the truth about us . . . I suffer from a severe case of "hubris," an overweening pride. Prometheus was punished by the gods forever and is still suffering in all of us for inventing fire and stealing it from the gods. I am forever punished by the gods for being given the fire and trying to put it out. The fire, of course, is you . . .

You are probably the best actress in the world, which, combined with your extraordinary beauty, makes you unique. Only perhaps Duse could match you (Garbo and Bernhardt make me laugh). When, as an actress, you want to be funny, you are funnier than W. C. Fields; when, as an actress, you are meant to be tragic, you are tragic . . .

. . . The belligerence that has developed between us is inexplicable. . . . Love, however (however much I deride it) is an overwhelming factor. It is something that will live with me forever with or without you. . . . It will not strictly be any of my business, but if for e.g. I happen to come across a snap of you in a nightclub laughing with another nameless group of people, I shall add some more pain to my already pained mind.

. . .

On November 28, 1973, Elizabeth entered the University of California Medical Center for yet another operation, this time to remove an ovarian cyst. Henry Wynberg arranged to spend the night in a room adjacent to hers while she recovered. But his presence wasn't enough. When she got word of Laurence Harvey's death while recuperating from her three-hour operation, Elizabeth felt such a profound sense of loss that she did the only thing she could do to make the pain go away. She called Richard and told him that she couldn't bear the idea of living and dying alone. Burton had once written to her, "If anybody hurts you, just send me a line saying something like 'Need' or 'Necessary' or just the one magic word 'Elizabeth,' and I will be there somewhat faster than sound."

The words Elizabeth uttered were, "Can I come back home?"

This time he took her call. Taking three days off from filming (and paying Ponti $45,000 for each day he missed), Richard flew from location shooting in Sicily to Los Angeles, an exhausting trip that took him by way of the North Pole. He walked into Elizabeth's hospital suite in Los Angeles and the first words out of his mouth were, "Hello, Lumpy, how are you feeling?"

Elizabeth, giddy with delight, answered, "Hi, Pockface."

"The next thing I knew," Elizabeth later recalled, "he was by my bedside and we were squeezing the air out of each other and kissing each other and crying. 'Please come back with me,' he asked. You've never seen anybody heal so fast. It was as if the Grand Maestro had placed a hand over my incision and healed me up."

Turning to one of Elizabeth's nurses, in his best Henry VIII voice, Burton declared, "I'm the husband. I want my bed."

Henry Wynberg discreetly left the hospital and drove himself home.

The next day, Richard wheeled Elizabeth out of the hospital. He was beyond caring what effect the sight of him pushing her in a wheelchair would have on their film careers. It was enough that she was all right, enough that they were leaving the hospital together. They flew back to Italy so Burton could resume filming.

Their reunion made news around the world. On NBC, news anchor John Chancellor wryly announced, "Elizabeth Taylor and Richard Burton are reconciling permanently—as opposed to temporarily." In London, workers at Madame Tussaud's Wax Museum dragged the Burtons' figures closer together, though not quite as close as they had been before.

The couple spent that Christmas at Casa Kimberly in Puerto Vallarta, where they had perhaps always been happiest, and Burton gave Taylor a 38-carat diamond. But until, and unless, Richard was able to finally confront his demons and stop drinking altogether, they were, in his words, "doomed fools."

Three months later, the Burtons flew to Oroville in northern California, where Richard began work on *The Klansman*, a movie for Paramount about racial violence in a small Southern town before the Civil Rights era, written by the well-regarded Southern chronicler William Bradford Huie. After a long hiatus, Burton was finally making a movie in the United States. His costar was Lee Marvin, the "better class of drunk" to whom he had lost his Academy Award for *The Spy Who Came in from the Cold* eight years earlier. Indeed, Marvin would prove a better class of drunk, staying relatively sober as he barely kept up with Burton's three bottles of vodka a day. Taylor was also drinking, but no one could touch Burton.

Despite being reunited with Elizabeth, Richard drank continuously, suicidally, from morning till night, by now unable to control the shaking in his hands. By now, he was in the final stage of alcoholism, a condition he still—amazingly—denied that he had. Nothing but a medical intervention could save him now.

In *The Klansman*, Burton played a Southern landowner gone to seed, complete with a limp and Southern accent, but the limp was real, due to Richard's recurrent gout. Lee Marvin saw how much Richard was suffering, once nearly bursting into tears when he couldn't get a line right. He was also in pain from acute sciatica and old injuries, which caused severe pain in his left arm and a constant hunching of the shoulders. "It was a wonder he could move at all," Lee Marvin later commented. "He had guts, and I admired that. He never complained of being in pain. I'd say, 'Rich, are you okay?' and he'd say, 'Just a little discomfort.' *Discomfort!* Jesus, the guy was in fucking agony!"

And, with his out-of-control imbibing, Richard began womanizing again. He started flirting with bit players in the production, and when word got out, young women began hanging around the set, hoping to be picked up by the famous actor. He met an eighteen-year-old waitress in front of the local jail, invited her into his trailer, and the next day bought her a $450 ring. The waitress, a former "Miss Pepsi of Butte County," made the front page of the local newspapers. He also briefly became involved with a thirty-three-year-old married woman with three children, until her husband showed up on the set, threatening to shoot Richard.

Even Burton knew he was out of control. Gianni Bozzacchi saw that Richard was tortured by his own cheating on Elizabeth, "which was only at the end, when the drinking became terrible," Bozzacchi recalled. "I remember Richard, with tears in his eyes, saying to me, 'Gianni, why do I do it? I love this woman so.' He wasn't just destroying himself with drink, he was destroying himself with guilt."

The journalists smelled blood in the water and flocked to the set. In the mid-1970s, alcoholics were still considered objects of scorn and the butt of jokes. The idea of alcoholism as a genetic disease, like diabetes, had not yet taken root in the public imagination.

Even the public relations liaison for the movie took advantage of the situation, realizing that any publicity for the film was better than none, and he invited the press to watch Burton's public disintegration. Reporters took delight in baiting the actor, yelling out, "Tell us about Dylan Thomas! Tell us something about Wales!" They then described Burton as a human wreck, scribbling down and printing his anguished, liquor-inspired words, which he tossed out like worthless coin: "My father was a drinker, and I'm a drinker, and Lee Marvin is a drinker. The place I like best to be in the whole world is back in my village in Wales, down at the pub, standing with the miners, drinking pints and telling stories. One drinks because life is big and it blinds you," he declaimed. "Poetry and drink are the greatest things on earth. Besides women. There's something to death, and something to truth, and we're after them, all our beautiful lives on earth. Liquor helps."

Elizabeth was horrified to see what was happening to Richard. She left for Los Angeles as soon as the news story of the $450 ring appeared in the press, after spending only a week on location. Ironically, Richard later credited Lee Marvin with saving his life. "I wouldn't have survived without Marvin," he told the actor and writer Michael Munn. "I would have drunk a hell of a lot more a whole lot quicker and wound up dead a whole lot sooner." Lee Marvin saw that Richard "was drinking not for the pleasure of it but because he had a great need, and I doubt he knew what that was himself. Maybe it was for Elizabeth. But whatever it was, he was in pain, and he drank to kill that pain. I used to do it, too."

The director, Terence Young, was also appalled to see what was happening to Burton. Young had directed two James Bond movies, and at one point Burton had been under consideration to play the secret agent, but now he had days when he couldn't "get a single line right. He tried again and again," Young remembered, "but it just wouldn't come out right. He was so desperate. It was painful to see this great actor disintegrating before all our eyes." Toward the end of

filming, Young had one more scene to shoot with Richard: his character's death scene. When the director saw him lying on the set, he
turned to Ron Berkeley, Richard's makeup man, and told him, "You've
done a great job with Richard."

"I haven't touched him," the makeup artist answered.

That did it. The director finally shut down the production and
brought in a doctor to examine Burton. His verdict: "This man is
dying."

Burton was rushed to St. John's Hospital in Santa Monica. Richard's
doctors told him he would be dead in two weeks if he didn't detoxify.
He had a temperature of 104 degrees, his kidneys were on the point of
collapse, and he was suffering from influenza and tracheo-bronchitis.
He was given emergency blood transfusions to cleanse his body of
alcohol. Richard would remain there for six weeks, hallucinating and
near death for the first several days. He often dreamed of his brother
Ifor, standing whole and upright before him, challenging him to make
up his mind: *live or die.* Later, as he slowly began to recover, he ran
into Susan Strasberg on the hospital grounds, the dark-haired young
actress with whom he had had an affair seventeen years earlier. She
barely recognized him. His hands shook violently, his face was ashen,
his body was frail. He was not yet fifty.

Elizabeth stayed in touch by phone, but she couldn't stand it anymore. She flew to Gstaad, where she quietly filed for divorce. On April
25, 1974, they publicly announced their plans to divorce, and Richard
let it be known he would give Elizabeth everything she wanted—
possession of the *Kalizma*, Casa Kimberly in Puerto Vallarta, $7
million worth of jewelry, all the priceless art they had acquired over
the years. She was also awarded custody of Maria, the much-loved
daughter they had adopted in 1964, who bore his name. He seemed to
want to divest himself of his entire life, though he made sure that his
immediate family in Wales—his twenty-nine sisters, brothers, in-laws,
nieces, and nephews—would continue to be provided for. He wanted
Elizabeth and all their children to be safe and well looked-after. That

was his role now, to provide for the extended family, which had grown huge, to be the father he had never had—because Dic Jenkins had provided for no one.

On June 26, 1974, citing irreconcilable differences, Elizabeth was granted her divorce in a small, wooden-frame courtroom in the Swiss town of Saarinen. Richard was still too ill to attend the proceedings, and was represented by a doctor's certificate. The judge asked the inevitable question he was required to ask: "Is it true that to live with your husband became intolerable?"

"Yes, life with Richard became intolerable," Elizabeth answered softly, dressed in a brown silk suit and wearing dark sunglasses. It had been so much more complicated than that—in fact, it had been the greatest adventure of their lives, but their ten-year marriage was now reduced to a line of stock dialogue. She told the judge that she had tried everything to keep their marriage together, but now it was over. Not her love for Richard, but their life together.

Twenty minutes later, she called Richard and asked, "Do you think we've done the right thing?" But for Richard, who couldn't imagine living without Elizabeth but who couldn't seem to stay sober when they were together, "the adventure of a lifetime" was over. Or so he thought. On June 27, Richard, now recovered and in recovery, sailed for Europe on the SS *France*.

Henry Wynberg joined Elizabeth on the *Kalizma* to cruise the Mediterranean, and Elizabeth, ever the survivor, attempted to recreate the life she had led with Burton, dining in Monaco with Prince Rainier and Princess Grace, spending time at her chalet in Gstaad. Wynberg tried to fill Richard's shoes, taking Elizabeth to soccer matches in Munich (instead of rugby matches in Wales), and bringing her home to meet his parents in Amsterdam (a replacement for Burton's sprawling family in the hilly dales of Pontrhydyfen and Port Talbot). And then there were the jewels: the $2,400 coral necklace (not quite the $1.1 million Cartier diamond that now bore Elizabeth's name). Wynberg had pleaded with the Beverly Hills jeweler to "make it bigger."

In August, Richard went back to work. Sophia Loren, ever solici-
tous of her troubled friend, got him hired to replace the actor Robert
Shaw in a television adaptation of Noël Coward's *Brief Encounter.*
Shaw had been released from the Carlo Ponti production to play the
salty shark-hunter on Steven Spielberg's *Jaws* (a role, incidentally, that
would have well suited Richard, and would have rejuvenated his film
career, bringing him to the attention of a new generation of moviegoers). But Richard no longer had the stamina for such a role, had he
even been considered for it. Instead, he played the romantic lead in
a slightly creaky production of a World War II–era romantic drama.
Burton looked frail and thin in the television film, and Sophia Loren
was too beautiful to play the ordinary middle-class housewife the role
called for, so the production was not particularly well received. Still
recovering from his medical ordeal, Burton now found himself in a
phase where he could only act with his sonorous voice: hence the historical figures he would continue to play, where he could stand still
and declaim great speeches.

Elizabeth, meanwhile, returned to Los Angeles, where she tried
living with a smaller entourage. "She was down to a secretary, a chauffeur, a butler, and Henry," noticed her old friend, the journalist and
liberal columnist Max Lerner. She leased an Italianate villa in Bel
Air, where she and Wynberg decided to launch a number of business
ventures—a diamond-selling enterprise and a cosmetics company.
It was an exciting new prospect for Elizabeth—a world she had yet
to conquer—and many around her thought that Wynberg (though a
prodigious lover in his own right) had become more of a business partner than a paramour. Liz Smith later noticed, when she visited them,
that Elizabeth didn't have any pet names for him, such as "darling," or
"sweetnose," or "dearest," or "fuckface," all endearments she'd used
with Richard Burton. And she made no attempt to hide her frequent
phone calls to Richard.

* * *

If Elizabeth tried to replace Burton with Henry Wynberg in a road-show version of their fabled life, Richard quickly became engaged to another Elizabeth—the thirty-eight-year-old Princess Elizabeth of Yugoslavia, recently separated from her merchant banker husband, Neil Balfour. A celebrated beauty, she was rumored to have been romantically linked to President Kennedy. Six years earlier, Princess Elizabeth had visited the Burtons on their movie sets in Paris. Burton had described her then as "pretty but impertinent," too quick to laugh when Rex Harrison blew a line, too pleased to go out with Warren Beatty when he asked her. But if you were going to follow up the most famous movie star in the world, a Yugoslav princess wasn't a bad place to land. And Richard wanted—needed—to be married, to have a sense of family around him, to even consider fathering children again. He was still depressed enough about losing Elizabeth that there were attempts to keep newspapers from him while he was filming *Brief Encounter*, because the tabloids were rife with stories about Elizabeth and Henry and the possibility that they might marry.

So, barely four months after his divorce, Richard announced his engagement. When Elizabeth received the news, she immediately suffered severe back spasms and had to be put in traction. She insisted that it had nothing to do with Richard's engagement, but it was part of her pattern to react to stress and setbacks in her life by becoming injured or ill. A hospital bed was moved into her Bel Air mansion.

Richard and Princess Elizabeth celebrated their engagement by touring the casbahs of Morocco, where Burton was surprised to hear himself greeted by turbaned old men as "St. Becket" or "Major Smith," his character from *Where Eagles Dare*, which, he discovered, had been a huge success in the cinemas of Tangier.

Due to her place in aristocracy, Princess Elizabeth introduced Burton to Lady Churchill, Sir Winston Churchill's widow. That October, he had begun filming a ninety-minute biopic, playing the great man in "A Walk with Destiny," a *Hallmark Hall of Fame* coproduction of the BBC and NBC (titled "The Gathering Storm" in the States). As he had for *Brief Encounter*, Burton was now only receiving $200,000 salary, plus salaries for two secretaries and the use of a Rolls-Royce during production. Still, it was a far cry from his former $1-million-plus-percentage salary, and he now realized how relatively broke he was, post-divorce.

By December of 1974, Richard's engagement to Princess Elizabeth had ended. While on location in the Riviera, filming *Jackpot*, a film that was never finished for lack of production funds, Richard had reunited with a beautiful African-American actress and model named Jean Bell. She was, in fact, the first black model to appear on the cover of *Playboy* magazine. Though she didn't have a part in the film, the actress had first met Richard on location for *The Klansman*. When Princess Elizabeth saw in an English newspaper a photograph of Richard and Jean Bell strolling arm-in-arm on the Riviera, all bets were off. Burton moved back into his house in Céligny, with Jean Bell beside him.

Elizabeth Taylor, meanwhile, was offered another film. In January 1975, she brought Wynberg with her to Leningrad, where she'd agreed to appear in the first Soviet-American coproduction, *The Blue Bird*, for a greatly diminished salary of $3,000 a week, plus a percentage of the gross. She ended up paying $8,000 of her own money to have her costumes redesigned. It was directed by seventy-six-year-old George Cukor, nearing the end of his long career (he immediately fell in love with a young Hungarian boy and lost interest in the movie), and it costarred another trio of beauties: Ava Gardner, Jane Fonda, and Cicely Tyson. Elizabeth played four different allegorical roles in the film: Mother, Light, Maternal Love, and Witch. Elizabeth and Wynberg (hired as a still photographer on the set) checked into the Leningrad Hotel, where Elizabeth promptly came down with amoebic dysentery from contaminated ice cubes and rapidly lost eighteen pounds. ("I never looked so good," she told Rex Reed, "but what a hell of a way to diet . . .") Wynberg nursed her and waited on her, and the couple had rashers of bacon flown in from London's Fortnum & Mason. When she got the news of Richard's broken engagement, Elizabeth immediately called him. They spoke for hours on the phone, Henry discreetly stepping aside.

Richard and Elizabeth had spent the past fourteen months in their parallel universes, appearing in films that would go bankrupt or fail at the box office, traveling with their new consorts, and speaking frequently with each other on the telephone. Now they agreed to meet in Lausanne, in neutral Switzerland, a place where they'd reunited once before at the height of *Le Scandale*. She flew to Gstaad, with Wynberg, while Burton remained in Céligny, with Jean and her thirteen-year-old son, Troy, whom Burton had enrolled in an exclusive Swiss school. Jean tried to keep Burton from returning to alcohol. He was mostly abstaining, but his hands still trembled, and he still suffered from gout, arthritis, and sciatica.

By August of 1975, Elizabeth ended her romantic relationship with Wynberg, though, almost as a going-away present, she entered into a partnership with him, leasing rights to use her image to publicize and sell cosmetics (their business partnership was eventually dissolved). She and Richard arranged to meet at her Swiss lawyer's office in Lausanne, ostensibly to discuss their financial settlement. But when he saw Elizabeth, he was struck by how beautiful she looked, newly slimmed down. And Richard, no longer bloated by alcohol, looked wonderful to Elizabeth. They fell into each other's arms, tears streaming. On August 21, their publicist, John Springer, announced that they were again in love.

Jean Bell left Céligny; Henry Wynberg flew back to London. Neither could compete with the star power of those they had, temporarily, replaced. And it wasn't just star power: Elizabeth and Richard had lived such extraordinary lives that there was no one else who could match them in their experiences and memories. They were the only two people who could even begin to understand what they had lived through. Like the handful of men who had touched down on the moon, they had no peers, and no one else with whom they could share the details of their mad, extravagant lives together.

Elizabeth had never stopped being in love with Richard. Maybe now, with "Liz and Dick" on the wane—their joint movie career was certainly over, and their separate careers were foundering—there would be a chance for Elizabeth and Richard. But, they soon discovered, "Liz and Dick" still caused near riots when they appeared in public. Elizabeth pressed Richard to remarry, but he was reluctant to go down that road again.

Nonetheless, the newly reunited couple flew to Israel on a grand tour to lend their somewhat tarnished glamour to a number of worthy causes. At a benefit concert in Israel, Elizabeth read the Story of Ruth, and Richard read the Twenty-third Psalm. Whenever they left the King David Hotel, they were mobbed by unruly crowds, mad to get a glimpse of the infamous couple. It was so bad that Henry Kissinger, then U.S. Secretary of State, who was staying at the hotel with his wife, Nancy, offered them use of his own security detail (seventy U.S. Marines and nearly a thousand Israeli troops). They declined, but the Kissingers were so starstruck that the Secretary of State threw a party for the couple.

After a week in Israel, they returned to Gstaad and made plans to attend a celebrity tennis tournament in Johannesburg, South Africa, another charity event to raise funds for a hospital. (Burton wrote to Kate the morning before leaving, "Tonight . . . we fly to Johannesburg . . . Everybody is terrified that superbly sober as I am, I may yet start sounding off on 'Apartheid.'") Throughout it all, Elizabeth kept leaving Richard little love notes, saying she would leave it up to him to decide what to do. She clearly wanted to remarry. Burton resisted, until Elizabeth went into the hospital to investigate an intestinal complaint. An X-ray revealed a spot on her lungs that her doctor thought might indicate cancer. For twenty-four hours, she was terrified. She would later write about the incident in a seventeen-page document, handwritten in ink in schoolgirl penmanship (and later published in the *Ladies' Home Journal*), "I thought all through the night . . . it's funny when you think you don't have long to live how many things you want to do, and see, and smell, and touch. How really simple they are." When she got the report that the shadow on her lung was caused by old scar tissue from having had a mild case of tuberculosis as a child, she was ecstatic. She wrote, "I gave him a Valium—he whispered poetry—we kissed . . . Happiness! I have my life back. I mean you, Richard."

That's when Richard got down on one knee and proposed remarriage. "I think I brought it up and he shied away sweetly," Elizabeth wrote. Richard gallantly asked, "Will you marry me?" Of course, she accepted. She later recalled, "[W]e sent everyone out of the room, including the children, and we got stoned." All their old habits were waiting for them, which is what, perhaps, Richard had wanted to avoid.

He went out that night and got drunk.

On October 10, 1975, Elizabeth and Richard—or was it Liz and Dick?—celebrated their remarriage with a ceremony on the banks of the Chobe River in the Chobe Game Reserve in Botswana, South Africa. "That's where I would like to be mated again," Elizabeth had written. "In the bush, around our kind." It's interesting that they chose Botswana as the site of their reunion. Besides being a place where they could walk in public unmolested by gawkers and photographers, Africa is often the place, symbolically, as the psychiatrist and writer Kay Redfield Jamison has noted, where people go to revivify their lives—its vibrant beauty has the power to heal old wounds. The night before the wedding, Elizabeth found herself as sleepless and full of anticipation as a young girl.

An African district commissioner from the Tswana tribe performed the twenty-minute ceremony, in which they were asked if they "understood the consequence of marriage." There was perhaps no other couple on earth who better understood the consequences of marriage.

The ceremony was "witnessed by two hippos" who emerged from the Chobe River, Elizabeth recalled. Richard wore a red silk turtleneck sweater and white slacks. The bride wore a long green dress ribbed with beads and bird feathers, which had been a gift from Ifor and Gwen Jenkins just four Christmases ago. This was the first time she had worn it, and she did so for Richard, to commemorate Ifor's memory, though it was not a memory Richard wished to revisit.

The only fly in the ointment was Richard's condition. He had woken up pink-eyed and slightly hung over the morning of their wedding. She made light of it in her *Ladies' Home Journal* article about the wedding, but what she failed to realize was that Richard could not stay sober and still be with her. Alcohol was the fuel that propelled their life together, and unless Elizabeth stopped drinking, Richard could not stay sober. The difference was, Elizabeth could handle alcohol, but it was killing Richard.

Elizabeth was not happy about finding her newly minted husband in this condition, but she wrote that, despite his flaws, "I love him, deeply and truly and forever," adding: "he has the most remarkable recuperative powers I've ever seen, which is probably why he is still alive. Thank God!"

The ceremony over, they piled into a waiting Range Rover and began their safari honeymoon. Elizabeth was ecstatic. She wrote a little note to Richard:

Dearest Hubs—

How about that! You really are my husband again, and I have news for thee, there bloody will be no more marriages—or divorces either.

We are stuck like chicken feathers to tar—for lovely always.

Do you realize we *shall* grow old together, and I *know* the best is yet to be!

. . . Yours truly, Wife

But the honeymoon was called off when Richard fell ill, diagnosed with malaria. A pharmacist named Chenina Samin (later shortened to Chen Sam), an extremely competent Egyptian woman in her early forties, was helicoptered in, and she nursed Richard back to health. Elizabeth was so impressed with her that she invited the striking, capable woman to join her entourage. She did so, becoming Elizabeth's secretary, publicist, and indispensable friend for the next three decades, replacing—if possible—Dick Hanley's loving but firm hand in Elizabeth's life. And Richard was restored to good health—for a while.

The press had a field day covering the wedding—Elizabeth's sixth, Richard's third. Ellen Goodman wrote in the *Boston Globe*, "Sturm has remarried Drang and all is right with the world . . . In an era of friendly divorces and meaningful relationships, they stand for a marriage that is an all-consuming affair, not a partnership. None of this respecting each other's freedom, but instead, saying, 'I can't live without you.' Wow."

On November 10, Elizabeth threw Richard a fiftieth birthday party in the Orchid Room of the Dorchester Hotel, back in London. Burton was still fighting for sobriety, and some felt that he did not look well—"like a man who wasn't really there," wrote one British writer who attended the party. Burton was the only one sipping mineral water among the 250 guests, but within weeks of their marriage, he would begin drinking again. He and Elizabeth went back to their old pattern of fighting and making up. One of their bodyguards, Brian Haynes, thought the marriage was doomed from the start. "But I could see that they seemed to need each other. . . . When he was away, she couldn't bear to be without him. They were often at each other's throats, and there was plenty of hard-core swearing on both sides."

When Elizabeth went back into the hospital for recurrent back and neck pain, she insisted that Burton stay with her. This time, he didn't want to. He felt pressured and harangued, and, given his attempts to stay sober, the pressure was becoming unbearable. Smoking a cigarette, he wheeled her into the hospital, and when the inevitable photographer asked for the couple to kiss for the camera, Burton refused.

In December, they returned to Elizabeth's Chalet Ariel in Gstaad for the Christmas holidays. As in Goforth's villa in *Boom!*, Elizabeth had an intercom system put in that connected her to her secretary's room and to the kitchen—but not to Richard's bedroom, located at the other end of the chalet. By now, Richard was back to drinking, prowling the house at night, chafing under Elizabeth's possessiveness. He managed to slip away to the nearby ski slopes with the ever-present Brook Williams, for a rare outing.

On the slopes, Richard happened to notice a tall, stunning woman who simply took his breath away. She was a green-eyed, twenty-seven-year-old former model named Suzy Hunt, in the process of divorcing the celebrated Formula One race-car driver, James Hunt. She was totally different from all the doe-eyed, raven-haired women he had been smitten with in the past—Susan Strasberg, Claire Bloom, Elizabeth Taylor.

She struck him with all the force of a new beginning. Elizabeth didn't know it yet, but Richard Burton had just met his future.

16
PRIVATE LIVES

"Everyone bought tickets to watch . . . 'Liz and Dick.'
And we gave them what they wanted."
—ELIZABETH TAYLOR

"I've never found a part as good as
playing the husband of Elizabeth Taylor."
—RICHARD BURTON

January 1976 was a turning point for Richard. Not only did he begin spending time with Suzy Hunt, he took on new representation in New York, the Austrian theatrical agent Robert Lantz. Robbie Lantz got him the opportunity to replace Anthony Perkins for three months in the lead role in *Equus*, a new play by Peter Shaffer. He had been thought of because it had been a lackluster season on Broadway that year, and even a somewhat faded movie star could add the excitement needed to sell tickets.

Alec McCowen had played the lead role of psychiatrist Dr. Martin Dysart in the original production at the Old Vic in London, and Burton's fellow Welshman, Anthony Hopkins, had preceded Perkins in the role on Broadway. The controversial play—about a troubled youth who blinds six horses, and the disillusioned psychiatrist who treats him—had caused a sensation on both sides of the Atlantic. The play included male nudity (the young man's) and disturbing subject matter.

Still living with Elizabeth in Gstaad, in separate bedrooms, Burton walked through the snow around the chalet, reading Shaffer's play, mesmerized by his beautiful speeches. He had always responded to the power of words, but he hadn't set foot on a stage since his triumphant *Hamlet* in 1963, when he had run the gamut of huge crowds and policemen on horses just to get into the theater, and his less than triumphant *Doctor Faustus* at the Oxford Playhouse in 1966.

When *Jackpot* couldn't attract the funding to complete filming, Burton must have felt that his movie career was virtually over. He continued to rail against the "unmanly" art of acting, but not only did he want and need the income, acting was still in his blood, still challenging, still the most satisfying thing he could do, apart from his deep reading and the hours he spent writing in his diaries. But he was sick to death of those European coproductions, those "Tower of Babel films," as he called them, in which half the actors spoke different languages. And all the international travel that was required! He wasn't lying when he told Elizabeth that he was a different man now, he was tired, he didn't want to live in the old way anymore.

But Burton was nervous about taking on another stage performance—especially because this time, he would be doing it entirely without alcohol.

He left Gstaad and flew to New York to begin rehearsing for a twelve-week run, moving into a twentieth-floor suite at the Lombardy Hotel on 56th Street off Park Avenue. Unlike the Dorchester, the Lombardy was and is a small, European hotel, neither grand nor grandiose. Brook Williams, who remained a loyal friend and personal assistant, accompanied him.

And so did Suzy Hunt. Burton had been struck by her beauty on the ski slopes of Gstaad, but his heart really went out to her when he next encountered the willowy blonde at a party. She was down on all fours, searching for a lost contact lens, and Burton had at first thought she was inebriated. He soon found out that Suzy, who had been educated at a convent, was quite straight when it came to any kind of intoxicant. The daughter of a brigadier solicitor, used to the huge crowds that had cheered her ex-husband, James Hunt, she was up to the challenge of taking on this world-famous man, removing him from Elizabeth's influence, and making sure he would never again drink himself to the brink of death.

Angered and humiliated by Burton's departure, Taylor took up with a thirty-seven-year-old advertising executive from Malta named Peter Darmanin. She had met him in a discothèque in Gstaad called The Cave, where she had gone with Chen Sam. Before Richard left for New York to appear in *Equus*, she'd warned him, "You have the guts of a blind burglar—you know they'll be gunning for you." Twelve years ago, it was Taylor who had given Burton the courage to go back on stage. Now she reminded him that he was fair game for the critics. They would be waiting for him with sharpened knives.

Perhaps as a retaliation for Richard's defection, Elizabeth made plans to sell the beautiful 25-carat pink diamond ring that Richard had bought for over $1 million and had given to her to commemorate their remarriage. She'd planned to use the proceeds to set up a hospital in Botswana. But when she got word from Richard that he wanted to see her, would she please come to New York and meet him at the Lombardy, she was suddenly hopeful. "Please come. I need you," he'd told her.

"When?" she'd asked.

"Now."

Perhaps, for a third time, they would patch things up.

From Switzerland, Elizabeth called Alexander Cohen, the play's producer (who had also produced Burton's *Hamlet* thirteen years earlier). She had a wonderful idea. Why not give a party to celebrate Richard's return to the stage, and combine it with her forty-fourth birthday on February 27, 1976? It would be an intimate gathering for thirty-six guests, held at Caffe da Alfredo in Greenwich Village. Cohen, who also produced the annual Tony Awards, knew how to put on a good show, so she left the details to him. There were even plans to have the Burtons cohost the Tony Awards that year.

Nervous and fearful about taking on such a large and difficult role in front of a live audience, Burton decided to test his stamina by replacing Tony Perkins in a Saturday matinee, though he was still rehearsing the part. That afternoon, just before the curtain lifted, a sonorous voice announced, "At this performance, the part of Martin Dysart will not be played by Anthony Perkins." The audience groaned their disapproval. The voice continued: "The part of Martin Dysart will be played by Richard Burton." The audience rose to its feet and cheered, welcoming Burton back to the New York stage.

Just before previews were to begin, Richard met Elizabeth at Kennedy Airport. She was bundled up in a fur coat and wearing dark sunglasses. They greeted each other with a big kiss, which was there for all to see the next morning in Liz Smith's syndicated column. But when they arrived at the Lombardy, Elizabeth checked into a separate suite. Word got out that she was in town, which made the cast and crew of *Equus* apprehensive—it was well known by now that Burton had trouble staying sober around Elizabeth. The rehearsals had gone well—and his stand-in performance for Tony Perkins had been triumphant—but it had been a difficult transition for Richard. "It was the first time in my life I'd been onstage without a drink," he later said. "I've never been so bloody scared." The stakes were high: he risked public humiliation, and with his film career in eclipse, he risked his livelihood as an actor.

When Elizabeth checked into the Lombardy for their anticipated reunion, she could tell right away that something was not quite right. He seemed distant and tentative. That's when he told her that he wanted a divorce.

"Immediately, everyone in every surrounding room started hearing incredible fights," Liz Smith recounted, "because Richard had only invited her to New York to tell her that he had fallen in love with Suzy Hunt."

"Why the hell did you have me come all the way here to tell me that?" Elizabeth wailed.

Elizabeth discovered that Suzy Hunt had been with Richard all along, that they had been seen around town, at 21, at Gallagher's Steak House in the heart of Broadway, shopping at Bloomingdale's, with Brook Williams acting as the beard. The more time Richard spent with Suzy, the more he felt that she was the right woman for him, at the right time.

Reporters lay siege to the Plymouth Theatre during a Monday-evening preview performance of the play. Liz Smith and her right-hand man, Denis Ferrara, remembered that a big mob of fans waited for Elizabeth outside the Lombardy. "She came out," Ferrara recalled, "and from a distance, she looked fantastic, and everyone goes, 'ooh.' But the closer she got, she looked like someone who had just been told that her entire family had been wiped out. Outside the Plymouth Theatre, even though it's Burton's return to Broadway, another mob was screaming, 'Liz! Liz!' It's her they wanted."

At Sardi's, after the performance, Burton stood up and embraced Suzy Hunt in front of Elizabeth. "That was the end," Liz Smith recalled. "When they emerged from Sardi's, Elizabeth was completely stoned and Richard was stone cold sober. He helped her get into the car, but she knew it was all over. She left New York the next day."

The marriage of the century was over. Instead of celebrating Elizabeth's birthday, Burton met with Suzy Hunt and Brook Williams at Mont St. Michel restaurant, to celebrate his new life—with mineral water.

When Burton's *Equus* opened on February 23, it was Suzy Hunt and not Elizabeth sitting in the audience, for what many would describe as a theatrical triumph. The audience adored Burton and again gave him a standing ovation; long lines queued for tickets, and all his performances quickly sold out. The reviews were mostly (though not entirely) ecstatic: " . . . the actor's performance in *Equus* seems to me the best work of his life," wrote Walter Kerr for the *New York Times*. Clive Barnes called it "a star performance." Suddenly, the sun was shining on Richard Burton again. Whenever he and Suzy entered a restaurant during the run of the play, they were applauded. Burton kept his promise to Alexander Cohen and appeared as a presenter at the Tony Awards, where he was given a special medallion with the inscription "Welcome Back to Broadway."

After Burton's triumphant opening night, Suzy Hunt went back to Richard's dressing room to congratulate him. What awaited her was a surprise: a message from Elizabeth. After the preview performance, Elizabeth had gone back to Richard's dressing room to congratulate him on his splendid performance. When she found the room empty, she'd taken an eyebrow pencil out of her purse and, like Gloria Wandrous in *BUtterfield 8*, wrote on his mirror: "You were fantastic, love." How long had that message from Elizabeth been there? And why hadn't Burton wiped it off? For the first time, Suzy realized that Elizabeth would remain a force to be reckoned with and, in some way, would always be part of Richard's life.

After agreeing to a divorce, Elizabeth flew to Los Angeles and checked into a Beverly Hills Hotel bungalow—it was too painful to face any of the homes she had shared with Richard—leaving it to Cohen to cancel the party she had planned and to announce that she would not be cohosting the Tony Awards. Back in Los Angeles, Henry Wynberg was waiting for her.

In the second, and final, divorce settlement, drawn up by Aaron Frosch, Elizabeth took everything: full possession of the *Kalizma* and Casa Kimberly, all the jewelry and the works of art. Richard kept the Everyman Library that Elizabeth had given him, and a small Picasso he had bought at auction in London just before he was fired from *Laughter in the Dark*. Richard kept his house in Céligny, which he had owned before the marriage, and he had the thousand volumes of his library moved there from the Gstaad chalet. Harder to untangle were their business interests and the corporations they'd founded together: Taybur Productions, Oxford Productions, their shares of Harlech Television, and the Vicky Tiel Boutique in Paris. Their legal representatives worked out the details.

At the end of the twelve-week run, Richard and Suzy traveled to Haiti as the guests of "Papa Doc" Duvalier. It's surprising that Burton would have accepted such an invitation, given how there had been death threats against him when he and Taylor had made *The Comedians*, an exposé of the brutal Duvalier regime. Perhaps Duvalier was just a movie fan all along, and Burton's star power trumped the faux pas of appearing in a political exposé. Perhaps Burton felt there were few places left where he could escape from Elizabeth's sphere of influence. He and Suzy bought a thirty-five-acre estate where they could hide from the world, and that was where Richard, on August 1, 1976, finalized his divorce from Elizabeth. He and Suzy married twenty days later, in a four-minute ceremony in Arlington, Virginia, just after she received her divorce from James Hunt. Between his divorce and his marriage to Suzy, Richard flew to Hollywood, where he filmed *Exorcist II: The Heretic* for John Boorman at Warner Bros. The reviews were so bad that his new wife told him, "You must never do anything like that again, not even to get a million dollars." Thankfully, he would follow this film catastrophe with the movie adaptation of *Equus*, earning his seventh Academy Award nomination. Surely, after all those near-misses, he would win this one.

The new Burtons settled into Richard's home in Céligny, and Suzy went into a bustle of activity remodeling and redecorating the house, making it comfortable for Richard and, hopefully, removing lingering memories of Ifor's accident. She cleaned out an attic room that had become a roost for pigeons and transformed it into a spacious haven for Richard to read, study, and write, with a log fireplace, comfortable chairs, a desk with a typewriter, and special bookshelves she had made along the length of the room that held the thousand volumes of Burton's treasured library. ("Was it not Francis Bacon who said books make the best furniture?" Burton was fond of saying.) That wasn't the only big change: she made sure that Burton's entourage—except for his friend Brook Williams—stayed away from him. She had decided that they were part of the reason Richard drank so much—they made it too easy for him. Kate Burton, years later, saw the good effect that Suzy'd had on her father's life, helping him to stay sober: "I think Suzy Hunt provided a very important gift to him. She made him able to leave Elizabeth."

Back in Los Angeles, Elizabeth was miserable. While Burton was being acclaimed, and publicly praising his young wife for giving him his life back, Elizabeth was drinking to excess, hiding out in the Beverly Hills Hotel. She decided to get on with her life. She leased a house and was seen around town with Henry Wynberg, but the bloom was definitely off that rose, as the used-car salesman was under indictment for rolling back the odometers on some of the cars he had sold. Even worse, he was hit with a morals charge in connection with a photo shoot at his home involving four girls from a Beverly Hills high school. Wynberg was ultimately given a ninety-day jail sentence on a misdemeanor conviction of contributing to the delinquency of a minor.

But Elizabeth's life was about to change. She met the Kissingers again, at a party in Palm Springs given by Kirk Douglas and his wife, which led to invitations to attend various charity balls in Washington, DC. It was the spring of 1976, the Bicentennial year, and Washington was alive with benefits and celebrations. There she met and had a brief but intense friendship with the Iranian Ambassador Ardeshir Zahedi, jetting to Tehran for a fabulous party at the Zahedi palace (under the Shah of Iran's regime, a few years before the Iranian Revolution). She drank champagne and vodka and dined on caviar. When she was invited to a reception at the British Embassy for Queen Elizabeth II, she agreed to go, but "the most beautiful woman in the world" did not have a date. She was provided with one: the chairman of the Bicentennial Committee, a wealthy Virginia Republican named John Warner Jr.

Warner's first marriage to the heiress Catherine Mellon had made Warner rich (his father-in-law had sided with him in the divorce, agreeing that women couldn't handle money). His father-in-law had also, arguably, helped bring Warner an appointment as secretary of the navy in President Gerald Ford's administration.

Warner was a tall, distinguished, politically well-connected country squire, who owned Atoka, a 25,000-acre farm in the horse country of Middleburg, Virginia. He had courtly good manners, and, curiously, bore a strong physical resemblance to both Richard Burton and Mike Todd—the large, squarish head, the rough but handsome features, as if he had been fashioned out of good earth. They began seeing each other.

When she got news of Richard's marriage to Suzy Hunt, Elizabeth was in Vienna, having taken the offer of a role in *A Little Night Music*, an adaptation of a Stephen Sondheim musical. She actually had to sing in the part, and, of all things, that heartbreaker, "Send in the Clowns," which she did gamely and self-deprecatingly. She cabled her congratulations to Richard, and she asked Warner to join her in Vienna. He did.

They were married on December 4, 1976. Soon after, Warner tested the waters for a run for the U.S. Senate, with Elizabeth's star power as his not-so-secret weapon. He eventually won his place in the Senate— by default, when his triumphant opponent in the Republican primary, Richard Obenshain, died in a private-plane crash. After winning his bid and becoming a U.S. senator from Virginia, Warner now had everything he wanted, and, like a good Republican husband who felt that a woman's place should be in the home, he asked Elizabeth to give up her career. She did—which didn't seem like a sacrifice after reading the scorching reviews of *A Little Night Music*.

Once the exhilaration of campaigning for Warner was over, there was little for Elizabeth to do. She noticed that her self-esteem was plummeting—her identity as a senator's wife was not enough for this world-famous, sophisticated, and brilliant woman. Richard had never treated her as just a wife, or a sex object, or a broad—he had always respected her intelligence and she had always been a full partner. But with Senator Warner, who spent most of his time in Washington, leaving her alone on their vast estate, she felt "redundant." She later reflected, "[L]ike so many Washington wives and like so many other women . . . I had nothing to do." The coup de grâce came when a contingent of Republican ladies took her aside and told her she could no longer wear purple—her signature color—because it was "too passionate." For a while she complied, putting aside her Halston outfits and adopting "sedate little Republican ensembles," as she put her passion in mothballs and played the role of the senator's wife.

Bored and feeling useless, Elizabeth consoled herself with eating and drinking to excess. So, with little to do in the Virginia country-side, she saw her weight balloon from 130 to 180-plus pounds. "Eating filled the lonely hours, and I ate and drank with abandon," she later admitted, as Halston designed larger and larger pantsuits for her to wear, in any color but purple. "During the early 1960s," she mused, "the Burtons' 'profane' romance vied with the 'sacred' one [the Ken-nedys'] in Washington, DC. The same papers that had given priority to the first photographs of Richard Burton and me on a beach over pictures of the Kennedys in the White House, now featured my new and unflattering measurements." For the first time in her life, she became the butt of cruel jokes—not about her many marriages, as in Oscar Levant's quip, "Always a bride, never a bridesmaid"—but about her appearance. Joan Rivers started it all on *The Tonight Show with Johnny Carson*, and the jokes didn't stop for years. The only person who didn't join in the laughter was Richard Burton. It was all right for Richard to tease her, calling her "my fat Jewish tart" or "Twiddle-twaddle," but not the rest of the world. Elizabeth later showed real class by sending Joan Rivers flowers and a note of condolence when her husband, Edgar Rosenberg, committed suicide.

Elizabeth made other sacrifices in her marriage, besides her career and her wardrobe, including selling her famous Taylor-Burton diamond to New York jeweler Henry Lambert to help out with their expenses (and to exorcise the lingering ghost of Richard in their marriage, perhaps). "It represented a different phase in my life," she explained. "The fun phase." Lambert paid her $3 million, twice what Burton had spent for it.

Elizabeth was used to a fabulous social life, but Warner preferred to live quietly. "John and I never had people in," she recalled, "and we hardly ever went out. Most evenings he'd say, 'Why don't you go upstairs and watch TV, Pooters?'" (He also called her his "Little Heifer.") Finally, she'd had enough. Elizabeth took her purple Halston pantsuit out of mothballs and wore it for a Republican ladies luncheon held in her honor. She knew she had to change her life.

When Elizabeth finally confronted herself, staring at her unflattering weight gain in the three-way mirror in the home she shared with Warner in Georgetown, she resolved to do something about it. She drew on her memories of Richard—their incredible, roller-coaster life together, their obsessive love—and those memories gave her "the strength to recreate a new dream." That dream would involve Richard, and it would bring them both back to the stage.

The idea may have been planted by a cocktail party conversation with Burt Reynolds, who told Elizabeth that as his film offers began to dry up, he started a dinner theater in Jupiter, Florida. He'd asked if she'd be interested appearing with him in a revival of *Who's Afraid of Virginia Woolf?* She declined the offer, but Elizabeth had always wanted to return to the stage after appearing as Helen of Troy in *Doctor Faustus*. She'd loved the risk and adrenaline rush of appearing before a live audience, but she knew she didn't have the training for the stage, and she certainly didn't have the voice. But she felt that that was something she could work on, just as she could work on slimming down.

Meanwhile, Richard was having his own problems. On March 29, 1978, he made his last trip to the Dorothy Chandler Pavilion in Los Angeles as a nominee for Best Actor for *Equus*—his seventh nomination. When the words "And the winner is—Richard . . ." rang out,

Burton started to rise from his seat. At last, the award was his! Then the presenter continued, " . . . Dreyfuss!" A look of pain and disbelief crossed his face. Thirty-year-old Richard Dreyfuss had won the Oscar for his comedic role in Neil Simon's *The Goodbye Girl*, and Burton was once again left unrecognized by the Academy for the part that had virtually saved his diminishing acting career. (He would, however, win a Golden Globe for his performance.) Perhaps it was true, after all, that Hollywood had never embraced him, and had collectively sided with Elizabeth in the divorce. And Burton had spent all those years making films in Europe, taking Elizabeth with him, away from Hollywood, for a decade. In a way, they never forgave him for marrying her, and they never forgave him for divorcing her.

After that, there would be a slew of bad-to-middling films: *The Medusa Touch*, *The Wild Geese*, *Absolution*, *Breakthrough*, the unfortunate *Circle of Two*, with sixteen-year-old Tatum O'Neal, and *Lovespell* (a film adaptation of *Tristan and Iseult*). He still hoped to play King Lear, the great Shakespearean role, and made plans with Alexander Cohen for the production. However, he didn't have the stamina for the eight-week run necessary to make a profit, so the production was canceled.

Through it all, Burton stayed sober, with Suzy Hunt watching over him, though at times he felt she watched over him too much, even to the point of reading his scripts and deciding which films he should make. She made some terrible choices, fueling the widely held belief that Burton had sold out his talent just to make a few bucks: *The Medusa Touch*, *Absolution*, *Breakthrough*, *Circle of Two*. Suzy fussed over Richard, combing and recombing his hair; she made sure the entourage stayed away; and she took over their duties, one by one, further isolating him. John Springer, Ron Berkeley, even his new agent Robbie Lantz found themselves out in the cold. Richard felt hemmed in, treated like an old man, something Elizabeth would have never done. Suzy was unhappy, too, whenever she ran up against the many reminders of Richard's former life with Elizabeth. While making *Ab-*

solution in 1980, they vacationed in Puerto Vallarta, which had by now become a bustling resort town. They ended up buying a villa, even though the reminders of Elizabeth were everywhere, such as a welcoming sign proclaiming THE MOST BEAUTIFUL PLACE IN THE WORLD, WHERE ONE OF THE MOST FAMOUS COUPLES FOUND LOVE.

In July of 1980, Burton was asked to appear in a revival of *Camelot*, for $60,000 a week, in a twelve-month American tour. It was a sentimental journey, not only for Richard but for the audiences that flocked to see him, still fascinated by the actor's past and his fabled marriage to Elizabeth. The play began its run in Toronto before coming to New York. When Suzy saw a picture of Elizabeth and Richard together, smiling, in a souvenir program being sold in Toronto's O'Keefe Center, she became incensed. "I want it out!" she said, so a small army of theater employees stayed up all night cutting the offending photograph out of the program. Another strain on the couple was that Suzy didn't know any of the boldface names who came to see Richard in the play and toasted him afterward. At a party thrown by the Kissingers, Richard had to explain to Suzy, sotto voce, who each of the notables were—that's Joe Alsop, famous political writer, that's William F. Buckley, that's Happy Rockefeller, Nelson's wife ("and very *un*-happy," he noted, after her husband died in the arms of another woman).

In New York for the opening of *Camelot*, Suzy was bothered wherever they went, as they were stared at and scrutinized. Basically a shy woman, Suzy couldn't get used to strangers examining her hair, her jewelry, her makeup, even following her into public restrooms to try to get a more intimate look. She didn't have Elizabeth's ability to remain private—to lower the veil—in public.

A pinched nerve in Richard's neck, and his old, persistent injuries, began to cause him considerable pain once the tour began. He found he couldn't use his right arm, and Suzy had to do all his packing for him, which he considered emasculating. King Arthur was a particularly strenuous role to begin with, in which he had to project to audiences in the thousands in giant amphitheaters, brandish a sword, and sing. He longed for "the panacea of a drink" ("A double ice-cold vodka martini, the glass fogged with condensation, straight up and then straight down and the warm food of painkiller hitting the stomach and then the brain and an hour of sweetly melancholy euphoria. I shall have a Tab instead. Disgusting," he complained.) He took painkillers for the pinched nerve, which made him nauseous, sometimes having to run backstage between scenes to vomit.

Shortly after opening night in New York, Richard seemed to lurch around the stage. Someone suddenly yelled from the audience, "Give him another drink!" The curtain was brought down and an understudy replaced Burton; hundreds of audience members angrily walked out of the theater. But Richard had not been drunk. He had taken a glass or two of wine with his old friend Richard Harris, who'd replaced him years ago in the film adaptation of *Camelot* when Richard had declined the role. The wine had mixed badly with the prescription painkiller he was taking.

Perhaps as a way to reassure the public that he was still very much in control of his faculties, Burton appeared on *The Dick Cavett Show* on four successive nights, where indeed he was witty, looked well, and comported himself with dignity and charm. For the rest of the tour, his performances were met with standing ovations. In fact, certain songs affected the public in strange and powerful ways. One man in the audience offered the cast $1,000 if they would just reprise the last scene of the play. When he sang "How to Handle a Woman," there wasn't a dry eye in the house, as audiences assumed he was, in his heart, dedicating the song to Elizabeth. In fact, there were rumors that she was in the audience during the show's run in New Orleans, and that Richard had, indeed, sung the song to her.

But the pain was finally too much for him, exacerbated by doing eight performances a week. He was down to 140 pounds, from 175. When the tour reached the West Coast, he collapsed after a show and was once again taken to St. John's Hospital in Santa Monica, on March

26, 1981, the very place that had saved his life seven years earlier, detoxifying him from alcohol. There, he underwent a risky surgery, a cervical laminectomy, on his neck. He was warned that the operation could leave him in even more pain. He was so desperate, however, that he took the risk. But the warning proved true: he was left in worse condition, in continuous pain. Richard had to drop out of the rest of the run of *Camelot*, and, as before, Richard Harris replaced him as King Arthur.

Suzy tried to nurse him back to health, but it wasn't pretty. Richard was hospitalized again on October 7, for a perforated ulcer. He was a bitter invalid, in constant pain, and abusive to Suzy. He hated his own behavior but could do nothing about it. She finally left, and on February 20, 1982, they announced their separation. In the ensuing divorce settlement, she ended up with the house in Puerto Vallarta and $1 million. He didn't blame her; it had all been too much for Suzy. But Elizabeth could have handled it.

In 1982, Burton took on the last of his "great men" roles, playing the august German composer Richard Wagner for an eight-hour television series directed by Tony Palmer and filmed in Vienna. Burton was not in good shape, smoking four to five packs of cigarettes a day, and beginning to drink heavily again. The mild epilepsy that had once been kept at bay, ironically, by alcohol, had now returned, and he suffered occasional seizures. For *Wagner*, he reunited with three of the greatest actors of the English stage—his heroes, his friends, and his bêtes noires Sir John Gielgud, Sir Ralph Richardson, and Sir Laurence Olivier. John, Ralph, and Larry. The only one at the table without a knighthood was Richard. He was supposed to have been their heir, "the greatest stage actor of his generation," but now Burton no longer had the stamina to play the tormented king of Shakespeare's greatest tragedy; he wondered if he would have the physical strength to carry Cordelia across the stage in her death scene.

Each of the four veteran actors took turns hosting dinner parties for the cast. Burton's was the last, given at the famous Palais Schwarzenberg in Vienna. Also present were director Tony Palmer and the great cinematographer Vittorio Storaro. It was a splendid evening of storytelling and mimicry and good humor, with Richard avoiding the wine sitting in front of him. Finally, he reached for a glass, and started drinking. The transformation was like Dr. Jekyll and Mr. Hyde. Richard turned on the "three knights" with uncharacteristic viciousness, Tony Palmer recalled. He called Olivier "a grotesque exaggeration of an actor. All technique. No true emotion." Gielgud was next, and Burton made snide remarks about his homosexuality (a sad and curious insult to the man with whom he had probably had an affair thirty-two years earlier). And he told Sir Ralph that his fabled timing was really just a result of poor memory, a "darting about" to read his lines from cue cards. The three old actors stared at him in silence. Despite shaking their heads over him throughout the years, as Burton had reeled from one terrible movie after another, they had always admired, even loved him. Afterward, Palmer recalled, Richard berated himself, moaning, "Oh, God, oh, God, I've gone too far!"

In December 1981, Elizabeth separated from John Warner, and Richard would finalize his separation from Suzy Hunt three months later. Those two marriages, Liz Smith believed, had been "big 'fuck-yous' to each other. Suzy Hunt was everything Elizabeth was not—tall, thin, and blond. And John Warner was this handsome, sober, distinguished, ex-navy secretary who became a senator. It was a continuous game of one-upmanship." But those marriages had been necessary. Burton had needed someone to help keep him sober and return him to a quieter life. Elizabeth's four years with Warner, in which she had relished living in a country estate and helping to get him elected to office, ended up showing her what she had always needed: a chance to perform, and an audience who could not get enough of her. The republic of her fans had never been a burden to Elizabeth—she had always connected with them, and like true royalty, she reigned because of their devotion.

Rumors of a possible reunion started flying again when Taylor came to London with *The Little Foxes* and Burton flew in from Vienna on a break from filming *Wagner*, to appear onstage in a reading of *Under Milk Wood*. Liz Smith thought at the time, "she'll have to get him back, because Richard couldn't resist the allure of Elizabeth."

Nine months earlier, on May 7, 1981, *The Little Foxes* had opened in New York for six months of sold-out performances, then toured New Orleans, Los Angeles, and now London. It was the first time the play had been performed on Broadway since Tallulah Bankhead had starred as the scheming, duplicitous Southern lady, Regina Giddens, in 1939. (The play's author, Lillian Hellman, had a fit when she learned that Elizabeth—whom she insisted on calling "Lizzie"—would take on the juicy role.) Despite a two-week bronchial infection, Elizabeth managed to perform in 123 sold-out performances. Mike Nichols had been concerned that she didn't have the vocal equipment to project onstage, but she proved everybody wrong. Though some critics sniffed, Elizabeth was nominated for a Tony Award.

So, on February 27, 1982, Elizabeth celebrated her fiftieth birthday in a gala celebration at London's Legends nightclub, hosted by Zev Bufman, a fifty-two-year-old Israeli producer who coproduced *The Little Foxes* with Elizabeth, and with whom she'd formed a theatrical production company, The Elizabeth Theatre Group. The guest list numbered 120, including international celebrities like Rudolf Nureyev as well as Elizabeth's children, Liza and newly married Maria Burton Carson, and Senator Warner's two daughters, Mary and Virginia. That night, Elizabeth looked wonderfully well—slim, triumphant.

Newly separated from John Warner, she arrived at the party arm-in-arm with Richard Burton.

They danced together that night, billed and cooed, and Richard drove her back in his Daimler to her rented townhouse at 22 Cheyne

Walk, in Chelsea. She invited him inside, and Burton laughed when he saw that she'd had the house redecorated, all in lavender. They talked together, as they had over the last four years over the phone, about their children: Maria, who had grown up to be tall, coltish, and beautiful; their grandchildren—on her side, not yet on his. And brilliant, bilingual Kate, who had graduated Brown University with a degree in international relations, but who decided to go into the family business, after all, and had enrolled in the Yale School of Drama. And the beguiling, boisterous Wilding brothers, Michael and Christopher, who finally seemed to be finding their way, to Burton's great relief.

The press was ecstatic to welcome back the two ex-lovers, and much speculation was given to their obvious delight in being in each other's company again. They missed "Liz and Dick," who made much sexier copy than Mrs. John Warner and the clean-living Burton.

The following night, Richard revisited his favorite Dylan Thomas radio play, *Under Milk Wood*, at a public reading at the Duke of York Theatre to raise funds for a memorial stone for the author in Westminster Abbey's Poets' Corner. Unbeknown to Richard, while he was reciting to a rapt audience, Elizabeth quietly entered the theater and slipped onto the stage, standing behind him. The audience was thrilled at the sight of her, and Burton wondered what the excitement was all about. Wearing jeans and a loose sweater, she suddenly upstaged him by curtsying and throwing a kiss to the standing-room-only audience. She then whispered to Richard, in perfect Welsh, "I love you."

"Say it again, once more, my petal. Say it louder," Burton answered.

Elizabeth, now addressing the audience, repeated the words: *"Rwy'n dy garu di."*

It brought down the house. Flustered, Burton lost his place in the text and apologized to the audience. It took a lot to knock this old pro off his pins, but Elizabeth had done just that. In the theater that night was a young Irish actor, Gabriel Byrne. It was, recalled Byrne, "the most unforgettable thing, perhaps the most theatrical moment I'd ever seen on a stage. I never forgot it."

Afterward, Richard took Elizabeth to dinner at the Garrick Club, a famous watering hole for theater people. The liveried waiters served Jack Daniel's on the rocks to Elizabeth and poured two double vodkas for Richard. He then drove her to her leased town house in her chocolate-colored Rolls-Royce, a gift to Elizabeth from Zev Bufman.

When they arrived, the couple was greeted, as usual, by Elizabeth's entourage. This time Burton took a stand and ordered them to leave. "Get out," he shouted, and they all scattered to other parts of the house.

Elizabeth took a long look at Richard and said, "Hey, Buster. You're thin. Aren't you going to kiss me?" Burton took her in his arms and kissed her.

"I can't believe it all happened with us," she whispered.

He stayed the night.

The next few nights, the couple were seen around town, and Burton seemed newly smitten by Elizabeth. He told one reporter, "Elizabeth and I are destined to get back together again. I can't live without her. I love the woman." He even penned a little poem on a napkin: "I know a lady sweet and shy,/Oft have I seen her passing by,/Beguile my heart I know not why,/And yet I love her 'til I die." But—still ambivalent—he told another reporter, "I couldn't take it with Elizabeth anymore. I am involved with her as an ex-wife and mother, and as a legend. She's a dear, sweet, wonderful legend—and a little bitch." Elizabeth was more guarded, or perhaps more coy, in her comments to the press: "I have had no contact with him and don't intend to. He is a figure of the past."

Yet it was Elizabeth who would find a way to bring them back together. Not as Elizabeth and Richard, but as "Liz and Dick."

Buoyed by the success of *The Little Foxes*, Elizabeth had looked for a play she could appear in with Richard by her side. She considered

Tennessee Williams's *Sweet Bird of Youth*, about an aging actress who takes up with a young lover, with the telling line, "There's nowhere to go when you retire from movies, except oblivion." But it wouldn't suit her purposes. "I knew the role of the fading Southern belle would suit me," she later observed, but there was no role for Richard, who "was too old for Chance," the young drifter played by Paul Newman in the film adaptation of the play. She settled on that delightful old chestnut for fading movie stars, *Private Lives*, by Noël Coward, who had always wanted them to take on the roles of Amanda and Elyot, the ex-married lovers who rediscover each other just after marrying other people. Noël Coward had written the play as a vehicle for himself and his favorite actress, Gertrude Lawrence. He'd knocked it out in four days while recovering from the flu in Shanghai.

It was a kind of siren call to Richard, who was already planning to do more theatrical productions, such as Eugene O'Neill's *Long Day's Journey into Night*, and as ever, he still hoped to take on *Lear*. Richard— sober and looking fit, if a bit thin—flew to Elizabeth's home in Bel Air to discuss the production. She offered him $70,000 a week for what would turn out to be a seven-month tour. Burton accepted.

For the first time in eight years, Burton returned to writing his diary, where he put down his trepidations about taking on the part. He was anxious about reuniting with Elizabeth in such a public way. He knew what he was getting into—the crucible of public attention and the frenzy of renown that followed her, and thus him, everywhere she went. Though he had mentioned to the press that they might get back together, he wasn't really sure it was a good idea. Part of him wanted to be with Elizabeth again, but he was apprehensive. Over the phone, Burton discussed the idea with Gielgud, who seemed to have forgiven him his earlier, intemperate remarks.

Sir John counseled against it. "You're not really going to do *Private Lives*, are you?"

"I expect Elizabeth will make me do it," Burton answered.

So Elizabeth and Richard announced their plans to reunite in a tour of *Private Lives* at a press conference at the Beverly Hills Hotel on September 23, 1982. The next morning, the newspapers got it right: "The Liz and Dick Show" was back in business. There was no backing out now, especially when the play was announced in the *New York Times* with an ad showing an enormous heart with an arrow through it, and the words: "Together Again." Elizabeth had always been a genius about publicity. "I'm ready for Nouveau York," she proclaimed.

They began rehearsals on the second week of March 1983, in the Lunt-Fontanne Theatre on West 46th Street, where Richard had triumphed in *Hamlet* a lifetime ago. Elizabeth moved into Rock Hudson's apartment in the Beresford on West 81st Street, with stunning views of Central Park. Burton checked into the Lombardy. The next day, Maria dropped by Burton's hotel with her new baby, and they went to visit Elizabeth in the Beresford. It was a happy family reunion. Burton looked around Rock Hudson's apartment and noticed—with a sneer, no doubt—that there wasn't one single book in the place.

Burton was still on the wagon, but John Cullum, who played the discarded spouse Victor Prynne in the four-character play, and who had been Laertes to Richard's Hamlet, was alarmed at how fragile Burton looked when he showed up for rehearsals. "He'd lost all the weight in his torso," Cullum recalled. "His voice was the same, but he didn't have the strength that he'd had, because he was always so virile. But he put himself through it." Cullum thought the whole experience was surreal. "It was a weird company," he said. "Let me tell you. She was the boss." Elizabeth later demurred, "Believe me, I've had the tact not to point out to Richard that now he's my employee," but Richard was well aware of it.

Burton recorded his frustration with trying to work with Elizabeth, who had gone back to her old bad habits. "E. . . . drinking. Also, has not yet read the play! That's my girl! . . . This is going to be a long seven months." But by March 27, something clicked and Elizabeth suddenly pulled it all together and "was tremendously better"; "for the first [time] I enjoyed rehearsals," Burton recorded.

Cullum also found it difficult to rehearse with Elizabeth, mostly because she didn't really want to rehearse. As an actress, Cullum believes, "Elizabeth was a natural. She was one of the most skillful film actresses you'd ever met. She just didn't have very much stage experience. For instance, when I first met with her, I suggested we run through the lines; she didn't want to do that, because I think her attitude was, it would take the edge off the performance. That's okay for film, but if you have to get jacked up for every performance, it's gonna kill you."

Cullum noticed, too, how Elizabeth couldn't handle certain lines during rehearsals. When she was having trouble with a reference to a hotel in Deauville on the French Riviera, "Richard started laughing, and Elizabeth just blew up and screamed, 'What in the hell are you laughing about, you silly ass!' And he said, 'Darling, we *stayed* at that hotel for over two months!' All the places in *Private Lives*—they had lived them."

The play opened in Boston on April 13, 1983, to a sold-out run, standing ovations, and three curtain calls for Elizabeth. Burton gave Elizabeth a long kiss at the end of the evening, and the audience went wild. Their entry into Boston via Logan Airport had been a reprise of their *Hamlet* tour, with large crowds greeting them, many waving copies of Kitty Kelley's scathing biography of Elizabeth, *The Last Star*, for Elizabeth to autograph.

The opening in New York on May 9, 1983, "was a circus," Brook Williams recalled. Crowds filled the streets around the theater, waiting for a sight of Elizabeth, who showed up with her pet parrot on her shoulder, which she kept in her dressing room and later took to bringing onstage with her in the final scene. The curtain of the Lunt-Fontanne Theatre was raised thirty-five minutes late, and the first intermission lasted longer than the entire first act.

Burton seethed backstage—he was the most punctual of actors; he hated to be late; he was a Spartan about things like that no matter what condition he was in at the time. He fumed in his dressing room (where he'd hung the Welsh flag on one of its red felt walls). Elizabeth was sober—she never touched a drop before the show—as she got ready in her lavender dressing room, complete with shirred chintz curtains, lavender towels, silk flowers, and a hundred-gallon aquarium. (Their specially redesigned dressing rooms were so spectacular that they were featured in *Architectural Digest*.) "Elizabeth would be there, chatting away, getting her makeup on, five to ten minutes before curtain," Cullum recalled, "and Richard would just be beside himself!" Brook Williams served Richard tea and made small talk, trying to calm him down.

"This just proves it," Burton complained to Brook. "I can never get together with that woman again." Elizabeth took so long to do her makeup, he started insisting that she be made up at her apartment before coming to the theater. (She often ended up doing it in the limousine on the way over.)

Despite first-night problems, the sold-out house rose to their feet and gave Elizabeth and Richard five curtain calls. Every opening night on the tour would be like that as the production headed west: Philadelphia, Washington, Chicago, Los Angeles. But what became clear from that first night was that audiences were cheering "The Liz and Dick Show" more than Noël Coward's witty play.

"They had lived *Private Lives*," Cullum realized, "and that's why it didn't work. It was a caricature." It was supposed to be a drawing-room comedy, not a parody, but there were too many parallels, just as there had been in *Cleopatra*, *The V.I.P.s*, *The Sandpiper*, *The Taming of the Shrew*, *Boom!*, *Divorce His Divorce Hers*. But now the parallels weren't dramatic; they were comic. The audience knew the public life behind the drama of *Private Lives*, so their repartee had a triple-entendre effect.

First of all, Elyot's new wife is named Sibyl (played by Charlotte Moore, who replaced Kathryn Walker). Lines like Amanda's "Poor

Sibyl. . . . I suppose she loves you terribly" and Elyot's "Not as much as all that. She didn't have a chance to get really underway" announced that the play was really all about Elizabeth and Richard.

When Elizabeth/Amanda tells Richard/Elyot, "Eight years all told, we've loved each other. Three married and five divorced," it just ran too close to the truth. And when Richard tells Elizabeth that she has "No sense of glamour. No sense of glamour at all," the audience guffawed. Elizabeth's line "I feel rather scared of marriage, really" brought another huge laugh and that weird feeling of being in a parallel universe. When Elizabeth asked, "How long will it last, this ludicrous, overbearing love of ours? . . . Shall we always want to bicker and fight?" Richard answered, "No, that desire will fade, along with our passion."

More truths were told, in the guise of Amanda and Elyot. Elizabeth: "I believe it was just the fact of our being married, and clamped together publicly, that wrecked us before."

Richard: "That, and not knowing how to manage each other."

Elizabeth: "Do you think we know how to manage each other now?" The audience's heads were spinning. When Elizabeth said, "This week's been very successful," looking out over the full house, "Liz and Dick" merged completely with Amanda and Elyot.

Though audiences lapped it up, paying $45 for the best seats, the reviews were the worst either had ever received in their long careers. The critics—not quite ready to embrace camp when they saw it—hooted and jeered. Frank Rich in the *New York Times* called it "a calculated business venture," a "trashily amusing old-time burlesque stunt," in which "Miss Taylor and Mr. Burton look whipped and depressed." He noted that Burton seemed "robotic" (he could barely move his arms and shoulders without pain). At one point, Burton/Elyot tweaks Elizabeth/Amanda's breast (or honks it, as one playgoer recalled), but does so, Frank Rich thought, with "the clinical detachment of a physician who's examined too many patients in one day."

James Brady compared Elizabeth's acting to "the Hitler Diaries—you don't believe it, but you gotta look." The *Christian Science Monitor* lamented, "They have become one word: Liz'n'Dick . . . condemned to be Antony and Cleopatra in an endless sequel of daily life . . . Their flight to personal freedom two decades ago has turned them into a kind of public slavery. They have become our dancing bears with permanent iron collars on their necks." *Variety* cruelly wrote, "*The Dance of Death* would have been a more appropriate choice." *People* magazine noted the play by running a tongue-in-cheek dictionary entry for "Lizandick":

> **LIZANDICK** ('liz n 'dik) *n. pl.* [contemporary usage fr. Liz and Dick, often followed by exclamation point, i.e., *Lizandick!*] 1. Archaic. Mythic American actress and Welsh actor whose names were eternally coupled despite their celebrated uncoupling(s). 2. Aging and ever expanding histrionic duo whose sum is greater than their individual parts, and whose mutual moves are perpetually played out in public (Did you hear that ~ started a limited-run revival of Noël Coward's *Private Lives* in Boston last week?) 3. Any pair of people who come together, split, come together, split, until they seem to make a profession of it or until their acquaintances move past empathy to ennui.

Elizabeth tried to avoid reading the reviews, but it was impossible. The *Boston Globe* notice brought her to tears ("a caricature of a Coward heroine, inside a caricature of an actress, inside a caricature of [Elizabeth] Taylor"). Cullum saw that "she was hurt, and she didn't quite understand why they were so vicious. But she was a trouper. You had to admire her, because they said awful things, and the delight with which they attacked a person who was so famous and so wonderful! They were enjoying it." The bad notices shortened the New York run of the play by several weeks, yet Elizabeth and Richard soldiered on. The *New York Post* screamed, "Liz & Dick: Damn the critics, full speed ahead!" and "It's Liz & Dick vs. the Critics."

In fact, the press had never had it so good. They were reliving their salad days as well, feasting on speculation over whether the couple would reunite, devoting whole columns to the phenomenon of "Liz and Dick." *New York Times* columnist Russell Baker got into the act, as did the *Daily News*'s Jimmy Breslin, who met Burton at the Lombardy for an interview. They discussed the actor's well-known battles with alcohol. "I wouldn't have missed any of it for the world," he said. "I have to think hard to name an interesting man who didn't drink." Burton also mentioned how appalled he was with the trend he'd noticed in New York restaurants to order just a small glass of white wine in lieu of real drinking. "When the hell did that start?" he asked Breslin, himself a two-fisted drinker. " . . . [T]he other night I heard a man say, 'I'll have a vodka martini straight up.' I turned to [him] and said, 'Well done. You're having a proper drink.' "

One night, Elizabeth and Richard went to Sardi's after the show, and Richard proceeded to give her notes on her performance. They both started drinking heavily. "It didn't take much to get Richard off the wagon," Cullum observed. "In any case, the next night, Elizabeth didn't show up, so he had to go on with the understudy. Richard was incensed. And she didn't show up on Thursday, and on the Friday and Saturday, he had to play two shows with the understudy. She was quite good, but he didn't contract to play with anybody else. And he knew that Elizabeth was ticked off because of the notes he'd given her. So he got more and more angry . . . And sure enough, Monday morning, which was our day off, he said he would not play anymore with the understudy. And he disappeared."

A few days later, the headlines read, "Richard Burton Marries."

Richard had flown to Las Vegas with his young assistant, Sally Hay, checking into the $1,000-a-night bridal suite of the Frontier Hotel. On July 3, 1983, he married Sally—a thirty-four-year-old Australian woman he'd met in Vienna on the set of *Wagner*. She had been the continuity girl on the production, and the two had become close during the seven-month shoot. She was slim, light-haired, intelligent, and gentle in manner—more like Sybil than Elizabeth. She even bore a noticeable physical resemblance to Sybil and to Kate. She was able to provide for Richard what he most needed at the time—companionship and attention to his health and comfort. She even traveled with a spoonlike instrument in her handbag that could be slipped into Richard's mouth to prevent him from biting his tongue during the epileptic seizures that occasionally recurred.

"She can do everything," Richard confided in Brook Williams, who was now with him constantly. "She can cook, type, do shorthand, there's nothing she can't do. She looks after me so well. Thank God I found her, Brookie." In his diaries, though, he would refer to her as "lovely Sally" or "sexy Sally" or "undo-without-able Sally," so the relationship wasn't merely one of care and comfort.

So Sally had stayed on after *Wagner*, and had moved in with Richard, and had accompanied him to New York. Elizabeth was not happy about it, but when he disappeared for three days and came back married to Sally, she was incensed.

"I think Richard really tried to get out of that contract then," Cullum recalled. "He just didn't like to be in a show that wasn't working." Cullum, too, tried to get out of his contract. In one scene with Elizabeth, Cullum realized that nobody in the audience was watching him. "I would look at the audience, and I could see they were just *riveted* to her. They couldn't believe that they were really up there—icons who had become alive. Richard was so powerful onstage, he could hold the stage with anyone. But he didn't really care—it bothered him that he had to work for her and she was the boss. At least that's the impression I got."

Elizabeth put on a brave face and even hosted a party, in Philadelphia, for the newly married couple. But after Burton's marriage to Sally, Elizabeth didn't seem to care anymore. "I began to crack," she later admitted. "My worst habits surfaced. I began overeating, drinking, and taking pills. The minute the curtain went down, Jack Daniel's was waiting for me in the wings."

Her weight gain was noticeable and many critics gleefully pointed it out. It was painful for Kathryn Walker, playing Sibyl, to see Elizabeth looking at herself in the mirror before going on and asking, "Do I really look fat?" She was "hurt, very hurt," Kathryn recalled, "and now they're throwing her to the lions, the way she's being directed. I don't know why she can't stand up to them."

But she did stand up to their director, Milton Katselas, who was brought in from Los Angeles, where he was an acting teacher and something of a guru. Cullum, who had worked with him years earlier, remembered that the director "came in almost professorial, talking about 'the humor and the comedy of Noël Coward.' It didn't take long for even me to figure out that he had just discovered him, and he was talking to Richard and Elizabeth, who *knew* Noël Coward and had spent a lot of time with him." Katselas was sent packing and was replaced with another director.

In private moments during rehearsals, Elizabeth had whispered to Richard how lonely she was, despite the attentions of her coproducer Zev Bufman, and Victor Gonzales Luna, a courtly, divorced Mexican lawyer and father of four, whom Elizabeth had met the previous year. Stung by Burton's defection after all the speculations in the press about a reunion, Elizabeth announced her sudden engagement to Luna. A photograph ran in the *Post* of the two couples at a party at the Café Royal in Philadelphia: Richard and Sally, Victor and Elizabeth, who gamely showed off her 16.5-carat engagement ring from Luna.

But all the joy had gone out of the tour for Elizabeth. "It became a twenty-four-hour nightmare," she later said. "It didn't matter that we didn't get good reviews. We still played to packed houses. No one was coming to see the English drawing-room comedy anyway. Everyone bought tickets to watch high-camp 'Liz and Dick.' And we gave them what they wanted." Elizabeth desperately wanted to stop the show, "to put an end to this torture," but they had contracts to fulfill.

Richard had had enough as well. While he was in Boston, he had received a phone call from John Huston, who wanted him to play the alcoholic but eloquent consul in Malcolm Lowry's powerful novel, *Under the Volcano*. It was a role especially well suited to Burton, that of a brilliant mind unraveling as his marriage falls apart. But Burton knew immediately that he would not be able to get out of his contract, and the part ultimately revived the flagging career of another great actor from the United Kingdom, Albert Finney.

Elyot was also proving a physically demanding role for the fifty-seven-year-old actor. Sally noticed with alarm that Richard was taking a beating during the playful pillow fight and love-play onstage. "She would just grab at him or throw her whole weight on him," Sally observed. "I could see the spasms of pain as he braced himself—just where he had that terrible operation." Some nights he would come offstage bleeding and Sally would have to reapply his makeup. While she cleaned him up, Richard would say, "That's our girl. She'll surprise us all."

The production limped to its conclusion in Los Angeles. Liz Smith reported on one of the last performances there, in the Wilshire Theatre, before it closed on November 6. She wrote, "The Liz 'n' Dick Show . . . known officially as *Private Lives*, is now mercifully just a memory. And what a memory!" By now, however, Elizabeth had pulled out all the stops. "They stepped on each other's lines," the columnist wrote. "They stepped on each other's feet. They camped, cornballed and generally carried on like mad things. Miz Liz . . . really let loose—winking, mugging, tossing breakfast rolls across the footlights. Needless to say, the audience LOVED her!"

What Liz Smith had seen, perhaps, and the other critics had not, was that Elizabeth had finally embraced her new role of queen of camp. She had always loved the big show—Mike Todd had taught her that—the spectacular entrance, the opulent furs, the eye-popping diamonds, fabulousness for the sake of fabulousness. She loved it, she celebrated it, she understood it. And perhaps the biggest reason why she and Burton could no longer be together onstage, was that, by now, Richard was tragedy and Elizabeth was comedy. Elizabeth realized it herself, saying at the time, "When we were able to be Richard and Elizabeth, the marriage worked beautifully. It's Liz and Dick that didn't work, because they were two people who didn't really exist." But now it was all they had left.

Privately, Elizabeth was not doing well. Audiences were surprised when they saw how much weight she'd put back on. She was taking so much medication, and drinking so heavily, that even her old friend and physician, Dr. Kenemer, refused to treat her any longer. In December, the ordeal of *Private Lives* finally over, she collapsed and was rushed to Cedars-Sinai hospital in Los Angeles, in physical pain from colitis but mostly "awash in self-pity and self-disgust," chasing down painkillers with Jack Daniel's. Victor Luna visited her in the hospital, but it was clear that their marriage plans weren't going anywhere.

Her old friend Roddy McDowall, along with her brother Howard and three of her grown children, Michael, Christopher, and Liza, all confronted her in the hospital. On December 5, 1983, they checked her into the Betty Ford Center in Rancho Mirage, near Palm Springs, for detoxification from drugs and alcohol. She shocked the world as the first celebrity to openly check into the now-famous treatment center, and Betty Ford herself, the former first lady and the clinic's founder, was Elizabeth's personal sponsor. Elizabeth announced that she had sought treatment for addiction, beating the tabloids to the punch. Burton would fight most of his life against admitting his alcoholism, yet Elizabeth, far more able to face hard truths, told the world.

After seven weeks of therapy and spartan living, Elizabeth emerged from the clinic, sober and eleven pounds lighter. When Burton, back in Céligny with Sally, saw a photograph of Elizabeth, newly transformed and looking radiant, he called to tell her how great she looked. He wanted to see her again. She was still his greatest pleasure, Burton admitted to his brother Graham Jenkins one evening in July at the Dorchester, when he was in London filming *1984*, his last movie.

"We've never really split up," he told Graham, "and I guess we never will." Elizabeth, still with Victor Luna, began dividing her time between a new home she'd purchased in Bel Air and her beloved chalet in Gstaad. At one point, they met up with Richard and Sally in a London pub, and Richard was gob-smacked at how preternaturally beautiful Elizabeth looked—uncommonly slim and radiant. But mostly they kept in touch through frequent phone calls. For a man who spent his whole life avoiding the telephone, he loved it when it was Elizabeth's voice at the other end. Sometimes they would discuss new projects they could do together, or tease each other, or revisit the past. "The bond between them seemed to defy all efforts, including their own, to make a clean break," Graham believed.

Then, in one long phone call from Céligny late in the summer of 1984, Richard did something he had never done before in his talks with Elizabeth. After hoping to meet again, either in London or in Gstaad or in Céligny, he uncharacteristically ended his call with, "Good-bye, love."

For Elizabeth, it had an eerie sound of finality to it, though neither she nor Richard knew that they would never see each other again.

EPILOGUE

"Richard and I lived life to the fullest,
but we also paid our dues."
—ELIZABETH TAYLOR

"You never get to be a great actor until you're dead."
—RICHARD BURTON

He was like an old wounded lion," the director Michael Radford recalled about filming Richard Burton in his adaptation of George Orwell's political novel *1984*. Burton was fifty-eight at the time, but he appeared to Radford "an old man. I got the impression that he just couldn't wait to die, that life had seeped out of him in some kind of strange way. What was important for him in his life had gone. I thought that he was dying while he was making the film."

He had not been their first choice to play O'Brien, the coldblooded party official who tortures Winston Smith in Orwell's novel. Unlike his time with Elizabeth, when he was everyone's first choice, when movies like *The V.I.P.s* were created specially for them, Burton was fourth on the list. The producers had first offered the role to his old rival Paul Scofield, but Scofield had broken his leg before filming began. They then offered the part to another ghost of Richard's past, the powerful actor Rod Steiger, a one-time husband of Claire Bloom, whom Richard had once loved. But Steiger had just had a face-lift, and it had not gone well. "We got a telegram from his agent," Radford recalled, "saying 'Mr. Steiger's face-lift has fallen.'" So they next offered $80,000 to Marlon Brando, but his agent told them, "Mr. Brando does not get out of bed for less than $1 million."

"Our producer, Simon Perry, said, 'He's given up serious acting then, has he?' That was the end of Marlon Brando," Radford remembered. They had to begin the fourteen-week shoot without an O'Brien, wary about hiring Burton, because they'd heard he was still drinking. Desperate, they finally approached him with the offer, sending the script by helicopter to Haiti, where he and Sally had bought property, just as he had with Suzy Hunt a few years before. He felt it was the only place he could live where he wasn't recognized on the street.

"He said yes, he loved the script, he got on a plane, he came to the set, and he said to me, 'I know I'm not the first choice, Michael, but I'll do my best.'" Radford was surprised that Richard and Sally turned up without an entourage, except for Brook Williams. And he was surprised to find Burton completely sober.

"He didn't drink at all during the making of *1984*," recalled Radford. "He really didn't." But Radford had his suspicions about Brook Williams, whom he described as having a "drinker's complexion. You know, purple nose and the cheeks with veins in them. He would be on set all the time, and he would bring these cans of Diet Coke, already opened, to Richard. Inevitably, there was an air of suspicion around the set that they were laced with vodka." Richard would often ask his director, "Would you like a drink, Michael?" Radford would take a little sip to see if it had any vodka in it. "That was the unwritten pantomime that went on, but Richard was absolutely sober, as was John Hurt," the intense English actor who played Winston Smith in the film, who also, at the time, had a reputation for heavy drinking.

Part of what made Burton seem so frail was the fact that he no longer had full use of his arms. One hand shook so much that Radford had to employ an extra just to grip Burton's hand and to help him lift up his arms. Whether it was the result of the beating he'd received years ago at Paddington Station, or the unsuccessful operation he'd had on his neck, or alcohol-deadened nerves, he was now like Faustus at the end of Marlowe's play, unable to lift his arms in prayer as Mephistopheles and Lucifer hold them down at his side.

"The other thing is," Radford believed, "his famous memory was actually gone. So, he was like a real old rep actor. And he had some long speeches to do. Suddenly, he'd go, 'I'm sorry, did somebody speak?'" Radford thought he might even have suffered a small stroke.

And yet, Burton gave one of the most powerful performances of his life in the brief but intense role of O'Brien, Winston's inquisitor and tormentor. Radford thought Burton was actually the most amazing actor he'd ever worked with. "Richard had that thing which Al Pacino has," Radford noticed, "which is that some way or another, he brings up the standard of everybody around him. He had a phenomenal presence on the set. He wasn't really interested in the psychology of the character. He was hopeless with props—none of this Marlon Brando stuff. He had this physical presence, but he also had this amazing voice. That was what held you."

His body of little use to him now, Burton was acting entirely with his eyes and his voice. It was as if his lifetime of triumphs and excesses, of joy and grief, had been distilled into a pure, pitiless performance. Like King Lear, the part that finally eluded him, the only thing left was self-knowledge. "It was gripping, really," Radford reminisced. "I'm so pleased that he was the guy I chose in the end. What I tried to do was get a sort of intimate performance out of him. I think I did."

Throughout filming, in an odd way, Elizabeth Taylor still haunted Richard's life. Three women turned up at the gates of the studio, all claiming to be Elizabeth—none of them looking remotely like her—and asking to see Richard Burton. Radford noticed that Richard and Sally seemed devoted to each other, but Richard often talked about Elizabeth in front of his wife in a way that must have been painful for her.

After *1984*, there would be one more role for Richard, in a tele-vision mini-series called *Ellis Island*, about the lives of European immigrants at the turn of the century. It was fitting that his last role would be as a father, as Burton took the part just so he could appear with his daughter Kate, now twenty-six and a successful actress. It was a last chance for a kind of reconciliation with the daughter he felt he had neglected, and who had once stood up to him, saying she would never see him again if he didn't stop drinking. Now he was sober. Two weeks after finishing *1984*, he was on a soundstage with Kate, where he watched her scenes with immense pride. Kate never felt closer to her father. At lunches on the set, or in Burton's trailer between scenes, he talked to her, she recalled, "about his childhood, his shame about some of the parts he'd been in, his shame over the drinking." They even discussed doing another film project together sometime in the future, but neither knew that for Burton, the future was now only a matter of weeks.

In Céligny, Richard's twilight life was decidedly quiet. He and Sally would rise around nine a.m., have tea, go into town for shopping and to have lunch. "He discussed many things with me," Sally later recalled. Once, when they were talking about his life with Elizabeth, he turned to her and said, "Did I really do all that? Did I really do the jewelry, the yacht, the plane? Did I do that?"

In early August, they got word that John Hurt was in Switzer-land, working on another film. He drove from Geneva to Céligny to have dinner with the Burtons. He stayed in the guest cottage, and the next morning they sat talking for a few hours. Burton seemed world-weary. John Hurt remembered thinking that Richard was still in the grip of an obsession with Elizabeth, and that it would never be over. Burton whispered to Hurt, *sotto voce* so Sally wouldn't overhear, "She still fascinates, you know." He had said the same thing to his brother Graham Jenkins on a visit three weeks earlier in London, at the Dorchester, during the filming of *Ellis Island*.

Burton had been sober for a long time now, but on Friday, August 3, 1984, the two friends went out drinking. Sally wasn't there—she had gone to the Café de la Gare that night. They found a comfortable bar with a soccer game on the television. Gianni Bozzacchi, the photographer who grew to love Richard Burton, tells a strange tale of what happened that night. According to Bozzacchi, Burton had words with another drinking patron. No one remembers what was said, but Richard was pushed and his head hit the floor. In the Swiss summer darkness, the scuffle spilled out into the street, but Richard couldn't lift up his arms to defend himself, just as his father couldn't defend himself, years ago, when his burned arms were strapped to his side and he was beaten bloody outside of the Miners Arms.

Bystanders wanted to take Richard to the hospital, but he refused. He was too used to having his every move reported, photographed, and broadcast around the world. He would go home instead, he insisted upon it.

The next day, August 4, Sally drove John Hurt back to his hotel in Geneva. Brook Williams was absent as well. When Sally returned, Richard complained of an excruciating headache, so she gave him some aspirin and he took to his bed around ten p.m. The next morning, Sally found him breathing with difficulty. She called the doctor, who arrived in twenty minutes, but didn't find anything particularly alarming. Nonetheless, Sally had him taken to the local hospital in Nyon, where they discovered something was terribly wrong. They sped him to Geneva, where doctors found that Burton had suffered a massive cerebral hemorrhage. Though they worked furiously to try to save him, Richard Burton died on the operating table. He was fifty-eight.

His death, Sally later said, "was a tragedy for us, but not for Richard. My feeling was that Richard had many lives in him, but not that of an old man." In fact, if the final operation had saved Burton's life, it would probably have left him paralyzed, wheelchair-bound, like his brother Ifor, and—even more terrifying—without the ability to speak.

To Burton, who loved language above all else, that would have been intolerable. He had long been celebrated for his voice, described by one film critic as "chorded and powerful, yet also famously musical. It was the outer edge of his authority and his fears." Burton himself had once described "the Welsh voice" as "the deep, dark answer from the valleys, to everybody."

Back home in Céligny, Sally found next to Richard's bed a few lines of Shakespearean verse he'd written down in red ink just before his cerebral hemorrhage:

> The multitudinous seas incarnadine,
> Making the green one red. . . .
> Tomorrow and tomorrow and tomorrow . . .
> Our revels now are ended. . . .

And then an unfinished line: *"Cap a pi . . ."*

Bozzacchi is alone in his belief that Richard was beaten the night before his death. There is no police report, and to this day, John Hurt won't talk about his last twenty-four hours with Richard Burton. In any event, he was gone.

Richard Burton's death was announced and made headlines around the world, and Sally made plans for his burial. Her first problem was how to handle Elizabeth Taylor. Her mere presence at Burton's funeral could turn the solemn event into a media circus, which Sally hoped to avoid. So Elizabeth was not invited.

By now, Elizabeth had left Gstaad and was back in Los Angeles. When she received the news of Richard's death, she fainted. Later, she would say, "I was still madly in love with him the day he died. I think he still loved me, too. I thought he'd always be there, at the other end of the phone. Even if we weren't together, I knew he was still in the world." She realized that she "would never hear his voice again, or see his face, his eyes . . . if I hadn't been to Betty Ford before his death, I don't think I'd be around. I loved him for twenty-five years."

Once she recovered, she called Sally, who told her to please stay away from the funeral in Céligny, where Richard was to be buried. Elizabeth did so, though their children attended the service: Michael, Christopher, Liza, Maria, Kate. They, too, had loved Richard and had called him father.

On August 11, 1984, a memorial service was held for Richard Burton in Pontrhydyfen. Again, Elizabeth was not invited. Five hundred people were in attendance, raising their voices in Welsh song. At the last minute, Sally relented and called Elizabeth to invite her to the memorial, but the invitation came within twenty-four hours of the service, so Elizabeth couldn't make it in time.

When Elizabeth finally arrived in Céligny on August 14, to visit Burton's grave, she found that Sally had been right all along—the paparazzi were lying in wait for her.

They were camped out at the gravesite, waiting for Elizabeth. She arrived at the ancient churchyard at dawn, with Liza and four bodyguards, in a gray Mercedes. She found her way to Richard's grave, so quiet that she could hear the sounds of a mountain river nearby. Suddenly, a phalanx of reporters and photographers ran toward her from behind tombstones and burial plots, their flashbulbs popping like mad in the dismal morning light. Her bodyguards opened bright umbrellas to shield Elizabeth from the horde and to give her some privacy, as she knelt at Richard's grave. The next morning, however, she managed to elude the press and return to the grave one more time. She would describe that visit "as one of the few occasions ever that Richard and I were alone."

Two days later, Elizabeth went to Pontrhydyfen to visit Richard's family. Richard would have been furious, because she was late. She arrived wearing the Krupp diamond, Richard's gift to her. Graham Jenkins picked her up at the airport and drove her to Hilda and Dai

Owens' house. When she arrived, the family assembled at Hilda's raised their voice in the Welsh song "We'll Keep a Welcome in the Hillside." Elizabeth was touched and told them all—Richard's Welsh family—that she felt she had come home. That night she slept in Hilda's humble front room, but she really felt like "the Princess of Pontrhydyfen," as Richard had once called her. When she left the next morning, she'd asked for a memento of Richard, a painting by his brother Verdun of the house Richard had been born in. It was his last present to her.

There would be one more memorial service for Burton, and this one Taylor was invited to (though Sally objected to her being seated with the family). Organized and presided over by Robert Hardy for fourteen hundred of Richard's friends, family, and colleagues, it was held at the St. Martin-in-the-Fields Church, Trafalgar Square in London, on August 30, 1984. When Elizabeth arrived for the magnificent service, dressed in black and wearing a black turban, all eyes were upon her as she took her place next to Cecilia, the woman who had been Richard's sister and his mother, his adored "Cis," the prototype for all the women he'd ever loved. Elizabeth, solemn and dignified, seemed to Hardy to be "a queen in mourning."

"What to do about Elizabeth" had been the topic of discussion in Céligny and Wales after Richard's death, but Elizabeth had always known what to do. She returned to Los Angeles, determined to get on with her life. She broke off her halfhearted engagement to Victor Luna. She turned down all offers to talk publicly about Richard Burton. The press had already written what they'd wanted about "Liz and Dick." After all, the Burtons had once made marriage seem glamorous—even dangerous. Even Larry King, years later, couldn't get Elizabeth Taylor to talk about Richard Burton. Elizabeth told the talk show host, "Those are *my* memories."

She would write two more books, *Elizabeth Takes Off (On Weight Gain, Weight Loss, Self-Image, and Self-Esteem)*, and *Elizabeth Taylor, My Love Affair with Jewelry.* Burton had always wanted to write and publish books, but except for a handful of published articles and two brief autobiographical works, no book was finished. He'd tried a novel, unfinished and unpublished, but it would turn out that the book he'd meant to write—the rich, deep, detailed story of his life—existed in his hundreds of pages of diary entries, notes for a novel never finished, but complete and revealing in themselves.

Elizabeth had starred in one more feature film before Richard's death, an Agatha Christie mystery called *The Mirror Crack'd*, in 1980, appearing with a number of aging, former A-list Hollywood actors: Kim Novak, Tony Curtis, and her dear friend Rock Hudson. When Hudson died in 1985 from the mysterious illness that was plaguing gay men at the time, Acquired Immune Deficiency Syndrome, Elizabeth mourned the wasting away of her once strapping costar in *Giant*. She was devastated by his death, and by the fact that he had tried to hide the nature of his illness, just as he had always had to hide his homosexuality in an era and a profession that wouldn't allow him to be who he was. Furious about the way the Reagan administration and her own industry were ignoring the pandemic, Elizabeth was determined to confront the disease that so many were dying from. She became the public spokeswoman for AIDS research, raising millions of dollars to develop a cure and treatment, and to change the public attitude about the disease and toward homosexuality itself. By 1992, she had done more to raise awareness of AIDS than any other American. When people were afraid of being in the same room with AIDS patients, Elizabeth often visited them at a hospital in Los Angeles. During one such visit, she delighted the patients by climbing into bed with a man being treated for AIDS. She said to the astonished fellow, "It's the perfect relationship! I don't want to get married again, and you're probably not interested in me." They cheered and applauded her for that. Richard would have been proud of her, and, in fact, she later said that her interest in AIDS research sprang in part from his hemophilia, and his shame over his early same-sex dalliances.

In 1988, after a relapse of prescription drug abuse, she returned to the Betty Ford Clinic. There she met a fellow patient, a tall, good-looking construction worker and former trucker named Larry Fortensky. Reader, she married him.

After fourteen years without a feature film, Elizabeth would next appear in a cameo role in the comedy *The Flintstones*, as Pearl Slaghoople, Fred Flintstone's shrewish, bejeweled mother-in-law. She would do a number of movies for television, finally appearing in Tennessee Williams's *Sweet Bird of Youth* in 1989 and in *These Old Broads* in 2001, mostly as a favor to her old friend and former "rival," Debbie Reynolds. She would discover that she really did have a head for business, launching two perfumes—Passion and White Diamonds—which would earn her more money than she had ever made in her film career. At $200 per ounce, Elizabeth Taylor's Passion was among the best-selling perfumes in America by the mid-1990s, making Elizabeth one of the richest women in the country.

Over the decades, many of her film performances have been reassessed, even those trapped in bad movies. The films of her European period bear a second look—she's genuinely moving in *Secret Ceremony*, for example, as the haunted mother of a drowned child. Her performances in her best films—*A Place in the Sun, Giant, BUtterfield 8, Cat on a Hot Tin Roof, Suddenly, Last Summer, Who's Afraid of Virginia Woolf?*—are now seen as exemplars of great movie acting. Burton knew what he was talking about when he called her "the greatest film actress in the world."

In 1998, there was one small coda to *Le Scandale* brought about by the death of Elizabeth's treasured friend, Roddy McDowall. The former child actor had known Elizabeth for fifty-six years, and had taken some of the most beautiful photographs of her. He had acted with Elizabeth in *Lassie Come Home*, he had acted with Richard in *Camelot,* and had been in Rome with Elizabeth and Richard in *Cleopatra*. As McDowall lay dying in his home in Studio City, California, sitting at his bedside were Elizabeth Taylor and Sybil Burton Christopher. He had been loyal to them both. Thirty-four years after *Cleopatra*, the old rivalry between the women no longer mattered.

In the 1980s, Elizabeth had famously befriended another cultural icon, the strangely boyish Michael Jackson. She felt a kinship with him, as both had been denied true childhoods, yet at the same time had been able to indulge their childish whims well into adulthood. She appreciated his genius as a performer, especially as she knew how shy and insecure he was at heart—not unlike Richard. And, like Richard, Michael Jackson scorned his physical appearance. Elizabeth was touched when the troubled star told her that his favorite role of Elizabeth's had been Helen Burns, the little orphan in *Jane Eyre* whose long, beautiful hair is shorn by Brocklehurst, the sadistic head of the orphanage. "You know, of all of my films, that was Michael's favorite," she reminisced.

She married Larry Fortensky in 1991 at Jackson's Neverland Ranch in California. But her marriage to Fortensky—her eighth, if you count Richard twice—lasted less than four years. She would later say, "After Richard, the men in my life were just there to hold the coat, to open the door. All the men after Richard were really just company." Elizabeth always considered herself married to Burton and has never changed the stipulation in her will that she be buried beside him.

In 2007, Elizabeth made perhaps her last appearance in a play when she performed A. R. Gurney's *Love Letters* with James Earl Jones at Paramount Studios. It was a charity performance to raise funds for mobile AIDS units, and when she was wheeled onstage, as she now often relies on a wheelchair, she was met by a standing ovation. Liz Smith was there, and she was as impressed as the audience was by Taylor's moving performance in a play that chronicles a long, loving relationship through the exchange of letters. Liz Smith noticed that if the crowd cheered her on her entrance "for her history and courage," by the end of the play, their standing ovation was for Elizabeth, the actress.

But then again, Elizabeth knew something about love letters. She received her last one in Bel Air. Richard had mailed it on August 2, 1984, so it arrived a few days after his death. It was waiting for Elizabeth when she returned from London, after attending Richard's memorial service there. It was his final letter to her, the one he had slipped away to write in his study at Céligny, surrounded by his books. It was a love letter to Elizabeth, and in it he told her what he wanted. Home was where Elizabeth was, and he wanted to come home.

She's kept that letter by her bedside ever since.

ACKNOWLEDGMENTS

F irst of all, we must thank Dame Elizabeth, whom "Age cannot wither, not custom stale," as Shakespeare described Cleopatra, Queen of the Nile.

When we first embarked on this venture, we happened to mention our proposed book on "the Taylor-Burton romance" to a young theater major who had recently graduated from college. Her response stunned us: "I never knew Elizabeth Taylor was married to Tim Burton!" It also stunned Dame Elizabeth when the story was told to her. Concerned that Richard Burton's name and legacy were in danger of being forgotten, she agreed to work with us, behind the scenes as it were, by making available a trove of some forty letters and notes written to her by Richard Burton. She also allowed us to see parts of her 1965 autobiography, *Elizabeth Taylor*, that she had suppressed for fear that they might hurt various people or disappoint her fans. As she has always refused to speak publicly about her affair with and marriage to Richard, we feel that this book is the closest we'll come to her thoughts and feelings on the "great love and tumultuous passion," in Burton's words, that first shook the world in 1962.

We must also express our gratitude to those closest to Elizabeth Taylor. We are respecting their wishes to remain unnamed, but their help and encouragement truly made this book possible. We salute your generosity of spirit, your insights, your wisdom, your impeccable hospitality.

We also want to thank Sally Hay Burton, Richard's widow, for her continued graciousness and many kindnesses to us. We are truly grateful for her permission to quote from Burton's published and unpublished works, including his diaries, letters, two poems, and several short stories and essays : "A Christmas Story," "Meeting Mrs. Jenkins," and "Traveling with Elizabeth." We also thank Elisabeth Bennett, archivist at the Swansea University Library, for her advice and guidance, and Melvyn Bragg, for his masterful life of Richard Burton and for permission, through Sally Hay Burton, to quote from Burton's diaries published in *Rich: The Life of Richard Burton*.

We also extend our thanks to Kate Burton, who gave us her blessing, and to many who met with us and allowed themselves to be interviewed, including those who helped us during the research and writing of "A First Class Affair," an article about the making of the Burtons' second film together, *The V.I.P.s*, which originally appeared in *Vanity Fair* magazine. They are Gianni Bozzacchi, Sally Burton, Gabriel Byrne, Linda Christianson, John Cullum, Denis Ferrara, David Frost, Henry Grossman, Robert "Tim" Hardy, John Heyman, Waris Hussein, Gavin Lambert, Brenda Maddox, Christopher Mankiewicz, Keith McDermott, Peter Medak, Mike Nichols, Tony Palmer, Liz Smith, Victor Spinetti, Richard L. Sterne, Rod Taylor, Gore Vidal, Elisabeth Woodthorpe, Michael York, and Franco Zeffirelli.

A particularly deep bow to the most gracious of men, Graydon Carter, for the pleasure of his friendship and the privilege of working for him at *Vanity Fair*; the incomparable Doug Stumpf, patient friend and editor nonpareil at *Vanity Fair*; and his indispensable editorial assistant, Christopher Bateman. To Ann Schneider, high priestess of photography at *Vanity Fair* and for this book, our deep admiration for your grace under pressure. To Chris Garrett, David Friend, and Beth Kseniak at *Vanity Fair*, for their wisdom and many kindness.

To our friend Dick Guttmann, who makes all things possible, we are forever in your debt.

Finally, where would we be without our indefatigable agents, Justin Manask in Hollywood and David Kuhn in New York, as well as David's able assistant, Billy Kingsland? Or our brilliant researcher, Eva Burch, and our transcriber, the poet Richard Lucyshyn? And our deepest gratitude to our editor, Rakesh Satyal, who brought his own considerable gifts to our effort, and to Jonathan Burnham, publisher of HarperCollins and a true prince of the city. Our book would have been much diminished without their enthusiasm and encouragement. It was a privilege to work with HarperCollins.

"I don't care what you write about me," Dame Elizabeth told us. "God knows, I've heard it all, just as long as you honor Richard." We hope that in telling their story, we have honored them both.

TWO POEMS BY RICHARD BURTON[*]

Sally Hay Burton discovered these two poems among Richard Burton's papers after his death. The untitled poem is a nostalgic farewell to Wales, written in a style influenced by his friend and countryman Dylan Thomas. "Portrait of a Man Drowning" was apparently written in November of 1965, while Burton was filming the bleak, Cold-War era film, *The Spy Who Came in from the Cold*. Neither poem has been published before now.

The mountain earth feels damp against my hand;
Around me sway a thousand sap-filled stalks
Of tender grass; The cows browse drowsily
Below me in the fields, and silly sheep
Bleat so pathetically. Dusk descends
And makes the cool earth cooler; lovers slow
In Sunday best drift past like ghosts of laughs
And murmurings; and some go up and some
Go down the mountain.

* published with permission of Sally Hay Burton

I see the gamblers hide behind some hedge or shade,
And play silently between dexterity
Of toil's blunt fingers shuffling dirty cards;
And panting greyhounds run a merry race around them
In the fading light.
There is no life stir now
There is no hub-bub of activity;
The rushing of the whispering waterfall
Breathes silence on the mad tormented valley.
The voices rise insidiously as is
The creeping dusk. "Abide with me," they moan,
A hundred coal-fogged voices harmoniously
Goad up in an ecstasy of melancholy magic;
All is still.
And there were things that made me;
Grew around the core of my young soul,
But I have other worlds for whom to weep;
I shall return no more.

—RICHARD BURTON

"PORTRAIT OF A MAN DROWNING"

Who can he be
That man alone in the saloon bar's corner?
Who can he be
That man alone, solitary, musing.
Remembering
What can he be?

The shoulders hunched.
The face pocked, rived and valleyed

With a lifetime's small tragedies.
The slanting mirror on the wall
Emblemed in Coope and Alsop
Reflecting his receding hair,
His thick shoulders,
His silent simian hirsute hands.

What is, what was the weight that sloped
Those hunching shoulders?
That man alone, solitary musing. Thinking
Of what can he be.
Nothing?

Or does he live again the nightmare
Of all the same he suffered and made others to suffer,
The torn promise, the shattered word,
His red hand caught in the emotional till,
The things he had never done and never would do now,
Lost lovely things. The hopeless things long lost,
The hot blush of childhood lies,
Love and hate and fear and love again and hate
And the ultimate terrible ineluctable wrath of God.
Does he hear the silent howl of death?

Hunched, solitary, silent.
That man alone in the saloon bar's corner
That man alone, solitary, musing,
Who can he be?
I lift my eyes from the bitter pint.
I see that man in the mirror.
That man is me.

—RICHARD BURTON, NOVEMBER 5, 1965

ENDNOTES

PREFACE

vii "I am forever punished . . .": Undated letter from Richard Burton, B-T Archive.

vii "Since I was a little girl . . .": Elizabeth Taylor, *Elizabeth Takes Off* (New York: G. P. Putnam and Sons, 1987), 83.

vii "the most vivid example . . .": Authors' interview with Liz Smith and Denis Ferrara.

viii "On the face of it . . .": Ibid.

ix "My blind eyes are desperately . . .": Undated letter from Burton, B-T Archive.

ix "Richard was magnificent . . .": Private letter to authors from Elizabeth Taylor.

CHAPTER 1: *LE SCANDALE*

1 "I did not want to be another notch . . .": Elizabeth Taylor with Richard Meryman, *Elizabeth Taylor* (New York: Harper & Row, 1965), original manuscript.

1 "How did I know the woman . . .": Paul Ferris, *Richard Burton* (New York: Coward, McCann & Geoghegan, 1981), 153.

1 "swank house. . . . It had been a hell of a year . . ." Burton notebooks, Melvin Bragg, *Rich, The Life of Richard Burton* (London: Hodder & Stoughton, 1988), 89.

2 "the most astonishingly self-contained . . .": Graham Jenkins, *Richard Burton, My Brother* (New York: Harper & Row, 1988), 5.

3 "I was so totally chaperoned . . .": Taylor, *Elizabeth Taylor*, 68.

3 "You and your studio . . .": Ibid., 16.

4 "When I met Nicky . . .": Elizabeth Taylor, *Elizabeth Taken Off* (New York: Berkley Books, 1987), 64

4 "Hey, Mac, get out of the way . . .": Lester David and Jhan Robbins, *Richard & Elizabeth* (New York: Funk & Wagnalls, 1977), 85.

5 "Todd's living up to his legend . . .": S. J. Perelman, *Don't Tread on Me* (New York: Viking Penguin, Inc., 1987), 172.

6   "Go on, hit me . . .": Donald Spoto, *Elizabeth Taylor* (London: Time Warner Book Group, 1995), 126.

7   "She's as wistful . . .": Oscar Levant, *The Memoirs of an Amnesiac* (New York: G.P. Putnam's Sons, 1965), 282.

7   "She was a woman who loved . . ." Eddie Fisher, *Been There, Done That* (New York: Thomas Dunne Books, 1999), 152.

8   "Blood Thirsty Widow . . .": Elizabeth Taylor clipping file, Academy of Motion Picture Arts and Sciences.

8   "Mike is dead and I'm alive!": David and Robbins, 99.

9   "Anyone who is against me . . .": Eddie Fisher, *Eddie: My Life, My Loves* (New York: Harper & Row,1981), photo insert.

9   "If Todd said steak medium rare . . .": David and Robbins, 98.

12 "I lost to a tracheotomy": Spoto, 247

13 "Don't do it.": Hume Cronyn, interviewed on DVD release of *Cleopatra*.

14 "I can be an actress or a woman . . ." Joe Mankiewicz, *All About Eve*.

14 "Why couldn't they let me . . .": David and Robbins, 68.

15 "small expenses": Ruth Waterbury, *Richard Burton, His Intimate Story* (New York: Pyramid Books, 1965), 107.

17 "tried homosexuality . . .": Burton's BBC Interview with Michael Parkinson, November 23, 1974, BFI Archive; Bragg, 258.

18 "rather full of himself," "cold fish eye": Taylor, *Elizabeth Taylor*, 103.

18 "a movie star but a genuine . . .": Ibid.

19 "a boxing poet": Emlyn Williams, interviewed in Tony Palmer's documentary, *Richard Burton: In from the Cold*.

19 "there was a lot of hemming . . .": Ferris, *Richard Burton*, 151.

19 "Has anybody ever told you . . .": Taylor, *Elizabeth Taylor*, 102.

19 "couldn't wait to go back . . .": Ibid.

19 "You're too fat": Waterbury, *Richard Burton, His Intimate Story* (New York: Pyramid Books, 1965), 112.

19 "so bloody marvelous": Ibid.

20 "He was kind of quivering . . .": Taylor, *Elizabeth Taylor*, 103.

20 "Joe, what's going on here?" to "not *doing* anything": Fisher, 205.

21 "who knows how much . . .": Fisher, *Been There, Done That*, 202–03.

21 "At some point after . . .": Fisher, *Eddie: My Life, My Loves*, 205.

21 "the busboy," Kitty Kelley, *Elizabeth Taylor: The Last Star* (New York: Dell Publishing, 1981), 199.

22 "I must don my armor once more . . .": Bragg, 145.

23 "Print it . . . Would you two mind . . .": Waterbury, 115.

23 "I am Isis . . . I am the Nile . . .": Joseph Mankiewicz, *Cleopatra*.

23 "Mike Todd . . .": Kelley, 201.

23 "From that first instant . . .": Mankiewicz.

23 "To have waited so long . . .": Ibid.

24 "Elizabeth was not used to . . .": Jenkins, 123.

24 "Even if he hadn't destroyed . . .": Fisher, *Been There, Done That*, 205.

25 "I adore this man . . .": Taylor, *Elizabeth Taylor*, 104.

26 "I lust after your smell . . .": Letter from Richard Burton, B-T Archive.

26 "Tell me the truth . . .": Fisher, *Been There*, 207.

26 "Elizabeth, who do you love?" anecdote: Ibid., 210.

27 "Eddie broke the cardinal rule . . .": Authors' interview with John Heyman.

27 "Ever since Richard and I . . .": Fisher, *Eddie: My Life, My Loves*, 211.

27 "What are you doing there?": C. David Heymann, *Liz: An Intimate Biography of Elizabeth Taylor* (Secaucus, New Jersey: Citadel Stars, 1996), 249.

27 "Elizabeth and Burton are not just *playing* . . .": Spoto, 264.

28 "incredibly patient and well informed . . .": Walter Wanger and Joe Hyams, *My Life with Cleopatra* (New York: Bantam Books, 1963).

28 "It seemed like everybody who worked . . .": Taylor and Meryman, *Elizabeth Taylor*, original manuscript, Private Collection.

28 "We'd spend weekends there . . .": Ibid.

29 "I feel dreadful . . ." anecdote: Wanger, 128.

30 "We drank to the point of stupefaction": Burton notebooks, Bragg, 365–66.

31 "I think Burton had finally . . .": Wanger, 217.

31 "I was a very sick girl": Taylor, *Elizabeth Taylor*, original manuscript.

32 "Row Over Actor Ends Liz . . .": *Los Angeles Examiner*, Taylor clipping file, Academy.

32 "I knew it before she did": Fisher, *Been There*, 219.

32 "LIZ, EDDY DENY SPLIT": Ibid., 212.

32 "I was lost": Spoto, 272.

33 "Eddie Fisher Dumped": Fisher, *Been There*, 223.

33 "that marvelous voice": Ibid., 217.

33 "Don't worry, Elizabeth . . .": Taylor, *Elizabeth Taylor*, original manuscript.

CHAPTER 2: VERY IMPORTANT PEOPLE

35 "I was damned helpless . . .": Sam Kashner, "A First-Class Affair," *Vanity Fair*, July 2003, 148.

35 "Gstaad is a lonely place out of season": *Ladies' Home Journal*, November 1965, 151.

35 "Warren, do you think Elizabeth Taylor . . .": Kashner.

36 "Tried again to get Elizabeth": Wanger, 146.

36 "erotic vagrancy": Kitty Kelley, *Elizabeth Taylor: The Last Star* (New York: Dell Publishing, 1981), 217–18.

36 "Miss Taylor and Mr. Burton . . .": Spoto, 273.

36 "sick of being chased": Wanger, 143.

37 "It's lunatic. Bessie Mae": Patricia Bosworth, *Montgomery Clift* (New York: Simon & Schuster, 1994), 370.

37 "In a few weeks": Fisher, *Been There*, 217.

39   "Being pulled through that mob . . .": Taylor, *Elizabeth Taylor*, original manuscript.

39   "Leez, Leez! Baci, baci!": Taylor, *Elizabeth Taylor*, 112.

39   "After my last shot": Taylor, *Elizabeth Taylor*, original manuscript.

39   "We tried to stay away . . .": *Ladies' Home Journal*, October 1973.

40   "making too many people": Authors' conversation with Taylor.

40   "the most miserable day . . .": Elizabeth Taylor, *My Love Affair with Jewelry* (New York: Simon & Schuster, 2002), 111.

40   "I was dying inside . . .": David, 35.

41   "Richard and I arrived . . ." anecdote: *Ladies' Home Journal*, October 1973.

42   Sybil Burton's attempted suicide and "severely retarded": mentioned in several Taylor and Burton biographies, including Tyrone Steverson, *Richard Burton, A Bio-Bibliography* (Westport, Connecticut: Greenwood Press, 1992), 40.

42   "I loved Richard so much . . .": Taylor, *Elizabeth Taylor*, original manuscript.

43   "Let Sophia stay in Rome!": Kashner, *Vanity Fair*.

45   "nice little shop" anecdote: Taylor, *Jewelry*, 56, 59, 63.

47   aware that Mankiewicz blamed . . .: Taylor, *Elizabeth Taylor*, original manuscript.

48   "arrogant hair . . . Imagine having . . .": Ibid.

48   "it left him with . . .": Authors' interview with Robert Hardy, August 23, 2007.

49   "She came from the valleys . . .": Ibid.

50   "One just hoped . . .": Ibid.

50   "show up for wardrobe fittings": Kashner, *Vanity Fair*, 141.

51   "He was one haunted boy-o": Ibid.

51   "The family wasn't happy . . . married to both women.": Ibid., 145.

52   "At her best, she was . . .": Interview with Hardy.

52   "the boozing was prodigious . . .": Bragg, 166.

52   "The drink was the problem": Kashner, *Vanity Fair*, 145.

53   "I know nothing about . . .": Bragg, 167.

53   "Everybody was extremely . . . after lunch—look out!": Kashner, 149–150.

54   "Richard loses his temper": *Ladies' Home Journal*, November 1965.

54   "I think the effect Burton had": Fisher, *Eddie: My Life*, 215.

54   "Mike [Todd] was a bit of a madman," Taylor, *Elizabeth Takes Off*, 71.

54   "my little Jewish tart . . . it was foreplay to them": Kashner, 150.

55   "You couldn't have been . . .": Ibid., 146.

56   "I was caught off-balance . . .": Ibid., 148.

56   "Burton and Taylor in their public adultery . . .": Bragg, 164.

57   "less an actress than a great . . .": David and Robbins, 143.

57   "The mountain of notoriety . . ." and subsequent reviews: *Cleopatra* clipping file, Academy of Motion Picture Arts and Sciences.

58   "She was the reverse . . .": Spoto, 268.

58   "wisely tried to ride it . . .": Bragg, 151.

58   "These were larger-than-life . . .": *Life*, April 1963, 63.

59   "Has it been his name . . ." and subsequent dialogue: Mankiewicz screenplay, *Cleopatra*, DVD.

59   "who stood always in Caesar's footsteps . . .": *Life*, 63.

59   "a masculine façade . . .": Ibid.

59   "who talks incessantly . . .": Kenneth Tynan's interview with Richard Burton, *Playboy*, September 1963.

60   "The ultimate desertion? . . .": Mankiewicz, *Cleopatra*, DVD.

CHAPTER 3: A YEAR IN THE SUN

61   "My father would never say . . .": Joseph Roddy, "Visit with Richard Burton," *LOOK*, January 28, 1964.

61   "Ever since I'd been ten . . .": Taylor, *Elizabeth Taylor* book excerpt, *Ladies' Home Journal*, November 1965.

62   "The happiest days . . .": Ibid., 15.

62   "National Velvet was really me": Kelley, 21.

63   "I will grow . . .": Ibid., 121.

63   "I worked harder . . .": Ibid.

64   "Oh, Elizabeth, darling . . .": Ibid., 23.

64   "I'm the son of a Welsh . . .": Kenneth Tynan, "*Playboy* Interview: Richard Burton," *Playboy*, September 1963.

65   "Which one?": John Cottrell and Fergus Cashin, *Richard Burton, Very Close Up* (Englewood Cliffs, New Jersey: Prentice-Hall, 1971), 6.

65   "The seven boys born to Dic . . .": Ibid.

65   "remarkable. Each and every one . . .": Authors' interview with Robert Hardy.

66   "To have Dadi Ni's boys . . .": David and Robbins, 26.

66   "I did it, even though . . .": Ibid.

65   "bridge over the ford . . .": Jenkins, 17.

65   "It was our parents . . .": Jenkins, 18.

66   "by dribbling [two] eggs . . .": Waterbury, *Richard Burton*, 16.

66   "Dic was a real sweet . . .": Cottrell, 8.

67   "the drinking was tremendous . . .": Ibid., 10.

67   Burned in a mine fire anecdote, Hilda Owen interviewed in Tony Palmer's *In from the Cold*.

68   "no ordinary woman . . .": Burton, *A Christmas Story* (London: Hoddard & Stoughton, 1964, 1989), 44.

68   "When my mother had died . . .": Ibid., 47.

68   "He was never smacked . . .": Jenkins, 21–22.

69   "quick to discover . . .": Ibid., 23.

69   "The chapel was our . . .": Ibid., 223.

69   "spoke the most perfect Welsh . . .": Hardy.

69   "a wild, breathy, passionate . . .": David, 27.

69   "The Welsh gift of language . . .": Cottrell, 11.

70 "the boy had spots": Jenkins, 31.

71 "Not having to act . . .": Ibid., 38.

71 "he had the rough good looks . . .": Ibid., 38.

72 "However often the advantages . . .": Ibid., 41.

73 "Burton's tragedy . . .": Joseph Mankiewicz interviewed, Palmer's *In from the Cold*.

73 " . . . a shrewd Welsh boy . . .": Kenneth Tynan, *Curtains* (New York: Athereum, 1961), 11–12.

75 "Before I met her . . .": Tynan interview, *Playboy*, and Hollis Alpert, *Burton* (New York: G. P. Putnam & Sons, 1986), 122.

75 "third-rate chorus girl": Kelley, 233.

77 "It's hard to believe . . .": Taylor, *Elizabeth Takes Off*, 74.

77 "like Never Never Land . . .": quoted in Lee Server, *Ava Gardner, Love Is Nothing* (New York: St. Martin's Press, 2006), 422.

77 "made equally unfit . . .": Ibid., 420.

78 "She wanted to be . . .": Jenkins, 142.

78 "You should be more careful . . .": Ibid., 143.

78 "When she left the room . . .": Ibid.

78 "In Mexico . . .": Ibid., 143–44.

79 "Get this maniac off . . .": Alpert, 133.

79 "there were more reporters . . .": John Huston, *An Open Book* (New York: Ballantine, 1981), 346–47.

79 "the great day when . . .": Ibid., 347.

80 "abandonment and cruel . . .": Kelley, 227.

80 "embarrassing her publicly": Ibid., 228.

81 "There is no more delectable . . .": Burton, "Dauntless Travellers," *Vogue*, October 15, 1971, 130.

82 "I used to spend all day": Kelley, 239.

82 "Richard lives each . . .": Axel Madsen, *John Huston* (Garden City, New York: Doubleday, 1978), 204.

83 "Everyone was drinking . . .": Server, 421.

83 "She can outdrink . . .": Kelley, 238.

83 "Richard, take a drink . . .": Ibid.

83 "with a few bottles . . .": Ibid., 239.

83 "sex, drinks, drugs, vice": Madsen, 206.

84 "a French tart": Kelley, 227.

84 "the street we live on . . .": "Dauntless Travellers," 130.

84 "the thrilling still music . . ." and anecdote, Ibid.

85 "We must have been . . .": Ibid.

86 "My father would never say . . ." and anecdote: Roddy, *LOOK*, January 28, 1964.

86 "Boys, our troubles . . .": Ibid.

98 "loved my shape . . .": conversation with Taylor.

98 "Where I was wrong," Jenkins, 143–44.

CHAPTER 4: NO MORE MARRIAGES

89 "You're the one they've come to see . . .": Ferris, 177.

89 "I say we will have no more . . .": Alexander Walker, *The Life of Elizabeth Taylor* (New York: Grove Weidenfeld, 1990), 274.

89 "Mike and I hope to have . . .": Spoto, 188, and *Elizabeth Taylor by Elizabeth Taylor*, original manuscript.

90 "He was simply splendid . . .": quoted in Steverson, 58.

90 "I can never repay him . . .": Burton's televised interview with Michael Parkinson, November 23, 1974, BFI Archive.

90 "so the beauty of the language . . .": Steverson, 94.

91 "isolated, apart, in a world . . .": Burton's interview with Kenneth Tynan, 1967; *The Spy Who Came in from the Cold* DVD special materials.

91 "I do feel that on the stage . . .": Ibid.

91 losing a thumbnail: Authors' interview with John Cullum, August 4, 2009.

91 "I bleed more than Laertes . . .": *New York Times*, June 17, 1964.

92 "I've been a bleeder . . .": Ibid.

92 "the best seat at the restaurant . . .": Parkinson interview, BFI.

92 "had a kind of private veil . . .": Ibid.

93 "Drink not the wine . . .": Alpert, 137.

93 "Ghastly crowds of morons . . .": Sir John Gielgud, *A Life in Letters* (New York: Arcade Publishers, 2004), 305.

93 "Mostly, she stayed in . . .": Authors' interview with Richard L. Sterne, February 10, 2008.

93 "read with such enormous energy . . .": Ibid.

93 "He had an amazing . . .": Ibid.

93 "Is there such a thing . . .": Burton's interview with Parkinson, BFI Archive.

94 "It's the deep, dark answer . . .": Ibid.

94 "was very quiet . . .": Interview with Sterne.

94 "We shall be sold out . . .": Gielgud, 304–05.

94 "Richard adored Sir John . . .": Sterne.

94 "directors are relatively . . .": Tynan interview.

95 "an unmitigated disaster": *Toronto Daily Star*, Richard Burton clipping file, Academy of Motion Picture Arts and Sciences Library.

95 "magnificent . . .": *Toronto Telegram*, Academy Archive.

96 "The crew adore him": Gielgud, 306.

96 "treated everybody . . .": Sterne.

96 "There was one performance . . .": Ibid.

97 "The first time I played it . . .": Tynan interview.

97 "You never knew . . .": Sterne.

97 "couldn't keep their hands . . .": quoted in Bragg, 187.

97 "everybody wanted to be . . .": Cullum.

97   "Physically, Burton was magnetic . . .": Sterne.
97   "Richard belonged to . . .": Ibid.
98   "Richard is at his most agreeable . . .": Gielgud, 306.
98   "Richard was so energetic . . .": Sterne.
98   "There were six of us . . .": Ibid.
98   "He didn't like to be touched . . .": Ibid.
99   "Elizabeth was always there . . .": Ibid.
99   "She couldn't have been . . .": Ibid.
100   "Elizabeth Burton and I . . .": *Los Angeles Times*, March 16, 1964.
100   "I say, we will have . . .": Walker, 274.
100   "We thought there was going to be . . .": Sterne.
101   "shouting, clawing admirers": *Herald Examiner*, March 23, 1964.
101   "was being pulled . . . to this extent": Ibid.
101   "a theatrical experience": *Los Angeles Times*, March 26, 1964.
101   "poetry and passion . . . .": *Boston Herald*, March 26, 1964.
102   "one of the very few actors . . .": Hume Cronyn, *A Terrible Liar* (New York: William Morrow & Co., 1991), 330.
102   "was enveloped in . . . Dickenliz": Ibid., 356.
102   Taylor would attend . . . : Steverson, 83.
103   "a great roar . . . 'Fuck you—' " anecdote: Cronyn, 358.
103   "Mr. Burton is without feeling" and subsequent reviews: Steverson, 82–83.
104   "We could tell something . . .": Sterne.
104   "I was tearing along . . .": Bragg, 197–98.
105   "We have been playing . . .": David, 149.
105   "I had been asking him . . . carry any money" anecdote: Sterne.
106   "It was always hard for him . . .": Bragg, 198.
106   "If she doesn't get bad . . .": Ibid., 196.
107   "Her makeup smeared . . .": Fisher, *My Lives, My Loves*, 217.
107   "was reminded of that time . . .": Sterne.

CHAPTER 5: IN FROM THE COLD

109   "I love not being me . . .": Taylor quoted in Bragg, 192.
109   "how would you like to travel . . .": Burton, "Dauntless Travellers."
109   "professional itinerants": Ibid.
109   "Travelling with Elizabeth . . . we separate countries into foods": Ibid.
111   "a turbulent red wine . . . enchanting wife beside you": Ibid.
111   "How would you like to . . .": Ibid.
112   "the new Mr. Box Office": *Time* magazine, Burton clipping file.
113   "For the money, we will dance": Spoto, 300.
114   "From the Beginning, They Knew . . .": Movie poster advertisment for *The V.I.P.s.*
116   "one of the biggest homes . . .": Peter Bart, "Picture Painting and Passion," *New York Times*, September 1964.

116 "would have ended . . .": *Hollywood Reporter*, December 16, 1964.

116 "a special unveiling": *Hollywood Reporter*, January 1, 1964.

116 "soggy, woolly, maundering . . . silly movie" and "sense of sin": *New Yorker*, July 16, 1965.

116 "the mess of windy platitudes . . .": *Saturday Review*, July 24, 1965.

116 "nice, taut little drama . . . bungalow": *Variety*, October 15, 1971.

117 "any poor soul": *Saturday Review.*

118 "It was my betrayal . . .": Dalton Trumbo and Michael Wilson, *The Sandpiper*, DVD.

118 "men have been staring . . .": Ibid.

119 "an elderly governess . . . royal visit": Bragg, 192.

119 bring Jessica into their household: Authors' interview with Gianni Bozzacchi, March 21, 2009.

119 estimated $50 million: Bragg, 195.

120 "The Black Dog—": Authors' interview with Michael York, May 15, 2009.

120 *hiraeth* . . . "a longing for": Bragg, 199.

120 "a chemical imbalance": Ibid.

120 thirty-seven tailored suits: Cottrell, 292.

121 "even today I can remember . . .": Claire Bloom, *Leaving a Doll's House* (New York and Canada: Little, Brown & Co., 1996), 48.

121 "Burton, who had an encyclopedic . . .": Ibid., 45.

122 "I haven't looked at . . .": Ibid., 87.

122 "Richard was tender . . . have received": Ibid., 93.

123 shattered and humiliated: Steverson, 116.

123 "As Jimmy, he was able . . .": Bloom, 107.

124 "hadn't changed at all . . .": Bragg, 200.

124 "nervous, but all right": Ibid.

124 "Burton was in the ring . . .": Ibid., 120.

124 "Taylor was extremely upset . . . having me around": Bloom, 119.

124 "Like the spirit . . .": Ibid.

125 "not just Shakespeare . . ." quoted in Bragg, 201.

125 "I can't go to a pub anymore . . .": Spoto, 307.

125 "It was without doubt . . .": David, 293.

126 "It was like a fair here . . .": quoted in Bragg, 187.

127 "I wouldn't be here now . . .": Spoto, 306–07.

127 "He had a bottle of scotch . . ." anecdote: Bragg, 202.

128 "No one makes an entrance . . .": Burt Boyar, *Photographs*, 105.

128 "Richard? . . . Yes, darling?" anecdote: Bragg, 202.

129 "nervous all day worrying . . .": Burton notebooks entry, Bragg, 203.

129 "Went tramping with Michael . . .": Ibid.

130 "an independent tornado": Taylor, *Elizabeth Taylor*, 143.

130 "that lovely and loving Liza . . ." undated note from Richard Burton to Elizabeth Taylor, B-T Archive.

CHAPTER 6: WHO'S AFRAID OF ELIZABETH TAYLOR?

133 "I *am* George.": Kelley, 250.

133 "Let's face it—a lot of my life . . .": *Elizabeth Taylor* excerpt, *Ladies' Home Journal*, November 1965, 81.

134 "all dark brightness . . .": Andy Warhol and Pat Hackett, *Popism: The Warhol Sixties* (New York: Harvest Books, 1980), 144.

135 "A terrifying position . . .": Authors' interview with Robert Hardy.

136 "the girls . . . in Brooklyn . . .": Warhol, 36.

137 "She's discontent": Edward Albee, *Who's Afraid of Virginia Woolf?*, DVD.

138 "When I saw the lines . . .": Kelley, 246.

138 "taken an abiding dislike": Jenkins, 157.

138 "You've only to read the first lines . . .": Ibid., 158.

138 "You'd better play it . . .": Kelley, 246.

138 "looked all wrong . . ." anecdote: Ernie Lehman's notebooks excerpt published in *Talk*, April 2000.

139 "Ernie, I'd have done this . . .": Alpert, 154.

139 "You don't know anything . . .": Ibid., 156.

139 "Fuck him! . . . But you know . . .": Ibid.

140 "A movie is like a person . . .": Leslie Halliwell and John Walker, ed., *Halliwell's Who's Who in the Movies*, 15th edition (New York: HarperResource, 2003), 348.

140 "In fact, we later lost . . .": Kelley, 248.

141 "somebody knows what I like": Alpert, 166.

142 "was especially tough on her . . .": Kelley, 249.

142 "a little harmless hilarity": *Saturday Evening Post*, October 9, 1965.

142 "Fear no more the heat o' the sun . . .": Poem and anecdote, Ibid.

143 "a very disturbing man . . .": Ibid.

143 "You have to carry me . . .": Ibid.

143 "7/6/65 . . . A very exhilarating day . . .": Lehman notebooks, *Talk*.

144 "as much weight as she could . . ." anecdote: *Saturday Evening Post*.

144 "a bit nervous . . . giving her a little kiss": *Talk*.

144 "Darling, everyone is so fantastic!" anecdote: Authors' conversation with Elizabeth Taylor.

145 "Elizabeth loves to fight . . .": Alpert, 173, and Kelley, 251.

145 "It was very cathartic . . .": *Elizabeth Taylor*, original manuscript.

145 "I am just constantly surprised . . .": *Saturday Evening Post*.

146 "I don't run out screaming . . .": Ibid.

146 "Richard had black days . . .": Ibid., 172–73.

146 "I can't act tonight": Alpert, 172.

146 "Looking back now . . .": Ibid., 172.

146 "it took the form of being abusive . . .": Ibid., 173.

147   "She was constantly punching him": Kelley, 251.
147   "I *am* George. George is me.": Kelley, 250.
147   "as though I were George": Alpert, 171.
147   "I am the Earth Mother . . .": Albee, *Who's Afraid of Virginia Woolf?,* DVD.
148   "I'm loud . . . And I'm vulgar . . .": Ibid.
148   "Musical beds is the faculty sport . . .": Ibid.
149   "In a wretched part . . .": quoted in Steverson, 54.
149   "I never had a better time in my life": Taylor, *Elizabeth Taylor,* original manuscript.
150   "I'm paying her a million . . .": Kelley, 253.
150   " . . . buying her a baby wolf." anecdote: Lehman notebooks, *Talk.*
150   "I finally know what it feels like . . .": *Talk.*
151   "no one under the age of eighteen . . .": *Variety,* June 1, 1966.
151   gave the best performance . . .: Kelley, 259.
152   "a marvel of disciplined compassion . . .": *Newsweek,* July 4, 1966.
152   "heroic calm . . . Burton simply soars . . .": quoted in Kelley, 259–60.
153   "career had become only a way": *Ladies' Home Journal,* November 1965, 149.
154   "We've got to stop moving around . . .": Ibid., 152.
154   "No, we're terribly proud of you": Ibid., 154.
154   "a perverse tease! . . .": Ibid., 152.
154   "go into semiretirement . . . not to be pleased.": Ibid.
155   . . . once, for instance, on shipboard": Ibid., 154.

CHAPTER 7: MARRIED LOVE

157   "I can't say it in words . . .": Franco Zeffirelli, *Zeffirelli* (New York: Weidenfeld & Nicolson, 1986), 216.
157   "We live in a blaze of floodlights . . .": Bragg, 242.
157   "Monty has even more problems . . .": Patricia Bosworth, *Montgomery Clift* (New York: Bantam Books, 1979).
158   "Though we were linked romantically . . .": Taylor, *Elizabeth Takes Off,* 63.
158   "Monty, Elizabeth likes me . . .": Bosworth, 395.
158   "a phony actor": Ibid.
159   "If Monty doesn't work soon . . .": Ibid.
159   "she would pay . . .": Ibid., 396.
160   "the first person to take her seriously . . .": Bosworth, 395.
160   "The world is round, get over it": Conversation with Elizabeth Taylor.
161   "The truth is": Kelley, 274.
161   "Mabel" or "Mabes," "Lumpy," "Twit Twaddle," etc.: Letter from Richard Burton, B-T Archive.
161   "Well, they got an earful": Taylor, *Elizabeth Taylor,* 131.
162   "I think you should go . . .": Kelley, 277.
162   "Martha completely took me . . .": Taylor, *Elizabeth Taylor,* 158.
162   "There is no deodorant . . .": Ibid., 124.

162 "Richard and I are going . . .": Ibid., 127.
163 "more interested in illicit . . .": Ibid.
163 "Is Liz Legally Wed?": *Movie Mirror*, 1965, Elizabeth Taylor clipping file, Academy Library.
163 "Liz Confesses: Burton's Ruining Me . . .": *Photoplay* 1964, Ibid.
163 "Richard Burton to Liz: I Love . . .": *Saturday Evening Post, The Taming of the Shrew* clipping file, Ibid.
163 "Is that Maria's mother? . . . in that way" anecdote: Taylor, *Elizabeth Taylor*, 148–49.
164 "Elizabeth Taylor Seeks" and " . . . Slash Taxes as Briton": Elizabeth Taylor clipping file, Academy.
164 "I love America,": Taylor, Elizabeth Taylor, 128.
164 "The marriage . . .": *Life*, February 24, 1967.
165 "Will you please stop . . ." bush baby anecdote: Zeffirelli, 200–01.
166 "I wondered if I was going to . . .": Ibid., 212.
166 "a Hollywood baby . . . a rich sheik": Ibid., 212–13.
166 "We had invested $2 million . . .": Burton notebooks, Bragg, 212.
167 "four children, dogs, cats . . .": Cottrell, 301.
167 "Where are the bosoms?": Ibid.
168 "didn't give a damn": Zeffirelli, 214.
168 "It was all very Douglas Fairbanks . . .": Ibid.
168 "Why can't we take on one death-defying . . .": Jenkins, 162.
168 "Elizabeth was very shy . . .": Cottrell, 302.
169 "maids, secretaries, and butlers . . .": Michael York, *Accidentally on Purpose* (New York: Simon & Schuster, 1991), 132.
169 "[her] morning was given over . . .": Zeffirelli, 215.
169 "French hours" to "'one-shot Liz' . . .": Ibid.
170 "We'll have to start . . . ordinary lead one" anecdote: Victor Spinetti with Peter Rankin, *Victor Spinetti, Up Front* (London: Portico, 1998), 180.
170 "I never gaped at anybody . . .": Burton notebooks, Bragg, 213.
170 "Albee was very flattering . . .": Ibid.
171 "Wonderful! A bus trip" anecdote: Spinetti, 182–83.
171 "the exquisite softness . . .": undated note from Richard Burton to Elizabeth Taylor, B-T Archive.
171 "I would sometimes find . . .": York, 132, and authors' interview with York.
172 "Richard bringing Elizabeth . . ." to "They gave me my chance": Interview with York.
172 "That M. Nichols really gets . . .": Burton notebooks, Bragg, 212.
173 "one of the most brilliant . . .": Taylor, *Elizabeth Taylor*, 161.
173 "I'm not sure I like . . .": Burton notebooks, Bragg, 212.
173 "the Jews of Britain . . .": Brenda Maddox, *Who's Afraid of Elizabeth Taylor?* (New York: M. Evans, 1977), 181.
174 "During the war . . .": Taylor, *Elizabeth Taylor*, 90.

174   "My great-grandfather . . .": David, 148.

174   "I was born a Jew": *LOOK*, January 28, 1964.

174   "You're not Jewish . . .": David, 148.

174   "Dear Sheba": Burton's undated note to Taylor, B-T Archive.

175   "Isn't it awful to have to tolerate . . ." anecdote, Zeffirelli, 218.

175   "It was one of those moments . . .": Burton notebooks, Bragg, 227.

176   "Sept. 24. [Monty's] companion . . .": Ibid.

176   "Rest, perturbed spirit—": Kelley, 256.

176   "What do you think . . .": Jenkins, 155.

177   "What other young couple . . .": *LOOK*, October 1966.

177   "Between scenes . . .": Ibid.

178   "My real name, of course, is Richard Jenkins . . .": Cottrell, 309.

178   "holding their Welsh cocks": Ibid., 310.

179   "As soon as that bloody . . .": Ibid.

179   "They can take . . .": Ibid., 311.

179   "We were only sad . . .": Ibid., 309.

180   "We had as much . . ." to "Elizabeth was not displeased": Burton notebooks, Bragg.

181   "In one of her better performances . . .": Hollis Alpert, *Time*, March 17, 1967.

181   "his first whiskery kiss" to "one long honeymoon": Bragg, 227.

182   "Thy husband is thy lord . . .": William Shakespeare, *The Taming of the Shrew*, Act V, scene ii.

182   "played it straight": Zeffirelli, 216.

182   "deeply moved" to "my heart is there . . .": Ibid.

183   "E. very ill from that bloody . . ." and following entries: Burton notebooks, Bragg, 226.

183   "the whole huge thing": Bragg, 229.

CHAPTER 8: SEDUCED BY FAUST

188   "I am madly in love with her . . .": Burton notebooks, Bragg, 235.

185   "I'm just a broad . . .": Taylor, quoted in Spoto, 320.

186   "This boy . . . will be a great actor . . .": Michael Munn, *Richard Burton, Prince of Players* (London: JR Books, 2008), 35.

186   "I have had many students . . .": Cottell, back cover.

186   "bloody a few noses . . . was coming up": Burton interview, Palmer's *In from the Cold.*

186   "When he came to Oxford . . .": Robert Hardy, interviewed in Palmer's *In from the Cold.*

188   "I remember the shock of thrill . . .": Cottrell, 299.

188   "her slow walk . . .": Cottrell, 300.

188   "with thunder and slaughter . . . the undergraduate actors": Ibid., 299.

188   "To praise most cordially . . .": Ibid.

189 "Richard seemed to be . . .": quoted in Palmer, *In from the Cold.*

189 "Why me?": Ibid.

190 "wolfish grin" anecdote: Kenneth Tynan and John Lahr, ed., *The Notebooks of Kenneth Tynan* (New York and London: Bloomsbury, 2001), 415–16.

191 "Marlon's immorality . . .": Burton notebooks, Bragg, 223.

191 "tacit connection between . . .": Peter Manso, *Brando, The Biography* (New York: Hyperion, 1994), 631.

192 "everybody became sloshed . . .": Bragg, 223.

192 "Richard likes you . . .": *Hollywood Lawyers*, 105.

193 "supremely fine actress . . .": Huston, *An Open Book*, 373.

194 "nearly half of the U.S. film . . .": Cottrell, 314.

194 "They say we generate . . .": David, 165.

195 "Kate came to stay . . .": Burton notebooks, Bragg, 217.

196 "Oh don't worry . . ." Sir John Gielgud interview in Palmer's *In from the Cold.*

196 "I'm just a broad . . .": Taylor, quoted in Spoto, 320.

197 "I used to be considered . . .": Authors' interview with Gianni Bozzacchi.

197 "I don't have to retouch . . .": Ibid.

197 "Richard was not that vain . . .": Ibid.

198 "You're really good, Gianni . . .": Gianni Bozzacchi, *The Queen and I* (Madison, Wisconsin: University of Wisconsin Press, 2002), 4–5.

198 "When I take pictures . . .": Author's interview with Gianni Bozzacchi.

198 "That's what the world . . .": Author's interview with Gianni Bozzacchi.

198 "If Botticelli were living today . . .": Bozzacchi, *The Queen and I*, 6.

198 "When you get injected . . .": Author's interview with Gianni Bozzacchi.

199 "perfect, an exquisite little doll . . .": Taylor, *Elizabeth Takes Off*, 51.

199 "Some beautiful people . . .": Ibid., 51–52.

200 "I was glad to leave Dahomey . . .": Piers Paul Read, *Alec Guinness, The Authorized Biography* (New York: Simon & Schuster, 2003), 472–73.

200 "a perfectly ordinary . . .": Bragg, 234.

201 "Elizabeth and I love . . .": Chandler Broussard, "On Location with Richard and Liz: Why They're Never Dull," *LOOK*, June 1967, 67.

202 "You took your life in your hands . . .": Ibid.

202 " 'Quicktake' Elizabeth": MGM short feature, "The Making of *The Comedians*," DVD special feature.

202 "when they are both off . . .": Norman Sherry, *The Life of Graham Greene, III,* (New York: Viking, 2004), 422.

202 "I hardly find him . . .": Read, 472.

203 "I can show you . . ." dialogue from *The Comedians*, DVD.

203 "Have you seen Richard Burton?" anecdote: Bragg, 235.

203 "E. is looking gorgeous . . .": Burton notebooks, Bragg, 234.

203 "I am madly in love . . .": Ibid., 235.

205 "I would never have dreamed . . .": *LOOK*, 69.

205   "Well, I must say . . .": Ibid.
206   "Do not burn the bridges . . .": Kelley, 261.
207   "He was always very aware . . .": Mike Nichols, Palmer's *In from the Cold.*
207   " . . . we heard that E. had won . . .": Burton notebooks, Bragg, 240.
207   "and never tiring of it . . . he needs that Oscar": Sammy Davis Jr., *Hollywood in a Suitcase* (New York: William Morrow & Co., 1980), 26–27.
208   "I drank steadily . . .": Burton notebooks, Bragg, 221.
208   "Elizabeth joined us . . .": Ibid.

CHAPTER 9: *BOOM!*

211   "[We are] a lovely charming decadent . . .": Burton notebooks, Bragg, 243.
211   "People don't like sustained . . .": Taylor, quoted in Alpert, 188.
212   "I can't say the word 'Bugger' . . .": David Caute, *Joseph Losey, A Revenge on Life* (New York: Oxford University Press, 1994), 238.
213   "Call me Tom": Bragg, 233.
213   "stupendously drunk . . . worse for wear" anecdote: Burton notebooks, Bragg, 241.
214   "overweight stars . . .": Caute, 226.
215   "ice-skating rink . . .": Taylor, *My Love Affair with Jewelry*, 36.
216   "SHE OUTLIVED SIX . . .": *Boom!* promotional booklet.
216   "Elizabeth Taylor is seriously considering . . . and not with crutches": Ibid.
216   "a picture-postcard sea": Graham Payn and Sheridan Morley, eds., *The Noël Coward Notebooks* (Boston: Little, Brown, 1982), 655.
216   "please feel completely free . . .": quoted in *Boom!* promotional booklet.
217   "Our credo might have been . . .": Taylor, *Elizabeth Takes Off*, 87.
217   "tighten up those muscles . . .": Ibid., 80.
218   "Creating a life with him . . .": Ibid., 87.
218   "My working relationship . . .": quoted in Caute, 226.
218   "very old and slightly . . ." and following entries: Burton notebooks, Bragg, 244.
219   "never lost his eye": Cole Lesley, *The Life of Noël Coward* (New York: Knopf, 1976), 508.
219   "before it's too late": Burton notebooks, Bragg, 245.
219   "I'm supposed to leap . . .": quoted in Mark Shivas, "Was It Like This With Louis XIV?" *New York Times*, October 15, 1976.
220   "a den of thieves" anecdote: Steverson, 168.
220   "looking infinitely sexy" anecdote: Burton notebooks, Bragg, 245.
221   "Not too bad . . .": Ibid., 238.
221   "canary, and not mustard" and description of yacht: Alpert, 186.
221   who relieved themselves all over the rugs: Kelley, 269 and Cottrell, 315.
222   "We are lunching with somebody . . .": Burton notebooks, Bragg, 260.
222   "Not bad for an old woman . . .": Ibid., 261.

223 "And possibly Ari Onassis . . .": Ibid., 260.

223 "how beautiful his eyes were": Ibid., 261.

223 "eyes in the back of her bum . . . a bit of a bore": Ibid.

224 "half a million pounds . . . get the money": Ibid., 265.

225 "How can he possibly . . .": Ibid., 241.

226 "How many nominations . . ." anecdote: Ibid., 242.

226 "touching it and staring . . .": Ibid., 263.

226 "When I got there . . .": Gielgud's interview, Palmer's *In from the Cold.*

227 "A terrible day . . ." anecdote: Burton notebooks, Bragg, 243.

228 "She is a nice fat girl . . .": Ibid., 238.

228 "The Burtons seem to revel . . .": Cottrell, 319.

228 "amazing how a couple . . .": *London Evening Standard,* quoted in Cottrell, 319.

229 "lost faith in faith": Greene, *The Comedians,* DVD.

229 "a character assassination . . .": Graham Greene and Richard Greene, ed., *A Life in Letters* (Canada: Knopf, 2007), 293.

229 "a country of voodoo . . .": Ibid.

230 "You must at some time . . . deserted film for the stage": David Lewin interview with the Burtons, Palmer's *In from the Cold.*

231 "*Doctor Faustus* is . . .": quoted in Cottrell, 319.

231 "*Doctor Faustus* becomes . . .": Pauline Kael, *Going Steady,* 41.

231 "absolutely the right . . .": *Los Angeles Times,* March 15, 1968.

231 "Her vivid personal imagery . . .": Ibid.

232 "if Faustus says 'gold' . . .": Kael, 41.

232 "No one sets out . . .": Jenkins, 160.

233 "I would lift up my arms . . .": Christopher Marlowe, *The Tragical Story of Doctor Faustus* DVD.

233 "anticlimactic and banal": Bosley Crowther, *New York Times,* February 7, 1968.

233 "got[ten] away with murder . . .": Burton notebooks, Bragg, 306.

235 "deep down in his desperate . . .": Ibid.

234 didn't really understand: Authors' interview with Gore Vidal.

234 "Scene by scene": John Huston, *An Open Book* (New York: Ballantine, 1981), 374.

CHAPTER 10: THE ONLY GAME IN TOWN

235 "I introduced Elizabeth to beer . . .": quoted in *Interview,* February 2007, 228.

235 "With Richard Burton, I was living . . .": Taylor, *Elizabeth Takes Off,* 87.

236 "It is a little melancholy . . .": *Time,* March 28, 1969, quoted in Steverson, 171.

237 "Yes, luv, we did spend . . .": Burton clipping file, BFI Archive.

237 "The Grand Duchess Vladimir . . .": Taylor, *My Love Affair with Jewelry,* 63.

237   "I thought how perfect : . .": Ibid., 49.

238   "deep Asscher cuts . . .": Ibid., 49.

238   "I adore wearing gems . . .": Ibid., 84.

238   "Is that the famous diamond?" anecdote: Taylor, *Elizabeth Takes Off*, 84–85.

238   "Elizabeth Taylor and Richard . . .": Maddox, 207–08.

239   "a kind of arrogance . . .": quoted in Maddox, 208.

239   "Dick [Burton] was too old . . .": Tennessee Williams, *Memoirs* (New York: Doubleday, 1975), 200.

239   "we'll all be proud of [*Boom!*] . . .": Losey quoted in Caute, 226.

239   "You're just wrought up . . .": Williams, *Boom!*, DVD.

239   "beyond bad, the other side . . .": John Waters quoted in *Premiere*, August 1992, 9.

241   "Richard Burton would be leaving . . . unprofessional": Cottrell, 323.

241   "like an immature bride . . .": Ibid.

241   "One would think . . .": Burton notebooks, Bragg, 384.

244   "Elizabeth had her uterus . . . completely helpless": Ibid., 255.

245   "lurid hallucinations . . . hush, he'll hear you": Ibid.

245   "a naughty girl" . . . "fuck off": Ibid.

245   "She is still asleep . . .": Ibid., 256.

245   "A child with Richard . . .": Taylor, *Elizabeth Taylor*, original manuscript.

246   "truly terrible": quoted in Maddox, 119, and *Secret Ceremony* clipping file, Academy Library.

246   "Her disintegration is a . . .": quoted in Maddox, 119.

246   "quite beautifully made . . .": *Secret Ceremony* clipping file, Academy Library.

246   "famous for her mammalia," *Secret Ceremony*, DVD.

247   "The paparazzi were now . . .": Authors' interview with Bozzacchi.

247   "I remember that he had . . .": Burton notebooks, Bragg, 256.

248   "He literally missed . . .": quoted in Cottrell, 326.

248   "After Cis, I loved Ifor . . .": Jenkins, 179.

248   "hero, brother, father . . .": Cottrell, 327.

249   "I tried it once": Bragg, 258.

249   "What could I say? . . .": Authors' interview with Liz Smith and Denis Ferrara.

249   "entertaining an officer . . .": Munn, 36.

249   "I will if you will": Bragg, 258.

250   "They must be out of . . .": Spoto, 326.

251   "her young & attractive . . . working without me": Bragg, 262.

251   "I have worked out . . .": Ibid., 262–63.

252   "The beating *they* took . . .": Taylor, *My Love Affair with Jewelry*, 99.

253   "All along I knew . . .": Ibid., 102.

253   "marred royalty . . . dervish": Burton notebooks, Bragg, 272.

253   "I'd better be off . . .": Ibid., 273.

253   "I'd like to be alone . . .": Ibid., 264.

253   "She asked if I would stop . . .": Ibid.

254   "like a wild animal . . .": Ibid., 277.
254   "He had made my mother . . .": *Interview*, 182.
255   "by lampooning his own . . . witless adaptation": quoted in Steverson, 172–73.
255   "She is a wildly exciting love-mistress . . .": Burton notebooks, Bragg, 277.

CHAPTER 11: "RINGS AND FARTHINGALES"

257   "It's just a present for Liz": Burton letter to Taylor, B-T Archive.
257   "Sometimes his joy was perverse . . .": *My Love Affair with Jewelry*, 90.
257   "So I'll have my two favorite . . .": Burton notebooks, Bragg, 278.
258   "My chief worry . . .": Ibid., 280.
258   "stoned daze . . . a murderous world": Ibid., 286–87.
259   "like a talisman . . ." and description of La Peregrina: Taylor, *My Love Affair with Jewelry*, 90.
259   "Sometimes his joy was perverse . . .": Ibid.
260   "exquisitely matched . . .": Ibid., 86.
260   "The last six or eight . . .": Burton notebooks, Bragg, 290.
261   "I was never sued . . .": Ibid., 262.
262   "What are you doing, Lumpy?": Ibid., 292.
262   "Elizabeth is now looking . . . returner of the ball": Ibid., 303.
262   "You will never, of course . . .": Burton letter to Taylor, B-T Archive.
263   "a lot of mediocre rubbish": Burton notebooks, Bragg, 262.
263   "I must have a son . . . I will have Anne": all dialogue from *Anne of the Thousand Days*.
264   "no rubbish and cunning": Burton notebooks, Bragg, 306.
264   "They have every shrug . . . longer than Hamlet": Ibid.
265   speculating that Burton and Bujold: Steverson, 179.
266   "a demonic charmer . . .": Burton notebooks, Bragg, 294.
266   "how marvelous E. would be": Ibid., 306.
266   "I am very jealous of E. . . .": Ibid., 305.
267   "all the godsons, goddaughters . . .": Ibid., 313.
267   "There is no question . . . odd jewel or two": Ibid.
267   "We'll nip over to Paris . . . books with photos by E.": Ibid., 313–14.
269   "not a bad record . . .": Ibid., 311.
270   "imitating a blue-gray . . . intolerant wife": Ibid., 308.
270   "They fought right from . . .": Authors' interview with Liz Smith.
270   "running rows . . . smattering of scholarship": Burton notebooks, Bragg, 315.
270   "the drinking fed the jealousy . . .": Liz Smith.
271   "If any man had done that . . .": Burton notebooks, Bragg, 315.
271   "We are fighting . . . separate ways pretty soon": Ibid., 316.
272   "cleaned up a little . . .": quoted in Steverson, 175.
272   "dared risky roles and . . .": Ibid., 176.
272   "rings and farthingales . . .": Burton letter to Taylor, B-T Archive.

272   "numbered, gleaming . . .": Burton notebooks, Bragg, 317.

273   "He'd have lived until . . .": Ibid., 320.

273   "long silences and deadly . . . red and masculine": Ibid., 318.

273   "[W]hat the hell's the matter . . .": Ibid.

273   "It will make my ugly, big . . .": Ibid.

274   "there was much more to life . . .": Ibid.

274   "I was going to get that diamond . . .": Ibid., 318–19.

275   "I wanted that diamond . . . Dallas, Texas": Ibid., 319.

276   Cartier's display ad in *New York Times*, Taylor, *My Love Affair with Jewelry*, 95.

277   "too soon made glad/ . . .": Robert Browning, "My Last Duchess."

277   "Well, that's not the sort . . ." anecdote, Taylor, *My Love Affair with Jewelry*, 173.

277   "It was more of a millstone . . .": Kelley, 267.

278   "The peasants have been lining up . . .": quoted in Maddox, 214.

278   "How many women have been criticized . . .": Ibid., 213.

278   "The Cartier diamond . . .": Ibid.

CHAPTER 12: FALLEN STARS

281   "Nobody but nobody . . .": Burton notebooks, Bragg, 324.

281   "We've lived like gypsies": Taylor, *Elizabeth Taylor* excerpt, *Ladies' Home Journal*, 81.

282   "How funny it will be . . .": Burton notebooks, Bragg, 267.

282   "None of the children . . .": Taylor clipping file, Academy Library.

282   "If you're a bad actor . . .": Burton notebooks, Bragg, 278.

283   "Very well. I shall stop . . .": Ibid., 325.

283   "break the back of . . .": Burton letter to Taylor, B-T Archive.

283   "The sun is bright . . .": Burton notebooks, Bragg, 326.

284   "You look marvelous!" anecdote: Ibid.

284   "I have to face the fact . . .": Ibid., 327.

284   "When he stopped drinking . . .": Authors' conversation with Taylor confidante.

286   "was like a second mother . . .": Taylor, *My Love Affair with Jewelry*, 212.

287   "We can't make a picture . . .": Walker, 307.

288   "The world has changed . . .": Burton notebooks, Bragg, 324.

288   "the world's costliest coat . . .": *Life*, Taylor clipping file, Academy Library.

288   "owed her performance . . .": Bragg, 320.

289   "The whole world makes fun . . .": Burton notebooks, Bragg, 328.

289   "My only chance is that . . .": Ibid.

290   "pink pills . . . They certainly eased the boredom . . .": Ibid., 329.

291   "Barbra Streisand who fancies herself . . .": Ibid.

291   "Who the hell voted for Wayne?": Ibid.

291   "In some ways, *Anne of the Thousand Days* . . .": Interview with Liz Smith.

291 "You son of a bitch . . .": Bragg, 174.

292 "I lost again . . .": Burton notebooks, Bragg, 329.

292 "If he had won the Oscar . . .": Liz Smith.

292 "The Million-Dollar Era . . .": Taylor clipping file, Academy Library.

293 "put a bandage around her . . .": Burton notebooks, Bragg, 329.

294 " 'Mia,' saying that . . .": Ibid., 332.

295 "would see, in person . . .": Ibid.

295 "she held the audience . . .": Ibid.

296 "hippie" . . . "to have a look" anecdote: Ibid., 335.

296 "a kind of super motel": Ibid., 324.

297 "sheep's eyes": Ibid.

297 "I aged another ten years . . . I love you, too, baby": Ibid., 338.

398 "Dearest Scrupelshrumpilstilskin . . .": Burton letter to Taylor, B-T Archive.

300 "another attack of gout . . .": Ibid.

301 "Dearest Toothache . . .": Ibid.

301 "Dear Long-way-away-one . . .": Ibid.

302 "Forgot the momentous news . . .": Burton notebooks, Bragg, 351.

302 "Don't forget you're always . . .": quoted in Alpert, 252.

302 "I get a bad notice . . .": Ibid.

302 "Missed yesterday . . .": Burton notebooks, Bragg, 352.

303 "They're remarkable . . .": Taylor, *Elizabeth Taylor* excerpt, *Ladies' Home Journal*, 81.

304 "Dearest Ivy League": Burton notebooks, Bragg, 397.

305 "pleased that it means we are . . .": Ibid., 333.

305 "an unmistakable aura . . .": Bernard Weintraub, "The Prime of Mr. Burton?" *New York Times*, December 6, 1970.

305 "It seems fairly ridiculous . . . Never": Ibid.

306 "She wants me to . . . approaching my prime": Ibid.

CHAPTER 13: BLUEBEARD

309 "All my life, I think I have . . .": Burton notebooks, Bragg, 367.

309 "No *Bluebeard* broads": Taylor quoted in Bragg, 407.

310 "The Burtons are protected . . .": Cottrell, 338.

310 "I will love you always . . .": Kelley, 298 fn.

311 "a ruthless survivor . . .": Walker, 309.

311 "We both let off steam . . .": *Ladies' Home Journal*, April 1971, 88.

311 "The people around her . . .": quoted in Spoto, 344.

311 "She's left the hotel . . .": Michael Caine, *What's It All About?* (New York: Turtle Bay Books, 2002), 313.

311 "the only actor I ever . . .": Ibid., 319.

311 "a living legend . . . real-life Alfie": Ibid., 312.

312 "Dear Twit Twaddle etc. . . .": Burton letter to Taylor, B-T Archive.

312   "I love you and . . .": Ibid.

312   "She didn't exactly encourage . . .": Munn, 195.

313   "squelching [her] real feelings . . .": Taylor, *Elizabeth Takes Off*, 100.

313   "bugger all" and "the most glamorous hooker . . .": quoted in reviews of "Under Milk Wood [DVD]," FilmThreat.com, April 12, 2008.

314   "To begin at the beginning . . .": Dylan Thomas, *Under Milk Wood*, DVD.

315   "After he'd had a few . . ." anecdote: Cottrell, 385.

315   "never heard Richard talk . . . an entire life": Gianni Bozzacchi interview.

316   "[T]he winning film of the moment . . .": quoted in Munn, 191.

316   "just sitting back and listening . . .": Ibid.

316   "The man Redford . . . a star": Burton notebooks, Bragg, 351.

317   "two heavyweight champions . . .": Bragg, 357.

317   "The quivering awareness . . .": *Ladies' Home Journal*, April 1971, 118.

317   "his latest and least . . . hope for": Vincent Canby, "Whatever Became of Richard Burton?" *New York Times*, June 13, 1971.

318   "My lack of interest . . . untrue": Burton notebooks, Bragg, 367.

318   "The old Etonians . . .": Ibid., 370.

319   "You know, it's really not . . .": paraphrased quote, Bragg, 367.

319   "This is the baby Richard and I . . .": Kelley, 281.

320   "I made it *up* . . .": Ibid., 282.

320   "My left hand and wrist . . .": Burton notebooks, Bragg, 359–60.

321   "Were it not, actually, for E.'s . . .": Ibid., 364.

321   "If I should go away . . .": Ibid., 371–72.

322   "Suddenly, something came . . ." anecdote: Taylor, *Elizabeth Takes Off*, 75.

322   "only Elizabeth drinks . . .": Burton notebooks, Bragg, 377.

323   "But he's *your* dog" anecdote: Ibid., 368–69.

324   "The virtual cessation . . .": Ibid., 381.

324   "E. is trying to press me . . .": Ibid., 385.

325   "slightly gaga": Ibid., 390.

326   "in a somewhat false . . .": Ibid., 387–88.

326   "the Duchess of Windsor and . . .": Ibid., 389.

326   "an hour or more of . . .": Ibid.

326   "cadaverous . . . Where's my Elizabeth?": Ibid., 389–90.

327   "making out": Ibid., 390.

327   "so that you can feel . . .": Taylor, *Elizabeth Taylor*, 173.

327   "with half a dozen . . .": Burton notebooks, Bragg, 393.

328   "[F]irm as they are . . .": Ibid., 404.

329   "like cats after cream . . .": Cottrell, 359.

329   "a genius . . ." Tammy Grimes quoted in Cottrell, 361.

329   "to be done with immense . . .": Burton notebooks, Bragg, 405.

329   "plays the organ . . .": Ibid., 406.

329   "If he sold himself . . .": Alpert, 204.

330   "both mercurial, jealous . . . will ever happen": Taylor, *Elizabeth Taylor*, 135–36.

331 "fell in love with her . . .": Taylor, *My Love Affair with Jewelry*, 50.
331 "He didn't make me look . . .": Burton notebooks, Bragg, 405–06.
331 "We would love you to come . . .": Ibid., 407.
332 "It cld be a step toward . . .": Ibid., 410.
333 "Love Is Everlasting": Walker, 314.
334 "by God, they're really good . . .": Burton notebooks, Bragg, 410.
334 "One day somebody else . . .": Taylor, *My Love Affair with Jewelry*, 73.
335 "Ifor is very near the end . . .": Burton notebooks, Bragg, 363.
336 "he was the nearest to a father . . .": Jenkins, 179.

CHAPTER 14: DIVORCE HIS DIVORCE HERS

337 "I shall miss you with passion . . .": Burton letter to Taylor, B-T Archive.
337 "Maybe we loved each other . . .": Taylor letter to Burton, July 4, 1973, Ibid.
337 "Richard needed their protection . . .": Alpert, 207.
338 "You remind me quite distinctly . . . Richard!": Ibid., 206–07.
338 "Hey Lumps, . . .": Burton letter to Taylor, B-T Archive.
338 "[Spencer] Tracy's drunks . . .": quoted in Alpert, 208.
339 "could see him getting older . . .": Ibid.
339 "You're so tough . . ." anecdote: Kate Burton's interview in Palmer's *In from the Cold*.
339 "She was stronger than Richard . . .": quoted in Alpert, 207.
340 "I owe the public who pays . . .": Taylor, *Elizabeth Taylor*, 174.
340 "My Darling, I think I'd better go . . .": Letter from Richard Burton, B-T Archive.
341 "Dear Eddie, please believe . . .": quoted in Alpert, 207.
341 "Get that woman . . .": Ibid., 208.
342 "Dearest Child, . . .": Letter from Richard Burton, B-T Archive.
343 "This is for Nathalie": Alpert, 209.
343 "It's a triumph of life . . .": Authors' conversation with Gabriel Byrne.
343 "I'm as thrilled by the English . . .": Burton notebooks, Bragg, 267.
346 "She had this extraordinary . . .": Authors' interview with Waris Hussein, March 18, 2008.
346 "charming and sober . . . colonized by England": Ibid.
350 "Now everybody is . . ." anecdote: Ibid.
354 "that blue nightie . . . lovely love": Letter from Richard Burton, B-T Archive.
354 "wonderfully nourishing sense . . .": Hussein.
354 "pirates on the main . . .": Bragg, 414.
354 "Continued with the same gifted . . .": Letter from Richard Burton, B-T Archive.
355 "he hated it": Hussein.
355 "astronomical . . . their every whim": Authors' interview with John Heyman.
355 "the critics were waiting . . .": Hussein.

355 "a matched pair of thudding . . . an autopsy": quoted in Kelley, 289.

356 "he's never more than . . .": all dialogue from *Divorce His Divorce Hers*, DVD.

356 "just went down . . .": Hussein.

356 "Years later, I met with . . .": Ibid.

357 "If there is one thing . . .": Maddox, 229.

358 "spellbound by the couple . . .": Dominick Dunne, "The Queen and I," *Vanity Fair*, March 2007.

358 "at the peak of . . . on the screen": Ibid.

358 "seethed on the sidelines . . .": Ibid.

358 "drank champagne . . .": Heymann, 313.

359 "I don't like the thought . . . offend me": Ferris, 230.

359 "Richard Jenkins, Richard Burton . . .": Interview with Gianni Bozzacchi.

360 "they fell out of love": Dunne.

360 "a mini-*Cleopatra*": quoted in Heymann, 316.

360 "So My Lumps, You're off . . .": Letter from Richard Burton, B-T Archive.

362 "They were like brothers . . .": Spoto, 351.

362 "Why did you ever . . .": quoted in Bragg, 417.

362 "I am convinced it would be . . .": Ibid.

CHAPTER 15: MASSACRE IN ROME

365 " . . . [I]f you leave me . . .": Letter from Richard Burton, B-T Archive.

365 "I don't want to be . . .": quoted in Kelley, 295.

365 "The last day of March . . .": Letter from Richard Burton, B-T Archive.

366 "Perhaps my indifference to . . .": quoted in Kelley, 291–92.

367 "I love you, lovely woman . . .": Letter from Richard Burton, B-T Archive.

369 "Can we get the hell . . .": Ibid.

369 "affectionate rows . . . he didn't love her": quoted in Gerald Clarke, *Capote* (New York: Random House, 1988), 270–71.

370 "BELOVED IDIOT. MISS YOU . . .": Letter from Richard Burton, B-T Archive.

370 "Elizabeth has always fancied . . .": Burton notebooks, Bragg, 206.

371 "Going out was *life* . . .": quoted in Spoto, 342.

371 "Well, first of all": Letter from Richard Burton, B-T Archive.

371 "Richard had so much . . .": Taylor, *Elizabeth Takes Off*, photo caption (no page number).

372 "I will not talk about . . .": Caute, 296.

372 "I have never quite got over . . .": Letter from Richard Burton, B-T Archive.

372 "You are too old a hand . . .": Caute, 296.

373 "risotto, roasted Palumbo fish . . .": Walker, 321.

374 "a Dior suit, matching handbag . . .": Kelley, 300.

374 "The stone had been offered . . .": quoted in Kelley, 300.

374 "[t]all and extraordinary . . .": Burton, "My Friend Sophia," *Ladies' Home Journal*, 1973.

375 "I knew he was flirting . . .": Taylor, *My Love Affair with Jewelry*, 118.

375 "Today is the second sad . . .": quoted in Bragg, 418.

375 "I don't want to be . . .": quoted in Kelley, 295.

375 "Gee, she has everything . . .": Ibid.

376 "Let's face it, I was . . .": quoted in Fleming, *Vogue.*

378 "You fuckin' English!" anecdote: Interview with Gianni Bozzacchi.

378 "He came onto the set . . .": quoted in Kelley, 299.

378 "Public pressure to be . . . . 'drinking problem' ": Dorothy Cameron Disney, "Elizabeth Taylor & Richard Burton: Why This Marriage Can't Be Saved," *Ladies' Home Journal*, October 1973.

378 "E. T. Burton. It may very well be . . .": Letter from Richard Burton, B-T Archive.

379 "You asked me to write the truth . . .": Ibid.

380 "If anybody hurts you . . .": Ibid.

380 "Hello, Lumpy . . .": Munn, 203.

380 "I'm the husband . . .": Ibid.

381 "Elizabeth Taylor and Richard . . .": quoted in Kelley, 299.

382 "It was a wonder . . . in fucking agony!": quoted in Munn, 207. .

382 "which was only at the end . . .": Interview with Bozzacchi.

383 "Tell us about Dylan Thomas! . . .": quoted in Alpert, 218.

383 "My father was a drinker . . . liquor helps": quoted in Bragg, 420–21.

383 "I wouldn't have survived . . .": quoted in Munn, 207.

383 "was drinking not for . . .": Ibid.

383 "get a single line . . .": Ibid., 208.

384 "This man is dying": Alpert, 219.

385 irreconcilable . . . "became intolerable": Walker, 323.

385 "Do you think we've . . .": Munn, 211.

386 "She was down to a secretary . . .": Walker, 323.

386 "darling," or "sweetnose," etc.: Ibid., 325.

387 "pretty but impertinent": quoted in Bragg, 269.

388 "I never looked so good . . .": quoted in Walker, 325.

390 "Tonight . . . we fly to Johannesburg . . .": Bragg, 397.

391 "I thought all through . . . got stoned": Taylor, early draft of "Richard Again," *Ladies' Home Journal*, February 1976. Private Collection.

391 "That's where I would like . . .": Ibid.

391 to revivify their lives: Kay Redfield Jamison, *Exuberance* (New York: Knopf, 2004), 320.

391 "understood the consequences . . .": Walker, 328.

392 "witnessed by two hippos": Taylor, "Richard Again."

392 "I love him, deeply . . .": Ibid.

392 "Dearest Hubs—": Letter from Elizabeth Taylor, B-T Archives.

393 "Sturm has remarried Drang . . .": quoted in Maddox, 233.

393 "like a man who wasn't . . .": quoted in Kelley, 321.

393 "But I could see . . .": Ibid.

CHAPTER 16: PRIVATE LIVES

395 "Everyone bought tickets to watch . . .": Taylor, *Elizabeth Takes Off*, 98.

395 "I've never found a part as good . . .": quoted in Jenkins, 242.

397 "You have the guts of . . .": quoted in Kelley, 323.

398 "At this performance . . .": Alpert, 235–36.

398 "It was the first time . . .": quoted in Bragg, 437.

398 "Immediately, everyone in every . . .": Interview with Liz Smith and Denis Ferrara.

399 "Why the hell did you . . .": Alpert, 233.

399 "She came out . . .": Interview with Smith and Ferrara.

400 " . . . the actor's performance . . .": *New York Times*, March 7, 1976.

401 "You must never do anything . . .": Steverson, 199.

401 "Was it not Francis Bacon . . .": Bragg, 441.

402 "I think Suzy Hunt . . .": Palmer's *In from the Cold*.

402 contributing to the delinquency: Spoto, 361–62.

404 "redundant . . . nothing to do": Taylor, *Elizabeth Takes Off*, 40.

404 "too passionate . . . little Republican ensembles": Ibid., 39.

404 "Eating filled the lonely hours . . .": Ibid., 44.

404 "Always a bride, never . . .": Oscar Levant, *The Unimportance of Being Oscar* (New York: G.P. Putnam's Sons, 1968), 120.

405 "It represented a different phase . . .": quoted in Spoto, 384.

405 "John and I never had people in . . .": Taylor, *Elizabeth Takes Off*, 44.

405 "Little Heifer": Spoto, 374.

405 "the strength to recreate . . .": Taylor, *Elizabeth Takes Off*, 88.

407 THE MOST BEAUTIFUL PLACE . . .: Steverson, 210.

407 "I want it out!" anecdote: Alpert, 248–49.

407 "and very *un*-happy": quoted in Bragg, 453.

408 "the panacea of a drink . . . Disgusting": Burton notebooks, Bragg, 451.

410 "a grotesque exaggeration . . . I've gone too far!": Ibid., 466–67.

410 "big 'fuck-yous' . . .": Interview with Liz Smith.

411 "she'll have to get him . . .": Ibid.

412 "I love you" anecdote: quoted in Kelley, 415.

413 "the most unforgettable . . .": Conversation with Gabriel Byrne.

413 "Get out" anecdote: Kelley, 416.

413 smitten . . . "I love the woman": *Private Lives* clipping file, March 2, 1982, Library of Performing Arts, Lincoln Center.

413 "I couldn't take it . . ." and " . . . a figure of the past": quoted in Kelley, 415.

414 "There's nowhere to go . . .": quoted in Maddox, 247.

414 "I knew the role . . .": Taylor, *Elizabeth Takes Off*, 97.

414 "You're not really . . ." and " . . . make me do it": quoted in Alpert, 261.

415 " 'The Liz and Dick Show' . . ." and " . . . Nouveau York": undated article, clipping file, Library of Performing Arts, Lincoln Center.

415 "He'd lost all the weight . . .": Authors' interview with John Cullum. August 4, 2009.

415 "E. . . . drinking. Also, has not . . .": Burton notebooks, Bragg, 472.

416 "Elizabeth was a natural . . .": Cullum interview.

416 "Richard started laughing . . .": Ibid.

416 "was a circus . . .": quoted in Bragg, 475.

417 "Elizabeth would be there . . .": Cullum interview.

417 "This just proves it . . .": quoted in Bragg, 475.

417 "They had lived *Private Lives* . . .": Cullum interview.

417 "Poor Sibyl. . . . I suppose . . ." and all subsequent dialogue: Noël Coward, *Private Lives*, Act II, scene i., *Collected Plays: Two* (London: Methuen Publishing, Ltd., 1999), 43.

418 "a calculated business venture . . .": *New York Times*, May 9, 1983.

418 "the clinical detachment . . .": Ibid.

419 "the Hitler Diaries . . .": James Brady, "Private Lives," clipping file, Library of Performing Arts, Lincoln Center.

419 "They have become one . . .": Melvin Maddocks, *Christian Science Monitor*, April 25, 1983.

419 "*The Dance of Death* . . .": *Variety*, "Private Lives," clipping file, Library of Performing Arts, Lincoln Center.

419 "Lizandick ('liz n 'dik) *n. pl.* . . .": *People*, May 23, 1983, "Private Lives," clipping file, Library of Performing Arts, Lincoln Center.

419 "a caricature of a . . .": *Boston Globe,* undated review, "Private Lives," clipping file.

419 "she was hurt . . .": Cullum interview.

420 "Liz & Dick: Damn the critics . . .": Amy Pagnozzi and James Norman, "Liz & Dick," *New York Post*, May 9, 1983.

420 "I wouldn't have missed . . .": quoted in Alpert, 261.

420 "When the hell . . ." anecdote: Ibid.

420 "It didn't take much . . .": Cullum interview.

421 "She can do everything . . .": quoted in Bragg, 469.

421 "lovely Sally . . .": Ibid., 471.

421 "I think Richard really tried . . .": Cullum interview.

421 "I began to crack . . .": Taylor, *Elizabeth Takes Off*, 98.

422 "Do I really look fat? . . .": Marie Brenner, "The Liz and Dick Show," *New York Magazine*, May 9, 1983.

422 "came in almost professorial . . .": Cullum interview.

422 "It became a twenty-four-hour . . .": Taylor, *Elizabeth Takes Off*, 98.

423 "She would just grab . . .": quoted in Bragg, 477.

423 "That's our girl . . .": Ibid.

423 "The Liz 'n' Dick Show . . . the audience LOVED her!": *New York Post*, November 14, 1983.

424 "When we were able to be . . .": quoted in *New York Post*, clipping file.

424 "awash in self-pity and self-disgust": Taylor, *Elizabeth Takes Off*, 99.
425 "We've never really . . .": Jenkins, 242.
425 "The bond between them . . .": Ibid.
425 "Good-bye, love": Conversation with Elizabeth Taylor confidante.

EPILOGUE

427 "Richard and I lived life . . .": Taylor, *Elizabeth Takes Off*, 85.
427 "You never get to be . . .": Cottrell, 366.
427 "He was like an old . . .": Authors' interview with Michael Radford, April 1, 2008.
428 "We got a telegram . . .": Ibid.
428 "Mr. Brando does not . . ." anecdote: Ibid.
428 "He didn't drink at all . . .": Ibid.
429 "The other thing is . . .": Ibid.
429 "Richard had that thing . . .": Ibid.
430 "about his childhood . . .": Bragg, 483.
430 "He discussed many things . . .": Kashner, "A First-Class Affair," *Vanity Fair*, July 2003, 151.
430 "She still fascinates . . .": Alpert, 265.
431 "Burton had words . . ." pub fight anecdote: Authors' interview with Gianni Bozzacchi.
431 "was a tragedy for us . . .": Bragg, 485.
432 "chorded and powerful . . .": David Denby, "Requiem for a Heavyweight," *Premiere*, February 1991.
432 "the Welsh voice . . .": Burton's interview with Michael Parkinson, BFI Archive.
432 "The multitudinous seas incarnadine . . .": quoted in Bragg, 487.
432 "I was still madly in love . . .": Anne Taylor Fleming, "Elizabeth: ACT II," *Vogue*, October 1987.
434 "a queen in mourning": Interview with Robert Hardy.
434 "Those are *my* memories": Elizabeth Taylor on *Larry King Live*, May 30, 2006.
435 "It's the perfect relationship! . . .": Anecdote from Elizabeth Taylor's confidante.
436 "the greatest film actress . . .": Burton letter to Taylor, B-T Archive.
437 "You know, of all of my films . . ." Authors' conversation with Elizabeth Taylor.
437 "After Richard, the men in my life . . .": Ibid.
437 "for her history and courage": Liz Smth, "Liz Taylor Performs *Love Letters*," *Variety*, December 3, 2007.
438 She's kept that letter anecdote: Conversation with Elizabeth Taylor confidante.

BIBLIOGRAPHY

BOOKS

Alpert, Hollis. *Burton.* New York: G. P. Putnam & Sons, 1986.

Bloom, Claire. *Leaving a Doll's House.* New York and Canada: Little, Brown & Co., 1996.

Bosworth, Patricia. *Montgomery Clift.* New York: Simon & Schuster, 1994.

Bozzacchi, Gianni. *Elizabeth Taylor: The Queen and I.* Madison, Wisconsin: The University of Wisconsin Press, 2002.

Bragg, Melvyn. *Rich: The Life of Richard Burton.* London: Hodder & Stoughton, 1988.

Brodsky, Jack and Nathan Weiss. *The Cleopatra Papers, a Private Correspondence.* New York: Simon & Schuster, 1963.

Burton, Philip. *Early Doors: My Life and the Theatre.* New York: The Dial Press, 1969.

Burton, Richard. *A Christmas Story.* London: Hodder & Stoughton, 1964, 1989.

———. *Meeting Mrs. Jenkins.* New York: William Morrow & Co., 1966.

Caine, Michael. *What's It All About?* New York: Turtle Bay Books, 2002.

Caute, David. *Joseph Losey: A Revenge on Life.* New York: Oxford University Press, 1994.

Ciment, Michael. *Conversations with Losey.* London and New York: Methuen Publishing, Ltd., 1985.

Clarke, Gerald. *Capote.* New York: Random House, 1988.

Coleman, Terry. *Olivier.* New York: Henry Holt & Co., 2005.

Cottrell, John and Fergus Cashin. *Richard Burton, Very Close Up.* Englewood Cliffs, New Jersey: Prentice-Hall, 1971.

Coward, Noël. *Collected Plays: Two.* London: Methuen Publishing, Ltd., 1999.

Cronyn, Hume. *A Terrible Liar.* New York: William Morrow & Co., 1991.

Dauth, Brian, ed. *Joseph L. Mankiewicz Interviews.* Jackson, Mississippi: University Press of Mississippi, 2008.

David, Lester and Jhan Robbins. *Richard and Elizabeth.* New York: Funk & Wagnalls, 1977.

BIBLIOGRAPHY

Davis, Sammy Jr., *Hollywood in a Suitcase*. New York: William Morrow & Co., 1980.

Ferris, Paul. *Richard Burton*. New York: Coward, McCann & Geoghegan, 1981.

Fisher, Carrie. *Wishful Drinking*. New York: Simon & Schuster, 2008.

Fisher, Eddie. *Eddie: My Life, My Loves*. New York: Harper & Row, 1981.

———. *Been There, Done That*. New York: St. Martin's Press, 1999.

Gielgud, Sir John, and Richard Mangan, ed. *A Life in Letters*. New York: Arcade Publishers, 2004.

Greene, Graham and Richard Greene, ed. *A Life in Letters*. Canada: Knopf, 2007.

Gussow, Mel. *Edward Albee: A Singular Journey*. New York: Simon & Schuster, 1999.

Heymann, C. David. *Liz: An Intimate Biography of Elizabeth Taylor*. Secaucus, New Jersey: Citadel Stars, 1996.

Huston, John. *An Open Book*. New York: Ballantine Books, 1981.

Jenkins, Graham. *Richard Burton, My Brother*. New York: Harper & Row, 1988.

Kael, Pauline. *Going Steady, Film Writings 1968–1969*. New York: Marion Boyars Publishers, 1994.

Kelley, Kitty. *Elizabeth Taylor: The Last Star*. New York: Dell Publishing, 1981.

Lesley, Cole. *The Life of Noël Coward*. New York: Penguin Books, 1978.

Levy, Emanuel. *Vincente Minnelli, Hollywood's Dark Dreamer*. New York: St. Martin's Press, 2009.

Maddox, Brenda. *Who's Afraid of Elizabeth Taylor?* New York: M. Evans, 1977.

Madsen, Axel. *John Huston*. Garden City, New York: Doubleday, 1978.

Mann, William. *How to Be a Movie Star: Elizabeth Taylor in Hollywood*. New York: Houghton Mifflin Harcourt, 2009.

Manso, Peter. *Brando: The Biography*. New York: Hyperion, 1994.

Morley, Sheridan. *Elizabeth Taylor: A Celebration*. New York: Applause Books, 1988.

Munn, Michael. *Richard Burton, Prince of Players*. London: JR Books, 2008.

Parkinson, David. *The Graham Greene Film Reader*. New York: Applause, 1993.

Payn, Graham and Sheridan Morley, eds. *The Noël Coward Diaries*. Boston: Little, Brown, 1982.

Perelman, S. J. *Don't Tread on Me: The Selected Letters of S. J. Perelman*. New York: Penguin Books, 1987.

Read, Piers Paul. *Alec Guinness: The Authorized Biography*. New York: Simon & Schuster, 2003.

Redfield, William. *Letters from an Actor*. New York: Limelight Editions, 1984.

Server, Lee. *Ava Gardner: Love Is Nothing*. New York: St. Martin's Press, 2006.

———. *Robert Mitchum: Baby, I Don't Care*. New York: St. Martin's Griffin, 2001.

Sherry, Norman. *The Life of Graham Greene, III, 1955–1991*. New York: Viking, 2004.

Smith, Liz. *Dishing Liz Smith*. New York: Simon & Schuster, 2005.

———. *Natural Blonde*. New York: Hyperion, 2000.

Spinetti, Victor, with Peter Rankin. *Victor Spinetti, Up Front* . . . London: Portico, 2008.

Spoto, Donald. *Elizabeth Taylor.* London: Time Warner Book Group, 1995.

Stanley, Louis. *The Dorchester: Sixty Years of Luxury.* London: Pearl & Dean Publishing, 1991.

Sterne, Richard L. *Richard Burton in Hamlet.* New York: Random House, 1967.

Steverson, Tyrone. *Richard Burton: A Bio-Bibliography.* Westport, Connecticut: Greenwood Press, 1992.

Taraborrelli, J. Randy. *Elizabeth.* New York: Warner Books, 2006.

Taylor, Elizabeth with Richard Meryman. *Elizabeth Taylor.* New York: Harper & Row, 1965.

———. *Elizabeth Takes Off.* New York: G. P. Putnam & Sons, 1987.

———. *My Love Affair with Jewelry.* New York: Simon & Schuster, 2002.

Thomson, David. *The New Biographical Dictionary of Film.* New York: Knopf, 2002.

———. *The Whole Equation: A History of Hollywood.* New York: Knopf, 2005.

Tynan, Kenneth and John Lahr, editor. *The Diaries of Kenneth Tynan.* New York and London: Bloomsbury, 2001.

Walker, Alexander. *Elizabeth: The Life of Elizabeth Taylor.* New York: Grove Wiedenfeld, 1990.

Wanger, Walter and Joe Hyams, *My Life with Cleopatra.* New York: Bantam Books, 1963.

Warhol, Andy. *The Philosophy of Andy Warhol (From A to B and Back Again).* New York and London: Harcourt Brace Jovanovich, 1975.

Warhol, Andy, and Pat Hackett. *Popism: The Warhol Sixties.* New York: Harvest Books, 1980.

Waterbury, Ruth. *Elizabeth Taylor.* New York: Appleton-Century, 1964.

———. *Richard Burton: His Intimate Story.* New York: Pyramid Books, 1965.

Williams, Gareth. *Valleys of Song: Music and Society in Wales.* Cardiff: University of Wales Press, 1998.

Williams, Tennessee. *Memoirs.* New York: Doubleday, 1975.

York, Michael. *Accidentally on Purpose.* New York: Simon & Schuster, 1991.

Zeffirelli, Franco. *Zeffirelli.* New York: Weidenfeld & Nicolson, 1986.

ARTICLES

Braddon, Russell, "Richard Burton to Liz: 'I Love Thee Not . . .' " *Saturday Evening Post*, December 3, 1966.

Brossard, Chandler, "Richard and Liz," *LOOK*, June 27, 1967.

Burton, Richard, "His Liz: 'A Scheming Charmer,' " *Life*, February 24, 1967.

———, "Travelling with Elizabeth, by Her Husband Who Loves Her in Spite of It," *Vogue*, April 1971.

———, "Dauntless Travellers: Mr. and Mrs. Richard Burton . . ." *Vogue*, October 1971.

BIBLIOGRAPHY

Denby, David, "Requiem for a Heavyweight," *Premiere*, February 1, 1991.

Disney, Dorothy Cameron, "Elizabeth Taylor & Richard Burton: Why This Marriage Can't Be Saved," *Ladies' Home Journal*, October 1973.

Elkin, Stanley, "Miss Taylor and Family: An Outside View," *Esquire*, November 1964.

Ferguson, Ken, "Richard Burton," *Photoplay*, November 1984.

Fleming, Ann Taylor, "Elizabeth: Act II," *Vogue*, October 1987.

Harris, Radie, "Broadway Ballyhoo," *Hollywood Reporter*, August 9, 1984.

Kamp, David, "When Liz Met Dick," *Vanity Fair*, September 2006.

Kashner, Sam, "A First-Class Affair," *Vanity Fair*, July 2003.

Lehman, Edward, diaries, published in *Talk Magazine*, April 2000.

Pepper, Curtis Bill, "I Don't Want to Be That Much in Love Ever Again," *McCall's*, January 1974.

Sischy, Ingrid, "*Interview* Loves Elizabeth Taylor," collection of articles and interviews, *Interview* Magazine Collector's Edition, February 2007.

Taylor, Elizabeth, "Richard Again," *Ladies' Home Journal*, February 1976.

Taylor, Noreen, "Peter Glenville Talks About the Burtons," *Vogue*, September 1967.

Tynan, Kenneth, "*Playboy* Interview: Richard Burton," *Playboy*, September 1963.

"The Man Who Knows Tells the Story of a Tumultuous Epic: *Cleopatra*," *Life*, April 19, 1963.

ARCHIVES

"B-T Archive": Letters from Richard Burton to Elizabeth Taylor, undated except where noted; private collection.

Elizabeth Taylor and Richard Meryman, *Elizabeth Taylor*, original unedited manuscript, private collection.

Richard Burton Archive, British Film Institute (BFI) Library, London, England.

Richard Burton clipping file, Margaret Herrick Library, Academy of Motion Picture Arts and Sciences, Los Angeles, California.

Elizabeth Taylor clipping file, Margaret Herrick Library, Academy of Motion Picture Arts and Sciences, Los Angeles, California.

Clipping files for *Ash Wednesday, Boom!, Cleopatra, The Comedians, Divorce His Divorce Hers, Doctor Faustus, Hammersmith Is Out, Reflections in a Golden Eye, The Sandpiper, The Spy Who Came in from the Cold, The Taming of the Shrew, Under Milk Wood, The V.I.P.s, Who's Afraid of Virginia Woolf?*: Margaret Herrick Library, Academy of Motion Picture Arts and Sciences, Los Angeles, California.

Private Lives clipping file, Library of Performing Arts, Lincoln Center, New York, New York.

DVDS AND VISUAL MATERIAL

David Lewin's interview with Richard Burton, *Becket* DVD, supplemental material.

Michael Parkinson's interview with Richard Burton, November 23, 1974, BFI Archive.

Kenneth Tynan's interview with Richard Burton, *Becket* DVD, supplemental material.

Tony Palmer, director, *In from the Cold*, VHS.

DVDs of *Anne of the Thousand Days, Ash Wednesday, Becket, Boom!, Cleopatra, The Comedians, Divorce His Divorce Hers, Doctor Faustus, Reflections in a Golden Eye, The Sandpiper, The Spy Who Came in from the Cold, The Taming of the Shrew, Under Milk Wood, The V.I.P.s, Who's Afraid of Virginia Woolf?*

INDEX

INDEX